Rodale books may be purchased for business or promotional
use or for special sales. For information, please write to:
Special Markets Department, Rodale, Inc., 733 Third Avenue, New York, NY 10017

Printed in the United States of America
Rodale Inc. makes every effort to use acid-free ∞, recycled paper ♻.

Charts by Ellen Gustafson and Kara Plikaitis

Book design by Kara Plikaitis

Library of Congress Cataloging-in-Publication Data is on file with the publisher
ISBN-13: 978–1–62336–053–5

Distributed to the trade by Macmillan

2   4   6   8   10   9   7   5   3   1   hardcover

We inspire and enable people to improve their lives and the world around them.
rodalebooks.com

★ *we the* ★ Eaters

If We Change Dinner, We Can Change the World

Ellen Gustafson

RODALE.

CONTENTS

DEDICATION iv
INTRODUCTION v

★ 1 ★

The Husk, the Cob,
and a Kernel of Truth

*The Heart of the Global Problem
with Corn*

1

★ 2 ★

Here's the Beef

*The 99-cent Burger Is the Most
Expensive Hamburger in the World*

31

★ 3 ★

Ruminations on Dairy

The People's Milk

55

★ 4 ★

Global Waves of Grain

*BMI, Borlaug's Wheat,
and Burger Buns*

79

★ 5 ★

Tubers and Fruits

*The French Fries, the Ketchup,
and the Orphaned World
of Real Vegetables*

103

★ 6 ★

The Sugar We Drink

How Sweet It Isn't

127

★ 7 ★

The Sweet We Eat

*Dessert All Day and Really Real Fruit
Flavors*

155

★ 8 ★

Reset the Table and *Really*
Change Dinner

*Beyond the Corn, the Meat, the Dairy,
the Wheat, and the Sugar Is That Single
Healthful Meal That Changes Everything*

179

CONCLUSION

*Action Steps: 30 Food Shifts to Better
Health and a Better World*

188

SOURCE NOTES 214

ACKNOWLEDGMENTS 225

INDEX 227

To my parents, who nourished me with good food and unconditional love, and to my husband, who is the best person I could ever imagine to share the table of life with.

INTRODUCTION

RUHIIRA IS A LUSH and isolated rural region in southwest Uganda comprised of clusters of villages and rustic commerce hubs spread out over a couple hundred square miles. Most of the roughly 40,000 residents live in the highlands, where mist gets trapped by the surrounding mountains, then settles like low-slung clouds over the verdant, rolling farmland and red clay soil of the valleys. Ninety percent of the population survive as subsistence-level farmers working land that is nutrient depleted, a result of poor farming practices and erosion caused by massive deforestation. Years of tree cutting to provide fuel for cooking and heat has impoverished the soil, and without key nutrients, crop yields decrease. This is a problem Ruhiira shares with much of Africa, where three-quarters of the farmland is severely degraded.

Houses in Ruhiira are commonly constructed of mud and wattle—a mixture of dirt and water applied to stick frames—and then covered in cow dung. Women and children transport water over long distances in yellow jerry cans to their homes for drinking and daily life, as men on old bicycles transport *matoke*—green Ugandan bananas—from the growing fields to the marketplaces.

The population of the region represents the poorest of the poor, with roughly half of the area's residents earning less than 2,100 Ugandan shillings, the equivalent of one US dollar per day. It is a region of sub-Saharan Africa that has been designated a United Nations "hunger hot spot." And in Ruhiira, many of the farmers fall tragically short even of subsistence: Roughly half the children under the age of 5 suffer from severe malnutrition.

Until just a couple of years ago, resources in Ruhiira were severely diminished. Seeds and fertilizer were as hard to come by as basic education and health care, or clean water. Tuberculosis and malaria were prevalent and pervasive. Farm equipment and bank loans were unheard of. Even an ox to pull a plow, for most farmers, was well beyond reach. And as lush as the landscape looks at first glance, the area is subject to overfarming and extended droughts. With little access to water for drinking, cooking, and washing, there is limited water to irrigate crops. Access to Ruhiira is via rough, unpaved roads, and it is 25 miles, and several hours, from the nearest city—a fact that both exacerbates and explains some of the region's most insidious problems. In short, it is difficult to live in Ruhiira, and it is exceedingly difficult to leave. And, other than the beauty of the landscape and the warmth of the people, there is little economic reason for anyone from outside the community to go there.

★ ★

I arrived in Ruhiira in May 2009 via a circuitous route. As a college student at Columbia University in New York City a number of years earlier, I had studied international relations, taking courses with names like Weapons, Strategy, and War; Middle East Politics; and US Foreign Policy. While studying abroad in Spain and traveling to Morocco in the spring of 2001, I experienced first-hand the growing anti-American sentiment among North Africans in what had once been American-friendly cities. The first time I saw anti-American graffiti in Madrid, it was sprayed on the side of a Burger King, and it was protesting our fast food colonialism—not our politics. In the fall of 2001, I was back at Columbia and living in New York, and when the attacks of 9/11 rocked our city, it felt tragically prescient that I was studying terrorism and the Middle East in this tenuous geopolitical climate. Seeing the world twist and turn, like the smoke and ash that rose for weeks from Ground Zero, was terrifying and surreal. We all knew everything had changed, but not precisely how—or by how much.

★ ★

My first job after graduation was at the Council on Foreign Relations, a think tank where I continued my focus on global security issues as the research associate for a group of senior, active-duty military officers. I was learning about the military from a front-row seat, researching the conflict in Afghanistan and the lead-up to the Iraq war. As a 23-year-old civilian, I flew in a plane for an aerial refueling, tried out night-vision goggles, saw an early-stage drone simulator, and landed in a plane on the deck of an aircraft carrier. Having lived through 9/11, this experience in itself was reassuring. It demonstrated to me the sheer might of America.

Armed with the experience and perspective gained from studying the US military, I left the Council on Foreign Relations and took a job at ABC News in its investigative unit, preparing research for reporters covering terrorist threats in the US and around the globe. There was one particular developing story I was pushing to get more play. This was during 2005 and 2006, and *New York Times* columnist Nicholas Kristof had begun sounding the call about the hunger and humanitarian crisis in the Darfur region of Sudan—part of the Horn of Africa also beset by terrorism and violence. While some mainstream reporting covered the conflict, and a few other outlets reported on the dire food insecurity plaguing the people of Africa's Sahel region, no one was connecting these two looming humanitarian and security disasters. Meanwhile, in my research for work, I had come across a compelling study about the connection between poor nutrition in students and their propensity toward violence. And then, in 2005, a devastating earthquake rocked Pakistan, affecting another food-insecure and terrorism-prone region.

This sequence of events got me thinking about an old African proverb: "A hungry man is an angry man." When I pulled up a map of the major hot spots of long-standing food insecurity and hunger around the world—the Horn of Africa and Yemen, the Sahel and Sahara regions, the Andes Mountains, the highlands of Central America, parts of South and Southeast Asia, and the countries of Afghanistan and Pakistan—I was staggered not by how *many* of these regions struggled with long-term violence—and, increasingly, terrorism—but by how *rarely* we connect that violence back to hunger.

> From that moment, I decided it made far more sense
> to make the world aware of the stories of the hungry,
> before they became the stories of the violent.

We've seen short-term food shortages and price hikes trigger violence throughout history, including in 2008, when global food prices spiked and violence erupted in 48 countries around the world. People who are hungry or lacking basic necessities are more likely to resort to violence in the short term as a way to protest and to get what they need. But when that hunger is systemic, so is the violence, and areas of *persistent* hunger are often the very regions where violence and terrorism have the deepest foothold. I became completely obsessed with this connection, so I left my job at ABC News and moved on, hell-bent on approaching terrorism and political insecurity from the ground up by combating food insecurity and hunger.

I took a job as a public information officer at the United Nations World Food Program (WFP)—the world's largest humanitarian agency, which is charged with feeding the world's hungriest people. With WFP, I saw the cascading effects, and the terror, of *real* hunger up close: off the maps and on the ground. My job was to raise Americans' awareness of global hunger and to get people engaged in the fight against it. I was based in New York at the UN headquarters, tracking hunger hot spots and relaying the data and stories from WFP's work in the field to the rest of the UN community, its corporate partners, and the media. This entailed working with WFP's celebrity ambassadors, who raised the profile of these stories and gave them the cachet the mainstream media needed to broadcast and write about problems like hunger in places like Ruhiira, Uganda. One of those celebrity ambassadors was Lauren Bush (now Lauren Bush Lauren), an honorary spokesperson for WFP who was focused on engaging young people in the conversation. A college student and a fashion model at the time (as well as the niece of one American president and granddaughter of another), Lauren had developed an idea to sell a tote bag that would include a donation to WFP to provide school food for hungry kids. It was a really good idea—use fashion and commerce to get young people involved in combating global hunger—and Lauren and I started scheming about how to connect our interests in fashion and entrepreneurship with our passion for making the story of the world's hungry more widely heard.

Our initial plan was that the WFP communications office at the United Nations (UN) would sell the bags and keep part of the earnings as a donation to support international school feeding, which gives children a free meal *and* gets them into school. But the UN passed on the idea, as it was too far outside their usual operations, and there was no real model for doing anything like it—at least, not back then, and not in the way we had envisioned it.[1] Undeterred, I

---

1 Unbeknownst to us, Blake Mycoskie was launching TOMS Shoes around the same time with a "buy one, give one" philanthropic model to provide shoes for children in regions of poverty.

encouraged Lauren to work with me outside of the UN structure to create a small company ourselves, one that would sell the bags and still return a big donation to support school feeding.

In 2007 we started FEED Projects in the corner of my Manhattan studio apartment, and our first product, the FEED 1 Bag, launched on Amazon.com that April. Each burlap and cotton bag we sold provided the funds to feed one child in school for an entire year. At the time, it was an audacious idea to think that a fashion brand could be built on making everyday consumer products that are embedded with a donation to do good, but in the first 4 years we sold enough bags to provide 60 million meals to children in many of those hunger hot spots around the world.

Those 60 million meals taught me a lot more about the might of America. And about the power of doing things yourself, and cutting to the root of a problem. But what I took away from the experience was this:

> The individual consumer, when working in the aggregate, has massive power to effect global change.

As a cofounder of FEED Projects, I headed to Ruhiira in 2009 to visit one of the Millennium Villages that FEED was supporting. Three years earlier, in 2006, the Millennium Villages Project (MVP) had come to Ruhiira, as it did to other pockets of extreme poverty throughout sub-Saharan Africa, with the admirable mission to change things for people living under such difficult conditions. The stated goal for the villages in the 10 countries where MVP set up camp is to cut poverty in half by 2015. In Ruhiira, the organization had already made substantial inroads toward improving education, facilitating access to clean water, training and assisting farmers, setting up a system for microlending, building medical clinics, combating malaria, and improving overall health care for residents.

I was there because FEED had partnered with MVP to provide "FEED Health Backpacks" for community health workers who travel on foot, walking door-to-door, up and down the steep dirt mountain paths, to provide home health-care visits to families throughout the region.[2] Each FEED Projects backpack is made of eco-friendly waterproof material and contains basic medical tools, including scales for weighing infants, oral rehydration salts to

---

2 The Community Health Worker Program is now being implemented around the world.

treat diarrhea, family planning methods, rapid diagnostic tests, and Coartem (artemether and lumefantrine) therapy for malaria, along with a training manual to use during health education sessions. By the time of my visit, Ruhiira, the hard-to-access hot spot of hunger, was being transformed into a hot spot of new-found hope.

To get to Ruhiira, we flew for more than 14 hours from New York and then traveled by car in one of the ubiquitous white Land Rovers used by aid workers all over Africa. On the way from the airport, we stopped for the night in Mbarara, which is located in western Uganda, about 180 miles southwest of Kampala, the country's capital, and about 25 miles from our destination. It is the closest city to Ruhiira, and it is home to dairy and banana farmers. *Matoke*, or plantain bananas, are Uganda's staple, and Uganda is the second-largest global producer in the world. But sadly, as we have seen in many regions of the world, even though a diet primarily based on a single food—like corn in Central America, rice in Asia, or *matoke* in Uganda—may provide adequate calories, it can also lead to micronutrient deficiency, sickness, and even death. Mbarara has the largest number of milk processing plants in Uganda, and a steel plant built by the Chinese, who also run many of the grocery stores in East Africa. A subsidiary of Miller opened a large-scale brewery, and there's a Coca-Cola bottling plant on Mbarara–Masaka Road that employs hundreds of local residents. Taking all this in from the car window, I was struck by the juxtaposition of burgeoning global industry and some of America's most iconic brands against extreme poverty and starvation.

The next morning, our group of aid workers, along with a few photographers and journalists who were covering the MVP, were picked up by car to finish the journey to Ruhiira. We knew that out in the field we'd have few food and drink options, so before leaving Mbarara we pulled over at a small, Chinese-run grocery store. As I entered, I was mainly concerned whether I'd find food safe enough to eat. I thought my best bet would be local fruit, like the *matoke*—something with the skin on, that we could peel, in order to avoid foodborne illnesses prevalent in the region such as cholera, dysentery, and typhoid.

But as I looked around the store, other than the *matoke*, I found virtually no fresh or local food to choose from at all. A wide assortment of white bread, doughnuts, pastries, and cookies filled shelf after shelf of the five aisles in the small shop—all imported products full of empty calories. Stocked next to the sweets were bottles of soda and all sorts of flavored water. Low on options,

I selected several bunches of yellow *matoke*, some plain wheat cookies, and Nutella.[3] Reflecting on it, I realized I had been in exactly the same predicament many times before as I traveled throughout sub-Saharan Africa, Asia, and Latin America. Nutritious food is hard to come by in many of these places, but even in the remotest areas—in a small hut on the side of a dirt road—you can buy a soda or a candy bar. In fact, it was common for local people, even in the most isolated areas, to offer aid workers a Coke or a Sprite as a welcome gesture. And across Uganda, along the roadways of the cities and larger villages, small stands sell exactly the same things I found in the store: *matoke*, Coca-Cola, candy, and processed white-flour "treats."

I had expected to find *little* food, and as always, I worried that anything prepared locally might not be up to Western standards of food safety. I even expected that I might be hungry for stretches during the trip. But I did not expect to find so little *nutritious* food, and so many empty calories.

In fact, what I found in Uganda was a version of what we have in every mini-mart, delicatessen, vending machine, and the inner aisles of every supermarket at home: a sizable assortment of sugar water to drink; salty, fried snacks; and a variety of sweet, processed treats made from refined wheat flour, preservatives, saturated fat, and sugar. Seven thousand miles from the 7-Elevens and Cumberland Farms, the gas station mini-marts and the vending machines of home, I found something sadly familiar, with a peelable skin made of *plastic*.

Standing in that small grocery store in Mbarara, I had an epiphany:

> The food options on the shelves of the store in Uganda carried far greater long-term health risks than the questionable pieces of "unsanitary" local fruit I had expected to find, and feared.

Somehow, our massive snack and drink companies had figured out how to get their processed corn, soy, wheat, and sugar products to those at the farthest reaches of extreme poverty, even as distribution of good-quality nutritious food remained an insurmountable problem. I have pondered how it was that we had created a global food situation where, for a complex set of reasons, it is nearly impossible for whole,

---

3 A 2-tablespoon serving of Nutella (37 grams) contains 200 calories, 11 grams of fat (3.5 of which are saturated), and 21 grams of sugar. That is roughly the same as a Mars almond bar or a small bag of Raisinets. In 2012, Nutella settled a false advertising class-action suit for $3 million after running ads claiming that Nutella is a healthy breakfast for children.

fresh food to compete in markets flooded with an abundance of high-calorie/
low-nutrition processed options. And it struck me hard that there was something
impossibly wrong with that.

Then, arriving back at JFK International Airport in New York 2 weeks later,
I experienced déjà vu. Unlike so many areas of Uganda, in New York there was
food available *everywhere*. But just as in Uganda, my options were pretty much
limited to processed forms of wheat, sugar, fat, and salt, as well as sodas or various versions of colorful, dye-infused sugar (or artificially sweetened) water. I
could buy a variety of white-flour pastries at Starbucks, or myriad salty/sweet/
fatty crackers, pretzels, chips, cookies, and candy at Hudson News. Or I could
buy a bleached-white-flour roll encasing processed meat crowned with wilted
lettuce and high-fructose corn syrup–laden ketchup, alongside fat-drenched
french fries from any number of fast food restaurants. In short, there was virtually nothing that was truly nutritious and healthy available to eat.

The term "food desert" was coined in the early 1990s to describe a rural or
urban area overrepresented by fast food and underrepresented by healthy and
affordable "real" food options, like those available in the outer aisles of a supermarket. Plainly, our food system has become so globally homogeneous that the
food desert I found myself in at an American airport bore an eerie resemblance to
that in rural Uganda.

The irony was not lost on me. When I was standing in a small market in the
middle of a continent that was literally starving to death, it seemed as if the
American food and food-aid system addressed these "pockets of extreme hunger"
by saying, "Let them eat cake." *Chemically laden, highly processed, nutritionally
empty, high-calorie cake.* And then the very system that had intervened to end
hunger and starvation added, almost as an afterthought, "And let them wash it
down with a Coke."

I had begun my journey with the premise that if we wanted to derail terror,
we had to start with food—but now it was clear that we were employing the
wrong food and the *wrong* food policy, and it wasn't working for any of us. Not
back in Uganda, and not here at home.

> Bad food can kill you just as surely as no food can.
> It just takes longer.

And it made me understand the depth and breadth of the bifurcated global
crisis, where hunger is inextricably intertwined with obesity.

Today, Americans spend an average of *90 percent* of their food budgets on processed food. Overproduction and overconsumption of bad food leads to a calorie-dense, nutrient-deficient diet, which leads to a slow, insidious demise. It creeps up on us in the form of obesity, cancer, heart disease, and type 2 diabetes. It creeps up on us in the form of degraded soil, a compromised environment, weakened local agriculture, and dead zones in our waterways. It creeps up on us in the form of depleted aquifers, superbugs propagated by agribusinesses' extensive use of antibiotics in livestock feed, superweeds resulting from the overuse of herbicides, and even a loss of real food variety in favor of tasteless, nutritionally void, genetically limited, and highly "engineered" products masquerading as food.

Consider that the Food and Agriculture Organization of the United Nations reports that between the years 1900 and 2000, the world lost 75 percent of its crop diversity. As a single example, India had 30,000 wild varieties of rice in 1950, but only 50 are expected to remain in 2015. Then consider that the US Centers for Disease Control and Prevention (CDC) reports an epidemic in global obesity even as global hunger continues to be a chronic and pervasive problem. The food systems we currently have in place aren't working. They are environmentally destructive, detrimental to local economies, and devastating to diversity and resilience as they make people in the developed world obese and keep the hungry world hungry.

And as much of this was happening, we failed to see what was coming.

THE 30-YEAR SHIFT RIGHT BENEATH OUR NOSES

Roughly 30 years ago (about the time I was born), a series of shifts—some well-intentioned—led to the current global food system and modern American diet. Around 1980, farming and food production, patterns of food delivery and consumption, even the way we *thought* about food careened off the tracks.

The food systems we live with today were formed by innovation, technology, and abundance. But they were also formed by food science that forgot what food is, and why we eat it. They were formed from farm subsidies and food aid that were intended to save farmers and save lives, but were destined to destroy them. They were formed from the farm consolidation that resulted from well-intentioned, misunderstood legislation. They were formed by the genetics of hunger—and the genetics of profit. And the system operated confidently under this principle: By producing cheaper, more shelf-stable food, it meant we could feed more hungry people.

That sounded like a solution.

In fact, it sounded like the *perfect* solution.

Yet it was a misguided measure that created an even bigger problem that has been 3 decades in the making. As a result, today America's largest exports aren't civilian aircrafts and semiconductors, intellectual property or even corn.

America's largest exports are bad food, bad food policy, crippling hunger, and escalating obesity.

★ ★

In the United States during the 1980s, a series of seemingly unconnected events laid the foundation for what would culminate in the catastrophic and cascading failure of the global food system that we now face. The massive consolidation of US agriculture, the widespread adoption of high-fructose corn syrup, the large government subsidies for corn production, the US Supreme Court ruling allowing patents on genetically modified crops, the reduction in public funding for agriculture and nutrition (in favor of corporate research funding), and the shift from international agricultural aid to US food aid based on sending excess grain abroad—these are just some of the key issues that played a part in building an industrialized, mono-cropped,[4] highly processed, inequitable food supply.

Though it seems as though we have abundant food choice, today 40 percent of all US animals are raised in the largest 2 percent of livestock facilities. Four companies (JBS Swift, Tyson, Cargill, and National Beef Packing) slaughter 85 percent of US beef cattle. Two companies (Monsanto and DuPont) sell more than 50 percent of US corn seed. One company (Dean Foods) controls 40 percent of the US milk supply.

Domestic production of a product that barely existed before 1980, high-fructose corn syrup (HFCS), increased from 2.2 million tons in 1980 to more than 9.1 million tons in 2012 as HFCS replaced more expensive sugar and seeped into our diet. And those 30-year changes haven't affected only the American eater. Since 1980 the US has cut its agricultural development assistance to Africa

---

4 The controversial high-yield, cost-efficient practice of growing one crop on the same land year after year has numerous detrimental effects—for example, it depletes the soil and increases dependence on pesticides as it limits us nutritionally to fewer and fewer crops.

by a whopping 75 percent, and we have been spending 20 times *more* on food aid to Africa than we have helping Africans develop sustainable ways to feed themselves (in that time, African corn production has fallen by 14 percent).

Back home, the CDC estimates that 75 percent of US health-care spending goes to treat chronic diseases, most of which are preventable and linked to diet—including heart disease, stroke, type 2 diabetes, and at least *one-third* of all cancers.

Wrapped in good intentions, we made a tragic series of mistakes. We redesigned our food and our farms in every possible way. We misdirected our food-aid policy. And we misunderstood the impact that these misinformed good intentions would have in the global marketplace.

We confused "any" calorie with a "good" calorie.

★ ★

In most cases, these changes in food production and food policy began as progressive innovations. And they suited our lifestyles. Processed foods, frozen dinners, instant coffee, and prebaked cakes and cookies freed up time for other things, including careers for women who were entering the workforce. We were sold on the idea that food and drinks could be outsourced from the home, and could be purchased and eaten anywhere we happened to be. Beyond convenience, these products were relatively cheap and abundant, and provided instant gratification to consumers, and larger and more stable profits to manufacturers. They even offered what we thought were health benefits. Artificial sweeteners were the magic elixir that would free us from weight concerns. High-fructose corn syrup would help keep food prices low, which meant more people could afford to eat. Shelf-stable food was a wonder of "modern technology," and food scientists created products that tasted good and were enriched and fortified to provide "all the nutrients" that we used to get from whole foods.

So we adapted—and, in the process, we forgot how food is supposed to look and taste. Cooking turned into reheating. "Big," "cheap," and "sweet" began to outweigh "nutritious" and "well produced" by an (un)healthy margin. Shelf stability trumped freshness. We ate more even as we spent less: The US Department of Agriculture (USDA) reports that Americans spent 23.4 percent of their disposable income on food in 1929, 13.2 percent in 1980, and only 9.8 percent in 2011—that's more than a 25 percent decline just since 1980. In the meantime, our health-care expenditures have moved in the opposite direction:

In 1960 we spent 5 percent of our income on health care, and by 2008, that figure had reached 16 percent.

As the decades rolled by, we dieted—high fat, low fat, no fat, low carb, no carb, Paleo, Mediterranean, raw food, South Beach, Atkins, vegan, gluten-free, and Skinny Bitch; we Nutrisystem-ed, Weight Watcher-ed, juice fasted, and gastric bypassed. We shook our heads in disbelief at reports of escalating childhood obesity, early-onset puberty, and the introduction of airplane seatbelt extenders and extra-large coffins as we overburdened the health-care system with obesity-related diseases. Our dinner plates got bigger along with our waistlines. Our expectations changed, and we hardly noticed. When Jamie Oliver tried to introduce plain white milk into a West Virginia school district in 2010, the cafeteria workers insisted the children wouldn't drink it; what was a treat a generation ago—chocolate milk—was now the new normal, even for breakfast. When, in 2012, Mayor Michael Bloomberg tried to restrict the size of large, sugary soft drinks in New York City, he was labeled a "nanny state" socialist. There was outrage; as consumers, we have been manipulated by sophisticated advertising and savvy marketers into believing that we are exercising freedom of choice and getting value for our dollar when we are offered government-subsidized, artificially cheap, half-gallon-size servings of soda. Yet those large sodas are often nothing more than bait, ploys by marketers to entice us as they successfully draw in more of our consumer food dollars by promising what appear to be irresistible bargains—bargains we fall for even as our health fails.[5]

Over the past 30 years, American international food-aid policies changed as well. We shifted from actual aid—helping the developing world improve agricultural practices so people could feed themselves—to dumping government-subsidized excess grain on the hungry world, which effectively crippled local efforts at sustainable agriculture and long-term sustainable solutions. As a clear example of this issue, Indonesia's foreign minister asked the US *not* to send shipments of rice after the 2004 tsunami devastated its coastal regions and killed close to 250,000 people; he knew it would cripple local rice farmers. Instead he asked for money from the US to use to buy local rice. Then in March 2010, Haiti's president, René Préval, asked America to stop sending subsidized rice after the earthquake—and we continued to ship it anyway, devastating the local rice farmers.

---

5 As we will discuss in much more detail, government corn subsidies played a big part in the switch to high-fructose corn syrup to sweeten soda, and the resulting artificial price structure around soft drinks and other sweetened foods.

★ ★

And that's just the tip of the iceberg.

There are currently a billion overweight or obese people in the world, and the number is escalating. There are close to a billion hungry people in the world, and another billion who are micronutrient deficient. And we can't seem to fix these problems.

Although the obesity epidemic began back in 1980, it's been escalating, and we now see this data *everywhere*.

But here is something most of us don't see:

> When I was in Uganda, a "pocket of extreme hunger," I saw an
> alarming number of people who were *obese*.

Traveling from the hungry rural regions into the bustling urban centers, one can see the shape of people change dramatically. In 2008, nearly a quarter of the adults in Uganda were overweight or obese—which means that Africa is headed from the coals of starvation to the fire of obesity at warp speed. In so doing, they are bypassing a critical step.

Being fed, well.

Although obesity and hunger look different from some angles, when we look at them closely we see how similar the two problems actually are.

Neither group is fed *well*.

★ ★

Coming face-to-face with that processed, sugar-filled cake in Mbarara was a wake-up call, and it sent me down a path that eventually led me to give a life-changing TEDx talk in NYC, right before my 30th birthday. I had been devoted to feeding the world's hungry but could not make sense of the coinciding timeline of the obesity epidemic that started the same year I was born—1980. Making the connection between hunger and obesity and their similar causes over the last 30 years became the nexus of the 30 Project, a way of advocating for long-term food system change by gathering thinkers and doers to dinner events around the country. Through these dinners, I was able to invite people working on hunger, obesity, and agriculture to meet each other (an amazingly new concept for many organizations involved in these food issues) and then come up with big ideas for how the whole system can improve for all eaters. Through this new work as an activist and public speaker, I met Danielle Nierenberg, a leading thinker on agriculture, hunger and poverty, and we joined forces to form Food Tank: The Food Think Tank, which has only just begun to shape the global food conversation.

Incidentally, speaking about the hunger and global security link also led me to meet my husband, a US naval officer, at a foreign policy conference. Being a military spouse adds a layer of patriotism, as well as frustration, to my work—our troops and their families should be able to eat more healthful, local foods here in the US, and the desperation of hunger abroad should not be the cause of violence and terrorism that send our military into conflicts in today's world of plenty.

From the shoppers in the market in Mbarara to the travelers in the airport snack shop in New York City to the whole generation of global youth fueling their bodies and minds with ubiquitous highly processed foods, the options most available to all of us seem to be built on the premise of "let them eat cake."

It has become clear to me that we can't just *feed* the world—we have to feed the world *well*.

This book is a call for a new constitution to build a more perfect food system.

A food system that is socially just, ensures domestic and global tranquility, promotes general health and welfare, and secures the blessings of good food to our posterity.

And it begins with these very powerful words:

We the Eaters . . .

In this book I will outline a vision to rebuild the fundamental systems that will bring real food to our tables and, in so doing, allow us to begin to create healthy market options for the hungry world. One incredible lesson I learned from FEED is that there is strength in the union of consumers. And that mobilizing a base of consumer dollars is a route to solving problems, and promoting freedom, and a formidable means to shifting power.

> Consumer spending in the US represents 70 percent of our gross domestic product—more than government and industry spending combined.

I contend that if we shift our own dinner plates, by spending our consumer food dollars differently, we can begin the process of rebuilding a food system that will have cascading benefits. One that will begin to reverse the global hunger and the obesity crisis as it provides better food and better health, and improves local economies and the environment as it increases access to education and, ultimately, provides a foundation for a safer world.

It is a vision for change that first coalesced for me when I laid a map of terror hot spots over one of food-insecure regions and saw that they were one and the same. And then it crystallized in a mini-mart in Uganda as I stood in an aisle with shelves of highly processed cookies and cakes on one side and chemical-laden sugar water on the other. For many of you, it will begin somewhere a whole lot closer to home.

And here is the best—and most powerful—part of all.

This change doesn't have to begin just in the hipster neighborhoods full of wheatgrass-shooting, edamame- and kale-munching vegetarians. It can begin right in your own backyard, at a good old American-style family barbecue. It is a change that can begin and end with a burger, a bun, fries, salad, and an ear of corn. It can be washed down with a cold sweet drink, and followed up with homemade cherry-apple pie.

"We the Eaters" is not a movement to take away your burgers
and fries. It's actually a way to get them back.

The Husk, the Cob, and a Kernel of Truth

The Heart of the Global Problem with Corn

FOR MANY EATERS, the iconic American hamburger takes center stage—or center plate—at a backyard summer barbecue. Since Americans eat upward of 40 billion hamburgers a year—that's almost 130 hamburgers per person, or about 2.5 a week—it is evident that the burger takes a star turn on our plates during the rest of year as well.[1] What we the eaters have to figure out is how to build a better burger, as part of a better meal, as a means to better health and a better world, so we can still have our burgers—albeit in a slightly altered but greatly improved form.

But we can't talk about how to create a better burger, or discuss how to improve the quality of meat, until we understand corn and the huge role it plays in food production. And the reason is that what we call corn—*Zea mays,* which descended from the wild native plant found in Mexico, Guatemala, and Nicaragua called teosinte—has evolved into one of the world's most highly cultivated grains. In fact, corn is a significant building block of the vast majority of our

---

1   Only about 13 percent of Americans don't consume meat in their diets.

food—one that is a critical component of those 40 billion burgers Americans eat each year.

The centrality of corn as an agricultural staple is no better demonstrated than by the fact that its name, *Zea mays,* is derived from the Arawak Indian word *mahiz,* which means "that which sustains life." The Arawaks weren't the only people to recognize the value in maize cultivation, either. An early account of European settlers observing the maize plant in the New World was published in George Sale's 1763 book, *An Universal History:*

> *The ear is a span long, composed of eight or more rows of grain, according to the quality of the soil, and about thirty grains in each row; so that each ear at a medium produces about two hundred and forty grains, which is an astonishing increase. It is of various colours, red, white, yellow, black, green, & [sic] and the diversity frequently appears not only in the same field, but in the very same ear of corn; though white and yellow be the most common.*

If we cut from the 1700s to today, when 812 million metric tons of corn are harvested around the world and corn is increasingly villainized as a significant agricultural and health problem, we the eaters are forced to wonder how we got from there to here.

As agriculturally significant as the corn *plant* is, it is by no means a singularly perfect food. Just as with the *matoke,* a diet of only (or mostly) corn, or any other individual food for that matter, would leave us deficient in important amino acids and micronutrients.[2] Even still, in many ways corn is truly an agricultural masterpiece. It is relatively easy to grow, prolific, versatile, and has the potential to yield more calories per hectare than any other grain—roughly 5 tons (up to 10 tons in favorable conditions), which far surpasses the 3-ton yield typical of rice and wheat.

---

2   Other than mother's milk, there is no single, nutritionally complete food. Eating a diet based on one food alone can lead to malnutrition and eventually organ failure due to a lack of essential amino acids. People who eat a diet composed of mostly corn can suffer from something called wet malnutrition—they get enough calories, but are lacking key nutrients—and that leads to stunted growth, irreparable cognitive impairment, and increased vulnerability to disease. This is problematic in many developing regions that are dependent on a single agricultural product—like the *matoke* in Uganda, or rice in much of Asia. Genetic engineering of rice to add vitamin A, and of corn (quality protein maize) are limited attempts to combat this problem.

Corn, especially in its early forms, was also a nutritional treasure trove—rich in fiber, carbohydrates, B vitamins, and naturally occurring, biologically significant antioxidants called phytonutrients. For the Iroquois Indians, and many other small farmers, corn would likely be planted side by side with its two "sisters," squash and beans.[3] The prickly squash vines would help keep predators away from the young corn plant, and its large leaves and thick, low-growing foliage served to tamp down weeds. The nitrogen-fixing roots of the bean plants replaced the nitrogen in the soil that was depleted by the corn; the corn plants in turn provided a natural support for the beanstalks to climb. After the harvest, when the corn, squash, and beans were eaten in tandem, they provided a nutrient-rich and nutrient-complimentary meal. And as is the case with many other grains, if there are compromised growing conditions resulting in a poor harvest, all is not lost. Today the entire corn plant can be harvested for silage[4] and used for animal feed, or to produce biofuel. And that is only the beginning of the myriad uses we have developed for *Zea mays*.

FARMER VERSUS FACTORY

To *really* understand corn, we need to imagine two scenes. The first is of farmers planting dried kernels saved from the previous harvest. It is an image of people with few tools to turn over the soil other than their own hands or perhaps a primitive hoe and trowel. The dried seeds are tucked into long rows, or small mounds of rich, tilled soil, and will yield a harvest of ears with multicolored kernels, from white and yellow to blue, red, purple, and black. Add to that tableau the hope held by these farmers that the real promise of these seeds—these kernels of corn—was that they would be able to provide enough food to feed themselves and their families and, just possibly, enough of a crop to trade or sell. This is an image with many faces: from the indigenous North Americans and New World Pilgrims of the past, to the malnourished farmers in Ruhiira or many other places in the developing world today.

The second scene comes from the heart of America's Midwest. Picture a

---

3   The Iroquois Indians planted what they called the "three sisters"—corn, beans, and squash—together in the same mound. This was symbiotic planting, as each plant aided the proper growth of the others—a system emulated by Michelle Obama in the White House garden.

4   Silage is a fermenting process performed by tightly piling entire corn plants (or other grain) in silos, or rolled in plastic shrink-wrap. This begins the process of fermentation to convert the grain for animal feed or biofuel use.

farmer from the Corn Belt of western Iowa. It's the land of large-production farms, where farmers plant thousands of acres of corn with massive machines, and where mile after mile of the rippling cornfields have the power to take your breath away with their sheer size and uniformity. A hundred years of US agricultural policies have favored large factories over small farmers. We have witnessed the fall from a peak of 7 million US farms in 1935 to roughly 2.2 million today. And when you drive through the Corn Belt, it is impossible not to be struck by the promise embedded in all that fertile land and those vast expanses of grain. It is a portrait that encapsulates the magnificence of America as an agricultural giant like no other, and one that attests to the fact that we have evolved a system of agriculture that gives us the ability to produce *so much food.*

Yet these two images, of two very different farmers planting corn under vastly different conditions, contrast more than just scale. They represent deep changes in farming and food production both here in America and around the world. And these two very different pictures are very interconnected.

What went wrong with corn, the grain known by early farmers as
"that which sustains life," isn't something wrong with corn itself.
It is what happened to agriculture along the way from those
first farmers to the farmers of today.

This leads us to another set of scenes worth setting. I've climbed to the tops of central grain bins heaped full of corn in the Midwest—and have driven from New Jersey to California "Instagramming" massive cornfields in every state along the way—and marveled at the large-production farms and the towns and met the people who live and farm there. And I've stood, thousands of miles away, on top of enormous mounds of stockpiled food aid: sacks of US corn–soy blend stacked to the rafters in grain storage warehouses in Rwanda and other developing countries in Africa. What struck me, and struck me hard, was that even though these two views were separated by continents and oceans and decades of agricultural advancement, from both of these divergent vantage points the view was essentially the same.

In both the American Midwest and in developing countries supported
by aid, I witnessed a population of very unhealthy people against a
backdrop of lots and lots of corn.

Although 87 percent of America's 2.2 million farms are owned by individuals or families, it doesn't mean they are all small. Just 8.5 percent of the farms today account for 63 percent of all agricultural output. That means that in the Corn Belt, the farms are often thousands of acres in size. Seeds are planted and irrigated, pests and diseases managed, and crops harvested by massive pieces of equipment such as computer- and satellite-guided tractors and combines, cultivators, and threshers. This is high-tech farming that most growers who have tilled land with a hoe or trowel in his or her own backyard, or driven a small utility tractor up a field on a small family farm, would not recognize. These are factory farms engaged in large-scale industrialized farming, where corn seeds are genetically engineered, patent protected, and royalty bearing. Where yields per acre for corn have been pushed from 54.7 bushels in 1960 to 161.9 in 2009.[5] This is the land of the mono-crop—where the wisdom reaped by the Iroquois tradition of planting corn, beans, and squash together to nourish both the soil and the people has long since been replaced by synthetic chemical fertilizers and pesticides. While companion planting, crop rotation, and grazing animals would make sense for the health of the plants, the animals, the soil, the overall environment, and ultimately the quality of the food, farmers can, with less effort, push yields higher and keep costs down in the short term by growing a single crop and using chemical fertilizers to compensate for the depleted soil, and herbicides and insecticides to manage disease and insects.

Meanwhile, nitrogen runoff from these fertilizers has flowed from the Heartland, down the Mississippi River, and severely polluted the waters of the Gulf of Mexico, creating what is referred to as a massive "dead zone" in the Gulf. This is just one of a plethora of environmental casualties resulting from the push to increase yields. It is viewed as a consequence that simply must be managed in the delta region, while it is rarely viewed as a consequence of what we put on our dinner tables.

Today corn is a nearly $65 billion commodity that is traded on the futures market and controlled by complicated legislation like the farm bill, with its tax subsidies, price manipulation, tariffs, acreage retirement, surplus management, and crop insurance. Moreover, the corn we grow today in much of this country isn't the sweet corn we the eaters shuck for our barbecues. It is a completely different crop called yellow dent corn, or field corn—one that can't be eaten

---

5   Agricultural scientists predict they can push yields to 275 bushels per acre by 2030.

unprocessed and is used primarily for animal feed, processed grain and cereals, cooking oil, corn starch, and to produce sweeteners such as high-fructose corn syrup, as well as industrial products—from ethanol for fuel to plastics, explosives, and paint. Much of the corn from the Corn Belt has come to resemble a factory widget, an industrial product that forgot long ago just about everything it knew about being a food that people eat as part of a healthy diet. Essentially, corn has become an asset class managed by gray suits, instead of a foodstuff grown by overalls.

> Corn, like sugar, wheat, and soy, is more an agricultural commodity or economic good than it is a food.

Here is one final visual.

The farmers in the first scene—from the indigenous people of North and Central America to the European colonists, to any of the early farmers who planted corn as it spread around the world in the 18th, 19th, and 20th centuries, to the new farmers from hungry regions of the world today—were, or are, thin. Really thin. Indeed, small, subsistence corn farmers are often hungry.

The farmers from the second scene, the farmers of the Corn Belt of today, are generally not thin at all. In Iowa, the iconic corn state where 92 percent of all land is in agriculture and 17 percent of the state's workforce is connected to agriculture, a full 67 percent of people are overweight, of whom 30 percent are obese—a number that is predicted to hit 54 percent by 2030. Sitting in a local diner a few years ago in Iowa, in the heart of the Corn Belt, the land of those industrialized factory farms, I watched as local farmers arrived, one after another, for lunch. (It was a lunch that would include no local food whatsoever; since industrial farms grow large quantities of corn, soybeans, and wheat for processing, there is virtually no food that people could eat as it comes off the farms.) And almost every last one of those farmers was obese. Way too many were morbidly so.

Now consider that 90 percent of the food eaten in the farm state of Iowa is imported from out of state. This is not unique to Iowa: 80 percent of Illinois's acreage is farmland, yet only 4 percent of what is consumed there is also grown there. Illinois has 76,000 farms and 950 food-manufacturing companies, and virtually *no local food*. If we throw away all the complicated conversations about what went wrong with corn and consider just a single image, and a single metric—that the very people who are growing our food and feeding us are fat and sick—it should be enough to stop us in our tracks. The profession that built this country, a profession that once required physical toil and a tough, strapping physique, one that produced *whole food* pulled from the earth and eaten as it came out of the ground or off the stalk, has evolved in such a way that even many of our farmers are not healthy. And that should be our defining image, because the farmers in the Corn Belt are effectively living in a food desert, where they are eating the same food that we are.

The difference is that the farmers in the first scene—the Iroquois, other Native Americans, and some farmers in the developing world today—ate corn in its natural state. The extent of their processing might have involved pounding the dry kernels into grain. In fact, the ancient Aztecs, and even traditional Central American corn farmers today, soaked corn kernels in a solution of water mixed with crushed limestone, seashells, or wood ash to soften the outer hull of the kernels so they could be more easily ground into flour. This process of nixtamalization increases the availability of nutrients such as calcium and niacin in corn and makes the corn meal a better food.[6]

Herein lies the crux of the problem with corn.

Today the vast majority of the corn (along with wheat and soy)
we eat in America is processed into a lesser, nutrient-depleted food.
Not a better one.

The irony is that because of misguided motives, this lesser "food" is actually considered a superior agricultural product.

★ ★

So what exactly can the current state of our Corn Belt farms and farmers teach those new farmers in Uganda, with their handful of corn kernels and all that hope? And what can the past 30 years of corn agriculture teach us about how to eat? The answers are embedded in these three questions: *How exactly did the corn we eat get so sweet? Why, and how, did corn get so industrial and cheap? And once it was rendered sweet, industrial, and cheap, what did we do with it?*

---

6   Nixtamalization makes the niacin in corn more available to human eaters. Despite the fact that this process, used to make healthier tortillas, originated in Mexico, the country has become a net importer of US-made tortillas—which are produced industrially and don't have the same enhanced nutritional profile.

CANDY CORN

The first step en route to the current problematic state of corn was that we took something "good" and tried to make it "better." On the surface, it made sense to make corn sweeter (it tastes better) and less colorful (yellow or white was perceived to look more appealing to eat).[7] This process began with early farmers hand-selecting seeds for desirable traits like heightened sweetness and uniform color, and ended in the labs of giant companies such as Monsanto, Cargill, Syngenta, and Dow that have been breeding corn (and other plants) for traits like resistance to diseases, pests, chemicals, and droughts; faster growth; qualities suited for animal feed; and, more recently, ethanol production. Along the way, we inadvertently selected some of the nutrients out of corn in favor of a higher starch and sugar content and "better" appearance, and, by introducing this kind of high-tech genetic engineering (GE), possibly opened a Pandora's box that could hasten a decline in human and environmental health.

Corn in the time of the Pilgrims and the first Thanksgiving was multicolored— yellow, blue, purple, green, red, even black. (This deeply colored corn was higher in anthocyanins, powerful antioxidants that have been shown to fight cancer, lower blood pressure, and reduce inflammation.) Overall, the corn of years ago contained a wider range of health-improving phytonutrients *and* had a much lower sugar content than today's corn. Today, the sweetest varieties contain up to 40 percent sugar. It got that way through natural mutation and selective breeding.

An ear of blue corn (try to find that at your local supermarket outside a bag of tortilla chips) has 99.5 milligrams of phytonutrients per 100 grams; bright yellow corn has 70.2 milligrams; an ear of white corn has only 1.54! The adage to eat the deepest-color grains and vegetables is backed by substantial science, but to placate sugar-loving palates and the false metric of lighter vegetative beauty, we have incrementally bred the nutrients out of corn (and most of our other food as well).

But why stop at sweetness when we can make corn "better" in so many other ways? This process was set in motion in 1980, with a Supreme Court decision (*Diamond v. Chakrabarty,* 447 U.S. 303 [1980]) allowing the patenting of genetically engineered bacteria (to be used to clean up oil spills) and, by default, other types of "proprietary" living things. With this legal precedent, plant

---

7   New corn growers in much of Africa express resistance to growing "yellow corn" because of the negative association they have made between the corn color and US food aid.

breeders could now patent and own the royalty rights to seeds. Of course, the main adopters of this technology were the groups that could benefit the most financially—for-profit corporations like Monsanto, Syngenta, and others. Now that we had the technology to do so, why not engineer the sweetest, highest-yielding, toughest, most weather- and disease-resistant crop of supercorn possible—as a means to feed the hungry world, and to lock in more secure profits for everyone, including the farmers, seed manufacturers, and food producers? Throw in higher protein—accomplished when quality protein maize (QPM) was introduced in the late 1990s—and it sounded like a biotech dream.[8]

BIOTECH DREAM, OR "FRANKENFOOD" NIGHTMARE?

For many patent holders, owning the commercial rights to the DNA of an important food crop is certainly a financial dream. There is a great divide between those who think genetically modified organisms (GMOs)—in which the DNA from two living things that would not be able to combine in nature is crossed— are a necessary route to an improved and secure global food supply and those who are concerned about the long-term consequences of what they have dubbed Frankenfoods.

Proponents of this technology believe it is beneficial to intentionally engineer seeds that produce plants with desirable characteristics, whether that means resistance to disease, pests, or drought, or any number of other attributes perceived to be better—all as a way to increase yields. Opponents of the technology, meanwhile, raise concerns that genetically modified (GM) crops will cause unforeseen health consequences and environmental damage, limit biodiversity, and inherently change the nature of plants and agriculture as they continue to be manipulated in "unnatural" ways. From an economic standpoint, the concerns center on fears that seeds will become the royalty-bearing intellectual property of large corporations, as seed patent holders squeeze out small farmers and food production becomes an even more corporate-controlled and profit-driven

---

8   In 2000, the World Food Prize was awarded to Surinder Vasal and Evangelina Villegas of the International Maize and Wheat Improvement Center for developing the GM corn plant with a higher amount of usable protein, called quality protein maize, as a solution for global hunger. On June 19, 2013, it was awarded to a group of scientists, including one from Monsanto, for developing the process of inserting foreign genes into the DNA of plants 30 years ago. (The World Food Prize has been criticized for its focus on industrialized agriculture.)

industry than it is today. Due in part to these concerns, Peru has a ban on GM crops until 2022, and they are legislated against, in some capacity, in numerous other countries, including Switzerland, France, Austria, Hungary, Greece, Bulgaria, and Luxembourg. Hungary recently burned 1,000 hectares of GM corn, and in March 2013 there was a March Against Monsanto in 436 cities in 52 countries around the world. Recently, even Mexico, our corn-loving neighbor to the south and the birthplace of modern seed breeding, banned the growing of GMO corn. Apparently, some people's idea of a biotech dream is an agricultural nightmare to many others.

★ ★

Since the 1980 Supreme Court ruling, when a company spends money to genetically alter plants, they can patent them. The patenting of GMOs functions a lot like the commercial hybrid seed market that's been consolidating over the past 30 years. It pushes farmers to either buy new seeds year after year, or pay royalties. From the dawn of agriculture, farmers have collected and saved seeds from each year's harvest to plant the following year. If the seeds are hybrids or patent-protected GMOs, farmers can no longer do that—at least, not without paying a yearly royalty, which makes it very tough for small farmers to grow food affordably. This has become an especially sticky subject since seeds and pollen are so hard to control: Monsanto has sued farmers who never planted Monsanto patent-protected seeds but whose non-GM plants commingled with the patented DNA the old-fashioned way—cross-pollinated by bees or via wind drifts from neighboring fields. Through no fault of their own, these farmers ended up with plants carrying the patented genes. To date, the courts have ruled in favor of the corporations—if you have GM plants growing on your land, you owe royalties to the patent holder, and it doesn't matter how they got there.[9]

> Just 30 years after seed patenting became legal and genetic engineering technologies started to spread, more than 70 percent of the processed foods we eat contain genetically engineered material, and almost none of them are labeled in the US.

---

9   In a twist, on June 6, 2013, a class-action suit was filed against Monsanto when "rogue" GM wheat not approved for sale anywhere in the world was found in the DNA of wheat on farmers' fields in the US, likely as a result of field testing conducted by Monsanto years ago.

That means that we the eaters who have concerns about eating GM foods will have a tough time determining what we can and can't eat.

★ ★

SPRAY AND PRAY?

One goal of genetic engineering was to create herbicide-resistant, or "Roundup Ready,"[10] seeds by embedding a gene in, say, a corn plant that would allow it to thrive despite exposure to weed-killing pesticides. Another was to control insects such as corn rootworm by inserting a gene in the corn that would produce a protein to kill the insect when it consumes part of the corn plant. This technology was intended to reduce the use of pesticides and allow farmers to grow more corn at a lower cost; indeed, industry regulators and Congress were told as much in 1996, as the first GM food crops were being introduced.

However, the most recent evidence shows that GM seeds have resulted in a *rise* in pesticide use, not a *decline*. How did that happen?

When farmers grow plants that can withstand the application of a weed-killing herbicide, they use the herbicide (in this case, Roundup) *more* frequently. More frequent application does several things. Initially, it reduces weeds, as it is supposed to; but that soon causes rapid evolution of the few weeds that can survive. With all the dead weeds, the resistant weeds have room to spread, and that means we are effectively breeding more and more new weeds resistant to Roundup. Thanks to fields upon fields of GM seeds, there are 23 known superweeds that are resistant to Roundup across thousands of acres of farmland in the US. The solution to that, in the eyes of the chemical companies that produce both the GM seeds and the chemicals sprayed onto them, is to create even stronger weed-killing herbicides, and to engineer new seeds that can withstand these new herbicides.

According to a study by the University of Washington, the continued use of herbicide- and pesticide-resistant seeds has boosted herbicide use by 25 percent and pesticide use by 7 percent. More pesticides are needed to combat the emerging numbers of superbugs, which have adapted to the protein in Monsanto's Bt corn, which was designed to kill the corn rootworm.[11] And those numbers are expected to rise dramatically.

---

10   Roundup is the trademarked name for Monsanto's version of the herbicide glyphosate.

11   Monsanto makes Bt corn, soy, cotton, and canola seeds embedded with the bacterium *Bacillus thuringiensis,* which kills the larvae of insects that damage the crops.

In the future, there will inevitably be more of the chemical glyphosate in the water and the air, as well as in the soil and our food. In addition, we will need new pesticides to combat the new weeds and bugs.

And why should we the eaters care?

For starters, there is evidence that high levels of exposure to glyphosate can cause damage to DNA and the nervous and endocrine systems, as well as birth defects, cancer, and early death in lab animals. Then consider that a more potent chemical herbicide that farmers may be forced to use if Roundup ceases working is 2,4-D, which is one of the active defoliant ingredients of Agent Orange. Yes, *that* Agent Orange—the one created by Monsanto and used to clear vegetation during the Vietnam War. From Monsanto's point of view, since it produces the seeds and the chemicals those seeds require, this is brilliant vertical integration with a proven track record of profits. But from the eater–consumer standpoint, it seems like a conflict of interest that chemical companies are now seed companies, pushing farmers to view their livelihoods as going to war with nature, even as it serves corporate interests more than their own. This is especially concerning when you consider that nature has some pretty efficient (and cheap) systems for weed prevention—things like mulch and crop rotation, the latter of which also helps promote crop diversity.

★ ★

But a central—and noble—goal of the GMO dream was to end global hunger and malnutrition.

In 1996, when less than 10 percent of corn and soy acreage in the US was planted with GM herbicide-resistant crops, it was estimated that roughly 944 million of the global population (16 percent) were hungry. By 2013, 85 percent of corn and 94 percent of soybean acreage in the US was planted with herbicide-resistant GM crops, and the number of the hungry around the world had dropped to 842 million (roughly 12 percent, or 1 in 8 people).[12]

Although the number of hungry around the world has decreased since the

---

12   Global hunger numbers are difficult to estimate, and averages hide the fact that some regions improve and others worsen. For example, despite improvements in some regions, in the October 2013 report released by the Food and Agriculture Organization of the United Nations, hunger in sub-Saharan Africa and West Asia had increased by 1 million since 2008–09.

widespread adoption of GM crops, there is broad consensus that the improvement has not been what was anticipated—nor has it been nearly enough. Nor is the drop in hunger a direct result of GM crops. In America, although hunger was thought to be nearly eliminated between 1960 and the late 1970s, by 1980 there were 20 million hungry people, and today—despite the GM corn and soy—there are more than 49 million hungry Americans. Internationally, we have not made the inroads necessary to reach the goal set forth by the 1996 World Food Summit to cut those hunger numbers in half by 2015, let alone reach the more aggressive 2001 Millennium Development Goal (MDG) to cut the number of the total population of hungry in half by 2015.[13] And in 2009 when the global recession hit, even with all those GM crops, hunger increased as more than 1 billion people went hungry.

Meanwhile, more and more eaters are growing concerned about the technology and would rather not buy GM food. Beyond the aforementioned animal studies related to pesticides, there is little conclusive data on how GM seeds will impact human health and the health of our planet in the long run. But what is clear is that in the years since genetically engineered seeds have been introduced, they have not proven to help the environment or end hunger, nor have overall general health outcomes improved. In fact, except for Hawaiian papaya and some squash, arguably all of the other GM food crops (alfalfa for cows, canola for oil, corn, cotton for oil, soy, and sugar beets) are ingredients that contribute to a less healthy diet and greater obesity. The correlation between the spread of GM crops and the spread of waistlines is hard to miss.

SO, GMO, WHAT HAVE YOU DONE FOR ME LATELY?

Since GM crops were first introduced in the marketplace, the numbers of obese and overweight people around the world have skyrocketed. Yet despite the compelling 30-year timeline GMO technology shares with global weight gain, the word "obesity" only recently began appearing in the various debates about GMO food. Even if there are no bulletproof long-term studies linking the consumption of GM corn and soybeans (and sugar beets and canola) to weight gain, we know that the increase in consumption of things like soda, snack foods, sweets, processed meats, and fast food are linked to the increase in obesity. *And* we also know that all of those foods are made with GM corn, and often with sugar and

---

13   The MDG's more aggressive target accounts for population growth.

canola oil. The goal of increasing yields of GM corn, soy, and sugar (and Canola and cotton for oil) is a proxy for increasing the quantity of junk food—and its partner, obesity. The system built on growing more and more of a few crops and decreasing dietary diversity has, at the absolute least, a strong correlation with worsening global health. Even if that is the only established connection between GMOs and human health, might that not be enough?

Or, better said by Jonathan Foley, the director of the Institute of the Environment at the University of Minnesota, "I worry that GMOs are sometimes the victims of reductionist thinking where the focus is on technology and business models, and less on the social and environmental impacts they may cause."

As we examine the outcomes of GMO technology, we are constantly weighing the good against the bad. The problem with this entire conversation is that we keep increasing the world's reliance on corn-centric agriculture when a look at the big picture of our global food system suggests that we shouldn't be planting more corn at all.

This brings into focus the biggest question about GMO technology: If GM seeds are being used to create more and more of the foods that we should not be eating, what is the endgame? Consider the stance taken by Margaret Mellon of the Union of Concerned Scientists, who explains that her "major concern about genetic engineering is not its risks, but that its over-hyped promises will divert resources from the pursuit of more promising technologies." When this concern is viewed alongside the comprehensive 2008 study by the World Bank and the UN that concluded that "GM crops would only play a small role in solving world hunger," we begin to see the scope of the problem.

★ ★

Now that we know how corn got sweet and how a modern-day version of that same technology is potentially making corn less healthy for us and for the environment, it's natural to wonder: How did corn become an industrial product, and how did it get so cheap for us to buy and so profitable for farmers to plant?

PILING UP THE (CORN) CHIPS

Even before GM technology, we made corn artificially cheap by removing just about all the free-market economics that normally set prices in the first place. A piece of legislation that started out as well intentioned and necessary, but wound up exploited and corrupted by politicians and profit-seeking opportunists empowered by corporate interests, gave farmers, not just seed and chemical companies, incentives to become corn-centric.

In order to protect against some of the economic risks of farming that were widespread during the Great Depression, Congress passed a far-reaching piece of legislation called the Agricultural Adjustment Act of 1933, which would later become known simply as the farm bill.[14] This legislation evolved out of an over-supply of grain crops in the 1930s when prices fell so low for corn and other crops that in Iowa farmers were burning their own corn to heat their houses because it was cheaper than coal. In fact, corn prices hit rock bottom, and the crop was rendered almost worthless. Farmers were losing their farms and filing for bankruptcy at record rates, a result of grain surpluses coupled with low demand, all of which was made worse by the broad economic effects of the Depression.

To stabilize supply and demand, and to help farmers get through the crisis, the legislation included payments to farmers to incentivize them to *not* grow crops on part of their land (manipulating supply) and gave the government power to buy and store the excess storable grain to be used later in times of need (manipulating supply *and* demand). Over the years, many other programs were established to control the grain market as a means to create a stable food supply for eaters and a stable financial situation for farmers. In 1983 the USDA's existing payment-in-kind program used "acreage reduction" to try to protect commodity prices after bumper harvests in 1981 and 1982. Facing surpluses of corn, lower domestic demand, and falling exports, the government paid a record number of farmers to leave their land unplanted. A separate initiative called the Conservation Reserve Program (CRP) also "rents" land from farmers as compensation to not plant, and the program accounts for roughly 30 million acres of unplanted farmland in America in any given year—even today. Further, agricultural commodity subsidies were put in place to help struggling US farmers and to feed the hungry by guaranteeing a certain price per bushel for crops *before* they are grown. In other words, if the price per bushel drops below the government-guaranteed price, the farmers receive a subsidized payment to make up the difference. Today

---

14 It took on this generic nickname in 1938. A new farm bill has been negotiated every 5 to 7 years since then. The most recent farm bill—the Agricultural Act of 2014—passed after 4 years of debate in Congress.

corn receives more subsidies than any other crop, although the most recent 2014 Farm Bill replaced direct crop payments with crop insurance.

All these programs are well-intentioned efforts to maintain a healthy economic environment for farmers and to stabilize crop prices. The CRP justifies this under the umbrella of "protecting the environment." When farmers leave acreage fallow, the use of chemical fertilizers is cut, waterways are less subject to pollutants, and wetlands and wildlife habitats are protected. So, it's evident even to the US government that chemically intensive agriculture is bad for the environment. But reflect back for a moment and consider that the transition to GMO-based agriculture is based on the premise that *we need to continue to increase yields so we can feed the hungry.* Yet we are paying farmers to *not* grow corn as we simultaneously invite for-profit companies to manipulate plant genes to increase yields in ways that may ultimately hurt farmers and eaters. In this light, genetically modifying seeds to produce higher yields by making them tolerant to polluting chemicals—when there are serious concerns about the health and environmental impact of the chemicals and the underlying technology while we are paying farmers to not plant corn—seems a little crazy.

> Once corn became a subsidized, lower-risk crop for farmers to grow,
> we started growing too much of it.

So we started finding more ways to use this falsely cheap option—we found more and more ways to use it for feeding people (processed food), animals (to produce meat and dairy), and, now, our cars (ethanol).

CORN, CORN EVERYWHERE, BUT NOT AN EAR TO EAT

So, we now have an overabundance of corn that is crippling us, and yet very little of it is actually eaten as fresh, unprocessed grain.

Broadly stated, the USDA and the farm bill function, in many ways, like the Federal Reserve Bank does when setting US monetary policy. The Fed implements, oversees, and manipulates monetary policy to stabilize the US economy as the dollar moves in the fluctuating global marketplace. Just like dollars, agricultural commodities such as corn, wheat, and soy are so vital to our survival that we use external artificial measures to stabilize them.

The ultimate effect of all these programs is the creation of a financial safe haven for growers of the most storable and calorie-dense foods—chiefly, corn, wheat, and soy—and an incentive to plant more and more of them. The farm bill established safety nets for certain agricultural products, like corn, that are not in place for other more perishable farm products, like fruits and vegetables. This is why corn, wheat, and soy are now everywhere, and in everything—it's been estimated that 77 percent of the food in supermarkets contains at least one of these products.

Since corn in particular became both financially safe for farmers to grow and artificially cheap, we found as many uses for it as possible. Corn in one form or another is used in livestock feed, soda, bread, peanut butter, jelly, salty snacks, sweet desserts, salad dressing, paint, candles, fireworks, antibiotics, aspirin, cough drops, monosodium glutamate, xanthan gum, and citric and lactic acids. Corn by-products are used to cool down superheated drilling bits used by oil companies, and can be used to remove cholesterol from milk and eggs. And corn is, in one form or another, an ingredient in far more of our foods than listed above, including the highly controversial manufactured sweetener known as high-fructose corn syrup.

Now, not all of these things are necessarily bad. In fact, much of it is a testament to ingenuity and science: *Look at all we can do with corn!*

But there are consequences for this "corn ingenuity" that are far-reaching. For example, the system of payments and insurance to commodity farmers skews government subsidies, helping the largest factory farms, not small local farms—a fact that contributed to the overall drop from 7 million US farms in 1935 to just 2.2 million today. This makes it hard to find locally grown food, mandates that crops be storable for long periods of time or used for processing, and increases transport costs and fuel use.

Those fuel costs are also manipulated by oversupply. Driven by the goal of oil independence, ethanol from corn came to be viewed as a promising, viable biofuel. Sadly, government mandates, which began in 2005, pushed for increased corn-based ethanol production and continue to do so, despite the fact that producing corn-based ethanol is not currently cost effective. Since the production of ethanol from corn actually requires a substantial amount of fuel (we need to fuel the tractors and trucks that grow and move the corn, and the factories that turn corn to ethanol, and we use petrochemical-based fertilizers and pesticides to grow the corn), fossil fuel use has not declined in a manner that makes ethanol sustainable. Yet 40 percent of the corn produced in the US today is now grown to produce ethanol—which, of course, pushes up the price of corn. Meanwhile, ethanol has a fuel economy 27 percent lower than that of gasoline. This lack of efficiency is technically offset by lower cost at the pump, but since ethanol is heavily supported by government subsidies to the tune of 45 cents a gallon, what all of this means is that corn-based ethanol ends up costing roughly 70 cents a gallon *more* than non-corn-based gasoline.

There is criticism that by growing corn to make ethanol we are inadvertently causing a shortage in corn—and other crops—available for food, and therefore creating an uptick in food prices. To combat this concern, the ethanol industry has started to create ethanol from the stalk and cob—cellulosic ethanol—as opposed to the current method of extracting the kernel starch. Once again, we have fallen deeper down the rabbit hole and are trapped in a corn conundrum. The corn ethanol business now employs 90,000 Americans, and with 40 percent of the US corn crop earmarked for ethanol, we are faced with what is viewed by most as a good idea that just didn't work out. But it is hard to exit without collateral damage. In June 2013 the president of Chevron stated that gasoline prices would likely rise as refiners exported more gasoline, thereby tightening the domestic supply, since refiners use increasing exports as a means to circumvent the Renewable Fuel Standard's (RFS) ethanol mandate. In other words, when the refiners can make more profit exporting gasoline because of ethanol mandates in the US, they will do that—which means in the US, supply goes down, and the price at the pump goes up.

★ ★

For we the eaters' purposes here, all we have to know is that the financial incentives and risk mitigation offered by our tax dollars keeps our agricultural system in the corn business. Farmers today can actually sell corn for less than it costs them to grow because of the subsidies we pay them with our tax dollars. This is precisely why so many of the products in the inner aisles of supermarkets and the pumps at the gas stations contain this one grain.

With corn now abundant and financially "safe" as far as agricultural products go, we keep finding even more ways to grow it, more places to dump it (foreign aid), and more ways to process it (cheap food and ethanol), with little regard for long-term consequences, even as new evidence suggests that all this corn overproduction is having a devastating effect on our health.

WHEN GRAIN BECAME (SUGAR) CANE: LIQUID CORN

"The stalk is jointed like a cane, is supplied with a juice, as sweet as that of sugar cane; but from the experiments that have been made, it appears to be uncapable of being rendered useful."

The Modern Part of an Universal History from the Earliest Account of Time, Volume 39, 1763

Well, that might have been what they thought back in the 1700s, but in the 1960s the government subsidies for corn helped the food industry create a really cheap and even sweeter source of sugar by isolating an enzyme from corn's starch and converting it into a highly concentrated "fructose syrup." High-fructose corn syrup (HFCS) became the elixir of the industrialized food gods. Manufacturers now had a source of sweetness that was less expensive than cane or any other form of sugar—such as sugar beets, honey, or maple syrup—and offered properties that increased shelf stability, including better moisture retention and a lower freezing point.

By the 1970s, HFCS was being produced at industrial levels, and the secretary of agriculture under Presidents Richard Nixon and Gerald Ford, Earl Butz, who objected to the acreage reduction programs of the farm bill, told farmers to plant corn from "fence row to fence row." And they did, amounting to a far-reaching "get big or get out" agricultural policy that began with the intention of increasing US food supply and farm income. And yet a few years later, in the 1980s, faced with a surplus of grain, we course-corrected once again by paying a record number of farmers to *not* plant corn; roughly half the Corn Belt sat unplanted as payments rolled in from the government.

Now consider what happened as a result. Before 1980, the US imported close to 45 percent of the sugar it consumed while producing only 55 percent domestically. In 1981 the government instituted price supports for US sugar beet and sugarcane producers, which shut our neighbors to the south, such as Mexico, Brazil, and the Caribbean nations, out of their biggest export market for sugar. By 2004 domestic production accounted for 87 percent of the US market for sugar. This means that US sugar, the kind made from sugar beets and cane, became much more expensive than it would have been if the price protections hadn't been in place. Because of rising domestic sugar costs, many food producers shifted to using cheaper HFCS instead, reducing even further the opportunities for foreign sugar farmers to sell to the US market. We interrupted the global sugar economy and, at the same time, inadvertently set off a nutritional time bomb. By 1984 both major soft drink companies had shifted from sugar to HFCS, opening the floodgates on the river of cheap, sweet drinks, candy, and snacks that would compromise the Western diet and global health.

★ ★

If we look at the role corn played in sugar consumption between 1980 and 2007, we can begin to understand why so many Americans got so fat—and how food became such a big problem for so many people.

Overall, available sugar for consumption rose from about 126 pounds per capita in the 1980s to 154.2 pounds by the 2000s. Cane and beet sugar consumption dropped from 86 pounds per capita in 1980 to 62 pounds in 2007. Yet, consider this:

The annual rate of consumption of HFCS increased from 19 pounds per capita to *56 pounds* (the USDA puts it as high as 63.8 pounds) —a jump that represents the single largest change in our diets between 1980 and 2007.

Now ask yourself this: How much corn syrup have you knowingly and intentionally eaten this week? According to the Census Bureau, each of us consumed 56 pounds of the stuff in the past year, which is more than a pound a week. But when was the last time you said, "I'll have the corn syrup?" or "How about a side of corn syrup?" By and large, we don't *choose* to consume corn syrup. But there it is, lurking in many of the processed foods we eat every day. Unlike our ancestors, who had to seek out nature's sweeter foods, like fruits, we have sugar available all day every day, even in salty and "healthy" foods. It's in our ketchup, salad dressing, yogurt, bread, pasta sauce, canned vegetables and fruits, and even so-called natural products like what you think of as maple syrup.[15] Perhaps most insidious is the fact that sugar, often in the form of HFCS, is also

---

15   Log Cabin, Aunt Jemima, Mrs. Butterworth's, and Kellogg's Eggo syrup all list HFCS and corn syrup as the first two ingredients and contain no actual maple syrup. Although many consumers think of these products as maple syrup, they are (appropriately) labeled as just "syrup."

lurking in most of our bottled drinks. Half of all Americans drink one sweetened beverage every single day, which adds 178 calories to men's diets and 103 to women's—almost none of which have any nutritional value.

Let's do some quick math. At approximately 1,300 calories per pound, the additional 37 pounds of HFCS consumption per person per year means that, compared to 1980, the average American has added an extra 48,100 calories to his or her diet in corn syrup alone. Since it takes 3,500 calories to gain one pound, this represents 13.7 pounds of weight gain per person per year. Subtract the calories for the 24-pound decline in our consumption of cane and beet sugar—or 8.9 pounds in added body weight—and you have 4.8 pounds per person per year in weight gain, or 48 extra pounds over 10 years. That means in the time it takes to reach age 30, an individual could, by this math, be roughly 144 pounds heavier than the same person a generation ago based only on an increase in sugar consumption, most of which is quietly added to our food in the form of HFCS.

★ ★

But it isn't just any old fat we've been adding to our waistlines. In 2010 researchers at Princeton University fed rats a diet high in HFCS and fed a control group an equal amount of calories from sucrose, or plain old cane sugar. Then they compared weight gain between the two groups. The rats eating the high HFCS diet gained significantly more weight; developed more "belly" or adipose fat, which is strongly correlated with heart disease; and had higher circulating triglycerides than the rats eating a sucrose supplement—even though they both consumed exactly the same number of overall calories and the same amount of sugar.[16]

The corn industry is printing disclaimers and running television commercials stating that there is a lot of "confusion about corn syrup" and "flawed methodology" in the Princeton study. But if you listen to the scientists, and if you look at your fellow Americans, and then you read the Census Bureau report on sugar consumption, it is pretty hard to not come to the conclusion that the food industry—and the government's good intentions—have inadvertently sabotaged us.

The reality is that sugar *should* be priced based on what it takes to sustainably grow it, to pay farmers and workers fairly, and to process and transport it. If sugar cost more, sweet food would cost more, and this would be a good thing.

---

16   In 2008 the American Medical Association said there was insufficient evidence that HFCS contributed to obesity more than any other form of sugar.

Once again, sweets might be occasional treats rather than a dietary staple. And HFCS *should not,* in all probability, be a food option in a health-focused consumer environment. Then again, we have to do *something* with all that corn.

As a quick aside, honey, which is the oldest-known sweetener and is arguably more healthful than refined sugarcane or corn, has also failed to escape the consequences of the industrial food-production system. First widely reported in 2006 in the US, colony collapse disorder has wreaked inexplicable havoc on bee populations, requiring farmers to arrange for trailer-dwelling beehives to be trucked in to pollinate their crops. Honeybee populations have declined from 6 million colonies 60 years ago to just 2.5 million colonies today. Ironically, many beekeepers have actually resorted to feeding bees cheap HFCS, and it is now believed that the sweetener may be interfering with the bees' immune systems and playing a role in the rapid decline of honeybees, even as the USDA reports that the honeybee population is "too low for us to be confident in our ability to meet the pollination demands of US agricultural crops."

AMERICA'S CORN FARMERS—
PROVIDING CALORIES FOR THE WORLD

Corn-sugar-induced obesity is only half of the story of how corn contributes to the malnutrition equation. The other half is unfolding in developing countries, where our corn policies end up perpetuating long-term hunger.

The farm bill dictates many other measures besides subsidies to farmers—it regulates programs like the domestic school lunch program and the Supplemental Nutrition Assistance Program (food stamps).[17] It also governs international food aid. And so another way the farm bill was used to create demand for corn was by creating markets for it in the developing world. Stockpiles of grain here at home, paid for by government subsidies and set aside to control supply and keep prices from plummeting, turned out to be an obvious source of food for people in need—one that could be sent as an "in-kind" donation from US farmers to the world. While this can be a productive measure in times of crisis such as famine and drought, starting around 1980, "food dumping" became the primary system implemented by the US to address the hungry, at the cost of programs we had in place to promote local agricultural development abroad.

---

17   The federal government changed the name of food stamps to the Supplemental Nutrition Assistance Program in 2008.

That's right: Even though corn becomes cheap feed for livestock, cheap food for people, and a bevy of other products including ethanol, we still have leftovers, which we put on ships and send to feed the hungry in the developing world. In the long term, food dumping, as opposed to agricultural assistance, puts local farmers in developing countries out of business, which only extends hunger indefinitely as it builds a culture of food *dependence* instead of food *independence*. Further, introducing our corn-based, processed-food diet into regions where other staples have traditionally provided nutrition destroys not only their health, but also their culture of planting and cooking those traditional foods. All of this is destructive, but it's hard to turn off the faucet when the money keeps rolling in—to the tune of $60 billion to $70 billion a year in corn agriculture alone.

In 2014, just like it had for the past 80 years, the farm bill (officially called the Agricultural Act of 2014) contained provisions for government subsidies for crop insurance, land retirement, food stamps, and aid programs overseas, among other things. Unfortunately, President Barack Obama's request for sweeping changes in the foreign aid program—to discontinue the practice of shipping US-grown agricultural products like corn, wheat, rice to areas of need—has been, by and large, rejected by Congress, except for a token allocation for local purchasing.

CORN, THE NEW GLOBAL CURRENCY

US farm subsidies and our food system have sabotaged hungry farmers in developing nations as they have sabotaged us here at home.

> The same food technology and agricultural policy that is fueling obesity in America is simultaneously perpetuating hunger in developing countries—even as it dooms certain populations in these regions to obesity as well.

Meanwhile, in the past 30 years, the international community decreased agricultural aid to Africa by almost 50 percent in favor of food aid. And between 1980 and 2008, the US Agency for International Development (USAID) cut African agricultural aid by 75 percent, in favor of shipping out US corn and soy on American ships. In so doing, we have created a cycle of dependence that will interfere indefinitely with the ability of local people to pull themselves out of poverty and hunger. There is probably no better public acknowledgment of this than former President Bill Clinton's apology in 2010 for making a "devil's bargain on rice" when he undermined farmers in Haiti by dumping US-grown rice from his home state of Arkansas in the form of food aid after legislating farm protections for Arkansas growers. Rice farmers in Arkansas collected $1 billion in subsidies from the farm bill between 1995 and 2011 as Haitian farmers were put out of business and American rice was given away for free (further exacerbating their devastation after the 2010 earthquake). With the compromises made on the newest farm bill, it seems we are locked into many of these same policies for the next 5 years.

We now use the developing nations as a market for our excess corn and other subsidized crops. Initially, this too was done with good intentions, as a means to help feed the hungry. But it backfired terribly. It is now a structurally flawed system in which we control the supply *and* create the demand as we inadvertently hurt local farmers who are trying, and now failing, to sell their produce in markets depressed by US excess. This is ironically juxtaposed against the ever-present availability of soda, processed-white-flour products, and candy of all kinds in even the smallest market huts across the hungry world. Those tiny market huts are also now often surrounded by cornfields. The farmers work hard, but have been trained to use our chemical-intensive, mono-cropping systems to grow grain. Despite all their efforts, the adoption of the US system means that tiny market hut is selling processed foods from the same huge companies that provide processed foods to the Iowa diner where I sat down to lunch in the Corn Belt. What could function as a regional or local food system, where people actually buy and eat their neighbors' crops and keep money in their villages to help them grow wealth, is actually a one-way street for capital to leave a community, and another one-way street for poor-quality food to enter.

Reconsider for a minute my original premise—that in order to address the global *terror* crisis, we have to address the global *food* crisis. As Nobel laureate Lord John Boyd Orr said, "You can't build peace on empty stomachs." I would add that you can't build peace by destroying local agriculture through food dumping, or creating agricultural dependence, continued hunger, and increasing rates of obesity. In fact, food assistance has been shown to contribute to enabling the length and severity of conflicts.

Yet for centuries, agricultural aid has been fraught with more than a bit of an unsavory history. Aid is fundamentally about the spread of agricultural innovations and technology to new places, but in many ways, it has been a mechanism for a form of veiled colonialism. There are countless stories of European colonists taking over the lands of "primitive people" and introducing new crops and techniques that were meant to either make the colonists money or placate the indigenous people (and usually both). The history of sugar in the Caribbean is one of the best-known examples of this type of agricultural imperialism, and corn is in many ways following in its footsteps.

Governments around the world are being taught to model their food and agricultural systems after ours, not only by investing heavily in growing mounds of their own corn, but by subsidizing fertilizers as well (as if we don't already know the environmental effects of heavy fertilizer use on water and soil).

> GM corn is now being touted as the solution to African hunger, despite our knowledge of how harmful the overproduction of corn has been to Western health, and as new health concerns surrounding GM seeds and food remain.

Traditional crops are being lost as more and more farmers in the developing world focus on planting this one nutritionally limited crop that is unlikely to stabilize their economies or improve local health and food security.

THE FUTURE IS NOT FOR CORN ALONE

To establish the future of global food security, we have to stop using corn yields as the key metric for success. And before considering just how much corn to grow, we have to look at real demand. The most important question is not "Can we grow more?" It is "Do we the eaters really want more corn-based sweets and snacks, industrialized beef, and other corn by-products in the human diet?"

Which circles back to Ruhiira, in Uganda, and the MVP village where they are now planting corn—Big Ag-style corn. At some time in the future, they may have to pay yearly royalties to plant patented seeds, even if the DNA from those seeds should happen to spread to their own crops. It also means that these farmers will become dependent on the fertilizers and pesticides that are necessary to grow these high-input seeds, which ultimately may be too expensive for them to sustain. So although the programs of helping farmers farm for themselves are better than the programs of dumping our subsidized grain on hungry regions of the world, we should have serious reservations that we may be starting a new cycle of dependency on less-nutritious, potentially harmful corn in new agricultural zones.

Admittedly, it is easy, as a well-fed American, to find fault with virtually any system of aid or assistance. If we give food, it suppresses local agriculture; if we plant corn, it may encourage the same long-term cycle of poor health we built here in America—unless we help those farmers to not fall victim to the same story. When I was in Tanzania, a Masai guide complained to me about all the Western food that had crept into the local traditional agriculture and was making people in his country sick in ways they had never been sick before. It's clear the system we have in place is not working for any of us—why replicate it?

★ ★

On the upside, there is no reason we can't improve this system, and continue to do so each step of the way, as we gain wisdom in hindsight from what went wrong in our own farming industry—while of course maintaining a sensitivity to the fact that if you are hungry, you don't care about agricultural policy or long-term consequences; you just want to eat now and feed your kids. This raises the following questions: Who is behind aid? And what are their vested interests?

The very companies that fund the nongovernmental organizations that are helping farmers in the developing world are the same Big Agriculture companies here in the US that established our current, flawed system of growing food. The renewed interest in "agricultural aid," at least judging from the kind of talk you hear at the World Food Prize, the World Economic Forum, and in the halls of Washington, DC, is driven by the same mono-croppers that have built the architecture of obesity in the West. These companies use aid dollars—from the Gates Foundation, the US government, and other sources—as yet another subsidized market to buy their products, whether those dollars are used to buy patented, royalty-bearing seeds, or pesticides. One way or another, America and its corporations—and, subsequently, our farms and farmers—are so heavily invested in corn, soy, and wheat that they can't back out.

But back to those unhealthy farmers in the Heartland. Corn is shipped from their fields as corn and comes back the same way it arrives in all of our towns and cities: by the tractor-trailer load, in the forms of processed goods like soda and snack foods, and cheap meat. In short, *bad food*.

Only a minuscule fraction of the corn grown globally is eaten as it comes off the stalk. And the corn we are growing in this massive, mono-cropped system isn't even the same product as the delicious sweet corn we can pick up across America in the heat of summertime. This, in effect, makes the simple act of roasting a locally grown ear of corn and eating it at your family barbecue, while avoiding all processed forms of the grain, an act of separatist sabotage.

> Eating an ear of whole, local, colorful corn is sort of like throwing a boatload of tea into Boston Harbor.

The unhealthy miles of corn in the Midwest contribute to the transformation of what should be vibrant regions of diverse agriculture in America into distressed, unstable food deserts as they compromise the environment, drive up fuel costs, and contribute to obesity in farmers and non-farmers alike. On a global level, our corn dumping and corn-centric agricultural practices disguised as food aid and farming assistance in the developing world are all part of a faulty system that needs to be restructured.

If you are just beginning to see that cheap food, brought to us by way of prolific, overabundant, artificially price-controlled, genetically altered corn, may not be so cheap after all, consider that the $90 billion earmarked for corn subsidies comes from our tax dollars. So any time we buy a piece of "cheap" food, we should be aware that we are paying a hefty upcharge for that "cheap" food with both our tax dollars and our health-care costs. Somewhere along the way, corn stopped being a delicious, healthy food and became a nutritionally stripped commodity. And it continued down a path to where it is now itself a glorified superweed.

We the eaters can demand corn how it should be: *a whole grain that is a healthy part of our diets.*

First, if we buy only corn meant to be eaten as corn—on a cob or as a whole grain in a lightly processed food—we will remove a lot of the highly processed and GM corn-based food from our diets, such as breads, canned soups, syrupy yogurts, and, of course, junk foods, as we also drive demand. If we won't buy it, they'll make less of it and, eventually, farmers will grow less of it. That's the way markets should work. We can shift our collective food dollars to the farms and farmers growing what we *want* to eat, and what is a better model for the rest of the world. We can go to a farm stand or a store and buy fresh ears of corn and then roast them at our backyard barbecues. The only corn on our dinner plates should still be in kernel form (and preferably have the husk attached). Those kernels should, in the most perfect world, be the most colorful we can find, or at the very least bright yellow—and every last one of them should come from a local and ideally a pesticide- and herbicide-free farm. We truly are a corn-fed country, as my cross-country Instagram photos suggest, because yes, every state in America grows corn.

★ ★

Another benefit to this approach is that none of us would be buying or consuming food that contains HFCS. If everyone in America decided today to refuse to buy or eat any product that contained HFCS, some very interesting things would begin to happen. For starters, companies would be forced to escalate their efforts to provide alternatives to HFCS-sweetened products, just like Heinz did with its Simply Heinz ketchup, and as Pepsi did with the introduction of Pepsi Throwback—both sweetened with cane or beet sugar. Something else rather interesting would happen as well: We would, in effect, be conducting a Princeton study of our own. We could be the lab rats *not* eating HFCS and watching as our weight likely goes down and our health improves. Not by changing our caloric intake or how *much* we eat, but simply by changing *what* we eat.

★ ★

As the following chapters will demonstrate, this story is much bigger than just corn. In the past 3 decades, an increase in industrial food processing, the loss of small- and medium-size farms, and the overproduction of subsidized commodity crops have left us with an overabundance of the wrong foods across the board. Consider what would occur if we dismantled subsidies that favor the overproduction of corn, soy, wheat, and cotton, and replaced them with incentives that encouraged more diverse, healthful agriculture. And then what would result if we applied the same sound agricultural programs in Uganda, and everywhere else in the world that needs assistance. We would begin to revolutionize the entire food system. We would use the power of free-market dynamics to our advantage. We need to deploy our consumer dollars, with purposeful, health-conscious, economically sensible, globally connected spending earmarked for good food *now,* instead of health-care costs later, as a means to realign the food system.

Here is some food for thought: The 33 percent rise in obesity in America predicted by 2030 will come with $549 billion in added health-care expenses. If the rate of the increase in obesity drops by only 1 percent, we would save an estimated $84.9 billion dollars in health-care costs. The conclusion is obvious: It costs far more to treat obesity than to prevent it in the first place, even if that means absorbing higher food costs in the short term.

> Even with all this corn hating, there is a more hopeful
> story to tell, too.

A few years ago, as part of the 30 Project dinner series I was hosting when I was trying to connect a variety of food activists in different communities, I found a group of passionate, change-hungry food activists right in the heart of the Corn Belt.

Sioux City, Iowa, is not the first town you would envision as having a progressive food scene. The downtown deterioration runs deep, and the options for healthy food, and entrepreneurialism, seemed dead on the vine. But just beneath the surface of this small American city lies an exciting future, driven by young people and business owners who want something *better*. With the help and leadership of a local Iowa State University Extension and Outreach program, which has the mandate to build up local food systems, and hosted by a local pastor in the community garden he started at his church, I was able to put together a delicious and hopeful dinner event, which included honored guest and food icon Mark Bittman and was set on a table built of reclaimed wood from old barns and hand-delivered by the farm family who made it. At dinner, the debate wasn't about how we could increase corn yields, or use all the corn we have, but rather how the region could grow all kinds of different foods to locally supply a new health- and market-driven agriculture system. Even in the heart of the Corn Belt, where "corn is king" and Corn Palaces seasonally decorated with corn art were built in the 1800s to glorify the crop, I saw so much hope for the future of farming and eating, and a brighter picture of a forgotten town. The fortunes of corn (and, later, meat stockyards and Tyson plants) did not keep the promise of vibrant, teeming urban centers to many cities of the Corn Belt, as much of the money has been drained out to the suburbs or corporate headquarters far away. Luckily, there's a new crop of food entrepreneurs, like Caturra Coffee Roasting Company, and leadership from an Iowa State University extension program called Flavors of Northwest Iowa, to support farm shares or community supported agriculture (CSA)[18] and local farmers, and even a community garden at a

---

18 CSA is the upfront, contracted buying of shares of the upcoming harvest by individual community members who share in both the bounty and the risk of farming.

prominent Episcopal church where local-food dinners are now regularly hosted. It seems like in the Corn Belt, all foods *except for corn* will be the roots of a better future.

THE BEEF IN THE CORN STORY

I opened this chapter by saying that we had to talk about corn before we could talk about beef. And the reason is that 40 percent of the corn grown in America isn't used to make HFCS, or produce ethanol for cars; it isn't even used to fill our cupboards with unhealthy corn-based food products. As bad as all of *that* is, the hidden part of the corn story is that all the subsidized corn we grow is used primarily to feed livestock: cows, poultry, even fish. That burger that needs to be made better is made of meat constructed in part by corn. And so is that farm-raised salmon that masquerades as heart-healthy wild salmon. Most of our meat and dairy products come from animals that were fed corn—not because it is good to feed them corn, but rather, for the same reasons cheap corn calories dominate every other aspect of our food and agriculture. GM corn-fed beef makes for an unartificially cheap and unhealthy burger, a very unhealthy eater, and an unhealthy world.

★ **2** ★

Here's the Beef

The 99-Cent Burger Is the Most Expensive Hamburger in the World

AFTER SPENDING THE DAY in the MVP community of Ruhiira, I was invited by a few local residents and food-aid workers from Mbarara to dine at a restaurant when we arrived back in the city for the night. I was eager to taste some local Ugandan cooking, and to get a feel for what people in this poverty-stricken area have the option to eat when they have enough resources to visit a restaurant. We headed to a roadside outdoor café that had plastic tables and chairs and the limited lighting typical of smaller African cities. Even though the few industrial fluorescent ceiling lights flickered on and off, they were a vast improvement over the total darkness of the surrounding areas.

When the waitress approached our table and offered us beer or soda to start, I felt, as I had so many times before, enormous frustration that in countries where clean water is a daily life-or-death issue for so many people, beer and soda can be found just about everywhere. I also knew that in many regions of Africa, beer drinking is generally reserved for men, and that it would be uncustomary for a woman to order a beer—but I did anyway. When the waitress returned to the table, she handed us our drinks, but instead of offering us menus or rattling off the specials, she simply asked each of us, "Goat, or no goat?"

When I naively inquired if there were any other options, she looked at me and repeated her question: "Goat, or no goat?"

It was clear that "goat, or no goat *was* the entire menu, and with my eyes now adjusted to the light, I cast a cursory glance around the restaurant. Indeed, it appeared that whether or not you got the goat, you got a plate of french fries and ketchup, but no locally grown vegetables. Any thought about engaging the waitress in the type of parlay common in American restaurants about dietary preferences ("I'd like the sauce on the side, steamed broccoli in place of the kale, *and* please tell the chef that I'm allergic to peanut oil, tree nuts, gluten, and don't like cilantro") was off the table in a country where the entire menu could be reduced to a binary question: "goat, or no goat."

Just for the record, I chose goat (and what I thought was the local Nile Special beer, even though I later learned the "local" brewery was owned by SAB-Miller, a South African conglomerate that owns Miller and Coors), and I can report that the beer was cold and the goat was delicious. It was cut into savory chunks and grilled on a simple spit over an open fire. The potatoes were the standard, thick-cut, deep-fried french fries you might get anywhere in the world, although the ketchup was a little sweeter and more watery than what we are used to at home. When I analyzed the meat, I deduced from past experience and my knowledge of local practices that the goat was grass-fed, and that everyone in the restaurant was eating meat cut from the same animal "family style." This is a less wasteful and more sanitary way to eat meat than cutting the meat from hundreds, or thousands, of different animals and then processing it in industrial plants and shipping it hundreds of miles across the country, as we do in the US to make cheap chopped meat for hamburgers.

> The goat I was served in Uganda was, most likely, a healthier meat
> than what is typically available in most American supermarkets,
> school lunchrooms, and restaurants.

Compared to a corn-fed beef hamburger in America, whether from a fast food restaurant or cooked at home, the piece of grass-fed goat meat I had in Uganda almost certainly contained fewer calories and likely no antibiotics, hormones, ammonia, additives, by-products, or preservatives. It had fewer bad fats, and had a lower probability of causing infection from E. coli. The animal was likely raised in a manner that was better for the environment and, ultimately, my own health, because it was raised locally (maybe even behind the restaurant) grazing on pasture grass, rather than eating GM corn in an industrialized feedlot a thousand miles away.

TO MEAT OR NOT TO MEAT?

Much like my dinner options in Uganda, the debate over sustainable, healthy diets in the Western world increasingly centers on a single question: "Meat, or no meat?" But since 87 percent of Americans currently eat meat as part of their diets and want to remain omnivores—and since the rest of the world is currently *increasing*, not decreasing, its meat consumption—it's clear to me that:

> The conversation we should be having isn't about "meat, or no meat,"
> but rather: "How do we eat meat *better?*"

The health of the people in many cultures that traditionally eat meat regularly—for example, the Masai people of Africa, and the Sardinians and Ikarians in the Mediterranean—is superior in many respects to the health of Americans following the modern American diet, which is heavily comprised of sugar, starch, and refined carbohydrates, as well as large quantities of factory-farmed meat. Still, as global demand for meat rises, there is enormous concern over how to raise more meat without destroying the environment.[1] A partial answer to this dilemma may lie in this question: *How is it that my meat options in a hunger hot spot in East Africa were by virtually every measure better than my meat options in the United States?*

Once again, the answer to that question begins with corn.

YES, MORE RUMINATION ON CORN

As I mentioned earlier, roughly 40 percent of the heavily subsidized and increasingly engineered corn grown in the US goes to feed livestock, not people. This has a long list of economic, environmental, and health ramifications. The 33.6 million acres of farmland in the US dedicated to growing corn for livestock feed means we have less pastureland available to raise cattle in a healthful manner—grazing on grass. All that corn production for animal feed also increases soil erosion, and soil

---

1   The leading cause of deforestation of the Amazon is beef production. The UN Food and Agriculture Organization estimates that almost 70 percent of the Amazon's forests have been cleared to create open land for grazing animals for human consumption.

and waterway contamination from the use of chemical fertilizers, herbicides, and pesticides. Because meat isn't locally raised, it takes fuel to transport young calves to the feedlots and then transport the "finished" cattle to slaughterhouses, as well as to transport the processed meat to the communities where it will be eaten. So our current system of industrial feedlot meat production also leaves a massive carbon footprint. Of equal significance is the diversion of resources such as land, capital, water, and manpower away from the cultivation of more nutritious and diversified, less industrialized crops. Growing so much corn for animal feed further entrenches us in the corn-centric, petrochemical-dependent food systems that have become the mainstay of US agriculture over the past several decades.

What is most telling, though, is that the biggest problem with feeding corn to livestock is incredibly simple and should have stopped us from adopting this practice in the first place:

> Cows are ruminants,[2] which means they are not biologically designed to eat corn. Put simply, eating corn makes cows sick.

Cows can't digest the high level of starch in corn, so they develop gas, bloating, infections, immune system depression, corrosion of the stomach lining, sepsis, acidosis, and liver failure—a set of bovine medical issues that could be avoided with proper pasture raising, but are now managed with prophylactic antibiotics, invasive medical procedures, and the hard fact that the cows don't have much need for healthy organs anyway since cattle raised for food in this fashion have massively truncated life spans.[3]

Since nature designed cows to eat grass, feeding them corn or any other grain would make no sense if it weren't for the fact that feed corn cuts the calf-to-table production cycle of beef roughly in half. Corn-fed cattle can reach market weight (about 1,000 pounds) in 12 to 14 months, a feat that would take 2 to 3 years if cows were raised grazing on pastureland.

You don't have to have a degree in agriculture economics to see the profit motivation behind the decision to feed corn to cattle. Beef yields have doubled

---

2   According to the Free Dictionary by Farlex: "Any of various hoofed, even-toed, usually horned mammals of the suborder Ruminantia, such as cattle, sheep, goats, deer, and giraffes, characteristically having a stomach divided into four compartments and chewing a cud consisting of regurgitated, partially digested food."

3   Cows can live about 15 to 20 years; dairy cows live less than half that time, and cows raised for beef are slaughtered just months after their first birthday.

because a corn diet fattens cows more quickly (just like it does to us), and the cost of producing a pound of beef has dropped proportionately. Remember as well that farmers are paid per bushel of corn, and that feedstock corn has been bred for high yields, which means growing corn for animal feed (or high-fructose corn syrup or ethanol production) provides a higher profit margin than growing lower-yield sweet corn for human consumption. That pursuit of higher profit embeds the farmers, and everyone else along the supply chain, in a system of growing this *specific* type of corn, which is inedible unless it is processed. Even though growing all that feed corn is damaging to the environment, detrimental to long-term agricultural and nutritional diversity, and terrible for the health of people and cows, we don't account for that in the price of our burgers. The fact that it takes 26.8 pounds of feed and 211.2 gallons of water just to make one pound of chopped beef, and that it takes additional petrochemicals and energy to produce the corn to make the feed to produce the meat, is irrelevant when the producers of that meat consider only one metric: More beef means more profit.

For those who do care, quite obviously, pasture raising is a whole lot nicer for the cows, and healthier for we the meat eaters. Compared to the meat from corn-fed cows, the meat from grass-fed cows is leaner, higher in omega-3 fatty acids and other healthy fats like CLAs (conjugated linoleic acids), and higher in vitamins C and E. Grass-fed beef is also lower in cholesterol and calories than its corn-fed counterpart, in part because the cow is walking around getting exercise. And of course, cows raised naturally produce more naturally flavored beef. But no one seems to care about these benefits when high yields of cheap, sweet corn and cheap, fat cattle are the cardinal metrics—not only for the food producers, but for we the eaters as well.

> Cows became just like the corn they are eating: a cheap commodity with higher yields, lower nutritional value, and a bevy of collateral health and environmental issues.

For consumers, subsidized corn fed to cows produces cows that are subsidized too. That paves the way for lower meat prices at the supermarket, and the beloved dollar menu at fast food restaurants.

★ ★

The problem with the math behind feeding corn to cattle is that it's only profitable if you don't consider the real costs: the cows' health, our health, the health of the environment, the livelihood of small farmers, and the hungry around the world. But it's easy to look the other way when corn is an almost $65 billion commodity supported by government subsidies[4] and powerful lobbyists—and the seductive fact that we can buy a burger from a drive-thru window for 99 cents.

On the other hand, it's tempting to argue that high yields of somewhat less nutritious and massively cheaper meat means, at least theoretically, that more people have access to the critical protein, micronutrients, and calories found in meat. According to the UN Food and Agriculture Organization, in developing countries since the early 1960s—and heavily weighted from 1980 on—meat consumption has more than tripled. In most parts of the world, the consumption of meat is a corollary to greater health; just ask the young African children exhibiting the swollen bellies of marasmus and kwashiorkor, both diseases of severe protein deficiencies. So the flip side of the anti-corn, anti-subsidy, anti-industrialized food systems argument laid out here is that, in the current system, subsidized, genetically engineered corn is a proven way to lower food prices on the shelf and at the drive-through, and lowering food prices allows more people to eat more meat, at home and abroad.

When we walk into a supermarket anywhere in this country, there is an *abundance* of food, including beef. And it is cheap. Really cheap. In 1980 Americans spent 13.2 percent of discretionary income on food; as I previously mentioned, today we spend a lot less than that—only 6 to 10 percent, depending on which statistics you use. Name any other country in the world, and that figure will be higher—much higher. In Kenya it's 44.9 percent; China, 33.9 percent; Peru and Russia, 29.1 percent; Saudi Arabia, 23.7 percent; Israel, 17.8 percent; Even in Norway, it's 13.1 percent.

> Americans spend a lower proportion of their income on food
> than citizens of any other country in the world.

There is no arguing that this system has produced an abundance of food that's inexpensive for the American consumer to buy. And yet, we are left with an

---

4   To understand just how big a role subsidies play, consider that in early 2013, a number of rice farmers in Arkansas who had been receiving subsidies to grow rice decided that if the subsidy programs for rice weren't extended in that year's farm bill, they would plow over their paddies and plant corn or soy instead. These were farmers operating high-tech rice farms with irrigation systems and satellite-driven tractors. The subsidies dictate what farmers plant and grow, and, therefore, what we eat.

almost unfathomable, perplexing mathematical problem. Over the past 30 years, while we were building systems of food production that resemble something closer to widget factories than agricultural enterprises, the number of hungry people in America has grown. Hunger has declined in some regions around the world (for example, parts of Asia), but worsened in others (much of Africa) as food insecurity and hunger still affect roughly 870 million people worldwide. During the same time frame, obesity levels have rapidly escalated, tipping the scales in many countries at well over 30 percent. (It's gotten so bad that on June 18, 2013, the American Medical Association finally reclassified obesity as a disease.) Somehow, having an abundance of cheap food, including cheap meat, has escalated obesity in a large segment of the global population while not reducing hunger around the world nearly enough.

> The industrialized food system that has created all of this cheap food has left well over a billion of us overweight and has not managed to feed the people who actually need affordable food—the hungry.

There is no better visual for this than to be looking at a multinational conglomerate's brown sugar water (Coca-Cola) and a multinational conglomerate's fermented grain drink (Nile beer) sitting next to plates of french fries in a hunger hot spot in an area of Africa that has limited access to a necessity as basic as water. That image alone should force us to consider why the shift to our consolidated, industrialized food system occurred in the first place.

SHORT AND FAT—THE LIFE OF THE MODERN "COW"

If we step back and examine the life cycle of an industrialized cow raised for beef, it is easy to see just how pervasive and problematic our corn-centric agricultural system has become. It is also easy to see why pushing corn yields to feed cows might not be in the best interest of anyone except the giant agribusinesses that now dominate our food system. In fact, if we take a hard look at factory meat production, we will see just how *expensive* cheap food is in general—and how expensive cheap beef is specifically.

Just as plants take energy from the sun and convert it into food through photosynthesis, cows have the ability to take energy from grasses such as alfalfa, clover, rye, and fescue and convert it into a high-quality protein through a digestive organ called the rumen. Plants photosynthesize; cows ruminate. Since humans can do neither of these things, it means that for us to eat beef we *need* plants to photosynthesize and we *need* cows to ruminate.

Up through the 1940s, we did just that. We let the grasses photosynthesize and the cows ruminate, and these two systems worked in tandem to produce high-quality protein. Cows were raised primarily grazing on pasture grass (or hay harvested and baled for the winter) as they were meant to, and their feed was essentially free. They hoof-compacted and fertilized the soil as they spread next year's alfalfa, rye, and clover seeds, or any other of the more than 700 species of native grass in their manure, until 3, 4, or maybe 5 years later when they reached kill weight and were taken to local slaughterhouses. If we ignore the trip to the slaughterhouse, this is an image that evokes a treasured bit of Americana—cows grazing freely on open fields of grass, providing a bucolic picture of healthy agriculture.

In the 1950s, farmers started to feed corn to cows because it is cheaper than grazing and it fattens cows fast. Today's factory-farmed cows are kept with their mothers to nurse and eat grass only until they reach about 6 months of age, at which point they are abruptly weaned and sold to feedlots to be "finished"—a farming term for fattening them up before they are sent to the slaughterhouse to be (and you have to love this term) "dispatched." During the last 5 to 6 months of their lives, these factory-farmed cows are kept shoulder to shoulder with thousands, often tens of thousands—even hundreds of thousands—of other cows in massive, fetid feedlots called concentrated animal farm operations, or CAFOs for short.[5] In these cow slums, they stand hock deep in manure, are fed a corn-feed concoction, administered daily doses of antibiotics (to prevent disease caused by their diet and living conditions), and given hormones and anabolic steroids to fatten them up even faster than corn alone can.[6] As we are feeding the cows the corn, the antibiotics, and the hormones, their meat is becoming less nutritious, but a more profitable commodity. They are also dying. But it hardly matters when their "dispatch" date is hovering just around their first birthday, a fact that means they only need their organs to function for a sum total of about 1 year.

★ ★

Since cows eat corn, sometimes even in the form of surplus, expired candy and

---

5   Think of a mall parking lot full of 100,000 cattle spanning as far as the eye can see.
6   Estrogen can add another 4 pounds a day in weight gain.

other cheap processed sweets like cookies made with HFCS and sold well below cost to feedlots, corn is now a huge part of both the hamburger and (because corn feed is also fed to dairy cows) the cheese on top of the burger as well. Once some enterprising cattle ranchers started feeding corn to cattle (generally the feed is a 70 percent corn, 30 percent soybean mix) and bringing them to market in half the time and at a much lower cost per head, the price of natural grass-fed beef, by comparison, looked like a high-end luxury good. The switch to corn feed and the consolidation of farms, slaughterhouses, and meat-processing plants impacted the pricing structure for beef in such a way that the industry found itself in a race to the bottom. The pressure was on to make profits by selling higher volumes of increasingly cheaper meat, at all costs. Which means that the small farmer grazing cows on pastureland, or even the small cattle rancher finishing with corn, was out of luck.

According to Kevin Dhuyvetter and Michael Langemeier, both formerly at Kansas State University's department of agricultural economics, the average farmer's profit from a calf-to-cow operation in Kansas was estimated to be $63.06 for each cow between 1997 and 2008. So the only way to make money raising beef cattle is with volume.

With all that volume, we the eaters have gotten a huge serving of cheap, highly subsidized meat. According to a report released by the Global Development and Environment Institute in 2007, "between 1997 and 2005, factory farms saved an estimated $3.9 billion per year because they were able to purchase corn and soybeans—the main components of most feed mixtures—at prices below what it cost to produce the crops. . . . Estimated savings to industrial hog, broiler [chicken], egg, dairy, and cattle operations totaled nearly $35 billion over the nine-year period." Ironically, it is not the farmers who grow the corn—nor those who breed the calves—who are profiting from this economic model, but rather the giant agribusinesses that have swallowed up all the smaller farms, as well as the cattle feedlot finishers, slaughterhouses, and meat-processing plants that can buy the calves on tight margins and the feed for below-market cost. The price of corn, measured against what it costs to grow, is such that many of the farmers I visited in the Corn Belt have to work off-farm jobs to support themselves.[7] The final irony is that these farmers often work as salesmen for the Big Ag fertilizer companies that are owned by the even larger Big Ag conglomerates that have come to monopolize the industry. Since margins are so tight, high

---

7   In 2000, 93 percent of farmers reported nonfarm income, compared to only 54 percent in 1970.

volume became critical for profit. And while consolidation is at the root of the problem, it is also the route to the desired outcome—cheap meat for consumers, and profit for agribusiness. When you consolidate, you reach profit not through quality, but through economies of scale.

And consolidate we did.

MEAT-OPOLIES

As I mentioned earlier, the number of farms in America has shrunk from a peak of 7 million in 1935 to just about 2.2 million today. The number of cattle slaughterhouses has dropped from more than 600 in 1980 to roughly 170 today. The US Department of Agriculture (USDA) pegs slaughterhouse costs about 30 percent lower in plants handling more than 1 million head of cattle than in "smaller" operations, which process 300,000 animals a year. Since the biggest cost of all for slaughterhouses is "cattle procurement," which the larger facilities can overcome through sheer volume, it follows that the biggest chop shops have the greatest chance to profit, and the little—or local—guy has almost zero chance of surviving. Facing such meat-opolies, there is little or no room for competition, so cattle ranchers have few options for competitive pricing when they bring their calves to market. A grass-fed beef rancher in Montana complained to me that the loss of local slaughter facilities meant that many farmers who are producing high-quality meat can't even get that meat to market—which means that not only do the ranchers have fewer choices, but so do the consumers.

When we consolidated the number of cattle producers, we also consolidated the animals, the manure, and the prevalence of disease.[8] Some CAFOs have manure "lagoons" and "pits" that hold tens of millions of gallons and stretch over many acres of land. The local roads and bridges can't handle the truck traffic to and from the CAFOs and need frequent repairs, and the air, water, and soil pollution through seepage and runoff is toxic, to say nothing of the working and living conditions for local residents and CAFO employees. All of this manifests as hidden costs footed by the taxpayers, even as we *think* we're getting cheap food. That bucolic picture of Americana—of cows grazing on grassy pastures—has morphed into something that looks much closer to a scene out of an agro–sci-fi horror movie.

For most of the steaks and burgers that we eat, the family farmer is not the

---

8   The United Kingdom, for example, spent roughly $20 billion over 3 years combatting an outbreak of hoof-and-mouth disease.

man behind the beef. A broad look at the meat and dairy industry shows a loss of more than 1.3 million cattle, hog, and dairy farmers in the past 30 years, along with the loss of millions of family grain farms, despite the fact that production of all these foods has risen dramatically. Three companies—Archer Daniels Midland, Bunge, and Cargill—control 90 percent of the grain trading around the world; DuPont (Pioneer) and Monsanto control close to 60 percent of the corn seed in the US; and 85 percent of HFCS is manufactured by only four companies as well: Archer Daniels Midland, Cargill, Tate and Lyle, and Ingredion. The consolidation of our food growers and our food processors leaves us with lots of cheap food, but less real choice and fewer options for innovation in the entrepreneurial ways of the farmers that built our country.

> Food today is produced in a less humane and *less human* way,
> with price the only real measurement of value. Let's face it:
> No farmer innovating on a small family farm would have
> conceived of something known as "pink slime."

Pink slime, as you may recall, is the controversial additive to ground beef that amounts to a foamy pink mixture of low-grade beef parts and, typically, ammonium hydroxide. If you're wondering why pink slime was invented in the first place, it was a way to reprocess "worthless" meat scraps into a salable product to make meat even cheaper. It's also blasted with ammonia to kill E. coli, making the meat both cheaper and "safer." The USDA buys 7 million pounds of pink slime for school lunch programs, and it was reportedly in up to 70 percent of all our ground beef until consumer outrage instigated by "food revolutionist" Jamie Oliver caused a swift pullback in its use. [9]

We the eaters are getting *really* cheap meat while farmers are facing impossibly tight margins; meanwhile the concentrated factory operations involved in finishing and selling beef are raking in the profits. Brazilian multinational JBS, which owns the iconic American Swift beef brand as well as 16 other beef brands (and 10 chicken and 5 pork brands), describes itself as the "largest animal protein company in the world." So much for real choice at the supermarket. Cargill sells beef under 14 brands and is a vertically integrated behemoth—it's

---

9   For the 2013-2014 school year, 2 million pounds of beef containing pink slime was ordered from the USDA, by a total of seven states—sadly, an uptick after the dramatic decline following Jamie Oliver's exposé.

involved in everything from making animal feed to trading sugar and cotton, managing mines and metals, and producing biofuels, vitamins, Truvia, HFCS, and antiperspirants. I can't say that list of business ventures makes me want to rush to the store to buy their burger meat.

The fact that feeding cows corn makes them sick en route to becoming cheap meat is viewed as nothing more than a manageable side effect, one that's far less expensive to deal with in the short term than it would be to raise cows by allowing them to graze out in the open on fields of grass. Fields of grass that, because of cascading economic effects, no longer exist because they were plowed over to plant feed corn.

THE REAL PRICE OF BEEF

If we step back for a minute from the dollars to the cows—the cows that are made sick from eating corn, are given prophylactic antibiotics to manage the infections that result from, among other things, eating corn and stewing in their own manure in overcrowded bovine ghettos—we can begin to see how the price of cheap meat is fundamentally deceptive.

> In the end, we are paying for cheap meat not only with our
> tax dollars, but also with our health, our children's health,
> and the health of the planet.

Consider for a moment that more than 80 percent of the antibiotics produced in this country go to treat livestock, not people. The antibiotics given to cows are a concern for a number of reasons, chief among them the fact that traces of these antibiotics wind up in our meat. These antibiotics then end up in *us* when we eat them. Further, 80 percent of the antibiotics fed to cattle end up in manure lagoons, and find their way into our streams and rivers—streams and rivers that feed our aquifers. And we know all too well the concerns of overexposure to antibiotics and the risk this poses for creating strains of antibiotic-resistant bacteria to go along with the superweeds, superbugs, and our supersized selves that have resulted from the proliferation of all that corn. What we don't yet know is how the past few generations, who have grown up with this antibiotic-laced meat and dairy, will fare later in life when the antibiotics we have don't work anymore.

Factory-farm practices and consolidation—especially as they relate to ground meat, where meat from thousands of animals can end up in one batch of hamburger—have also increased the risk of foodborne disease. We are seeing a rise in E. coli outbreaks, and specifically antibiotic-resistant strains of the bacterium—despite the valiant effort of using ammonia-treated pink slime to stem the problem.

Meanwhile, however, the tide seems to be changing on antibiotics. In 2013, the Food and Drug Administration started moving toward issuing voluntary reductions. Consumer demand has pushed big players such as Chipolte Mexican Grill, Hyatt Hotels, and Bon Appetit Management Co. to serve antibiotic-free meats, which then prompts innovation in the highly controlled and consolidated meat markets.

★ ★

Consolidation has, more than likely, also taken our food in many directions we the eaters would rather not know about—including labor, immigration, and quality-of-life issues arising from poorly paid, poorly treated, and poorly regulated farm-industry workers.

Since we all know it's not a farmer who's processing our meat on a factory "disassembly" line, it's telling to examine who is actually doing this work. In the time of Upton Sinclair's 1906 novel *The Jungle,* the new immigrant labor from Eastern Europe were employed in the slaughterhouses, doing dangerous work for a meager wage. With Sinclair's graphic exposé came a series of food safety laws (the Meat Inspection Act and the Pure Food and Drug Act of 1906) and antitrust interventions that served to improve working conditions for slaughterhouse workers as it also fostered competition within the agricultural sector.

From the early 1900s to the late 1970s, beef production was by no means perfect, but hundreds of local slaughterhouses supplied beef regionally across the US. Today only 13 large slaughterhouses supply most of the nation's beef, and a new group of immigrant labor—mainly Hispanic—is now exploited in these facilities.

Almost every step of the industrial meat supply chain degrades someone or something: the cows, the land, the farmers and industry workers, the consumers, and the communities these industries operate in.

Many communities with meatpacking plants see significant growth in non-native, non-English-speaking populations, many of whom are illegal, undocumented workers living and working under deplorable conditions. These conditions have become a breeding ground of abuse and fear, and are infested with drug operations, corrupt officials, and complicit corporations abusing an easily exploitable and vulnerable workforce as the communities suffer. Sadly, instead of paying Americans fair wages to do the work, corporate lobbying power and massive corruption allows these companies to hire undocumented, underpaid workers to process our meat, and it is we the eaters, aka we the taxpayers, who ultimately underwrite that cheap labor. These immigration policies, and this abuse and corruption, are just one more subsidy, one more hidden cost, we all pay to have cheap meat.

High-yield corn and government subsidies weren't the only elements at play in all this consolidation. Advances in technology, from tractors to refrigeration to better roads, all helped the industry move toward industrialized production of cheap meat, as did efforts to increase yields during World War II, when there were fewer able-bodied men to work the fields. But to an even larger degree, it was the needs of the fast food start-ups of the 1950s that set off a chain of events that took over and profoundly affected every aspect of how we grow, supply, and consume food.

THE HAMBURGER'S HELPERS

Today hamburgers are a $40 billion industry in the US alone, dominated by McDonald's, Burger King, and Wendy's. The burgers sold at most of these establishments are sourced from cattle grown to kill weight in CAFOs on a diet of mostly corn and soy. This diet creates more fat in the form of coveted "marbling," which is often augmented with injectable fillers, chemicals, and flavorings such as "finely textured lean beef," the industry name for pink slime.[10]

If you read up on the history of the hamburger, you will find a lot of paternity claims. But trying to figure out who was the first guy to slap two pieces of bread around a flattened patty of beef is far less interesting than unraveling the

---

10 In 2012 McDonald's dropped pink slime from its beef products, as did a number of other fast food restaurants like Taco Bell and Burger King. (Wendy's never used it.) In addition to pink slime, in early 2013 an exposé of the global meat industry found that some ground beef coming from European factory farms was actually full of horsemeat.

disruptive impact that the fast food culture, starting in the 1950s, had on our entire system of growing and producing food. Secretary of Agriculture Earl Butz's legislative philosophy to "get big or get out" by growing more corn wasn't the only force pushing us toward consolidation and overproduction. Fast food was doing it, too. And it spread to all aspects of US agriculture.

The *real* story of the hamburger as we know it can't be told without a giant nod to the fast food chains. One after another, between 1948 and 1956, young risk takers like the McDonald brothers, Carl Karcher, William Rosenberg, Glen Bell, Dave Thomas, and Harland Sanders founded, respectively, McDonald's, Carl's Jr., Dunkin' Donuts, Taco Bell, Wendy's, and KFC. These entrepreneurs had dreams of making food affordable, convenient, and, of course, *fast*. Sure, William Rosenberg undoubtedly knew that doughnuts did not a healthy meal make—but it's unlikely that the hamburger honchos thought they were setting America on a fast track to obesity and health issues with their fast and easy food options. This was just a welcome part of postwar prosperity and progress.

These franchised, factory-like fast food chains needed a consistent source of cheap beef—and cheap everything, really—here in America, and then, as the fast food empires expanded, around the globe. So they created them. And an examination of how McDonald's entered the Russian market in the 1990s gives us a good idea of what happened in the US back in the 1950s, and what happened as we replicated the fast food business model as a way of producing all of our food.

A consistent source of beef and controlled prices are critical to maintaining the brand equity of fast food chains. So when McDonald's opened its flagship store in Moscow's Pushkin Square in 1990, they didn't throw up some golden arches, toss some cabbage pies in the deep fryer, and source meat and potatoes from local suppliers. They brought in cattle from Holland and potatoes from the US, loaned capital to local suppliers, set up their own trucking fleet, started their own cattle-raising farms, and created a "McComplex" to handle all the processing of beef, bread, condiments, and shakes. McDonald's knew that if you want cheap and consistent, you have to control the suppliers,[11] not use existing local supply chains. And if you read Eric Schlosser's *Fast Food Nation*, you can see how the growth of these brands as they evolved here in America a few decades earlier impacted not just the culture and the economy of farming, but

---

11 Cargill opened a $490 million chicken facility south of Moscow to supply McDonald's chicken nuggets in June 2013.

also the very structure of the food industry and food production. All of these changes worked in a radical way to impact our health—*even if we don't eat in fast food restaurants at all.*

★ ★

McDonald's buys more beef in the United States than any other company. And in an overview for *Business Today* on the impact McDonald's had on Russia's agriculture when it entered the country in the 1990s, author Ravi Krishnani concluded:

> *"Many agricultural experts are of the view that McDonald's had changed the way Russians ate and now the 'Corporation' is also deciding what should be grown in the country. The crop preferences of McDonald's have led to shortage* [sic] *of other crops which should be otherwise grown."*

That is exactly what had happened here in America several decades earlier, and in the 1990s it was happening on the other side of the planet: Every aspect of food production was changing in order to produce cheap, less nutritious "fast" food products.

Today McDonald's dominates the fast food market share in Russia, and its fast food cadre of peers like Domino's, Subway, and Carl's Jr. have followed close behind—not only in Russia, but now in China and even sub-Saharan Africa as well. When I visited Moscow's flagship McDonald's in 1994, it struck me as a higher-end version of the franchises we had in the US (there was loud music playing and a lot of shiny stainless steel, rather than bright colors and plastic playgrounds), but more important, it was perceived as a welcome beacon of capitalism. But really, it seems like another example of fast food colonialism convincing eaters that this is what the "free market" tastes like. Just as we have been lining up for fast and cheap food over the past 6 decades, the Russians were lined up around the block—some waiting for more than 10 hours in subzero temperatures—for opening day.

THE DOLLAR MENU IS OUR DOLLAR

Consumer dollars are the driving force behind these brand takeovers of our food and agricultural systems, both here and abroad, and that happened because we the eaters forgot why we eat food in the first place. So it's hard to completely "blame" the fast food factories for the fact that we eat there. However, it is an opportunity to rethink what we are doing. We should be asking ourselves: *Do we want to use our dollars differently?* Because the same collective consumer dollars that built the fast food industrialized food complex can take it down too. In fact, the Millennial generation has started to do precisely that: Here in the US, there has been a 16 percent decline in Millennials' consumption of McDonald's since 2007.

★ ★

As consumers, we should recognize that with fast food, and with all food, it is high consumer demand that drives sales. Our continued demand is what's sustaining the food systems originally built by fast food, then replicated by Big Ag empires for all food production.

> We created a corn-based "fast feed" market for cows,
> and a corn-based fast food market for people, by moving
> our dollars away from nutrition and toward cheap and easy.
> Now we have to shift them back.

McDonald's is continuously retooling its menu to lure Millennials and the health conscious (offering salad—albeit with HFCS dressing, and often deceptively unhealthy[12]—and, in New England, organic coffee) as it continues to expand into emerging markets. The same unhealthy food system continues to be replicated around the world in the form of chain restaurants and cheap food in some countries, and agricultural aid and GMO seeds in others. Even still, the consumer's power to implement change is impressive—and often underestimated.

When Jamie Oliver called the food industry out for its use of pink slime, we all revolted, and many food companies reacted immediately. The same thing has started to happen with HFCS, as more and more manufacturers, fearful of consumer pullback, are switching to alternative sweeteners. Even McDonald's has

---

12   McDonald's Premium Southwest Salad with Crispy Chicken has 450 calories and 21 grams of fat. That is roughly equivalent to a double cheeseburger, which has 440 calories and 23 grams of fat, or a Steak and Egg McMuffin, with 420 calories and 23 grams of fat.

changed incrementally for the better in response to consumer pressure, using local beef in Norway and free-range eggs in the UK. In 2014, McDonald's announced that by 2016 the chain would begin purchasing "verified sustainable beef"—it's incredible language from such a big player, even if we don't exactly know what that means yet. When the chain restaurant Chipotle instituted a program of sourcing higher quality and more healthful and ecologically sustainable agricultural products, revenue rose tenfold, even though it had to raise its prices. We need to use these success stories as a motivational model for how to change so much more.

CHANGING THE MEAT CALCULUS

Some of the dominant health and environmental questions of this century will likely be these: Is obesity solely a result of an abundance of cheap food causing massive overconsumption? Or did we alter the food itself in such a detrimental way that it fundamentally changed how food interacts with our bodies? And, finally, how can we meet the demand for meat that continues to rise around the globe with high-quality, pasture-raised, healthier meat?

There are so many places to start looking for answers to these questions. And it can feel overwhelming. The food manufacturers and advertisers are telling us that obesity and the diet-related health issues that result from being so overweight are our fault—that our weight is just a matter of personal choice and a lack of self-control. Science is telling us that we engineered so much nutrition out of our food as we industrialized it and made it cheap that we introduced obesity-generating elements like Bt corn, HFCS, and high-fat, wrong-fat, corn-based meat to our diets. And our behavior and economics prove that making food irrationally cheap pushes rational consumers to eat too much.

★ ★

As we contemplate what to eat and the answers to these questions, we should look closely at how much we are really paying for cheap meat. The problem lurking in today's bargain-priced beef is that the same flawed system that works to make cows fat and sick likely works to make *people* fat and sick, too. And that feat—making us fat and sick—was accomplished with the same misguided goals that were applied to raising cattle: increasing the yields and lowering the prices of our food, at all costs.

As long as fast and cheap are the only objectives, fat and unhealthy
will be the outcome. Whether you walk on four legs or on two.

Although most eaters note the higher cost of "healthier food" with frustration, we have been lulled over the years into expecting bargain basement food
prices all the time. In 1984, Americans spent roughly 13 percent of their income
on food. Americans also spent roughly 8 percent of their disposable income on
health care that same year. Today those numbers are flipped: We spend around
8 percent of our income on food and 15 percent on health care. This begs the
question: *Have health-care costs risen inversely to food costs simply because health care
got more expensive and quality food costs went down, or are we spending more on
health care because we got sicker due to cheap food?*

The rise in obesity and the diseases related to it say it all. From 1980 to
2008, obesity rates in the US doubled for adults and tripled for children, and we
got sicker as a result: The number of Americans diagnosed with diabetes in that
time frame more than tripled, from 5.6 million to 20.9 million.

But now consider "expensive" meat. The average American eats 67 pounds
of beef a year and if we paid $5 a pound more for the beef we buy, that would be
$335 dollars per capita, or $1,340 per family of four, for higher beef costs. Yet, as
we recoil from the thought of paying more for food, remember that Americans
spend $245 billion a year on diabetes care alone. That's $7,900 per year per diabetic, or $31,600 for a family of four diabetics.

That $335 for better beef might be the cost of a trip to the doctor.

Medical costs for the obese are estimated to be $1,429 higher per year. For
a family of four obese people, obesity-related medical costs would run on average
$5,716. With $5,716 you could buy three whole grass-fed cows, butchered and
cut into steaks, roasts, and burgers, and individually wrapped for your freezer—
about 1,200 pounds of beef. But that family of four eating 67 pounds of beef
each needs only 268 pounds of beef, which means that theoretically (even though
it wouldn't last that long) a single, grass-fed cow could supply them with enough
beef for four and a half years. The status quo, of course, is that that family could
continue to buy cheap meat, and cheap food in general, and keep those dollars to
the health-care column of their family budget.

Here is another way to frame it: If food costs a bit more, we just might eat a
bit less. When we eat less, we might get smaller and healthier—and need less to
fill us up.

So in a nation where the conversation centers on the binary question of "meat, or no meat," the answer for many who want to eat meat is simply to eat *small* quantities of *good* meat. That 99-cent hamburger is a wolf in a cow suit. In fact, it is the most expensive hamburger in the world.

While it is now apparent that cheap meat isn't really cheap after all, and fat and unhealthy is *not* what we want for our families, we don't want a population of hungry and malnourished people in the developing world either. However, we can't conflate American overconsumption of cheap, subsidized meat with the steady growth of meat consumption in the rest of the world. In the 1980s and '90s, there were fears that meat consumption in the West would continue to rise and we would not be able to meet increasing global demand without engaging in expanding our current degrading farming practices. But then, quite abruptly, the growth in meat eating in the West paused. And then it started to slowly decline. Today in the West, we are eating less meat, likely for both health and economic reasons, and among Millennials in particular (today's trend-setting demographic and, of course, the key consumers of tomorrow) there are more vegetarians and flexitarians (reducing but not eliminating meat consumption) than their grand-parents could have imagined. These younger eaters are choosing less meat overall, and more of what they do choose is grass-fed and organic. And they are not likely to spontaneously change that pattern as they age. This may just be the major folly of the yield-obsessed scaremeisters of Big Food—that they miss the counter-trend sneaking up on them.

For that reason, we can be hopeful that as Americans gradually reduce their meat consumption and begin to eat higher-quality meat, the wild projections of even more CAFOs, more corn-fed cows, and more degradation of the land than we have today might not materialize. But beyond that, there is still the practical issue of how we can actually produce enough meat to feed the world *well* if we abandon these unhealthy high-volume practices. And one answer to that question may surprise you.

CAN MEAT SAVE THE WORLD?

In the 1950s, Allan Savory, a biologist, environmentalist, and animal lover born in Rhodesia (now Zimbabwe), concluded that the only way to save the grasslands that had been reduced to desert in his homeland by grazing herds of elephants was to cull the herds by 40,000 animals. He would later call this conclusion "the saddest and greatest blunder of my life," because even though they killed the elephants, the grasslands didn't return. Savory then dedicated his life to figuring out why.

"Desertification," or the process of land turning from grassland to desert, is a global environmental crisis involving two-thirds of Earth's landmass, from the plains of East Africa and the grasslands of Asia to the national parks in the American West. Environmentalists and climatologists blame desertification on overgrazing—either by domesticated livestock, or by herds of local wildlife increasingly confined to smaller tracts of land as we develop and agriculture takes over the open land. It makes complete sense. We can literally see that when there are too many animals on a pasture, the grass is eaten down to the dirt and the land is left bare. Ranchers and herdsmen must move their animals to new pastureland as they wait for the overgrazed grasslands to return. We then implement techniques like pasture burning (a billion hectares of land are burned in Africa every year for this purpose) to attempt to more quickly restore the grasses to the pastures and the carbon to the land. By and large, that doesn't work well either.

But Savory's research and commitment to figuring out how to restore the planet's grasslands led him to an astonishing conclusion. Turning back the clock of environmental history, Savory realized that what *used to* roam Earth were much larger, very compact herds of animals and predators than we have now, moving to new land as they grazed and trampled the soil, leaving behind a covering of manure. He realized that what we now perceive as overgrazing and degradation of the land by *too many* animals is actually the result of *too few* animals. In other words, Savory believes that we got it all wrong. He believes that to repair our pastureland, we need to allow much larger herds of cattle to graze on it and put more grasslands back into rotational grazing, not remove the animals as we have been doing. He says that in order to restore the environment, we must "do the unthinkable": *"Use livestock, bunched and moving, as a proxy for former herds and predators and mimic nature."*

Savory now teaches and implements a system of "holistic planned grazing," whereby he uses large herds of livestock in the same patterns that used to occur in nature with undomesticated wildlife, to restore the pasturelands and feed populations of the hungry with high-quality meat and dairy. And it is working remarkably well. Savory sees *more pastured animals* and *more grass-fed organic meat* on the great natural plains of the world as the answer to desertification and hunger, not fewer animals or more animals fattened on corn. He sees *more meat*, not less, as a way to serve the hungry, keep carbon in the soil and out of the atmosphere, and simultaneously reverse global warming. If we heed this advice and implement healthy pasturing systems that restore grasslands as they provide a high-quality source of protein for the world, we can begin to change our health, feed the hungry, and repair the environment. Although Savory's work and theories have many critics, it seems that with proper land management and better farming practices, coupled with less and better meat consumption in the West, we can create an "omnivore's solution" as meat consumption increases in the developing world and the global population settles somewhere, healthfully, between "stuffed and starved."[13]

LET'S STILL EAT BURGERS; LET'S JUST EAT BETTER ONES

What I am advocating is eating smaller production, more local, grass-fed meat from animals that were raised in a way that respects the farmers, the environment, the eaters, and the animals.[14] There are ever more options available to be able to do this, both in restaurants and supermarkets where it's getting easier to find grass-finished beef, wild fish, and free-ranging poultry. As consumers, we are letting the stores and restaurants know that is what we value, by sending our food dollars in a direction that is healthier for us, the environment, the farmers, and the industry workers, as well as the livestock. The same dollars that built the "dollar menu" and the CAFOs can help rebuild the great ranchlands and pastures of the world and support the next stage of sustainable meat production.

Truly innovative solutions and businesses are already being built to push the meat-production system in a better direction. Cow shares, where a few families buy a whole grass-fed organic cow and divide it up for their freezers, help save lots of money for the consumer and direct more profit directly to the farmer. Cornell University and the New York State Agricultural Extension system are pioneering meat-locker shares to be paired with cow shares in upstate New York, basically offering a room of big freezer chests that families who lack freezer space can use to store their meat. Whole Foods Market has instituted a more robust information system about meat for consumers, and Costco has a growing selection of

---

13   *Stuffed and Starved* is the name of Raj Patel's 2008 book highlighting the link between the overweight world and the hungry world.

14   To ensure the grass-fed meat you're buying truly is grass-fed, look for the American Grassfed Association (AGA) label. Eatwild.com provides an excellent state-by-state list of sources.

fresh and frozen grass-fed organic meat—no doubt a result of pressure from we the eaters who want to eat better meat.

Despite the role of meat as the main focus of many restaurant meals, more and more chefs are shifting to less meat overall, as they develop recipes where meat plays a smaller role, or no role at all. Many of the ethnic foods that are popular today—Middle Eastern, Mexican, Greek, Spanish, and Thai—can be made in the traditional way with meat as a side dish more than a mainstay on the plate. Cookbook author, food journalist, and *New York Times* columnist Mark Bittman introduced the concept of eating vegan before 6:00 p.m. ("VB6"), eschewing all animal foods until dinnertime and, in an interview on *60 Minutes*, Spanish-American celebrity chef José Andrés called meat "overrated" and said that vegetables and fruits are "so much sexier." Today many top chefs are helping to promote Johns Hopkins Bloomberg School of Public Health's Meatless Mondays campaign, which started in 2003 as a way to promote taking a day off from eating meat for health reasons. (It's also a very easy way to save money for high-quality meat on another night.) Meatless Mondays has spread globally to 29 countries and reached restaurants, schools, and home dinner tables.

As we cut back on meat consumption in the West, we can also cut back on *how much* we eat in general, and how much we eat out. In 2004 Americans spent half our food dollars eating outside the home, the bulk of which was at fast food restaurants. This simple act of reclaiming our kitchens will instantly improve our diets—restaurant meals are generally more caloric than homecooked meals—and free up funds to buy better-quality food to cook at home. It will also reenergize and reestablish the value of the family dinner table as the hub of the home, as it simultaneously works to engage us in a lifestyle that values food. Instead of feeling helpless and overwhelmed and yet again succumb to fast food, we the eaters can begin to make an impact on this massive problem by diverting our consumer dollars in different, healthier directions. The act of grilling homemade burgers is especially empowering when we consider that the money spent on food in one year in America represents a larger dollar figure than the total dollar amount of all the farm subsidies combined.

★ 3 ★

Dairy

The People's Milk

WHEN WE THINK about the role dairy plays in a backyard barbecue, the cheese on top of—or tucked inside—the burger is likely what comes to mind first. It's unclear who was the first person to put a slice of cheese on a cooking hamburger, but Louis Ballast of the Humpty Dumpty Drive-In in Denver, Colorado, tried unsuccessfully to trademark the word "cheeseburger" back in 1935.

Cheese, of course, starts with milk. And that means that the same corn feed and cattle-rearing conditions that produce nutritionally degraded and artificially cheap meat also produce nutritionally degraded and artificially cheap dairy products—including milk, cheese, cream, butter, yogurt, and ice cream—and for pretty much the same reasons. The grain-based diet fed to dairy cows in CAFOs produces dairy products with compromised nutrition for the simple reason that there are critical nutrients in grass that find their way into the milk of grass-fed cows that are missing from corn—and, as you might expect, from the gummy bears and stale cookies and other low-grade components that can find their way into cattle feed as well. And these farming practices diminish the quality of our dairy products beyond the impact that they have on nutrients.

Since dairy cows, just like cattle raised for beef, aren't supposed to eat corn in the first place, those that do often get sick. To combat this, they too are often given antibiotics. So unless we buy organic milk and milk products (certified organic milk must come from cows not treated with antibiotics or growth hormones), there can be traces of these antibiotics, and higher levels of pus and bacteria, in both the milk we drink and the milk products we eat. As important as these issues are, and as parallel as they are to the problems with meat production, there are other unique factors related to milk production and milk consumption that make the story of dairy every bit as complex, and disturbing, as the story of meat.

Just as the goal in corn and meat production was to increase yields, the same mandate pertained to milk. There were roughly 12 million dairy cows in the US in 1970; in 2007 that number was down to about 9 million. With a 25 percent reduction in the number of dairy cows, the only way to get more milk was to increase per-cow yields, which we (of course) did very successfully. Production per cow roughly doubled during that same time frame, from 9,700 pounds of milk in 1970 to almost 19,000 pounds in 2007. This was accomplished, in part, by implementing improved agricultural practices such as breeding cattle that are heavy milk producers,[1] but also by introducing dairy practices that are unhealthy for the cows, reduce the quality of the milk, and affect the health and nutrition of the consumers of those milk products. For instance, overmilking leads to udder infections, on top of the infections already caused by the corn-based diet, which leads to an even greater amount of unnecessary bacteria and pus in the milk and degrades the quality even further. Then there is the highly controversial use of Posilac, a synthetic version of bovine growth hormone (rBGH) developed by Monsanto and now owned by a division of Eli Lilly and Company that is barred in many countries around the world but is used on about 17 percent of the dairy cattle in the US to stimulate higher milk yields in order to generate higher profits for milk producers. Ask yourself this: Since rBGH is known to adversely affect the health of cows and to raise levels of insulin-like growth factor 1(IGF-1) in humans who drink the milk from those cows (IGF-1 is a hormone involved in the growth of cells, including cancerous tumor cells), would anyone not profiting from this milk think it's a good idea for anyone to drink it—especially children?

WHO MOVES THE CHEESE (AND MILK)?

All of these variables harm the milk we drink, and the milk products we eat. But

---

1   Holsteins are the most prevalent breed of dairy cows in the US and are prolific milk producers.

as important as these issues are, there is a much bigger story behind dairy. That bigger story lies with we the eaters, and a critical, coincident, and dramatic shift in our dairy consumption patterns. So while it might make sense to begin a chapter about milk and cheese on a farm with "a female dairy bovine that has calved at least once," an animal known to us simply as a cow,[2] I am beginning instead back in Africa, with an unlikely pair: Noah, a Masai tribesman whom I met in Tanzania, and Nestlé, the Swiss multinational conglomerate that defines itself as "the world's largest nutrition, health, and wellness company."

Nestlé may call itself that, and it certainly is large, but most consumers around the world know it as a company that sells a long list of processed foods. Foods like dehydrated chocolate milk products, ice cream, chocolate cereal, instant coffee, candy, and diet and baby foods under a plethora of brand names, many of which are unlikely to bring to mind "health and wellness." Nestlé is, after all, parent to a list of brands that includes, among others, Hot Pockets, Stouffer's, Nesquik, Milo, Coffee-Mate, Dreyer's, Chocapic, Nescafé, Butterfinger, Kit Kat, Lean Cuisine, and Good Start infant formula. And if you visit the Masai in Tanzania, you would think Noah would be about as far removed from Nestlé as anyone could possibly get.

The Masai are traditional herdsmen who live in an area spread over almost 62,000 square miles in eastern Africa, in a region referred to as Maasailand. They reside in small huts made of mud and cow dung in northern Tanzania and southeastern Kenya, where they support themselves as seminomadic cattlemen seasonally moving their grazing herds from lowland to highland pastures. Their economic and social culture centers around livestock (in particular, cattle) to such a large degree that the size of a man's herd is a measure of his wealth, and their diet is heavily based on fresh milk and meat, supplemented increasingly—especially in recent years—with a few local vegetables and legumes, along with a porridge made from either store-bought or locally cultivated maize.

The Masai people have recently been plagued with malnutrition, wasting,[3] and food insecurity as the grazing lands for their herds of cattle, goats, and sheep have suffered from rising droughts and have been reduced in size as a result of agricultural expansion and an increase in land earmarked for game preserves. The Masai culture is currently at a crossroads, as they try to choose between

---

2   A heifer is a female bovine that has not yet calved.
3   Low weight for one's height resulting from malnutrition, and marked by a critical loss of muscle and fat.

traditional tribal practices and the lure of the modern world. Today local Masai dairymen still carry raw milk in metal containers around the countryside on bicycles, but on special occasions and at ceremonies where the Masai would traditionally celebrate by eating meat and drinking the blood of cattle, now more and more, they drink Coca-Cola and Fanta soda instead.

Noah was raised drinking fresh, raw milk (unpasteurized and non-homogenized) collected directly from his family's own cattle. This milk was sometimes augmented with cattle blood, sourced by tapping into the jugular vein of a steer with an arrow and siphoning off blood, then packing the entry hole with mud to stem the bleeding. This fresh blood would then be mixed together with fresh milk in a drink they call *kule naa-ilanga*.

I'm telling Noah's story because he lives in a region of Africa that has the third-highest number of cattle on the continent, and he grew up drinking raw milk and *kule naa-ilanga*, immersed in a culture where a man's wealth is measured by the size of his cattle herd. But now, instead of traditional milk, he drinks a powdered cocoa and malt-flavored Nestlé product called Milo.

Milo adds about 120 calories (for 3 tablespoons) to the calories in a cup of milk, but the drink loses a lot of protein, calories, and calcium if it is mixed instead with water, which is how I watched Noah prepare it for himself right after he made a cup of local hibiscus tea with raw local milk for me and some of his other guests. One cup of whole cow's milk contains about 146 calories, 7.9 grams of fat, 7.9 grams of protein, 12.8 grams of sugar, and a fourth of the daily required calcium for an adult. While it may sound unsavory to us, 100 grams of cow's blood has 95 calories, 13.7 grams of protein, 242 milligrams of calcium, and 18.8 milligrams of iron. Noah's new drink, Nestlé's Milo dry powder, has 3 grams of fat and 20 grams of carbohydrates per serving, including 7 grams of sugar. The ingredient list includes milk powder, barley malt extract, sugar, cocoa, sodium phosphate, dicalcium phosphate (added calcium), soy lecithin, vitamin A palmitate (added vitamin A), thiamine hydrochloride (added B vitamins), ferrous fumarate (added iron), and artificial flavor. [4]

Even though chocolate-flavored milk might sound better to us than blood-flavored milk, replacing traditional foods with junk foods, even

---

4   Manufacturers make health claims for foods, using words such as "fortification" and "enrichment," which in some cases solves critical public health problems but in others allows companies to add vitamins or other nutrients to otherwise unhealthy foods. More on these claims later.

fortified junk foods, is not a good solution for anyone. *Except, of course, the manufacturers, who profit by opening new markets for their sweet, salty, and/or high-fat products.*

In reality, Noah might have been nutritionally, and perhaps economically, better off when he was drinking milk and blood straight from his herd. And he would *definitely* be better off if food companies entered his marketplace with varieties of unsweetened, healthy foods.

Once again, this story illustrates how health and nutritional shifts that began in the developed world's industrialized food-processing businesses are now embedded even in the farthest reaches of the developing world, where large populations of the "rising billions" are a multinational marketer's dream. We are all transitioning from eating whole foods as they come out of the ground and off the farm, to eating highly processed food products that diminish our health, our communities, and our environment, whether we live in America or Tanzania.

The interesting parallel here is that, just like Noah, Americans have cut way back on drinking whole, minimally processed milk, too. And that decision, no matter which side of the equator or economic spectrum you are on, unequivocally correlates with the decline in our individual and collective health.

> For both the Masai and Americans, this decline
> in health is a result of what we substituted for whole milk
> when we stopped drinking it.

For Noah, it was the instant, sweetened, fortified cocoa drink Milo. For us, it was actually a few things that are a whole lot worse than that.

HOW AMERICANS LOST THEIR MILK MUSTACHES

Americans switched to low-fat and fat-free dairy products during the "fat is bad" era that began in the late 1980s, and continued through the 1990s. Meanwhile, we started eating more refined carbohydrates and upped our intake of fat from different categories of food, possibly without realizing just how much we were actually eating, or how badly it would end for us. With support from the medical community and the USDA, we staunchly believed this shift was okay, as long as we didn't drink whole-fat milk.

US MILK AND CHEESE CONSUMPTION PATTERNS[5]

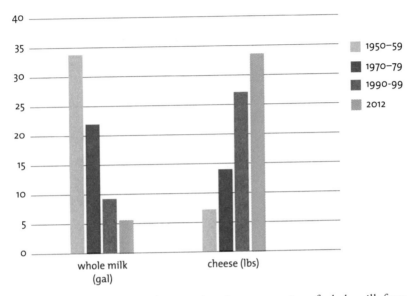

The graph shown here depicts a drop in consumption of whole milk from 33.5 gallons per person in the 1950s to only 5.2 gallons in 2012. This shift was partially offset by an uptick in low-fat and fat-free consumption (low-fat milk consumption rose from 2.9 gallons in the 1950s to 15.3 gallons per person in the 1990s—a lot of that in the form of low-fat chocolate milk), but was completely dwarfed by a dramatic rise in cheese consumption, from 7.7 pounds per person in the 1950s to more than 33 pounds in 2012. Fundamentally, we replaced milk with soda (both sugar sweetened and artificially sweetened) and other forms of sugar water like sports, energy, and juice drinks, and we started eating a lot more cheese. Note that Americans are not eating an ounce or two of real cheese added to a salad, or as a substitute for desert, as the French do. We are eating cheese at fast food restaurants: in Godzilla-sized servings of pizza, atop cheeseburgers, and in the form of fried mozzarella sticks and the like—and, often, as "cheese food products" that aren't actually cheese at all.

According to the Centers for Disease Control and Prevention (CDC), the percentage of kids drinking *any* milk daily fell from 76 percent in 1978 to 42 percent in 2010, and of those drinking it, many were consuming fat-free. Amazingly, this 30-year drop in children's milk consumption coincides with the explosion in childhood obesity. Researchers at the University of Virginia found

---

5   Chart complied from data collected from the USDA.

that kids who drink fat-free or 1% fat milk had higher body mass index numbers—the common measure of body fat based on weight and height—than those who drank whole or 2% milk. This might be attributable to the fact that a glass of plain old whole milk (which has 4 percent fat) makes for a filling addition to a meal, and leads to eating fewer other calories. A 2013 study in the *Journal of the American Medical Association Pediatrics* finally confirmed that, given low-fat flavored milk's high sugar content, it's better for kids to drink plain whole milk. Studies at Boston Children's Hospital and Brigham and Women's Hospital, also in Boston, reinforced this speculation—lower weight in children correlated with higher-fat milk consumption, confirming what many natural foodies have been saying for years: It's just better to drink milk in a more natural, full-fat form.[6]

> Ironically, at the same time our fear of fat drove us away from whole milk, our *total* fat consumption rose dramatically.

The consumption of added fats and oils (those not occurring naturally in food like milk and meat) was 67 percent higher in 2000 than it was in the 1950s. This rise is due largely to an increase in consumption of fried foods and highly processed snack foods like cookies and baked goods, as well as salad dressings and cooking oils. In this same time frame, we started eating more of our meals out of the house, and increasingly at fast food restaurants.

TODAY WE EAT OUR MILK

That 146-calorie glass of whole milk was villainized as being so unhealthy that we successfully avoided it, and largely replaced it with sugar water (soda), sweetened low-fat milk, and cheese products. Again, not plain "cheese," but rather, highly processed concoctions like "extra cheesy" pizza with a two-cheese crust and a four-cheese topping—products like the Cali Chicken Bacon Ranch dubbed one of the "American Legends" pizzas at Domino's. It's a product that weighs in at a shocking 670 calories per slice, or 4,020 calories for the whole extra-large pie with a "Brooklyn" crust. Based on calorie count alone, that extra-large pizza represents 27½ 8-ounce cups of milk.

To give you an idea of the forces we are up against as we try to make better food choices, consider that Dairy Management Inc. (DMI), a nonprofit

---

6   Whole milk contains between 3.5 percent and 4 percent fat.

organization established in 1995 in partnership with the USDA with the sole mission of increasing dairy consumption and facilitating its distribution here and abroad, is working incredibly hard to promote every aspect of the US dairy industry. On the surface, lobbying groups like DMI make good business sense, and there is nothing inherently wrong with them. These companies conduct industry-wide (rather than brand-specific) marketing and public relations, and they exist not only for big commodities like dairy, corn, and cotton, but also for relatively esoteric foods and fibers like watermelon, mushrooms, honey, popcorn, and even mohair. They execute campaigns that can get prunes renamed "dried plums," or remind kids that "Milk. It does a body good," and that cotton is "the fabric of our lives." But they are also responsible for running ad campaigns telling us that HFCS is no different from cane sugar[7] and that this is the "summer of cheese" as they push products in a way to increase sales but not necessarily to promote health.

All of these organizations are funded by farmers and agribusinesses within each industry, through a direct tax called the "commodity checkoff program." DMI does everything from helping to redesign supermarket dairy aisles in order to increase sales, to connecting dairy producers with the restaurants and manufacturers that need their products, to advertising dairy-based diets promoting weight loss. DMI even helped Domino's with market research and a launch strategy to introduce that mega-fat, mega-calorie, mega-cheese line of pizzas in 2009 after the company's earnings hit a slump.

Domino's wanted to sell more pizza, and US dairy farmers wanted to sell more cheese. So the two collaborated on a marketing campaign paid for with DMI funds (in this case, $12 million) collected from a mandatory tax on dairy farmers to help launch and promote Domino's American Legends line of "cheesier pizzas." With this campaign and new product introduction, Domino's saw its sales soar, and the dairy farmers sold a lot more cheese.

It happened yet again: first with corn, then with meat, and then with milk and cheese. A few Big Ag players and lobbying groups at the top have successfully pushed we the eaters toward the wrong foods, ultimately sending us to the doctor as they head to the bank. The net result is that we've forgotten how to eat, as a whole lot of people were profiting by diverting us away from healthy natural, whole food and toward unhealthy processed food. We had the USDA telling us

---

7   In May 2012 the FDA turned down the Corn Refiners Association's request to get HFCS renamed "corn sugar."

to cut back on whole-milk dairy consumption as DMI was selling us record numbers of "cheesier" pizza pies.

In the 1970s Americans' overall calorie intake was significantly lower (by roughly 530 calories a day) than it was in 2000, and it was even lower than that in the 1950s, when most everyone drank whole milk. Insert a proliferation of pizza, and by 2011 mozzarella consumption in the US reached an all-time high, topping out at 11.4 pounds per capita. The irony in this is that there is nothing inherently wrong with eating real cheese, even high-fat cheese like mozzarella, in moderation, especially if it's produced from healthy, pasture-raised cows. In fact, as we will see in the following pages, there are a whole lot of nutritional reasons we *should* eat cheese and drink whole-fat milk. But what's wrong is *how* we are eating that cheese and drinking that milk. A 1-ounce serving of fresh cow's milk mozzarella has 86 calories and, if it comes from a pasture-raised, pasture-finished cow, it is rich in protein, fat, vitamins, and micronutrients.

IT DOES A BODY GOOD—SOMETIMES

A body of evidence suggests that how the cow is raised is the most important part of the "Got Milk?" question. Just as grass-fed, grass-finished beef is healthier than grain-fed beef, milk products from pasture-raised, pasture-finished cows is nutritionally superior to milk products from grain-fed cows. Meat from grass-fed animals has a better vitamin profile than that of their grain-fed counterparts, and grass-fed cows produce milk products that are higher in vitamins A and E. Also, the milk of pastured-raised cows is higher in conjugated linoleic acids (CLAs), and having high levels of CLAs in your diet is believed to help you lose weight and may even cut your chances of getting cancer or suffering a heart attack.

Here's the shocker for people who switched to low-fat and fat-free dairy products: The highest concentration of CLAs are found in whole milk—and, more specifically, whole-milk products from grass-raised cattle.

The cancer-fighting properties of whole milk products from grass-fed cows come not only from the higher levels of CLAs, but also from the ideal balance of essential fatty acids (omega-3s and -6s). The disruption of this fatty-acid ratio is yet another negative outcome of industrial milk production. *Because of their diet, grain-fed cows produce milk with relatively higher omega-6 levels than grass-fed cows, and the high level of omega-6s interferes with the metabolism of the healthful omega-3s.* To compensate, dairy products, along with breads and cereals, are fortified with omega-3s; many people also take over-the-counter or prescription fish oil supplements to provide the omega-3s we used to get from eating full-fat, pasture-raised dairy. In our nutritional and environmental downward spiral, the production of those fish oil supplements (both in pill form and as food additives), which now generate $6 billion per year in the US and $25 billion globally, have negatively impacted the ocean ecosystem,[8] despite the fact that recent medical studies have demonstrated that in supplement form, omega-3s deliver questionable health benefits. It is almost incomprehensible that $25 billion is spent on supplements, fortification, and enrichment by a population reluctant to spend a few dollars more for organic grass-fed whole milk, which would provide those omega-3s in the first place.

As for drinking low-fat or fat-free milk, since some of the important nutrients in milk such as vitamins A, D, and E are fat-soluble, we can't absorb those vitamins when the fat is removed from the milk. As a result, low-fat and no-fat milk have to be fortified with factory-made vitamins to compensate for the loss of vitamins that would be in whole milk from cows that were raised healthfully in the first place. Ironically, those vitamins added to nutritionally stripped milk are then marketed to consumers as an "additional nutritional benefit."

In one final blow to the nutritional profile of factory-farmed milk, even more essential nutrients are lost because, once again, we pushed the yields; and, it seems, when milk *quantity* goes up, *quality* goes down. In other words, cows that are grain-fed and raised in industrial factory CAFOs produce *more* milk than their pastured counterparts, but that higher volume of milk likely contains *fewer* nutrients overall.

As with corn and meat, our farming practices coupled with our consumption patterns have rendered dairy a lesser food.

★ ★

When I asked Noah why he drank Nestlé's Milo instead of local, fresh milk, he told me he never really gave it much thought. He said Milo "tastes good" and is "really cheap," and then he just shrugged and said he "got hooked." My gut tells me that you might get a similar response to the same question posed to a Domino's pizza eater, and a low-fat chocolate milk or soda drinker too. They probably

---

8   Harvesting Antarctic krill for its omega-3s has impacted the population of whales, seals, and penguins that feed on that krill.

didn't give that order of pizza, chocolate milk, or soda a whole lot of thought. Besides, it tastes good, it's cheap, and they're hooked.

To give you an idea of just how far we fell off track and how far we have strayed from real food en route to industrialized food, consider this:

Ingredients in organic, grass-fed milk: milk

Ingredients in organic, grass-fed mozzarella: whole milk, citric acid, and rennet[9]

Ingredients in Domino's "Pizza Cheese"—which is what I'm assuming is what we think of as mozzarella: part skim mozzarella cheese (pasteurized milk, cultures, salt, enzymes), modified food starch, cellulose (to prevent caking), nonfat milk, whey protein concentrate, flavors, sodium propionate (a preservative).

Of course, your "pizza cheese" always comes with a crust [the Handmade Pan Crust contains enriched flour (wheat flour, iron, thiamine mononitrate, niacin, riboflavin, folic acid), water, butter flavored white shortening flake (palm oil, natural butter flavor, and soy lecithin), vegetable oil (soybean oil, citric acid), sugar, salt, less than 1% dough conditioners (sodium stearoyl lactylate, whey, enzyme [with wheat starch], ascorbic acid, l-cysteine, with silicon dioxide added as processing aids), yeast (yeast, sorbitan monostearate, ascorbic acid)] and some Hearty Marinara Sauce [which contains tomatoes, tomato puree (water, tomato paste), carrot puree, onions, celery puree, romano and parmesan cheese (cultured milk, salt, enzymes), sugar, salt, garlic, butter, spices, chicken base (chicken including natural chicken juices, salt, chicken fat, sugar, maltodextrin, hydrolyzed corn gluten, dried whey, natural flavoring, yeast extract, turmeric for color), olive oil, citric acid, and xanthan gum].

Looking at these ingredients should begin to demonstrate how the long lists of added ingredients in all the processed foods we eat work together over our lifetimes to compromise our health. And that list doesn't even include any of the "flow-through" chemicals and additives like antibiotics, growth hormones, or pesticides that may originate with the production practices of these base ingredients.

CONSOLIDATION—THE "BIG CHEESE"

Despite the growth in national cheese consumption, the number of dairy farms in the US has declined dramatically, from around 650,000 in 1970 to roughly 90,000 in the early 2000s, and about 54,000 today. Average herd size per operation

---

9   Rennet is an enzyme used in cheesemaking.

increased from about 20 cows to 100. Fewer farms that are larger in size, with higher output per cow, took milk in the same direction as every other crop in agriculture: larger operations, a degraded product, and cheaper prices, as massive consolidation across the food industry became the norm. This makes it hard for the small farmer to compete, and for we the eaters to find healthy, well-raised food.

If it's hard for small, local farmers to compete with Big Ag in the US, it's even harder for small farmers in Tanzania to produce fresh milk at prices that can compete with a processed product from Nestlé. Nestlé has the same economies of scale enjoyed by other industrialized food companies; plus with Milo in Tanzania, they have shelf stability, chocolate flavor, sweetness, and affordability going for them. Throughout Africa, they, along with many other big international brands, also have the perception of "modern" on their side, which denotes something more in terms of safety and nutrition than perhaps it should to consumers in the developing world. The local Masai dairyman, with his metal can of fresh milk resting on the handlebars of his bicycle en route to market, has a tough time competing with the likes of Nestlé.

And even though multinational companies like Nestlé are entering these emerging markets all around the world with agricultural development programs under the guise of "helping" local communities, in the end they are often pushing our CAFO-based dairy production system on local farmers as they make in-roads selling unhealthy processed foods. Sadly, if there is progress in curtailing hunger, it is often with a diet that has put people on a fast track to obesity. And more often than not, these efforts don't lift the local economy much either. Even so, the processed-food companies do manage to enter into these emerging markets and sell products that generate enormous profit for themselves. Undercutting the local milk producers—"the people's milk," as local milk is referred to around the world—with a cheap, chocolate dry-milk powder, is not a long-term gain for the local people—not for their economy, and not for their health, no matter how many social and agricultural development programs are used to dress it up.

This is especially true for milk, because milk is a gateway food for both eaters and local farmers. You don't have to look any further than Nestlé's efforts to market infant formula to see just how much of a gateway food milk really is. Nestlé has been highly criticized—and has since conceded and repented—for its approach to selling baby formula, especially during the 1970s, when the company aggressively marketed formula to new mothers living in impoverished regions, often by giving away free samples to women whose only real (and truly free) hope for their baby's survival was successful breastfeeding.[10]

Nestlé products are now sold in every country in Africa, and many of them claim to be nutritious because they are "fortified." This is the same route companies took in the US to convince us that sugary, chocolate cereal is a viable and nutritious option for a toddler's breakfast; add some vitamins and minerals to nutritionally stripped food, and you can make impressive health claims, whether it's with Cocoa Puffs in the US or Milo in Tanzania. What I am criticizing here is the practice of adding a few vitamins to high-sugar/low-nutrient foods and marketing them as healthful, then selling them to malnourished people (or well-meaning mothers anywhere). This should not be confused with programs that fortify *healthy* whole grains and food staples—for example, the short-term addition of micronutrients to a diet where no other real food options are available, or the addition of iodine to table salt, which helps prevent brain damage related to micronutrient deficiencies.

★ ★

Tanzania now has a milk production board promoting consumption of dairy products. And even though the country has the third-highest number of cattle in Africa, there is an ongoing push to inseminate the local livestock with higher milk-producing breeds of cattle. Neither of these things is independently terrible, but the concerted effort to flood the market with milk has led to a drop in price—which is bad for a local group of herders like the Masai—and to a higher consumption of milk-based junk foods. Even in China, where there was traditionally very little cheese in the diet, the rapid growth of fast food has led to a huge increase in demand for dairy, roughly doubling in the past decade. But in many regions of the world, just like here in America, it's the wrong kind of dairy—the kind that comes out of a factory, not off a farm.

---

10   In the 1970s and 1980s, when Nestlé initiated a program to give away these free samples, the instructions on the formula were written in English. The women had no stoves to sterilize bottles or water, and therefore no clean water with which to mix the powder. They also had no income to support months of formula feeding when the samples were finished. When their own milk dried up, many women diluted the formula with unsterilized water to make it last longer, and their babies got sick, and some even died. Nestlé has since signed the International Code of Marketing of Breast-Milk Substitutes, although global boycotts of Nestlé due to its marketing practices regarding infant formula are still ongoing.

THIS IS YOUR MILK ON DRUGS

As I touched on earlier, one way to get cows to generate a lot more milk is to inject them with recombinant bovine growth hormone (rBGH), the genetically engineered product developed by Monsanto.[11] rBGH is a synthetic form of naturally occurring BGH, both of which increase an "insulin-like growth factor" or IGP-1 in humans, which affects the growth of cells (and has inconclusively been linked to cancer cell growth). The *only* benefit to using the hormone injections is increased milk production. And just like growing high-yield corn and producing high-yield beef, creating high-yield milk increases profits as it lowers the quality of the product.

The FDA approved rBGH for use in the United States in 1993, even while it was outlawed for use in (and in imports to) the 28 countries in the European Union (EU),[12] as well as Canada, Japan, Australia, and New Zealand. Ironically, the FDA approved rBGH *to increase milk production* even though seven years earlier, the USDA instituted a program to slaughter more than 1 million dairy cows in order to *lower* milk production by 7 percent, because we had too much milk. This mirrors the same convoluted thinking and market-intervention used when we push corn yields while simultaneously paying some farmers to not plant corn.

While using rBGH increases milk production, it also leads to fertility problems in cattle and a 50 percent increase in hoof problems or "lameness." The synthetic hormone also increases udder infections (mastitis) by an additional 25 percent above the increase caused by their corn diet, unsanitary confinement in CAFOs, and overmilking—a collective set of practices that, as stated earlier, increases antibiotic use in dairy cows, as well as the amount of infected matter that ends up in our milk. Even if we don't care about the health and well-being of cows (and arguably we should have concern for living things), these facts should raise plenty of concern about the impact rBGH has on us when we consume milk and milk products produced by cows injected with the synthetic hormone.

The FDA has been highly criticized for its handling of the approval of rBGH, as many of the panel members had affiliations with Monsanto, and many of the studies and data they used are viewed by those outside the FDA as

---

11   Also called rBST.
12   Fearing a link between elevated IGF-1 levels and breast and prostate cancers, the EU voted against allowing importation from the US of milk products treated with rBGH.

questionable at best. Since using more rBGH would mean that farmers would likely need more antibiotics, it seemed like the industry's lobbying efforts might have been at play when, in 1994, the FDA approved a hundredfold increase in the allowable use of antibiotics in cattle. Increasing antibiotic use in animals helped Monsanto market rBGH, but was also problematic in the long term, as strains of antibiotic-resistant bacteria continued to develop. In 2000, the *New England Journal of Medicine* reported the appearance of an antibiotic-resistant form of salmonella contracted by a 12-year-old boy, concluding that "antibiotic-resistant strains of salmonella in the United States evolve primarily in livestock." Since that is how these antibiotic-resistant strains develop, we need to be very careful about the health of our livestock—and yet we're not.[13]

The good news for we the eaters is that when consumer groups raised concerns over rBGH milk and milk products, many countries banned its use, and many companies and consumers here in the US refused to buy milk from dairy farmers using the hormone. (Of note is that the USDA reports only about 17 percent of dairy cows were injected with the hormone in 2007, down from 22 percent in 2002.) Many retailers, including Walmart, Costco, Kroger, Safeway stores in the Northwest, and Publix Super Markets, refused to sell the products. Most of the milk sold by Dean Foods, which handles a whopping 40 percent of the nation's milk supply, is also now rBGH-free. Starbucks and Chipotle Mexican Grill products are also free of rBGH. Facing mounting opposition, and further hampered when they couldn't get "rBGH-free" labels to be outlawed, Monsanto in 2008 sold the rights to rBGH to Eli Lilly for $300 million. Once again, this demonstrates just how powerful the consumer can be as a collective force for change in the food space, and it should encourage all of us to continue to leverage that power as we move forward.

MILK: RARE OR WELL DONE?

Traditionally, milk, like all agricultural products, was locally produced. Without refrigeration and transportation, there was no other feasible option. We went from the backyard cow, to the local farmer down the street, to regional milk

---

13   Researchers found links that strongly suggested the people who developed Cipro-resistant bacterial infections from 1996 to 2004 had acquired them by eating pork contaminated with salmonella. The FDA recognized the seriousness of the threat and banned fluoroquinolones from veterinary use in September 2005.

sheds (the local dairies that serviced a particular region or urban area), to massive consolidation and CAFOs. Facing spotty refrigeration, growing demand, and rapid urbanization, the late 1800s and early 1900s became a time of corner-cutting and industrialization by milk producers. Truly toxic products like "swill milk" emerged when industrial dairy operations set up shop next to whiskey distilleries in order to use the corn mash waste from whiskey production as feed for their cows. This still-alcoholic, nutritionally deficient mash made the cows that ate it produce thin, blue-hued milk, which often caused sickness and death in babies, along with rampant fear of the possibility of broad contamination of the milk supply.

It was during this time that New York City, America's largest population center, established the New York Milk Committee to oversee the city's milk shed and prevent the swill milk dairies from poisoning children with their deadly blue milk. Faced with the question of how to protect consumers from producers who were, even then, focused on higher yields and cost control rather than on quality, safety, and taste, the committee decided against farm-level regulation and moni-toring (an on-farm oversight system to make sure dairies were clean and well managed) in favor of a new technology from France: pasteurization.

This was, in effect, the first big win for industrial dairies. They could keep up with many of the unhealthy practices they had been engaging in, and now simply boil the "dirty" milk to make it safe, ridding it of the bacteria and other pathogens that were causing outbreaks of diseases like listeriosis, typhoid fever, tuberculosis, diphtheria, and brucellosis. Today everyone agrees that milk pro-duced in the unsanitary conditions of factory farms needs to be pasteurized, but many small, family-run and often organic dairies want to produce raw milk for consumers—which they are frequently prohibited by law from selling.

Although raw milk is legal throughout the EU, it is illegal in one form or another in a number of US states. Some states outlaw it altogether; others allow raw milk to be sold only from sheep and goats; still others allow raw milk from cow shares. Advocates of raw milk believe there are sweeping health benefits inherent in grass-fed, unpasteurized (and locally produced) milk, and want to drink it. These benefits arise first from the healthy way the cows are raised, and second from the lack of pasteurization. Along with destroying any unhealthy bacteria, the high heat of pasteurization destroys the healthy bacteria (or probiot-ics, as they're often called) that are present in raw milk, and it also interferes with the enzymes, vitamins, and protein in the milk. Proponents of raw milk also believe that there are nutrients present in milk—including those lauded CLAs—that are destroyed during the pasteurization process. Although there is little current scientific proof, proponents of raw milk believe it promotes overall robust health, and helps prevents everything from allergies, autoimmune diseases, lactose intolerance, asthma, and even eczema. Yet at the same time the debate over legality continues, unsanitary, antibiotic-laden, and poorly fed cows are pumping out unhealthy quantities of milk from infected udders—but since it is pasteurized, the FDA leaves these producers alone.

★ ★

Today, with the consolidation of the industry and farms, as well as tricky labeling laws, it's nearly impossible for most consumers to know where their milk comes from. Even in Tanzania, where Noah talked about how traditional people consumed milk from their own herds, there is a push for milk imports in the form of unrefrigerated, ultra-high-temperature pasteurized (UHT) milk that has been heated to destroy bacteria, most of which comes from unsanitary, higher-intensity farming practices. Perhaps the biggest reason we should be talking about raw milk is that it symbolizes growing consumer concern about the adulteration of all of our foods, as we the eaters question the overall impact industrialization and factory farming has had on our health. Perhaps we should start by agreeing that milk should be, at the very least, pastured, as we individually weigh the benefits and risks of pasteurization.

THE DAIRY DEBATE IS GLOBAL

I could just as easily have started this story about milk thousands of miles northwest of Tanzania, with the Dutch dairy-farming family I met in Nova Scotia while leading a regional food policy group at the local agricultural college. I spoke with the husband and wife owners, who emigrated to Canada from the Netherlands with their four small children, looking for fertile land to farm. This sounds like a story from a hundred years ago, yet they moved to Canada only in 1993. Today they are raising 150 cows on grass and hay silage, and were just about to install a robotic milking system when I met with them on their farm. Along with a cup of hot tea served with their own raw milk, they gave me insight into the issues facing medium-sized farms in Nova Scotia. It was a story that could have been told by dairy farmers anywhere in the world; their complaints were *that* universal. Consolidation makes it difficult to compete on price.[14] They believe in the ethical treatment of animals raised for food. They fear they won't be able to keep their agrarian lifestyle intact for the next generation. They face frustration that big-box, processed "junk" is sold legally as food, while the sale of their fresh, raw, unpasteurized whole milk is illegal where they live.

These are not easy issues. The CDC reports that in the US between 1998 and 2011, there were 138 reported outbreaks of bacterial illnesses resulting from raw milk that created 2,384 cases, 284 hospitalizations, and two deaths. On the other hand, the CDC also reports that 112,000 people in America die annually from obesity-related diseases such as stroke, diabetes, and heart attacks, or roughly 1.5 million deaths in the same time frame. And that likely underrepresents the obesity problem, as the CDC recently lowered the estimate of the number of obesity-related deaths by about two-thirds, from more than 300,000 per year—not because of a decline in obesity, but because we got better at treating heart disease.

These Dutch Canadian farmers pointed out that the Dairy Queen down the street from them can "legally" sell a whole range of sugar-steeped sweets marketed as "dairy." One of the products that Dairy Queen sells is an item called a Turtle Pecan Cluster Blizzard, which, for a large, weighs in at 1,470 calories and has 82 grams of fat. As we watched a couple of obese teenagers (who, based on the averages, were likely raised drinking low-fat milk while eating a diet of high-fat, highly processed food in Canada, just as in the US) walk past the farm, the farmers commented that your chance of contracting obesity from fast food is quite a bit higher than the probability of contracting salmonella, listeria, or E. coli from their raw milk. And they have a point. Just being born in the country that conceived of Dairy Queen puts your chance at obesity at close to 35 percent, even if you never dig a spoon into something called a Turtle Pecan Cluster Blizzard.

I have heard this same story from farmers around the world: Competition with "big and consolidated" is almost impossible, the small farmer has been mar-

---

14   The Canadian dairy farmers told me there had been between 800 and 900 farmers in this region of Nova Scotia just 20 years ago; that number has dwindled to about 220 today. The week I was there, the local milk processor was bought by a big national brand, Agropur, which is following in the footsteps of Dean Foods in the US. Dean Foods now owns 40 percent of the US milk market.

ginalized, and our beautiful rural farming communities have become food deserts that have evolved very quickly into pockets of morbid obesity.

I am not advocating that everyone drink raw milk—that would be irresponsible and impractical in a country of more than 300 million people—but I *am* advocating that we look more closely at the dairy products we are consuming, and that when we include milk in our diets, it should be the real kind, from a pasture-raised, pastured-finished cow, not out of a tin from Nestlé or a plastic cup from Dairy Queen. And it should be locally produced, by a dairy farmer who works to create a product from healthy cows that aren't fed unnecessary antibiotics and hormones, and aren't overmilked in favor of output over nutritional quality. Locally produced milk is wholly feasible and better for everyone, whether Masai or American.

BETTER BUTTER?

Although butter has been a nutritious staple of many traditional diets for thousands of years, it has become as much of a dietary lightning rod as whole milk. Indeed, the consumption patterns of the two are pretty similar—butter has been every bit as villainized for being unhealthy and high in fat as whole milk.

In the 1870s, a product of food engineering called oleomargarine was created that had a mouthfeel and taste similar to that of butter, but was made with less expensive vegetable oils. This marvel of science was white in hue, but dyed yellow to resemble the real thing. When the dairymen saw this cheap impostor infringing on their market, they successfully passed the Margarine Act of 1886, which taxed margarine and required licenses to manufacture it. A few big dairy-state legislatures also passed laws that required margarine to be dyed bright pink—a savvy industry push to ensure that consumers knew it wasn't real butter. The "pink laws" were overturned as unconstitutional, but shortages of butter during World War II pushed margarine back into the American kitchen; it was sold in its original white color, along with a package of yellow dye to be mixed in at home. This innovation, which encapsulates so perfectly the transition from real food to cheap, processed food products, has managed to survive and thrive, even as the original premise that "oleo" was somehow better for us has been debunked.

Although the low-fat, anti–saturated fat trend (as well as the cheaper price, due to subsidized corn and soybean oil) pushed many people toward margarine in the past half-century, today a new understanding of the harmful effects of consuming trans fats—margarine was made by hydrogenating oils to render them solid at room temperature—is pushing natural butter and other more natural fats like olive oil slowly back to the top.[15]

But it's not happening fast enough for many of our tropical forests. Slathered on our toast now is another oil that can be processed and hydrogenated into a butterlike substance: palm oil. Although most eaters have never even heard of it, the production of oil from palm trees has led to the devastation of tropical rain forests and the decimation of tribal and traditional farming regions. Processed palm oil is yet another example of a "food" that is not healthy for we the eaters, nor is it healthy for the communities on the other side of the world who are victims of its industrialized production.

SAY "CHEESE"?

If pink slime had a counterpart in the cheese business, it would be processed cheese. To make processed cheese, unusable scraps of Cheddar are combined with sodium phosphate and then "processed." This began in 1903, when entrepreneur James Kraft was selling cheese out of a wagon in Chicago and eventually experimented with rehomogenizing scraps of cheese, adding some chemicals and canning it, and calling it "process" cheese to distinguish it from "natural" cheese. This new product was shelf-stable and easily transported, and it became part of the daily rations for soldiers in both world wars. By 1930 Kraft had taken over the US cheese market, selling more than 40 percent of all cheese (or, rather, "cheese") consumed in the country. In 1931, the American Medical Association gave Kraft's Velveeta processed cheese its seal of approval. To this day, these neon orange, cheeselike products remain a mainstay of many American diets.

Real orange-yellow butter and cheese gets its color from high vitamin A content, which comes from the high vitamin A concentration (beta-carotene) in the grass and forage diet of the cows. Traditionally, in June, as the first new grass of many Northern Hemisphere temperate climates appears, cows that were fed hay all winter move outside and start eating a diet of fresh forage again. This first grass is extremely high in vitamin A, among other things, and gives cow's June milk a distinctly yellow hue. When that beta-carotene-rich

---

15 In October 2013, the US government announced plans to mandate that all trans fats in the form of partially hydrogenated oil, which are linked to an increased risk of coronary heart disease, lose their status as "generally regarded as safe," which would dramatically reduce their use in processed foods in the coming years.

milk is made into cheese, it gives Cheddar its well-known orange color.[16]

People used to be connected enough to the farm to know that the yellow-orange cheese was healthier, so when processed cheese was formulated—just as with margarine that was dyed yellow—cheese processors made their cheese orange to communicate to consumers that it was nutritious. The orange in today's dairy products is now mostly FD&C yellow food coloring, since the vitamin A in our milk is added after the natural form is destroyed during pasteurization (and is often missing in the first place due to lack of grass feeding and removal of fat).

After its massive commissioning of Kraft canned process cheese and other shelf-stable commodities for American soldiers during World War II, the US government had some leftovers. At the same time, around 1946, it moved to codify a program providing free or reduced-price lunches for American kids in need. Ironically, the National School Lunch Program got its start after young men showed up to boot camp too skinny and malnourished to be able to serve in the military. (Today, just 7 decades later, we now have the military's top brass fighting to make school lunches healthier and less caloric, since our nation's young people are all too often considered "too fat to fight.")

Through the new school lunch program, the government purchased mass-produced and shelf-stable food products, which gave them a permanent place in the food system. Dairy had a strong lobby, and processed cheese was a perfect candidate for government purchase. Eventually, lobbies for the hungry and the dairy industry began working in tandem to push government food stocks to be incorporated into the welfare system, school lunch programs, and the military. As the government bought more processed cheese, the quality became inextricably linked with these programs, and the phrase "government cheese" became synonymous in slang (and rap lyrics) for government assistance.[17]

NATURAL, ORGANIC, LOCAL MILK: THE "GATEWAY" DRINK

The system that has developed around the production of milk and other dairy products offers a good example of why it is time to reconsider the processing done

---

16   Today Organic Valley cooperative actually sells a "limited edition May-September pastured butter" that is heralded for its deeper yellow color and grassy flavor.

17   The practice of including 5-pound bricks of cheese in monthly government food allotments was phased out in the late 1980s.

to all our food, which takes it a long nutritional mile from where, and how, it started. And we the eaters are beginning to do so incrementally.

Responding to fears about growth hormones in milk brought to our attention by the hugely publicized controversy over Monsanto's rBGH, we the eaters are responsible for the meteoric rise of the organic milk industry. While genetically engineered products started populating supermarket shelves, tinkering with milk was more than many of us could take. Even as milk sales started flattening in the 1980s, the sales of organic milk increased. Today many young American parents, who might not have the resources or time to cook their own meals or shop at farmers' markets for produce, are choosing organic milk from Walmart. In fact, all around the world, organic milk has been shown to function as a gateway food for other healthier foods, as consumers understand its value for their families' health and how it shines a light on just how far our food has changed.

Today there are legions of eaters who are demanding something different even beyond organic, whole-fat milk. Despite the recession, in 2011 food analysts at the NPD Group noticed that the market for artisanal cheese and pricey Greek yogurt continued to surge. Supermarkets such as Hy-Vee in the Midwest have launched cheese clubs, and Kowalski's Markets in the Minneapolis–St. Paul region and many other places around the country, now have classes on how to make your own fresh mozzarella (a far cry from how Americans are typically eating our most popular cheese). In the same vein, frozen packaged pizza—one of the biggest dietary sources of dairy—showed signs of a sales slump in 2012, except for one bright spot: natural and organic brands like Newman's Own and Annie's. And across the country, organic, healthier pizza chains are expanding, such as Fort Lauderdale's Pizza Fusion, which has grown to include restaurants in Colorado, Florida, New Jersey, North Carolina, Ohio, and Saudi Arabia, and New York City's Wild, which has expanded to Las Vegas.

★ ★

As much as artisanal cheese and even the word "organic" carry connotations of "fancy" and "expensive," organic milk and goat cheese have the potential to be the Wi-Fi and smartphones of the food space. As with access to information, access to healthy food is no longer only for those with the most economic means, and increased demand has resulted in wider accessibility. In fact, beginning in 2000, more organic food was being sold in large supermarkets than in any other venue. A Missouri report on artisanal cheese notes that "specialty cheese grew by 94 percent from 1993 to 2004." Surveys show that three-quarters of all American households have purchased organic foods, and among the younger demographics the number is higher. And these organic shoppers include people from ethnically and economically diverse groups. As we age, we the younger eaters will continue to bring our passion and commitment to healthy food and our global mind-set with us. It's hard to imagine the Millennial CSA member of today becoming the Kraft Singles and Lunchables Mom of tomorrow, especially as more young entrepreneurs build the companies that make eating well easier and more convenient.

I should note that there are many reasons why people elect to not eat dairy at all. From the standpoint of health or ethics (lactose intolerance, or being vegan by choice), the availability of soy, rice, almond, coconut, cashew, and hemp milk, and associated products, makes dairy-free an increasingly accessible option. And a healthy one too: A 12-year Harvard study of 78,000 women demonstrated that high dairy consumption led to twice the risk for osteoporosis, suggesting that dairy can actually leach calcium from our bones (although in a study this large it's not known exactly what kind of dairy these women were eating). The researchers stressed how important it is for all of us, whether or not we consume dairy, to get protein and calcium from vegetables, whole grains, nuts, and legumes, like beans and greens, and not just from animal products like meat and milk (also, of course, to exercise, not smoke, avoid salt, and get enough vitamin D).

But since the conversation in this chapter is for those who *do* consume dairy, but might not realize they are consuming it in the *wrong way,* here's the bottom line:

> If we want to consume dairy, it should be whole, unsweetened milk and real, whole cheese and yogurt in reasonable quantities, from healthy cows, raised eating grass.

We the eaters should make a commitment to eat all our dairy products as close to how they come out of the animal as possible. Look for 100 percent grass-fed dairy products with certification by the American Grassfed Association, Food Alliance, or USDA, as well as certified organic brands that display the USDA organic logo or carry state or regional organic certification. Try to find and visit a local dairy farmer and support them by buying their products as directly as possible, or look for a local brand of milk that buys from farmers in a co-op model (Organic Valley is the biggest one) so that you have reassurance that the farmer got a decent price and lives not too far from your neighborhood.

Then go ahead and make (or buy) that pizza we all crave, with a crust made from organic whole wheat, yeast, and salt; cheese made from a grass-raised, grass-finished cow; and some organically raised heirloom tomatoes. And by all means, put a slice of real, whole-milk, organic, pastured, naturally orange-colored cheese on top of that burger made from grass-fed, pastured beef.

Global Waves of Grain

BMI, Borlaug's Wheat,
and Burger Buns

IN THE MOUNTAINS surrounding Quetzaltenango, the second-largest city in Guatemala (called Xela by local residents), lies a rural region populated by poor, often nutritionally stunted, indigenous Mayan people. Children with stunted growth are under normal height for their age, and it is estimated that stunting affects 200 million children under the age of 5 around the world. Sadly, Guatemala has the third-highest rate of nutritional stunting in the world—it affects more than 54 percent of the children.

A few years ago, on a trip with the UN World Food Program, I had the opportunity to serve lunch to a group of local schoolchildren in a village outside of Quetzaltenango, a lunch composed of a sweet, enriched milk porridge made with American corn–soy blend food aid. FEED was beginning to sell some beautiful Guatemalan ikat products to benefit local school feeding and nutrient fortification, and *Marie Claire* magazine was coming with us to see the programs we were benefitting in action. As we poured the sweet porridge (and tried to look natural as a photographer snapped away), all I could think about was what a sad turn of events this represented. The ancestors of these children were members of a civilization that was likely the first to domesticate and cultivate maize, and now they were relying on North American corn, in the form of food aid, as their staple food, as they suffered from stunted growth and wasting (low weight for height).

We began our story about wheat in the region that is the birthplace of—yes—corn. Because as you will soon see, while dependence on American grain has spread around the world through exports and food aid, the economies of a handful of food mono-crops have become deeply intertwined—and conspire to create more food insecurity.

More than 10,000 years ago, the ancient Mayans of this region developed highly sophisticated and dynamic agricultural practices that ranged from raised terracing and swidden (fire-fallow cultivation, also known as slash-and-burn agriculture) to forest gardens.[1] These agricultural practices transitioned humans in this region from a nomadic life of hunting and gathering to one of settlements, farming, livestock raising, and crop cultivation. The earliest archaeological evidence for maize cultivation dates to more than 9,000 years ago, not far from Guatemala, in the Central Balsas River Valley of southern Mexico. Ever since, this region of Latin America has had an agriculture-based history and economy where corn and beans have been the mainstays of the diet.

Yet despite modest population increases in Guatemala from 1984 to 2001, this country, where at least half of the population is employed in the agriculture sector and pervasive food insecurity and crippling malnutrition affect well over half the population, began growing *less* corn, beans, rice, and wheat and *importing more* of them. This raises the question: *Why would a country with such a rich history in agriculture and an abundance of fertile soil, which now has a struggling and poverty-stricken population, grow less of its staple foods?*

There are a number of economically progressive reasons that could be the impetus for a shift like this. For example, broad-based economic growth driven by advances in agriculture *could* mean that some farmers transitioned to higher-paying, nonfarm jobs. But that's not what happened.

A critical factor in the decline of the production of corn, beans, wheat, and rice in Guatemala was that, due largely to both the North American Free

---

1   A forest garden was an unplowed, cultivated agricultural system used by the Mayans that uses all of the levels from the ground to the forest canopy to cultivate food, medicine, spices, and more, in a sustainable, biodiverse manner. It is the basis of today's permaculture movement.

Trade Agreement (NAFTA), a law that President Clinton signed in 1993, and the Central American–US Free Trade Agreement (CAFTA) that President Bush signed in 2004,[2] the price of imported corn from the US was less than what the farmers in Guatemala could grow it for themselves. Priced out of the marketplace, local farmers could neither sell their corn into the Guatemalan market nor export it. Many farmers in rural communities dependent on selling commodities in urban areas, and to local processors, were undercut by these cheap imports. Coupled with protracted civil conflict that pushed the poor and vulnerable to the less fertile highlands, the already fragile regional food systems began to crumble. Chronic hunger was rampant, and as the US continued to sell cheap corn into the market, it also dumped shipments of soy–corn mix in the form of "free" food aid. The subsidies, consolidation, and earmarks that allowed US farmers to sell corn at a cheaper price per bushel than it cost them to grow it meant that farmers in Guatemala didn't have a prayer in such an artificial pricing environment.

> One thing that we the eaters don't often realize is that US subsidies and price supports affect international farmers and markets as well.

Crop cultivation patterns in Guatemala provide a real-time example of what happens when the US floods export markets with subsidized crops while simultaneously dumping free food aid. It may sometimes alleviate a short-term hunger crisis, but it can also suppress local agriculture and economic growth in the long term. There are a plethora of examples of this in other developing countries as well. When a starving Haitian saw the food-aid sacks from the US offloaded into towering piles on a pier in Port-au-Prince after the 2010 earthquake, the *Global Post* reporter Donovan Webster, who was standing next to him, asked why he didn't just take some of the free grain. The man, understanding the long-term impact of food aid in Haiti, responded with a heartbreaking statement: "I'm not *that kind of* hungry."

---

2   On December 8, 1993, President Clinton signed into law the North American Free Trade Agreement, a trilateral treaty between the US, Canada, and Mexico intended to ease trade, create jobs, stop illegal immigration, and help local economies throughout North America. But it is ultimately viewed to have had a detrimental effect. Guatemala is a member of the Central America Free Trade Agreement (CAFTA), which now has an import duty of 10 percent on corn from the US.

★ ★

In Guatemala, as long as US corn prices stayed low, importing subsidized cheap corn wasn't *that* bad. In fact, at least theoretically, it opened the door for the cultivation of other crops with higher profit potential. Instead, corn prices suddenly spiked, in part because a drought in the US pushed corn prices higher, and in part because the US government introduced legislation that stipulated that 40 percent of subsidized corn must now be earmarked for ethanol production.[3] This mandate provided substantial price support for corn back in the US, but tightened the global supply of corn available for food and raised the market price for yellow dent corn, grown not only for ethanol, but also for animal feed, cornmeal, and a whole lot of other processed, corn-based products. Throw in some not so inconsequential factors affecting the local health and the economy of Guatemala—such as poor education, inadequate infant nutrition,[4] and micronutrient deficiency (even when there is adequate caloric intake), plus a lack of irrigation, political turmoil, institutionalized racism, inequitable distribution of land, and the influx of American fast food restaurants—and this evolves from a story about food imports affecting local agriculture to an illustration of a massive, unintended failure of the complex adaptive system of global food production. Because today, although Guatemala is a net importer of corn, hunger and food insecurity have *increased*.

CHILDREN OF THE CORN

There are very few Americans who would connect seemingly isolated events—a drought in Kansas, an uptick in September corn futures, the fact that the gasoline we put in our cars now contains 10 percent ethanol—and suspect that these variables could collude to cripple the food economy of a Central American country, and result in children thousands of miles away suffering from malnutrition and stunted growth. Many of us probably think ethanol is good. Its purchase is patriotic because it makes us *less* dependent on foreign oil, *doesn't it?* And a drought in Kansas couldn't have such a big ripple effect—don't we *stockpile* corn? And doesn't American food aid feed the hungry around the world even when there are droughts?

---

3   US government subsidies for ethanol of 45 cents per gallon expired on January 1, 2012; they are now considering proposed subsidies for the production of cellulosic ethanol. But more important to the price of ethanol is the Renewable Fuel Standard, which mandates acreage under production for corn, and which nearly tripled the price of corn futures when it was instituted.
4   According to the World Bank, only 16 percent of infants in Guatemala get adequate calories.

And aren't corn futures just some fabricated derivative used by a bunch of commodity traders in Chicago to hedge profits and losses? An uptick in the price of corn futures can't possibly affect hunger in children in Central America—*can it?*

★ ★

This statement, from the 1989 congressional report titled *Agricultural Progress in the Third World and Its Effect on U.S. Farm Exports,* says it all:

> *"To be effective, agricultural policy must be comprehensive—that is, its scope must include policies for the production, distribution, and consumption of food along with other agricultural policies, since all types of agricultural production compete for many of the same resources."*

Unbeknownst to most Americans, subsistence farmers in developing countries are competing for many of the same resources as American Big Ag corporations, and are profoundly affected by the mandates and ramifications of the pro–Big Ag policies contained in legislation like the farm bill. Also unbeknownst to most Americans, the hungry in developing countries represent a profit stream for companies selling American agriculture products—a profit stream that accounted for half the global exports of grain from the US in 1987, up from one-third in 1970. This failed system pits the small farmers of the world against the giant US agribusinesses that are dependent on the developing world's hungry for a significant portion of their revenue.

And it gets worse. Many poor countries are plied with American-style agriculture "aid," a proxy system for pushing poor countries to solve their hunger issues by planting the same commodities that we are way too dependent on in the West. As this kind of agriculture develops in a poor country, the short-term successes can include an increase for some in per capita income, which creates higher demand for processed food as people move to nonfarm jobs in the cities. Thus, hunger *plus* food aid equals a further revenue stream for US agriculture, as these increases in per capita income then drive the US export market of processed foods.

All this means that a lot of our aid programs for agricultural development are not as noble and altruistic as they might seem on the surface. Most of us are unaware that more than 50 percent of US food exports now go to developing countries—countries that *pay* for them. The developing world is the most significant market for American farm products.

This system was put in place in 1954, when President Dwight D. Eisenhower established Public Law 480, which was essentially a way to create export markets for excess US agricultural products. In 1961 President John F. Kennedy amended PL480 to direct it toward goodwill and humanitarian efforts, calling the legislation Food for Peace. But the law requires that the majority of the help we give to feed the world's hungry must be actual food purchased from American farmers, and be shipped on US-flagged ships to the hungry country. This is far more expensive (and far less sustainable for developing healthy food systems) than if we were using US aid dollars to buy diverse and healthy foods locally from farmers in the developing world. But that, of course, would seriously affect the profit stream for US agricultural products.

What started as humanitarian aid based on surplus crops back in 1954 became an ingrained business model that binds our national generosity with profits for a large segment of our agriculture sector. And looking at the motivational factors behind aid, agricultural development, and the farm export market provides a window into understanding the story of what happened over time, and on a global basis, to wheat.

Consider that according to the UN Food Program, Guatemala has the highest level of malnutrition of any Latin American country, and the fourth-highest level of malnutrition in the world. As reported earlier, a staggering 50 percent of children under the age of 5 are malnourished or have stunted growth. Even worse, malnutrition among indigenous children is estimated to be closer to 70 percent. Complexities such as guerilla wars in the 1980s, coupled with institutional racism levied against the native Mayan people, have economically marginalized many indigenous Guatemalans, literally pushing them up into the highlands where there is less fertile land, irrigation is not a feasible option, rainfall is inadequate, and farming is exceedingly difficult. Guatemala also has a policy of land ownership that leaves the bulk of the best agricultural land in the hands of a few large landholders.[5]

These are enormously complicated and intertwined issues, and as American

---

5   In Guatemala, 70 percent of the land is owned by just 2 to 3 percent of the population. Therefore, for example, the sugar crop benefits a few large landowners and not the bulk of the population. Coffee growers in Guatemala are often small farmers, but coffee prices are such that these small farmers are struggling to compete on price when global market dynamics make it impossible to do so.

consumers, we're not connecting the dots between ethanol, food aid, drought, corn futures, and the intricacies of Guatemalan social, political, and economic policies. But researchers from Tufts University did connect a few of the dots, and they estimate that "Guatemala alone absorbed $91 million in ethanol-related costs, in part because its import dependence [on corn] grew from 9% in the early 1990s to nearly 40% today." In other words, as demand for ethanol pushed corn prices higher in the US, that meant higher corn prices for the Guatemalans, who had stopped growing their own corn because our imported corn *used to be so cheap.*

What I have outlined here is a brief explanation of a very complex global economic system that is, on the surface, centered on corn, but it is equally about wheat. Because as this corn story was transpiring, prices for tortillas doubled, and Guatemalans began transitioning to eating a more Western diet. A diet that included an abundance of highly processed wheat products.

WHEAT: THE OTHER WHITE GRAIN

Guatemala is the only Central American wheat producer, and it went from producing 50,000 metric tons of wheat in 1980 to just 5,000 metric tons in early 2000. While production declined, wheat *consumption* in Guatemala during this time frame actually rose at a higher rate than corn consumption, which means that Guatemalans from the fertile crescent of maize began eating more imported wheat to go along with all that imported corn. Between 1998 and 2002, there was a *362 percent* increase in wheat exports from the US to Guatemala.

What's more, as impossibly incongruent as it might seem in light of Guatemala's malnutrition, hunger, wasting, and stunted growth, in the past 30 years Guatemala has also developed a staggering obesity problem.

In fact, in the past 30 years, Guatemala's obesity rate has quadrupled. Guatemalan women have the highest obesity rate in Latin America (37 percent). And Guatemalan teenagers, who eat the most wheat- and meat-heavy diets—often in the form of fast food hamburgers—don't fare much better. Today, 67 percent of Guatemalans 15 and older are overweight, of whom 29 percent are obese.

In my experience, when you travel to Guatemala, your food options include more wheat than corn. In the city of Xela, located not too far from the Pacific

Ocean and just a few miles from where I was serving US food aid to those children, the main restaurant on the old city plaza is an American/Texas-themed pizza parlor. One roadside fast food restaurant serves the typical bread-heavy sandwiches that you'd get anywhere in America; another roadside stop features pasta as the only vegetarian option. And when I headed out to dinner with some of my hosts at an upscale international restaurant, it served wheat-based, not corn-based, pitas to accompany the meal.

Although the urban haves, and the rural or slum-dwelling have-nots, might seem miles away from each other geographically, the newfound love of fast food and processed wheat crosses income lines. Top fast food chains like Subway (hail, the hoagie roll!), McDonald's (with its ubiquitous burger buns), and Starbucks (with its assortment of pastries, alongside sugar-laden drinks) dominate the market. A quick look at the menu of even a Guatemalan chain like Pollo Campero confirms that wheat is heavily favored in almost every dish—starting with the breading around almost every piece of "pollo." Even in Guatemala, the home of Mayans and maize, fast food tortillas are often made from wheat, not corn.

In a country as large and developed as America, we don't usually see obesity side by side with stunted growth, wasting, and malnutrition, yet I saw it frequently on my trips to Guatemala. And there are some very specific biological reasons that obesity *quadrupled* in Guatemala against the backdrop of malnutrition. There is evidence that once growth is stunted due to poor nutrition as a child, it is easier to become obese later in life due to changes in the manner in which malnourished individuals are able to oxidize fat. This means that people in developing countries who have poor nutrition in childhood are at far greater risk than we are in America of becoming obese, and developing obesity-related illnesses, when they eat an abundance of poor-quality processed foods later in life. Consider that in the documentary *Super Size Me,* it took the filmmaker Morgan Spurlock (who did not suffer from nutritional stunting) just 1 month to gain 24½ pounds by eating all of his meals at McDonald's, yet it took him 14 months on a vegan diet to lose that weight. So now imagine what happens when fast food franchises open in countries that have populations suffering from hunger and malnutrition, and consider that today 90 percent of the fast food franchises in Guatemala are foreign, and US franchises have more than 80 percent of the market share. No matter where we look, the system fails the people of Guatemala every step of the way. In terms of diet, health, and nutrition, Guatemalans don't seem to have a fighting chance.

When speaking about Guatemala, Chessa Lutter, the regional advisor for the Pan American Health Organization, observed that "the same type of diet that is heavy in carbs and cheap fats, which makes kids short and anemic, also makes adults fat." According to José Andrés Botrané Briz, a food security expert in Guatemala, "A person can have 12 tortillas and a Coke and will not be hungry, but they won't be well nourished." And a study conducted in Guatemala shows that just a 10 percent increase in the consumption of highly processed foods translated to a 4.25 percent increase in body mass index.

This shift from traditional, homegrown corn that local people turned into tortillas with the help of lime and water to highly processed forms of de-fibered white wheat flour, in addition to the many iterations of deep-fried food cooked in cheap oil, has taken a massive toll on the people of Guatemala. It is documented that a primarily corn-based diet provides limited micronutrients—it's low in protein, iron,[6] and niacin—if it is not nixtamalized and complemented with other foods.[7] Yet a fast food diet of highly processed wheat-based foods, even those fortified with the missing nutrients, is actually, in many ways, a lateral nutritional move, taking one set of disease vectors—malnutrition, stunted growth, micronutrient deficiency—and trading them for another: obesity, heart disease, and diabetes. Today we see people in developing countries like Guatemala moving from hungry to obese in a single generation, as the interplay of stunted growth, early malnutrition, and a newly adopted Western diet wreak even more havoc on their health than on that of Westerners. In 1994 Barry Popkin, professor of nutrition at the University of North Carolina at Chapel Hill, called this new phenomenon "nutrition transition."

But nutrition transition as populations rapidly move from malnutrition to obesity, and the introduction of highly processed wheat products in developing countries, are only a small part of the wheat story. The main reason I introduced wheat by writing about Guatemalan corn production and the rapid transition of a culture to the Western diet is because it provides such a dramatic picture of what can go wrong when interconnected systems fail. It illustrates just how entwined American agriculture, American agricultural and food-aid policy, American ethanol production, and American dinner plates are with hunger *and* obesity in the far reaches of the world. And wheat is perhaps the best example of

---

6   A major health issue in Guatemala is anemia and iron deficiency, which can lead to mental deficiency and poor school performance. Corn flour is high in phytic acid, which interferes with iron absorption and therefore results in insufficient iron bioavailability.

7   Nixtamalization releases niacin, or vitamin B_3, which prevents pellagra and reduces protein deficiency.

an agricultural commodity with both catastrophic system failures and ground-breaking system successes.

THE GRAIN THAT SAVED A BILLION LIVES

What corn was to the Mayans, Aztecs, Incas, and other peoples of the Americas, wheat was to the people in many other regions of the world. The domestication of wheat began roughly 10,000 years ago in the Fertile Crescent—the region known today as Iraq, Jordan, Lebanon, Israel, Palestine, Syria, and parts of Egypt, Turkey, and Iran—after which it spread to Greece, Cyprus, and India, and then to Germany, Spain, China, and beyond. Just as corn did in Central America, wheat allowed humans in other regions of the world to transition from nomadic hunter–gatherers to agrarian cultivators of food. In terms of land area, wheat is now, by far, the largest crop cultivated in the world; it is grown on more than 240 million hectares.

Fast-forward from 10,000 years ago to the 1940s and 1950s. Norman Borlaug, who would later be dubbed "the father of the Green Revolution" and the "man who saved a billion lives" and would win the Nobel Peace Prize in 1970 for his groundbreaking work in wheat breeding and cultivation, was working at the International Maize and Wheat Improvement Center in Mexico. This was a joint venture between the Mexican government and the Rockefeller Foundation to breed new varieties of wheat. Over several decades, Borlaug bred new wheat varieties that produced dramatically improved yields. His early research produced varieties that were resistant to a plant disease called stem rust, which was plaguing Mexico's wheat crop at the time, and these new plants resulted in increased yields of roughly 20 to 40 percent. He then went on to crossbreed semi-dwarf varieties of wheat based on work originally done on rice in the Philippines, and he was able to generate varieties with even greater wheat yields, in part because the shorter, robust stalks of these dwarf plants he had propagated could hold up heavier grain heads without falling over in wind and rain. Via a technique he called "shuttle breeding" (he had to shuttle back and forth between distant growing fields), Borlaug was able to grow two harvests of wheat varieties in a single season by planting in separate regions and climates in Mexico; this expedited the process of creating new varieties. These new plants increased yields yet again, and on top of that, he now had plant varieties suited to different climatic regions and soil conditions, which opened the floodgates for planting wheat in a wider range of soil and climatic conditions around the world.

By 1963 Mexico harvested a wheat crop six times the size of the one harvested in 1944. In the years leading up to this harvest, Mexican farmers had shifted to planting 95 percent of their wheat crop with Borlaug's short, sturdy, semidwarf, and disease-resistant wheat varietals. Borlaug then took this stunning new technology to South Asia, specifically India and Pakistan, where famine was ravaging the population. The same thing happened in South Asia that had happened in Mexico. For the first time, food production actually exceeded the rate of population growth. Wheat yields more than doubled, which meant that concerns about long-term food supply and Malthusian[8] fears about our ability to produce enough food to feed the world's growing population were quelled. Borlaug not only believed that this was a proven route to ending starvation and famine, but also that his high-yield wheat varieties would slow down deforestation. Obviously, we would need less land to farm if we could double, even triple, wheat yields.

Recognizing that regions of food insecurity are also hotbeds of violence, Borlaug viewed his work—and so did the world—as a solution to not only feeding people and improving the environment, but also to bringing peace and diminishing violent conflict. When Borlaug was awarded the Nobel Peace Prize in 1970 as recognition of his work to "provide bread for a hungry world," he was lauded for the role that ending hunger plays in the achievement of world peace.

> *"This year the Nobel Committee of the Norwegian Parliament has awarded Nobel's Peace Prize to a scientist, Dr. Norman Ernest Borlaug, because, more than any other single person of this age, he has helped to provide bread for a hungry world. We have made this choice in the hope that providing bread will also give the world peace."*[9]

After introducing these new wheat varietals and the farming practices they required, first in Mexico and then in India and Pakistan, Borlaug brought his farming techniques to Latin America, the Near and Middle East, and, in recent years, to several countries on the African continent, where many regions have seen yields double and even triple in size. Imagine, if you can, the magnitude of this: Farmers transition to these hybrid semidwarf varieties, and yields increase

---

8   *An Essay on the Principle of Population*, Thomas Malthus's 1798 work espousing concern over the exponential growth in population outpacing the arithmetic growth in food supply.
9   Presentation speech by Mrs. Aase Lionaes, chairman of the Nobel Committee.

from 20 to 40 bushels of wheat per acre up to 80 bushels per acre. Borlaug continued his work for decades until his death in September 2009 at age 95, and is single-handedly credited with impacting global hunger and global harmony by saving hundreds of millions, perhaps even a billion lives—not for personal profit, but for the good of mankind.

Yet Borlaug is not without his critics, who view him as the father of mono-cropping, a farming practice that is heavily dependent on petrochemicals[10] and other costly investments, from machinery to fertilizers to seeds and pesticides (costs that have put many a farmer into debt). We know that mono-cropping increases the number and severity of pests and degrades the soil, which we then correct with pesticides and chemical fertilizers, which further degrade the soil, and harm the health of the air, the waterways, and we the eaters. We know that people are healthier when they eat diverse diets, and the planet is healthier if biodiversity is maintained, yet we continue to move to a system of mono-cropping because it is a system that is perceived by many to be the quickest route to the high yields deemed necessary to feed the world's escalating population base.

Borlaug's critics blame him for helping to create the Big Ag business model and making it difficult, if not impossible, for small farmers and diverse cropping systems around the world to compete. Indeed, the high cost of inputs like seeds, pesticides, and fertilizers, and the resultant increase in farmer debt, has been implicated in the financial demise of many small farmers all over the world. Then again, supporters of Borlaug would argue that it is easy to forget, when you are not starving and your children are not starving, what it means to save even one person, let alone a billion, from famine and starvation.

When I met Borlaug in 2006, he was giving an acceptance speech at an Auburn University awards dinner at the UN headquarters in New York to a university audience interested in agriculture, nutrition, and ending global hunger. That evening, he repeated his oft-quoted line "Take it to the farmers" and his call to engage and listen "to the young people!" When he did so, I was reminded of just how revolutionary a thinker he had been during his career, and that no matter where you may stand on the Green Revolution, his strength was that he

---

10   Nitrogen-based fertilizer is made from anhydrous ammonia, ammonium nitrate, and urea in a process that now consumes roughly 3 to 5 percent of the natural gas in the world, and irrigation piping is manufactured from petrochemical-based plastics.

refused to accept the status quo. Unfortunately, many benefactors of the agricultural technologies and farming systems Borlaug developed are part of the Big Ag food system and staunchly believe we should strictly abide by those scientific advances of more than a half-century ago, rather than move forward as we learn from and refine them. This is, of course, mainly because these benefactors are now financially profiting from those advances and will continue to do so as we maintain and expand the current system.

> Yet the status quo view of feeding the world is based on growing more and more of the few foods that we know how to grow more and more of, and that are proving to be bad for our health.

Now that we see the realities of the continued hunger and explosive obesity epidemic that these high yields and cheap commodities have contributed to, it's imperative that we think differently about what the focus of our food systems research should be as we move forward.

★ ★

Another very smart scientist, Albert Einstein, is miscredited with this quote:

> *"The definition of insanity is doing the same thing over and over again and trying to get a different result."*

TOMORROW'S PROBLEMS, YESTERDAY'S SOLUTIONS?

At the time of his groundbreaking work, Borlaug had been tasked with finding a solution to the question of how to produce enough calories to adequately feed an increasingly hungry world. Essentially, his mandate was to increase wheat yields. Today, if we actually listen to many of the malnourished farmers and the populations of hungry and overweight people, we would see that they are now approaching scientists with a *different* question and a different set of problems. As much as the Green Revolution and all that wheat saved so many lives, thanks to Borlaug's visionary thinking and brilliant body of work, it is time to step back and reassess some of these long-standing practices to better address new issues.

We need to focus on how to grow and eat better food,
not just increase yields.

Clearly today, as we saw in Guatemala, our massive global reliance on a few food crops (wheat, corn, rice, and soy) are colluding to make people and economies *dependent,* rather than self-reliant. It is a system that often makes people both more hungry and more obese, as this dependence on mono-crops negatively impacts our long-term health.

Overdependence on monocrops can also lead to political instability
and violence that stems from food insecurity.

Take Egypt. Forty-five percent of the population lives on $2 per day, and Egypt is the largest wheat importer in the world. Bread represents one-third of an Egyptian's total caloric intake. In 2007, when a global grain shortage caused wheat prices to soar, there were bread riots in Egypt and throughout the other wheat-importing countries in the Middle East. These are countries where an uptick in the price of bread can leave a large portion of the population to starve.

The same thing happened in 2010 when a crippling drought destroyed Russia's wheat harvest and, to keep the price of bread stable at home, Russia banned wheat exports. Global wheat prices doubled from $157 per metric ton in June 2010 to $326 per metric ton in February 2011. Once again, this had measurable negative impacts on the diets and well-being of the populations dependent on wheat imports to live. Violence erupted in many countries in the Middle East again, and the social unrest, the overthrow of governments, and the eruption of wars throughout the region came to be known as the Arab Spring. At least one of the contributing factors to this instability and violence is theorized to be the escalating price of wheat. *A hungry man is an angry man,* and dependence on a single crop can lead to starvation, social unrest, and even war.

Once again, these are enormously complex systems, but to completely understand the significance of Borlaug's impact on wheat farming and global hunger, it is necessary to understand the current thinking and where the Green Revolution is headed today.

And it is headed to Africa.

★ ★

Africa, to a large degree, missed the first Green Revolution, in part due to a lack of infrastructure, including irrigation and transportation; in areas of drought, for example, you can't grow crops that require petrochemical fertilizer if you don't have the water to dissolve the chemicals. Under both praise and criticism, the Bill and Melinda Gates Foundation and the Rockefeller Foundation formed the Alliance for a Green Revolution in Africa (AGRA), and Monsanto teamed up with AGRA to give out free seeds through a complex network of grants and nongovernmental organizations—free patent-protected seeds that require petrochemicals and, eventually, royalty payments, even when there is a drought and the plants die because many of these farmers still have no water to irrigate with. (Monsanto recently agreed that the seeds would be royalty-free "indefinitely," but there is a lot of skepticism surrounding that statement based on the company's behavior around the world.)

Demand for wheat in Africa grew by 45 percent from 2000 to 2009. In 2012 the continent imported 40 million metric tons of wheat, at a cost of $12 billion. Also, wheat cultivation is very tempting from a financial standpoint, since a metric ton of wheat in Zambia sells for $350, compared to a metric ton of corn, which is priced at $150 (though the profits are potentially offset by higher input costs from seeds to fertilizers). Herein lies the problem. We now know about the long-term impact of higher input costs and the increased loss of small farms. We know that polyculture (growing a variety of plants) is a better long-term solution to global hunger and health than monoculture. We know this because when Borlaug fed a billion people, we learned a lot about how we might improve what he started. So many now believe that before we bring monocropped wheat (or corn) farming on a large scale to Africa, we should think twice about the long-term consequences and consider the possibility of a Greener Revolution, one better suited to the new food needs of the 21st century. Of course, those thinkers are pitted against a very profitable and very embedded system populated by people who don't want it to change.

FROM PLANT PROPHET TO PLANT PROFIT

Traditionally, if a farmer simply collects the seeds from the strongest or most heat-tolerant or most productive plants from each year's harvest, whether he desires sweeter fruit, or early ripening, or a larger plant, the farmer is selectively crafting "better" plants (called landraces) for the area's microclimate through a form of "aided" natural selection, while enjoying a free source of seeds to plant in successive years. Many small farmers rely on seed saving, referred to as "brown bagging," as a free source of seeds, one that represents a significant cost savings, especially for poorer farmers in developing countries.

Hybridization, which is what Borlaug engaged in to create semidwarf wheat, is a more sophisticated process that involves the intentional crossing of two plants by a farmer, a plant scientist, or, increasingly, seed manufacturers like Cargill, Heinz, and Monsanto. This works by selecting two plants with desired characteristics and cross-pollinating them, thus creating a hybrid. These hybrid plants have DNA from both parent plants, and some will exhibit, or express, the desired trait, say, drought tolerance, early maturation, shorter stalks, larger seeds, or higher yields. But if the farmer were then to collect seeds from the harvest of these hybrid plants, successive generations of *those* plants would *not* have the desired traits of the parents, since the seeds of the hybrid plants revert back to the original plant's characteristics. So farmers growing hybrids can't collect the seeds from each year's harvest and are forced to buy new seeds each successive year. The trade-off, of course, is that if the hybrid plant has traits that are so desirable that the resultant harvest can command a higher price when brought to market, then increased crop revenues offset the input costs of higher seed prices. This has proven to be profitable for some farmers and problematic for others, especially smaller farmers and farmers in developing regions where the input costs of hybrid seeds, and the additional costs they incur—such as fertilizer and pesticides— have been too steep to absorb upfront, *even if the end product is a higher yield, a superior crop, and, ultimately, a higher income.*

★ ★

One step beyond hybridization is the process of genetically modifying organisms. Remember, in GM crops, the DNA from two living things that *would not be able to combine in nature* is crossed. In the case of Monsanto's Bt corn, for example, DNA from a *bacterium* known as Bt (*Bacillus thuringiensis*) is inserted into a *plant* (corn).[11] *The corn plant now contains DNA from a bacterium.* This new technology

---

11 Because of this, Bt corn is actually classified by the EPA as a pesticide. That's right: a corn plant is considered a pesticide.

was fueled by the 1980 Supreme Court ruling that allowed companies like Monsanto to patent, own, and profit from creating new living things by modifying genetic material.[12] Adding to this legislative foundation, in 2013 President Obama signed what has been referred to by critics as the Monsanto Protection Act, or the Farmer Assurance Provision (since farmers could continue to grow GM crops), which insulates Monsanto from financial litigation if GMO crops are found, in the future, to cause harm to consumers.

Traditionally, when a farmer buys seeds, the seed manufacturer would, in effect, get a single fee. The farmer then grows the crops and "saves" some seeds for next year's plantings, thereby reducing cost in successive years while hand-selecting and breeding plants better suited to his land. When hybridization and GM seeds became prevalent, the biological reality of hybrids (farmers can't save seeds) and the legal structure around GMOs (you owe a royalty to the patent holder) changed in a manner that allowed the developers of these hybrid plants to sell new seeds year after year, and with GM products, to collect royalties for the life of the patent.

All of this would completely change the profit structure and motivation of those involved in agri-science, plant breeding, and food production in fundamental ways.

HERE WE GO WITH GMO . . . AGAIN

Decades after Borlaug hybridized wheat in the mid-20th century, Monsanto began genetically engineering crops. With this new technology, and the protective legislation to shield it, why not take the groundbreaking work of scientists like Borlaug and bring it to the next level?

Along with GM corn, sugar beets, canola, soybeans, and alfalfa, Monsanto developed a GM wheat variety called MON 71800. But in May 2004 an interesting thing happened: Monsanto pulled MON 71800 out of its development pipeline, even though the FDA had approved it for use. International buyers had made it clear they would not buy GM wheat, or wheat products, from the US, or anywhere else. These buyers were responding to pressure from consumers who did not want to buy products made from GM crops; they included the European

---

12 The Supreme Court ruled in favor of Monsanto, agreeing that a seed patent could "last beyond the first planting." Patents on living material have since expanded from bacteria and plants to human DNA. In a case revolving around Myriad Genetics and the BRCA1 and BRCA2 genes, on June 13, 2013, the Supreme Court ruled that human genes *cannot* be patented.

Union, Asia, Japan, the UK, and Malaysia. Currently, there is no approved GM wheat growing in the world today.

But one of the significant differences between GM corn and GM wheat that concerned farmers is that the pollen from wheat has a greater potential to drift. In 1999 a shipment of wheat to Thailand from the US was found to contain some of the DNA from MON 71800, and in May 2013, Monsanto's GM wheat was found growing in a wheat farmer's field in Oregon. Monsanto could claim industrial sabotage; the other possibility, since Monsanto grew MON 71800 in test fields in the US, is that the DNA did what DNA does—it spread itself.

That is one of the biggest objections to GM seeds; that GMO technology is a system that can and very well may perpetuate on its own. And when we analyze the US food-aid system from its earliest form to its current state, we see how systems can get away from us. Putting grain on a US ship and sending it to a hungry region of the world seems not only productive, but also simple and morally correct. But when we see how the system of food aid eventually became corrupted and of questionable long-term value to the people it is supposed to help, and how those reaping the benefits shifted priorities within that system, we find that we are now stuck in an ineffective system that we can neither retreat from nor easily dismantle. GMO technology creates a system that has one goal (higher yields) and one owner (the lab that creates the seed) and the resultant level of myopia is what scares the world most about GMO technology.

If companies like Monsanto own the seed patents; control the petrochemical market of fertilizers, pesticides, and herbicides required to grow them; use the legislative protection of the US Supreme Court to guarantee the legality of the financial structure surrounding those seeds; and are protected from lawsuits if the GMO technology proves to be damaging to our health—all while preventing consumers from knowing which foods contain GM ingredients by influencing labeling laws . . .

> . . . then the farmers, and we the eaters, become serfs to a new type
> of colonial landholder—Big Agribusiness—that now effectively owns
> the land and has taken control of our diets by proxy.

In 2009 Monsanto, the world's largest seller of seeds, announced it would upcharge 42 percent for its seeds the following year because of increased yields. Yet that was based on *expected*, not necessarily *harvested*, yields. Higher yields don't always materialize, and profit is influenced by many global and environmental factors beyond the seeds themselves. A drought in Russia, a poor harvest of corn, a spike in oil prices that affects the price of fuel for tractors and the cost of making petroleum-based pesticides and fertilizers—all of these factors impact crop prices.

Another heart-stopping statistic is that 270,000 farmers in India have committed suicide since 1995. There is concern that a contributing factor to this humanitarian tragedy may be escalating seed costs related to GM crops—in some cases a jump of *8,000 percent*—which has also contributed to increasing debt as India's farmers transitioned to GM crops. Then there is the fact that 5 million Brazilian farmers were awarded $2 billion in April 2013 by Brazilian courts as part of a class-action lawsuit over inequitable yield-based royalties charged by Monsanto. Through a series of shifts both right below the ground and right below our noses, seeds, which used to be free, have become the intellectual property of corporations—and very expensive.

★ ★

Unfortunately, one of the most fundamental conversations about food, food systems, and hunger is a conversation grounded in basic math. Earth is only so big, and in order to keep pace as the global population grows, we must either cultivate more land (of which there is a limited quantity), stem population growth, or increase food output on the land we have in a healthful manner, as we simultaneously figure out how to be more efficient and prevent waste—since more than a third of all food grown around the world today is lost to waste and doesn't feed anyone.

To produce enough food for everyone, the math doesn't work any other way. When Thomas Malthus introduced *An Essay on the Principle of Population* in 1798, he raised the question: Will technology be able to advance at a greater rate than population growth? Or, to frame it more specifically: Will advances in agricultural science allow us to produce significantly more food using our existing space? Or, more basically: Can we feed the world?

Malthusian thinkers have often focused this question solely on yields, or the quantity of calories that come from a hectare of land. We the eaters have seen the folly of that math.

The question on the table today is: Can we feed the world healthfully?

The Green Revolution has been criticized for its dependence on chemical fertilizers, the damage it causes to the environment, its destruction of crop and food diversity, and its unequal impact on small farmers with limited resources. One of the greatest criticisms of its legacy is that while crop yields are up substantially, and a billion people were saved from famine and starvation, we built an agricultural system that is not providing healthful and diverse foods in a long-term or sustainable way. Perhaps it is now our responsibility to not let the massive system-wide success of Borlaug's wheat become a massive system-wide failure simply because we adopted his high-yield varietals while refusing to adopt his tenacity, his forward thinking, and his determination to reject the status quo when it can be improved.

★ ★

Sadly, the conversation we hear about wheat in America today centers on its role in the US obesity epidemic. Wheat has been villainized in recent decades as a "fat-producing carb." The first line of wheat defenders will contest that wheat itself is nutritious, but that it has been stripped of its nutrients as it is taken from a much more healthful whole grain and turned into low-nutrient white flour for bread and processed food. White flour that is further diminished as it is incorporated into highly sweetened, often high-fat junk food products like packaged cakes, cookies, and breads made with HFCS. And then diminished even more when these products are fortified to put back some of the lost nutrients (but none of the fiber) so food manufacturers can make health claims that proliferate, for example, in the cereal industry, where sugar-based, low-nutrient, wheat-based grains are directly marketed to children as healthy breakfast foods.

★ ★

Herein lies yet another problem.

When you are starving, when your children are starving,
you don't care about the economics and politics of food—you might
not even care about your long-term health. You care about getting
food, and nothing else.

It is then a responsibility of the non-hungry world to get our food systems right so we can figure out how to help the hungry world feed itself well—both now and for the long term. We need to eat in a way that builds a better system, so that the needs of the hungry world can be met along with ours. In the process of getting those high yields, we compromised the quality of the wheat being grown. We focused only on how the world could eat *more* wheat. As it stands today, to have an even *greener revolution*, one better suited to our current needs, just as with corn, meat, and milk, we the eaters have to focus on how to eat wheat *better*.

THE WHEAT WE (USED TO) EAT

Before Americans got so fat, just as we used to drink a lot more whole milk, we used to eat a whole lot more wheat. In 1900 per capita consumption of wheat flour in the US was roughly 225 pounds. That declined throughout the successive decades to bottom out, roughly around 1975, at 110 pounds per person. The primary reason was that improvements in transportation and refrigeration led to a wider availability of more diverse types of food, including vegetables, fruits, and meats.

Wheat consumption then began to rise again through the late 1970s and 1980s and into the 1990s, hitting about 150 pounds per person around 1997, as the dietary doctrine of the time pushed eaters back toward grain consumption and away from meat and dairy (animal fat was being touted as the causal factor in heart disease). But even at 150 pounds of wheat per person in 1997, we were still well below the 225 pounds consumed per person in 1900. In the mid-1990's, the nutritional thinking shifted, and the tides turned against wheat. Carbohydrates were villainized as unhealthy, and the massive popularity of low-carb diets took a toll on wheat sales. By 1997 those decades of modest growth in wheat had ended.

Even though we used to eat more wheat, we were baking our own bread. In 1890, 90 percent of the wheat consumed in the US was used in home-baked goods, and only 10 percent came from commercially baked products. That dramatically shifted by 1945 to 60 percent from commercially baked products, and then to roughly *90 percent* by 1990. In other words, we went from eating *no* commercially processed wheat products to eating *nothing but* commercially processed wheat products. And with those processed wheat products came a whole lot of other non-nutritious, calorie-dense, health-threatening ingredients.

★ ★

Not only did the *way* we eat wheat change, as we processed it into whiter and whiter flour, the plant itself changed too. For scientists to breed those coveted semidwarf varietals of wheat required thousands and thousands of crossbreedings over many years. They genetically engineered the size of the kernel and the height of the plant, and in the process they also altered the proteins and nutrients of the wheat to the point that, according to William Davis, the cardiologist who wrote the best-selling book *Wheat Belly,* eating two slices of even the whole wheat bread of today spikes blood sugar higher than a Snickers or Milky Way candy bar.

Davis advocates eating no wheat *whatsoever,* as a way to prevent and even reverse heart disease, as well as a multitude of other ailments from obesity to diabetes to osteoarthritis. Whether we agree with him or not, at the core of his argument is the fact that there were alterations in the genetic composition of the new hybrid, semidwarf varietals (particularly to a protein called gliadin) bred in corporate labs since the 1960s.[13]

When you read the science behind the chemical and genetic changes to the semidwarf wheat plants, it becomes abundantly clear that today one of the problems is that the hybrid wheat that emerged after thousands of crossings by scientists (and even exposure to "chemical, gamma ray, x-ray mutagenesis") is a very different grain than the wheat of the past. Unlike the corn we bred for HFCS and ethanol, which require much more processing to make it edible for humans, these new varietals of wheat actually taste good. And all that wheat in the form of processed foods is making us fat and sick, even those of us who didn't suffer as children, like the people in Guatemala, from malnutrition and stunted growth.

BETTER BURGER BUNS

At this point, if you are a meat eater, you have (hopefully) committed to eating only grass-fed burgers; and, if you enjoy dairy, perhaps with a slice of whole-milk cheese produced by a local, pasture-raised cow. But for this burger to be that iconic American sandwich, it needs to be majestically seated between two halves of a bun.

---

13 For starters, Davis contends that the protein binds to opiate receptors in the brain, which stimulates appetite.

If we compromise by cutting out all of the highly processed wheat products in our diets, and instead use a whole grain bun (perhaps one baked with heirloom wheat varieties[14] mixed with other whole grains) as part of our less frequently consumed, healthier burger, we will likely see changes to our health. By directing our dollars toward different wheat and wheat products, we will also be working with other eaters to move the entire food system closer to providing eaters with the best version of our favorite foods.

Diet trends such as low carb and Paleo have already shown how powerful changing consumer demand can be. Some fast food chains now serve burgers planted between two lettuce leaves, and products like quinoa and brown rice are increasingly offered as alternative grains everywhere from high-end restaurants to Costco aisles. Quinoa is a great example of the power of today's consumers; as the grain has increased in popularity, it has raised awareness about the effects—both positive and negative—on the impoverished regions that the crop is imported from. Demand for other grains such as oats, the ultimate healthy breakfast cereal, and barley or rye provide both good diversity for our diets, and good diversity for farmers and the soil. Healthier types of wheat consumption have become more accessible with the introduction of products made from sprouted wheat (wheat grains or seeds that have been allowed to start to grow their next wheat plant before they are ground up into flour), and products in which wheat flour is mixed with other nutritious grains. The sprouted grain bread market is led by Food for Life, a California company that uses biblical references in its branding and philosophy (something you might not expect from a popular health food brand). But the namesake Bible quote for its Ezekiel 4:9 bread encapsulates how wheat might reclaim its place in the agricultural and dietary landscape:

> *"Take also unto thee wheat and barley, and beans, and lentils, and*
> *millet, and spelt, and put them in one vessel, and make bread of it."*

Doing "God's work" might not be how my two friends Katie Baldwin and Amanda Merrow would describe their operations at Amber Waves Farm. Baldwin, who used to work with me at the Council on Foreign Relations, also

---

14   There is an increasing movement toward planting heirloom wheat varieties such as kamut, spelt, and einkorn. Heirloom wheat flour varieties are available from a number of sources for home bakers, such as Heartland Mills and Anson Mills (which has a recipe for hamburger buns made from heritage wheat on its website); Whole Foods Market carries Heritage Einkorn flour breads as well.

moved on from global political issues to food security issues, but she went all the way back to where food starts—with the sun, seeds, and soil—to become a farmer. She and Merrow founded Amber Waves Farm in Amagansett, New York, in 2008 on the east end of Long Island, after an apprenticeship with long-time farmer and writer Scott Chaskey. The farmers decided that one thing missing from the local food movement in their corner of New York state was the ability to make a fully local pizza, including the crust, or a local loaf of bread— something that many residents and farmers alike thought was virtually impossible with the climate—but they decided to try. In 2009, they launched the Amagansett Wheat Project and the have successfully harvested hard red wheat, soft white wheat, and soft red wheat in July of every year since and have local chefs and bakers clamoring for their organic wheat berries and stone ground whole wheat flour.

The Amber Waves farmers live the slogan of the young farmer group Greenhorns: "Serve your country food." As members of the growing young farmers movement and entrepreneurs, they use diversification to limit the inherent risk of agriculture and also run a mixed-vegetable CSA, participate in farmers' markets, and sell locally grown produce to restaurants. On top of that, they use their farm to teach school groups and families in the community about food and food production, fostering a connection between how food grows and what we eat. This is a critical element missing in our food systems today: connecting the farmers with the community and the eaters with the food. Amber Waves Farm is bringing locally grown wheat back to the region, partnering with bakers to produce bread from their harvest; and their diversification techniques seem to be working. In 2010, when a tomato blight hit the East Coast, their heirloom tomatoes were flourishing. In 2013 they donated 10,000 pounds of produce to local food pantries. By creating a food production and food distribution loop that keeps the food close to where it is grown, they keep the food dollars in the community, too. We the eaters need we the farmers to bring our daily bread—and daily vegetables—to our tables in healthier, locally produced forms.

The more we think about the diversity that could (and should) fill our plates and stomachs, the less of a role one crop like wheat will play. Although bread has played an important nutritional and cultural role around the world, to quote another Bible verse, "Man cannot live on bread alone." Today we probably say it best when we sit down to a delicious meal at a really nice restaurant: Don't fill up on the bread.

★ **5** ★

Tubers and Fruits

The French Fries, the Ketchup, and
the Orphaned World of Real Vegetables

EVEN BEFORE DR. BORLAUG began crossbreeding wheat at the International Maize and Wheat Improvement Center in Mexico, plant breeders in the seed and agriculture departments at H.J. Heinz were crossbreeding tomatoes in Bowling Green, Ohio.[1] In 1936 Heinz began selectively breeding tomatoes for high yield, viscosity, intensity of color, and firmness, creating hybrid tomato plants whose fruit characteristics suited each of its product lines, as well as the growing conditions of microclimates within North and South America, Europe, and Australia. By 1995 a division at Heinz, now called HeinzSeed, was employing plant breeders and agricultural scientists and dominating the processing tomato seed market in North America, as Heinz continued to expand internationally en route to becoming the dominant force in the global tomato market.

Heinz, like many large food manufacturers, contracts with local growers to plant its own hybrid seeds and deliver fruit to its specifications, ensuring quality

---

1   Tomatoes are technically a fruit, but I am including them here in the discussion of vegetables because of taste and culinary use patterns, which is the logic the US Supreme Court used in an 1893 trade case that classified tomatoes as a vegetable.

(and quantity) control at each step along the supply chain. Contract farming also provides some security to farmers who know that, as long as they abide by the corporate agricultural production mandates, crop sales are prearranged ahead of the harvest—and even ahead of planting. Through this system, Heinz provides its growers in the United States, Canada, China, Southeast Asia, India, Spain, Portugal, the Middle East, Africa, the Caribbean, and Latin America with 6 billion seeds a year (or seedling plugs started in a Heinz greenhouse that are ready for machine planting), and contracts with them to produce more than *2 billion tons* of tomatoes for Heinz's brands of juice, canned tomatoes, paste, and ketchup. Heinz also breeds hybrid tomato seeds and plants for farmers to sell as fresh produce under two brands: HeinzFresh, tomatoes that are bred specifically for supermarket produce sections in different global regions with characteristics of "firmness for transport" and "vine-ripe shelf life," and HeinzHeritage, a separate line of fresh tomatoes bred specifically for farmers' markets.

For almost 8 decades all around the world, Heinz has systematically bred and field-tested its tomatoes for each product category they have developed a market for. Heinz has also worked toward advancing and promoting sustainable farming techniques, including soil restoration, water conservation, and farming and plant breeding methods to reduce petrochemical fertilizer and pesticide use. This includes breeding tomatoes that are disease and pest resistant, and developing specific agricultural practices to help farmers deliver the product quality and high yield that Heinz expects. All of these things seem like reasonable, beneficial, and perhaps even honorable contributions to agriculture science and the broader food landscape.

★ ★

The juicy, round red tomato is actually a vast species with thousands of plant varieties that bear fruit in almost every color from white to yellow to purple to pink. But the tomatoes that end up on our plates don't tend to have anywhere near that genetic diversity. Even though all 50 states can grow tomatoes and 40 to 50 years ago growers and processors existed from Delaware to New Mexico, today California grows 96 percent of US processing tomatoes and one-third of ones that are sold "fresh." Heinz, along with seed companies Monsanto and Bayer CropScience, provide a full 90 percent of all tomato seeds that California farmers use.

The massive consolidation (sound familiar?) of tomato plant breeding has dramatically reduced the number of tomato varieties that most of us eat. One study published by Rural Advancement Foundation International suggested that the number of tomato varieties sold by the US commercial seed houses was 408 varieties in 1903, but by 1983 the number housed in the National Seed Storage Lab was just 79 varieties. Of course, Heinz isn't the only company involved in practices that diminish crop diversity. Nor is the tomato the only agricultural crop losing ground to the homogenized needs of large food processors and the increasing demands of we the eaters for cheap, uniform, readily available food.

Since then, a renewed interest in "heirloom" or older, unique (and more delicious) varieties has pushed seed companies to expand their offerings and there has been a 30 percent increase in fresh tomato consumption since 1985. But the vast majority of Americans are still eating just a handful of tomato varieties . . . because most of our tomatoes come out of a bottle, jar, can, or on top of a fast-food burger or pizza.

Americans still eat three-fourths of their tomatoes in processed form, and processed tomato consumption has been on a steep rise since the 1980s as we eat more pizza, salsa, and ketchup.

As we lose crop diversity, our food supply becomes more vulnerable to catastrophic demise due to pests or diseases, and we the eaters have fewer options when it comes to taste, flavor, and even nutrition. The same study by Rural Advancement Foundation International found a dramatic loss of lettuces (497 to 36 varieties), cabbages (544 to 28 varieties), and peas (408 to 25 varieties). The list goes on. Even our farm animal breeds have become less diverse.

The UN Food and Agriculture Organization (FAO) estimates that from 1900 to 2000 we lost a full 75 percent of crop diversity globally. As we saw with varietals of corn and wheat, loss of crop diversity has been happening across the board, as large corporate agricultural giants are spending tens, even hundreds of millions of dollars breeding proprietary plants. To their credit, they're also often initiating programs to improve overall farming techniques and soil conditions, developing pest- and disease-resistant plants, reducing fertilizer use, and improving irrigation techniques for their growers; Heinz, for example, in the Xinjiang region of China, where they have partnered with China's largest tomato processor, is breeding plants with the objectives of high yield, "firmness of transport," and "vine ripe shelf life," *and* they are instituting soil improvement and water conservation programs as they increase the income of rural farmers in the region.

This all sounds good at first blush, and these are goals that often serve the immediate needs of local farmers and we the eaters (even as they better serve a business that requires crops that are easy to transport and shelf stable). But these are not practices that necessarily support long-term agricultural, economic, and environmental needs, nor do they create the healthiest foods with the best taste and highest nutritional content. Then again, Heinz never really stated that as its goal in the first place. The aim of large agribusinesses and food-processing companies is to make a profit. And herein lies the difference between Borlaug's wheat and Heinz's ketchup.

When the endgame is corporate profit, the needs of we the eaters are often underserved. Borlaug bred wheat for the starving world, while Heinz was monocropping tomatoes by producing—and getting us to buy, and eat, all in the name of profit—more ketchup.

WHAT'S THE MATTER WITH KETCHUP?

Heinz uses more tomatoes each year than any other company in the world, and today more than 30 percent of processed tomatoes globally are grown with Heinz seeds. Heinz sells *650 million* bottles of ketchup each year; even more impressive, it manufactures *11 billion* single-serving ketchup packets that are sold to retailers of prepared food, primarily at fast food restaurants and convenience stores. This, in turn, has led Heinz to hone a proprietary interest in potatoes, specifically the kind of potatoes that are so frequently paired with ketchup: the iconic (and, in its current form, far from healthy) American french fry.

What is most interesting about this is that Heinz, the agricultural seed giant, the world's dominant tomato grower and processed tomato producer that manufactures all of that ketchup, has a vested interest in increasing sales of french fries, not only by dominating the at-home market with its own brand of processed frozen french fries, called Ore-Ida,[2] but at restaurants and takeout windows as

---

2   Ore-Ida manufactures numerous frozen processed potato products, including the legendary Tater Tots. *Three and a half billion* Tater Tots are eaten each year in America.

well. And with our help, they have done an impressive job: *Presently 25 percent of all vegetables consumed in America by kids are frozen, processed french fries.* And those fries, by and large, go hand-in-hand with ketchup, which makes dominance in this market sector a win-win for Heinz.

★ ★

From a consumer standpoint, hands down the most compelling things about frozen, processed french fries is that these fries are loaded with fat and salt and are cheap and ubiquitous, a set of attributes that push we the eaters to eat them in large quantities.

The most interesting thing about ketchup, meanwhile, is that it isn't eaten as a standalone "food" but paired with another product—often, fried potatoes. The second interesting thing about ketchup is that when we eat out, it's free.[3] As restaurants can't put it on the menus as an item for sale, Heinz knows ketchup is inextricably linked to, and is an important driver of, french fry sales.

When Heinz saw marketing data indicating that people were ordering fewer french fries at drive-thru windows than they ordered as walk-in, sit-down customers, Heinz determined this was due to a "ketchup delivery problem" that needed to be solved. Through consumer research, Heinz isolated the problem, determining that people found it hard to squeeze ketchup out of a little packet while driving. They also deduced this delivery problem extended to everyone in the car, since many customers didn't want their kids making a mess. So in 2011, Heinz stepped in with a solution, after spending millions of dollars to redesign the packet delivery system: the "Dip and Squeeze" packet. It placated consumer preference to dip (the packet lies flat and the top peels off) rather than just to squeeze ketchup onto fries, while also providing a less messy option for eaters in cars.

Heinz knows it makes more money if it controls the tomato seeds, the tomato growers, the irrigation, the pesticide and fertilizer application, the processing—basically, the whole supply chain all the way up to and including the ketchup delivery system. The bottom line is Heinz makes more money if fast food companies and other retail outlets sell more french fries. And they will go to extraordinary efforts to get us to eat them.

---

3   In 2013 it was reported that some McDonald's franchises in Manhattan were charging customers for extra servings of ketchup.

EVERYONE IS A FRY GUY

Heinz, the manufacturer of all those little plastic ketchup dispensers, the company that is so worried about the decline in sales of french fries at the takeout window, is the same company deciding which varieties of tomatoes the world should be growing. These factors, when taken together, affect the types of food that are available for us to eat. Companies like Heinz are indirectly making food decisions for us by limiting our options via mono-cropping, and inundating us with highly processed, highly replicated foods. And they have succeeded to such a large degree that the question "Would you like fries with that?" is as much a part of American food culture as the 1950s diner and apple pie. Indeed, french fries are now such a large part of the global foodscape that they dominate restaurant plates even in Uganda.

Which brings me to food—not crop—diversity as it pertains to the potato, not just in the US, but also around the world. As previously noted, Guatemala is home to the highest malnutrition rate in the Western Hemisphere, as well as a recent and dramatic increase in obesity. In 2006 the American french fry made up 35 percent of that country's imports of fruits and vegetables. That's right: *35 percent.*

Heinz, through Ore-Ida, sells 1 billion pounds of potatoes a year, and a lot of the ketchup to go with them: they control 60 percent of the US ketchup market, and an even greater share overseas.

> The fast food industry, and companies like Heinz, basically
> took the nutritious potato and the nutritious tomato and
> made them into a fat, salt, and sugar delivery system
> called french fries with ketchup.

In the perfect Modern American Diet trifecta, the processing of the potato supplies the fat and salt, and the ketchup provides the sugar. One tablespoon of Heinz ketchup contains 4 grams, or 1 teaspoon, of sugar. (One Dip and Squeeze packet has 6 grams of sugar, or 1½ teaspoons.) The ubiquitous 38-ounce bottle translates to 56 tablespoons of ketchup, or 56 teaspoons of sugar. That means a 38-ounce bottle of ketchup has almost the same amount of sugar as a six-pack of soda. And there is a good chance that sugar is high-fructose corn syrup to boot. Meanwhile, the process of turning a potato into french fries is estimated to diminish its nutritional value by more than 50 percent.

But we the eaters are not off the hook in this equation. Heinz is making fries and ketchup, and fast food companies are frying and salting potatoes, only because we line up out the door, around the block, and around the world to order them. It doesn't help the situation that they are available everywhere, very cheap, and often at the expense of more healthful options. Even still, we the eaters are responsible for ordering every last one of those fries, along with demanding, by eating in our cars, Heinz's newfangled ketchup delivery system. The problem with potatoes and tomatoes is the same problem with every other crop: It starts as a problem with what and how we are growing, and ends up as a problem with what we are choosing (and what choices we have) to put on our dinner plates. Just take a look at what happened to how we eat potatoes.

Total potato consumption has actually *dropped* from 122 pounds per person in 1970 to 110 pounds in 2011, as the *type* of potato consumed changed dramatically. We cut consumption of fresh potatoes almost by half, and increased

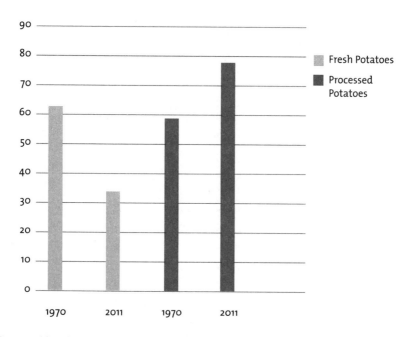

Chart created from data collected from the National Potato Council

consumption of processed potatoes by 16.3 pounds per person per year. (In 1996, at the peak of processed potato eating, the average American consumed 95.1 pounds of processed potatoes.) The USDA reports that 88 percent of french fries and 60 percent of the ketchup we consume are eaten *away from home*. We shifted *what* we were eating (fresh became processed) and *where* we were eating it (in a restaurant instead of at home). What makes this shift even worse are the cultural food associations that we the eaters need to be aware of—*because the food marketers certainly are.*

Researchers at the University of Oregon and Michigan State University report that Americans strongly associate salty and calorie-dense foods such as pizza, burgers, and fries with the consumption of soda. They report that this is a *culturally learned behavior.* (For example, the Japanese prefer green tea, not soda, with calorie-dense food.) What this means is that if we order fries, not only do we get the high calories and high fat *they* deliver, we get the added sugar of ketchup *and* likely wash it all down with soda (more sugar and empty calories), thereby making those french fries even worse for our health because of what accompanies them.

Now think for a moment about your own consumption patterns. If you order takeout pizza or fast food burgers, do you drink soda with them, or milk or water? By and large, junk food in general, and french fries and ketchup in particular, are not often paired with nutritious foods—or drinks. And to demonstrate just what a slippery slope this is, when those researchers offered kids raw vegetables with water, or raw vegetables with soda, the kids ate fewer raw vegetables when they were accompanied by soda. Even when we select food, it seems that one bad choice will lead to another.

DO YOU *REALLY* WANT FRIES WITH THAT?

A 16-year study of eating patterns of 52,000 people in Singapore published in 2012 revealed three stunning observations. The first is that consuming just two fast food meals a week increased death from coronary heart disease by a staggering 56 percent. Further, if participants ate at an American-style fast food restaurant four or more times a week, that number escalated to 80 percent. But there was one more lesson: When these study participants ate at fast food restaurants, excluding potatoes (french fries), their overall consumption of vegetables declined, mirroring the findings of the University of Oregon and Michigan State University study with kids and soda and vegetables.

★ ★

Scientists tell us that if you offer a toddler a wide variety of healthy foods, they may eat mostly melon one day, and mostly meat or bananas another day, but over the course of a week or month, they will eat a healthy and nutrient-balanced diet—*assuming the choices they are given are all healthy options.* And scientists also tell us that if you offer newborns sugar water or plain water, they will overwhelmingly choose the sugar water. When we serve fries with a meal, those fries replace something else. And those fries are likely to be paired with the other unhealthy options available in the food deserts of fast food restaurants and school lunchrooms, and on our dinner plates. There are very complicated inborn and culturally learned factors influencing our food choices. So we have to ask ourselves:

> Since those french fries are likely to be paired with a soda or a shake, but not with broccoli or kale, are we effectively creating unhealthy mini food-deserts on our dinner plates and in our pantries?

To provide a different set of statistics to showcase just how many french fries we eat, McDonald's alone buys 3.4 billion pounds of potatoes a year, and they use only a few varieties: Russet Burbank, Shepody, Ranger Russet, and Umatilla Russet.[4] All those potatoes are washed and machine cut, then blanched and sprayed with dextrose (corn sugar) to make them sweeter, sodium acid pyrophosphate so they will retain color, and two other chemicals, tert-butylhydroquinone (TBHQ) and dimethypolysiloxane. They are then frozen for shipment to franchises, where for years they were fried in 7 percent cottonseed oil and 93 percent beef tallow (which can withstand high heat and adds flavor) until word got out and vegetarians (logically) complained. McDonald's switch from beef fat created a kitchen sink-like list of ingredients: "potatoes, vegetable oil (canola oil, soybean oil, hydrogenated soybean oil, natural beef flavor [wheat and milk derivatives], citric acid [preservative]), dextrose, sodium acid pyrophosphate (maintain color), salt. Prepared in vegetable oil (canola oil, corn oil, soybean oil, hydrogenated soybean oil with TBHQ and citric acid added to preserve freshness), dimethylpolysiloxane added as an antifoaming agent." The fries contain both wheat and milk

---

4   J.R. Simplot Company of Boise, Idaho; Canada's McCain Foods; and Omaha-based ConAgra Foods are the three main potato suppliers to McDonald's.

ingredients in the "natural beef flavor," which they had to figure out how to re-create when they took out the tallow.

★ ★

A medium order of McDonald's french fries has 380 calories, 19 grams of fat, and 270 milligrams of sodium. When we add 3 tablespoons of Heinz regular bottled ketchup to that order of fries, we can tack on another 60 calories, 480 milligrams of sodium, and some HFCS along with "regular" corn syrup.[5] And to think that this was originally meant to be a side of vegetables.

Now consider this: A raw potato weighing the same 117 grams as a medium order of McDonald's french fries has only 90 calories, about a tenth of a gram of fat, and only 7 milligrams of sodium.

> Once again, it's not the potato, and it's not the tomato.
> It's what we do to it that's the problem.

THE POTATO BEFORE IT WAS A FRY

The potato, perhaps more than any crop, has a complex socioeconomic and political history. *Solanum tuberosum* is the botanical species from which the thousands of cultivated potatoes originally derived. Potatoes arrived in Europe from South America via the Columbian Exchange—the widespread transport of living things, including people (among them, slaves), plants, and animals; disease; and cultural elements between the Americas, Africa, Europe, and Asia, beginning with the discovery of the New World.

Although initially viewed with skepticism, in Europe the potato largely put an end to famine, which was prevalent from the 1500s to the 1800s. The potato stabilized the food supply, and without the population loss to waves of mass starvation there was rapid population growth across the continent.

Since potatoes are propagated vegetatively, the "seeds" planted for each subsequent year's crop are some of the potatoes a farmer grew the previous year. The

---

5   The ketchup in Heinz's Dip and Squeeze packet, as well as most of its bottled ketchup, contains HFCS; Simply Heinz and Heinz Organic use non-corn sugar. In October 2013, after Bernardo Hees, former CEO of Burger King, was named the new CEO of Heinz, McDonald's announced it would be dropping Heinz as a supplier.

farmer "plants" one potato in the ground (buried whole if the potato is small, or cut into pieces if it is large), and 2 to 3 months later that single potato yields a harvest of many. From the standpoint of potato genetics, this is essentially cloning, so all the potatoes planted one year are genetically identical to the potatoes from the previous year if all the seed potatoes were selected from the farmer's own harvest. The genetic similarity of potatoes is not a good thing when it's time to fight disease. When a fungus or pest strikes, varied genetics within a species of plant allows for the likelihood that some plants will be resistant to this new disease or pest, and will survive.

Historically speaking, there is no single crop that better illustrates for we the eaters the importance of crop biodiversity than the potato. The well-known Irish potato famine of 1845 and 1846, which to a lesser degree dragged on for 7 more years, caused the starvation of 1 million Irish, and the emigration of another million who could no longer sustain themselves at home. Ironically, this famine was caused by the fact that potatoes, which had initially alleviated famine, were the main source of calories for most of the population of Ireland. The problem, however, was that only a few cultivars of potatoes were planted, mainly a varietal called the Irish Lumper. Lumper potatoes were able to grow in poor soil and produce high yields, but they weren't resistant to a fungus identified (in the spring of 2013 from saved DNA) as a previously unknown strain of *Phytophthora infestans,* now called HERB-1. At the time, the fungus was simply known as "late blight," and when it appeared on potato plants across Ireland, it wiped out the crop, essentially turning the country's entire harvest to slime.

Today, even as potato diversity has declined globally, indigenous women in the Andes region of Peru are saving and cataloging wild seed potatoes so we don't lose genetic diversity of this important crop forever. There are potato gene banks maintained around the world: the US Potato Genebank's Potato Introduction Center in Sturgeon Bay, Wisconsin; the Institute of Crop Science and Seed Research of the Federal Agricultural Research Center, Braunschweig-Völkenrode in Germany; the N.I. Vavilov Research Institute of Plant Industry in St. Petersburg, Russia; and the International Potato Center (CIP) in Lima, Peru, which has close to 7,000 landraces. The CIP has seed potatoes, germ plasma, and DNA stores in a country where it is believed that a single Peruvian farm field contains a variety of potatoes that "exceeds the diversity of nine-tenths of the potato crop of the entire United States."[6]

---

6   Karl Zimmerer, an environmental scientist at Pennsylvania State University.

Even with these important efforts, diversity across the board, *for all of our crops,* is declining because of the direction our food systems are taking us—a direction that heightens the risk that these mono-cropping practices will send us down the path of the Irish potato famine once again. By limiting genetic diversity, the dominance of only a few varieties of corn, rice, and wheat as single crop answers to famine expose us to the same unknown frailties as the potato did. Complexity and genetic diversity are what make our agricultural systems—and diets—work, and every time we try to narrow a crop to one cultivar, or use one chemical as a solution to soil or plant health, we are ignoring the protective measures of nature's inherent complexity, and are putting our crops, and our health, in jeopardy.

SAVOR THE FLAVOR OF GMO VEGGIES?

A tomato ripening on the vine is the final stage of natural fruit production that begins with a seed that becomes a plant that flowers; the flowers are pollinated, produce a small green fruit, then a larger green fruit; and then that fruit finally develops a rich color, which signals that it has reached peak flavor and ideal nutrient and sugar content. The extraordinary attention vintners pay to grape ripening for wine making, carefully measuring and monitoring the Brix (sugar content of the grapes) in order to determine the precise time to harvest the grapes, should indicate just how critical hang time is for the flavor development of fruit.[7] From the standpoint of taste, it is ideal to let fruit ripen on the plant, tree, or vine. But if plant-ripened tomatoes are harvested, say, in Chile or California and then shipped in containers on freighters or in tractor-trailer trucks to New York, the tomatoes are a moldy puddle of mush by the time they reach supermarket shelves. As a result, much of the fruit we eat is picked green and ripened with ethylene gas sprayed in transit.[8] While ethylene is a natural plant hormone released by the plant to ripen its fruit, for commercial use ethylene is made from

---

7   In wine making, the ideal sugar content of the fruit is mandatory not only for flavor, but also for purposes of alcohol conversion.

8   Climacteric fruits like tomatoes, apples, melons, apricots, pears, mangoes, avocados, figs, papayas, and bananas release ethylene to ripen and are capable of ripening after they are picked. The reason you can ripen a green tomato by placing it in a confined space (like a paper bag) with a ripe piece of fruit—say, an apple—is because the ripe apple releases ethylene gas, which the bag traps, signaling to the tomato to produce ethylene as well.

natural gas and crude oil. So those red tomatoes (and the yellow bananas) that look "vine ripe" when we buy them likely got that way from the application of a man-made plant hormone, not from natural hang time in the sun. While ethylene gas is not dangerous per se, it is a replication of a natural process, and the practice of picking unripened produce reduces both taste and quality.

A couple of scientists armed with a genetically modified tomato produced by a California company named Calgene were supposed to change that. The tomato, called CGN-89564-2, or Flavr Savr, was the first FDA-approved and commercially produced GM food for human consumption, and it was a tomato that was engineered to have a slower ripening process. This would carry over to a reduced chance of *over-ripening* during transport, which would give the tomato the desired longer shelf life. The longer shelf life would, in turn, provide the opportunity for farmers to let the fruit vine ripen, which would make it taste better.

The problem with the Flavr Savr tomato was twofold. First, the technology involved slowing down the ripening process, but not the fruit *softening* process, which meant the fruit would still "go soft." This, as you can imagine, presented all sorts of harvesting and shipping problems. The second problem with Flavr Savr was that it was produced not by farmers, but by a biotech company that wasn't focused on taste (the original tomato was considered bland, but was later improved), and who were neophytes in food manufacturing and distribution, so they had all sorts of cost-control problems on top of issues of quality. When Calgene was bought by Monsanto (which was interested in Calgene's other biotech developments), the Flavr Savr tomato was discontinued.

So much for high-tech GM tomatoes—unless, of course, you consider the cholesterol-reducing tomatoes under development by Alan Fogelman, a professor and researcher at UCLA. He reports that consumption of this new tomato (which is not yet on the market) results in a reduction of plaque buildup in arteries by producing a peptide that mimics the actions of HDL cholesterol. So due to a megadose of convoluted thinking, we may soon have a GM tomato to lower the high "bad" cholesterol many of us have from eating all this poor-quality processed food that the food systems produce in the first place.

SORRY, WASHINGTON—FRIES AND KETCHUP AREN'T VEGGIES
Right now the US government recommendation for we the eaters is to consume four to six servings of vegetables every day. Yet the findings of one of the most

important studies of American dietary intake, the National Health and Nutrition Examination Survey, paints a dismal picture of what we are actually eating. Even when counting potatoes, jelly, and orange juice as fruits and vegetables, only 3.5 percent of women, 2 percent of men, and less than 1 percent of teenagers actually manage to meet the federal government's nutrition guidelines. Worse, a 2010 study by the National Cancer Institute found that *almost 40 percent* of calories consumed by children (2- to 18-year-olds) were empty calories—fats and carbohydrates that function to make them gain weight, but that don't provide any nutritional value.

Of course, what we eat is very much connected to what we grow, both in the West and in the developing world. A recent study from the Union of Concerned Scientists found that only 2 percent of US farmland is used to grow fruits and vegetables. How can we do what the USDA advises and "fill half of our plates with fruits and vegetables" if those foods constitute only 2 percent of what we are growing?

> Quite simply, we the eaters must change the landscape of food—and the foodscape of our dinner plates—by buying and eating more fresh, local, unprocessed vegetables.

When I sat down to write about vegetables in America, it was hard to imagine that I might need to consider french fries and ketchup—and even plain pizza—as a significant source of "vegetables." Because of the press it received, most of us are aware that condiments like ketchup and ingredients like pizza sauce have been classified as vegetables by the USDA, for the sad reason that this nuanced distinction would save the government money in the school lunch program. In 1981, during Ronald Reagan's presidency, Congress cut $1 billion from the subsidized school lunch program, and the USDA took some creative license with categorizing foods in order to stay within budget but still allow school districts to meet nutritional mandates. Schools have to serve meat, milk, bread, and two servings of fruit and vegetables for a meal to qualify for government money. By classifying pickle relish or other condiments such as ketchup as a vegetable, they could save on, say, peas and lima beans. There was outrage, of course, from the media and the public, but the truth is that the school food workers and nutritionists knew all too well that kids weren't eating those unappetizing mushy peas and plain lima beans anyway. This expensive debate over what constitutes a vegetable continued for years. During the Clinton presidency, it was suggested that salsa should count as a serving of vegetables; in 2004, under President George W. Bush, it was batter-coated french fries that earned the distinction as not just a vegetable, but also a *fresh* vegetable—and not just by Congress, but by a federal judge as well. And in 2011, Congress voted that 2 tablespoons of tomato paste on pizza was allowed to count as a vegetable in our children's school lunches.

Somehow, we are missing the bigger problem: No matter what we call it, and no matter how it's classified, these foods, and these food policies, are not helping our kids any more than a GM tomato engineered to reduce high cholesterol is a welcome addition to a food system that likely caused the high cholesterol in the first place.

There is a very big reason we don't eat more fresh vegetables in America, and it isn't because they aren't delicious. It's because fresh vegetables are an *orphaned* food.[9] From 2000 to 2008, vegetables grown in the US accounted for 14 percent of all cash crop revenue, but, as noted, less than 2 percent of cultivated acreage. Half of the vegetables grown in this country are grown for processing. As for tomatoes, three-quarters of them are consumed as processed fruit. Meanwhile, many other healthy vegetables are largely ignored by Big Ag. Without the interest of large food companies, fresh vegetables and fresh vegetable eaters have very few champions, which is a big part of the reason why we don't eat more of them. In other words, what we eat has been dictated in large part by companies deciding which foods have the most potential profit.

According to the USDA, 75 percent of the vegetable farms in this country are harvesting fewer than 15 acres of crops, and those small farms account for 90 percent of US vegetable production. From the standpoint of a nutritious food product, fresh vegetables have a lot going for them. But in terms of their value as an *agricultural* product in the current system, fresh vegetables—with the exception of the processed trio of corn, potatoes, and tomatoes—have a lot going *against* them. Vegetables are subject to spoilage and difficult to brand before they are processed, which means that nobody with any heft in the food space, especially not the large food manufacturers, are pushing fresh broccoli and spinach and eggplant on us. Vegetables (and fruits) are also classified as "specialty crops" by the USDA and are therefore not beneficiaries of commodity-style subsidies. As

---

9 "Orphaned" is a term often used to refer to diseases that affect only a small number of the population and are ignored by the pharmaceutical companies because they do not have enough profit potential. In the ag sector, it also means underutilized.

a result, today not a single US state meets the federal guidelines for fruit and vegetable consumption.

Most of us have eaten ketchup, lunchroom pizza sauce, and bland supermarket tomatoes. But how many of us, on a regular basis, eat locally or homegrown heirloom tomatoes fresh off the vine—maybe a Pruden's Purple, or an African Queen? And how many of our kids have eaten heirloom tomatoes? Better yet, how many of them have *grown them*? That locally grown heirloom tomato is very different in taste and nutrition from Heinz tomato ketchup or the supermarket tomato bred for long shelf life, and when we consider that, it becomes a whole lot easier to understand why kids (and many adults) *think* they don't like vegetables.

In many cases, they've never actually eaten a real vegetable, or had a chance to see them grow. I'm talking about vegetables that are a far cry from the mushy canned version served, and then scraped into the trash, in school cafeterias. Luckily, there are an increasing number of we the eaters from all walks of life who are working from the ground up to change that. And the reason this is so important has more to do with food education, health, and ultimately the preservation of the genetic diversity of plants than with nutritional superiority or sophisticated palates. Instead, it involves completely changing how we, along with the next generation, fundamentally *think* about food.

VETERANS OF THE VEGGIE WARS

Among this group working to move us in a healthy direction by including more and better vegetables in our diets are a number of renegade food revolutionaries. Two of them, Ron Finley and Stephen Ritz, are as outspoken and as unlikely healthy food advocates as you could imagine. Both of these men are introducing real vegetables to an equally unlikely group of kids—kids who live in communities where fresh tomatoes, or fresh vegetables of any type, are hard to come by. The closest many of these kids ever got to a real tomato, at least until they met Ron Finley or Stephen Ritz, was a tomato that made its way onto a school lunch tray or into a fast food restaurant in the form of pizza sauce or ketchup. Pizza sauce or ketchup that were made from tomatoes bred, grown, and processed for "ease of transport" and "long shelf life," then had their sugar content amped up with HFCS as they were converted into processed foods the USDA and Congress decided qualify as cost-saving ways to feed "vegetables" to American children.

Ron Finley grew up, and then raised his own sons, in South Central Los Angeles, where he made a career as a clothing designer to the stars. He received a standing ovation after his 2013 TED talk, in which he lamented the fact that he saw "wheelchairs lined up like used cars" for sale on the sidewalks and in the storefronts of his neighborhood, a typical low-income, urban American food desert with a high concentration of residents suffering from both poor nutritional health and escalating obesity. It's a place, says Finley, where the fast food restaurants and liquor stores seem to go hand in hand with declining health and rising crime. It is a neighborhood where, as he put it, "the drive-thru was more likely to kill you than the drive-by."

The difference between South Central LA and a lot of other poor communities is that it is located about a million nutritional miles, but only a 20-minute drive, from the culinary highbrow and weight-conscious city of Beverly Hills. Even with this proximity to wealth, Finley found he had to drive 45 minutes round-trip just to buy an affordable organic apple, let alone fill a shopping cart with healthy food. One day, while driving past his increasingly obese and sick neighbors who were living among abandoned lots where, by his account, "dialysis centers were popping up like Starbucks," he decided to do something about it.

Outside Finley's house in South Central is a strip of land running between the road and the sidewalk, which he estimates measures about 10 feet wide and 150 feet long. It is a strip of land that, as a homeowner, he is required by the city to maintain. In an act of utter defiance and desperation, he ripped out the grass and planted vegetables along the street. When his plants began to flourish, the city wrote him a citation, and told him to pull up the vegetables and replant the grass. Finley was incredulous, and pointed out to city administrators in charge of sidewalk and median strip maintenance that LA owns 26 square miles of vacant lots, which he said could sustain over 725 million tomato plants—and in case they hadn't noticed, obesity in his neighborhood was "five times higher" than in the surrounding, more affluent areas.

They were unimpressed, and the city of Los Angles issued Ron Finley a warrant for growing food in the sliver of dirt, crabgrass, and dandelions that separates the street from the sidewalk in a community where fast food restaurants spring from the concrete like invasive weeds. He circulated a petition on Change.org, got 900 signatures, and the city backed down. Ever since, Finley has been inciting what he calls "a gangster movement of gardeners" planting "food graffiti" in what is a food desert in one of the toughest and least well-fed neighborhoods in America. A self-made clothing designer now has people from his community growing and eating vegetables, which he gives away for free, in an effort to change this food desert into what he says someday could be a "food forest." And he's doing this not for profit, but rather so the people in his neighborhood can take a step toward reclaiming their health. In his TED talk, Finley argued that growing your own food is like printing money, and told the crowd that if they want to make a donation to his cause, or if they want to meet with him, they should show up on his street in South Central—and they better bring a shovel and be prepared to work.

Twenty-five hundred miles across the country from Ron Finley is Stephen Ritz, a sixth-grade special-education teacher living and working in the South Bronx—the poorest congressional district in the country. Stephen Ritz was teaching overaged, undercredited IEP[10] kids, many of whom were either in foster care or homeless and living below the poverty level, how to grow vegetables in their classroom (and we're not talking kindergarteners with bean seeds and paper cups).

Ritz then took his students outside the classroom, to plant fruits and veggies in vacant lots and median strips throughout the South Bronx. Next, he had his students grow food on specially designed vertical garden walls with LED lights inside the school, and then on the rooftops of buildings in this nutritionally orphaned community of New York City. His students were invited to plant an edible wall of food at NBC headquarters in Midtown Manhattan, and inside the John Hancock building in Boston. Next, they were planting food systems on the rooftops of beach houses in the land of Wall Street hedge fund managers in Southampton, New York. As Heinz breeds perfectly red tomatoes that can withstand traveling long distances in tractor-trailers, Stephen Ritz is growing tomatoes for "zero miles to plate" in an initiative he calls the Green Bronx Machine.

As of this writing, Ritz's students have grown 25,000 pounds of vegetables. In addition to feeding fellow students and teachers in their school and the senior citizens in their community, these "overaged, undercredited" kids were selling their produce at farmers' markets and earning—or, as Ron Finley described it, "printing"—money while building life skills, self-esteem, and physical health. These youth had higher attendance and graduation rates, and they were going to

---

10   Individual Education Program curriculum classification designates special-education students in public schools.

college because of one teacher's enthusiasm, the skills they developed, and the contacts they made while building edible walls and digging in the dirt. They were finding jobs in construction while still in high school, and they were finding themselves by growing food in the cracks and crevices, median strips, walls, and rooftops of the South Bronx.

Like Ron Finley, Stephen Ritz created an oasis of real, healthy, nutritious food in the desert of empty calories and processed fast food that has overrun our communities and schools, especially in economically depressed urban areas. In this same desert, these two men have planted hope in the form of microgreens, melons, heirloom tomatoes, and seed potatoes. Ron Finley summed it up best: "If kids grow kale, kids eat kale."

Half way around the world, in the shadow of Mount Kilimanjaro outside of Arusha, Tanzania, a school for former street children has a flourishing garden growing vegetables (along with growing fruit and coffee and raising animals) for themselves and a local tourist lodge. The school's agriculture lessons come daily after academic classes and the garden is supported by a central New York Slow Food group as part of the Slow Food Foundation's Thousand Gardens Project. Slow Food is an international organization committed to good, clean, and fair food and its Thousand Garden Project members from disparate corners of the world are seeing the connection between healthy local gardens and small farms growing vegetables as an essential part of the solution to both hunger and obesity. Even WFP, the world's largest food aid agency, is funding and supporting school garden projects to help students access local vegetables. In the ultimate example of Ron Finley's "Guerilla Gardening," I first saw in Kibera, the large slum in Nairobi, Kenya, the brilliant use of food aid grain sacks filled with soil and repurposed as urban vegetable planters.

From New York City and Los Angeles to Arusha and Nairobi, urban vegetable gardens are reconnecting eaters to healthy food, but urban gardens are only a start of the shifts underway to grow more of what we need to be eating.

WHAT'S RIGHT WITH KENTUCKY?

Although agriculture and rural-life champion Wendell Berry has been a Kentucky man his whole life, the state has not exactly been a model for healthy agricultural systems (unless you want to count the financial success of cancer-causing tobacco). Louisville is home to Yum! Brands (which owns KFC, Taco

Bell,[11] and Pizza Hut), as well as, perhaps fittingly, the health-care giant Humana.

While I was working at the World Food Program, Yum! Brands started a partnership with the organization, and recruited celebrity spokesperson Christina Aguilera to encourage people to add a few dollars (or cents) to their Taco Bell bills, which would be donated to WFP for school food programs. Around the same time, the US hunger nonprofit Feeding America launched an anti-hunger campaign on Snickers bars. Together, these marketing campaigns represent an inescapable irony—that we are pushing people who eat at unhealthy fast food restaurants and who buy candy to donate money to children suffering from one of the world's great injustices—childhood malnutrition and hunger. This underscores the point that none of us are fed *well;* not the Taco Bell patrons and candy buyers who are increasingly likely to be overweight, and not the hungry around the world.

★ ★

Admittedly, with its history, Louisville is an unlikely place to emerge as a foodie haven. But in 2000, when the USDA mandated a 45 percent cut in the amount of tobacco Kentucky farmers are allowed to grow—and spurred on by changing habits, greater education about health outcomes, and further government regulation of cigarettes (are you listening, Big Ag?)—many farmers had to change what they were growing or lose their farms. Instead of following Earl Butz's Big Government maxim of "get big or get out," they now had to rediscover their inner entrepreneur and "innovate or die." Today some Louisville tobacco farmers have become organic meat and vegetable producers. From the current mayor[12] down to the newest crop of young farmers, there is a community-based sense of purpose behind rebuilding the local food economy in Kentucky, even as the state ranks among the worst 10 for obesity, diabetes, and heart disease.

Today vegetable acreage is growing at a rate of 10 percent a year, with sweet corn, pumpkins, tomatoes, and green peppers topping the list of food crops. A young husband and wife team founded the regional company Green Bean Delivery, which provides Kentucky, Indiana, Ohio, and Missouri with

---

11 Taco Bell, to its credit, announced in July 2013 that it would be phasing out kids' meals with toys.
12 Mayor Greg Fischer oversees a "Healthy Hometown Healthy Eating Committee."

year-round organic and local food delivery. This initiative, along with similar companies like Farmigo, Good Eggs, and Veritable Vegetable in San Francisco, are expanding around the country to offer people a whole new model for how to buy good food away from the end caps and middle-aisle monocultures of the supermarket. And increasingly, even in those big supermarkets, grocers around the country are slapping "locally grown" stickers on produce and dairy products; in Kentucky you see "Kentucky Proud" stickers and displays, which help direct consumers toward local food options. A whole new area of downtown Louisville, NuLu, is sprouting delicious farm-to-table restaurants that are helping to keep young people, and their innovative energy, in the city.

★ ★

There are literally thousands of stories like this, and some of the most inspiring things I witness as I travel the world are these ground-up efforts by ordinary people as we the eaters form a more perfect union in the most unlikely places and in the most unlikely ways. These are not food executives or plant scientists, but rather ordinary people who are declaring independence from the industrialized food systems that have served us one too many poor-quality processed meals. They're doing it in the bare patches of earth between the roadway and the sidewalks in South Central LA, on the rooftops and in the abandoned lots of the South Bronx, in the rich soil of the Andes, and in the farm fields of Kentucky and Amagansett, New York. Ron Finley says "gardening is my graffiti," and Steve Ritz hopes to grow "green walls" as well as a new crop of good, healthy jobs for today's hungry youth; the group of women in the Peruvian Andes saving seed potatoes call it a way of life. It's a fledgling grassroots revolution by a subgroup of we the eaters who are taking back their health, their children's health, their communities, and their cultural dignity—as well as their inalienable right to eat real food, and lots of diverse vegetables pulled directly from the soil. Food grown with taste, nutrition, and quality in mind, and left unprocessed. So when we read about the risks of mono-cropping and the loss of crop diversity, and we contemplate the long-term implications of the privatization of seeds and the consolidation of growing and processing food, we should consider that we have left our health, our children's health, and the health of our planet in the hands of those who will profit most from poor food decisions—like fast food or processed fries with ketchup.

EAT THE GOOD NEWS

Compared to the 1970s, in 2000, overall vegetable consumption in the US was actually up. Although a big percentage of the rise in vegetable consumption is processed potatoes (frozen french fries), which rose more than 60 percent over this time span, consumption of fresh vegetables increased as well. We went from eating 147.9 pounds per person in the 1970s to 201.7 in 2000. It's a small step, but it's a hopeful one.

So what can we the eaters do to be part of the changing landscape of vegetables? It's simple, really. Eat more green and yellow and red and orange and purple locally grown vegetables. And eat *better* and *fewer* fries. And make them at *home*. From orange, blue, red, and brown potatoes. With extra virgin olive oil, pastured organic butter, or fair trade coconut oil, not trans fats and sugar. Serve them not quite so often, and alongside a whole lot of green and leafy foods. And maybe try to grow some of your own.

Despite what some try to say, kale, broccoli, and heirloom tomatoes are not actually trendy or reserved for the "haves" and the hipsters. Growing up, my mom learned from her mom and her grandmother that a daily fresh salad, even a simple one of lettuce, celery, and carrots, was essential for good health. My grandmother, being a child of the Great Depression, knew that to ensure nutrition in the down times, growing a small vegetable garden would give her family cheap access to fresh foods. So my mom always planted a garden as a way to save money on fresh vegetables all summer and then to have frozen containers of homemade pesto, tomato sauce, and soup for the winter. Planting greens in a window pot or a small tomato plant on your patio is actually less hipster and more historical—homegrown food was always a way to save money on food, and as a side benefit, you can't grow a french fry or a ketchup packet on a tree.

Homegrown vegetables have historically been part of the solution for farmers, too. Many industrial farmers still grow a garden, but often this is not embedded in the way we think about agricultural development. Sadly, vegetables are not high enough on the global agricultural aid radar at all. For the hungry world to share in this long-term nutritional rebalancing and better health, local vegetable production, and not just corn yields or mono-cropped wheat, will have to be part of the solution. Along with home gardens, creating local and regional food markets and farmers' markets for a variety of vegetables will help create healthy food systems everywhere. From Bogotá, Colombia, to Boise, Idaho, to Botswana, farmers' markets and small-farm vegetable production are a big part of the solution to hunger *and* obesity. And maybe someday, a new form of Big Ag will emerge, one unlike the current conglomerates, instead a cooperative effort of we the eaters wielding our power to change food from the ground up, using technology-based solutions such as smartphone-app-based food distributors instead of bioengineering. A system that will respond to the demands of we the eaters, with a diverse supply of much better food.

★ 6 ★

The Sugar We Drink

How Sweet It Isn't

IF YOU'RE NOT DRINKING a beer with that burger of yours, you'll likely be drinking something sweet. A typical backyard barbecue will often include an ice-filled cooler brimming with cans or bottles of soda, or a couple of those ubiquitous family-size 2-liter plastic bottles sitting right on the picnic table. Not so long ago, drinking soda was reserved for special occasions, and those drinks at that barbecue represented a real treat. Even in my house when I was growing up in the 1980s, when my dad was a chemical engineer working for PepsiCo and we could get Pepsi *for free,* soda was served only on special occasions. And my family was not unique. Over the past 30 years that has changed. Many of us went from drinking a small soda occasionally to drinking much larger servings of sweetened beverages on a regular basis, often every day. Even kids.

The amount of total *added* sugar (sugar not found naturally in fruit, vegetables, or dairy products) that we consume in our diets has risen from 6.3 pounds per person per year in 1822 *to more than 100 pounds per person today,* with an 18.2 percent rise between 1980 and 2005. As easy as it would be to blame this increase on desserts, today the USDA reports that only 12.9 percent of the added sugar calories in our diets come from grain-based desserts like cookies, cakes, doughnuts, and pastries. And those sugar-based cereals that get so much heat? As bad as they are—and they are bad (some sweetened cereals are more than 50 percent sugar)—only 3.8 percent of those added sugar calories come from ready-to-eat cereals. Which means that the largest source of added sugar lies somewhere else.

We're drinking it.

For both adults and children, the largest source of added sugar in our diets is sweetened beverages, especially soda. In fact, almost half of the added sugar we now consume comes from sweetened soda and energy, sports, and fruit drinks. The American Heart Association recommends that women consume no more than 6 added teaspoons of sugar per day, and men no more than 9 teaspoons; the USDA suggests an 8-teaspoon max for someone who eats 2,000 calories a day. Yet a single 12-ounce can of soda contains approximately 10 teaspoons of sugar, and a large soda typical of a fast food restaurant has about twice that amount, roughly 17 to 20 teaspoons of sugar.

> Wherever you look, the message is clear:
> We now drink way too much sugar.

This dramatic rise in sugary drink consumption occurred largely for two reasons, one financial and the other biological. The technology to mass-produce high-fructose corn syrup (HFCS) cheaply from government-subsidized corn provided the supply of cheap sugar, and, as we are about to see, our innate preference for sweet foods and the addictive qualities of sugar fueled the seemingly insatiable demand. Cheap supply and high demand meant low-cost soda for consumers, and high profit for manufacturers. As we are now finding, over the past 30 years this increase in soda consumption didn't just coincide with an epidemic of global obesity, type 2 diabetes, heart disease, and a whole slew of other health problems—it *caused* it.

The Harvard School of Public Health reports that in the US since the 1970s, caloric intake from sugary drinks more than doubled. They note, too, that one sweet drink per day raises the risk of death from a heart attack by 20 percent, and one to two per day increases the risk of type 2 diabetes by 26 percent. From 1989 to 2008, caloric intake from sugary drinks for kids ages 6 to 11 rose 60 percent, and 91 percent of this age group now consume sweet drinks (up from 79 percent). Sugary drinks are now also the largest single source of calories for teens, representing an average of 226 calories per day. Wherever you look, the data are overwhelming.

★ ★

Soda consumption, and its attendant diseases, didn't just explode here in America. Soda has become the most widely available drink in the world. In fact, soda is available in many regions that don't have basic necessities like clean water, electricity, or roads. Today, through a massive distribution machine and unprecedented brand power facilitated by high consumer demand and low cost, Coca-Cola is sold in 200 countries—more than are represented at the UN, or that signed the Millennium Development Goals to end extreme poverty. Beverage companies spend more than $3 billion per year marketing sweet drinks in the US, with about half a billion directed at children ages 2 to 17. And in Africa, where Coke has the dominant share of the sweetened beverage market, the company has established distribution networks called manual distribution centers (MDCs), which use bikes, pushcarts, and boats to deliver soda to remote, poverty-stricken areas unreachable by other means. It is truly stunning to observe the lengths to which they will go to sell every one of us a Coke.

Sadly, it's not just American kids who are developing a taste for supersweet liquid sugar. On my first trip to Rwanda, to visit the World Food Program School Feeding sites supported by the FEED 100 bags (which were being sold at Whole Foods Market stores across the US), I visited a number of elementary schools where kids were eating corn–soy-blend porridge, sometimes flavored with locally grown vegetables. As non-Rwandan visitors and honored guests, we were offered a highly valued treat—bottles of Coke or Sprite. I don't drink soda, but it would have been rude for me to turn down the gift. I couldn't help but notice when I sat with some of the students eating their lunches that they were looking longingly at my green soda bottle, as I was looking longingly at their local vegetables.

I felt the deep irony that even as I was working to improve the nutrition of these children, I came from the country that made young people around the world think soda was a valuable and "cool" offering, when in fact it leads them down a path to obesity and disease. It seemed sadly foreboding to have been gifted a bottle of soda by young, eager Rwandan students who now, through school meals, have so much promise for success and health—promise that may very well be ruined someday by a soda habit.

LIQUID SUGAR

In the broadest sense, sugar in our diets comes in two forms. There's the relatively small amount of sugar that occurs naturally in the foods we eat, like the lactose in milk, the fructose in fruits and vegetables, and the glucose we metabo-lize from carbohydrates. The second source is the now relatively large amounts of added sugars, which primarily includes sucrose (table sugar) from sugarcane or sugar beets and HFCS from corn—both disaccharides composed of fructose and glucose.

Since sugars found naturally in whole foods like milk and fruit come "pack-aged" with other nutrients like protein, fiber, and calcium, these sugars are more healthful than added sugars, which now represent anywhere from 16 to 25 per-cent of the total calories consumed by Americans. Since the added sugars in many foods and drinks like soda aren't bundled with any nutrients, they become problematic when we eat too much of them, which is largely a factor of all the processed foods we consume. Take, for example, a 20-ounce Coke.

> The 17 teaspoons of added sugar in a 20-ounce Coke is the same amount of sugar found in roughly 3 pounds of carrots, 7½ oranges, 230 stalks of asparagus, or 531 cups of spinach—with none of the nutrition those whole foods offer.

★ ★

Up through the 1970s, sugarcane was the primary commercially available sweet-ener used by manufacturers to sweeten foods and beverages. Although the US produces a lot of sugar domestically, we were, and still are, one of the world's largest importers of sugar as well. At the time, the US sugar growers lobby pushed the government to approve a sugar subsidy, raise import tariffs on imported cane and beet sugar, and establish quotas for imported sugar to protect themselves from cheap imports. These changes, all of which occurred around 1980 (like so many other wrong turns in our food system), made cane and beet sugar much more expensive. Since scientists could now effectively manufacture HFCS in large, industrial quantities from corn, a subsidized crop we were grow-ing in abundance, these factors colluded to dramatically change the US sugar market. Using cheap HFCS to sweeten foods became a financial advantage for both food manufacturers and consumers, and it was about to dominate the US sweetener market.

In the early 1980s, both Coke and Pepsi switched from sweetening soda with sucrose (refined from sugarcane or sugar beets), which is 50 percent glucose and 50 percent fructose, to using the new and cheaper HFCS 55, which is 45 percent glucose and 55 percent fructose. My dad was responsible for managing the process of switching the sweetener from sucrose to HFCS in his positions at PepsiCo, as production manager and plant manager from 1980 to 1984, and he can tell us firsthand how HFCS worked to make soda cheap, why it stayed that way—and that neither he nor his engineering and production floor colleagues likely had any idea what the repercussions would be: "We thought we were doing a great thing for the customer, and of course for the business, by using this new, more locally available and cheaper sweetener," he says. "I was proud to be working for one of the most admired companies, and I could have never imagined the unintended consequences of our work in the production plant on public health."

THE 99-CENT PRICE POINT

At the time, there was excitement. The main benchmark of success for the engineers at PepsiCo was that this switch from sucrose to HFCS would keep the retail cost of a 2-liter bottle at 99 cents. Soda is price sensitive, which means that as the price goes up, consumers buy less, and anyone in marketing knows that the penny jump from $0.99 to $1.00 is a big one for consumers.[1] So this shift from expensive sucrose to less expensive HFCS was perceived as good for Pepsi, and also good for consumers. And it was a strategy that worked. Soda sales surged; the soda companies made more money, and consumers got what they wanted too. Cheap soda. *Lots of it.*

Adjusted for inflation, soda is 33 percent cheaper today than it was in 1978. If you go back even further, using the US Bureau of Labor Statistics Consumer Price Index inflation calculator, a 6-ounce Coke that cost a nickel in 1934 would cost 87 cents in today's dollars. That means that the large, 32-ounce Coke at McDonald's *should* run you $4.64. But it's priced nowhere close to that. At McDonald's a large soda is about $1.79; at a supermarket, it's a whole lot less than that. Even in much of Africa today, a Coke costs the equivalent of 20 to 30 cents, which is about the price of a local newspaper. In fact, the National Institutes of Health refers to soda in Africa as an "affordable luxury."

---

1   A study by the USDA in July 2010 highlights this price sensitivity, estimating that a soda tax of 20 percent would reduce consumption of soda and result in a weight loss of 3.8 pounds for adults and 4.5 pounds per child per year.

★ ★

Based on the price of soda, you might be inclined to think that all food costs less today than it used to. But as the price of soda declined in the US, naturally sweet, fresh fruit, instead of getting cheaper, got more expensive.

> In fact, fresh fruit was 46 percent *more expensive* in 2008
> (adjusted for inflation) than it was even in 1978.

Fresh vegetables became 31 percent more expensive in the same time frame. While healthy foods *inflated* in price, unhealthy foods like soda *deflated,* largely due to the price supports for corn and the resultant switch to HFCS. As a population, we began to gradually shift our perceptions of what constituted good value in food. And good value was now a big, cheap, sugary drink.

Although my dad feels guilty about it now after seeing the global health outcome and knowing how detrimental HFCS turned out to be (remember the 2010 Princeton study that found higher obesity rates in rats eating HFCS than in rats eating sucrose?), at the time no one thought the switch from expensive cane and beet sugar to cheap HFCS would impact our consumption patterns, or our health, so dramatically. There was no thought that the constitution of HFCS itself might pose a health problem, or that if we made sweet foods and beverages like soda cheaper, we might eat and drink so much of them that we would create serious global health epidemics. Quite fairly, though, my dad looks back at his time as a young chemical engineer at a large and widely respected brand with pride. He helped make the bottle lighter, worked to engineer the cans to use less aluminum, and managed the removal of the black cups on the bottoms of 2-liter bottles in order to make them more recyclable. I'm quite sure that many good people who worked in jobs like his didn't realize the long-term consequences of what they were doing at the time, which was to improve the bottom line, and provide consumers with what they wanted—inexpensive sweet food.

Many businesspeople like my dad, who is now an organic community-supported agriculture (CSA) member and a soda abstainer, have learned the same lessons we have. Take Mike Roberts, for example, a former global president and COO for McDonald's. In 2011 he started Lyfe Kitchen, a restaurant franchise and product line of healthy, high-quality, locally sourced, organic food. It's promising and hopeful to see shifts like these from industry insiders. But back in the 1980s, unfortunately for we the eaters, the chemical engineers, marketers, and corporate executives working for the soda and fast food companies were, frankly, *too good* at their jobs. They were able to make food and drinks that weren't good for us irresistibly tasty and irresistibly cheap. And none of us—not the industry leaders, and not the eaters—knew how bad the outcome would be.

SWEET: FROM SCARCE TO SUPERFLUOUS

In nature, raw sugar and naturally sweet foods like fruit are hard to find. Until the technology to extract sugar from corn was mastered, sugar was also relatively difficult and expensive to refine. But as the price dropped for sugar products, it became financially feasible for us to eat more of these sweet foods, and it became more viable for food manufacturers to profit by selling them. According to the National Health and Nutrition Examination Survey data on food intake, between 1999 and 2004 the average American consumed 22.5 teaspoons of added sugar each day, with roughly half of that attributed to sodas and fruit drinks. By 2005 the USDA would report an even higher number: We were eating, on average, *30 teaspoons of added sugar per day,* compared to their recommended 8 teaspoons. There is some debate over the way these figures are calculated, as statisticians try to account for waste (for instance, a percentage of what is produced is lost to industry waste, and how much of the soda you buy do you not finish drinking?), but use any figure or data source you want, and there is no question that many of us are consuming a lot more added sugar than we used to—about 100 pounds of it a year.

★ ★

While the 10 teaspoons of sugar in a 12-ounce drink would be bad enough, manufacturers are now selling drinks in 20-ounce bottles, and larger. Even though they label those bottles as two and a half servings, this is generally disregarded, and we are drinking these "big gulps" as if they are single servings. So if you think you couldn't possibly eat or drink 30 teaspoons of sugar a day, consider this: One large 20-ounce soda gets you well over halfway there. (One teaspoon of sugar equals four grams, the measurement soda companies use, though the metric is meaningless to most Americans.)

When it comes to sugary drinks, the contents of the bottle are insanely cheap. Restaurants and manufacturers can offer these larger drinks as "value for the dollar" to the consumer, but it doesn't cost them very much more than a small serving would. Pepsi figured that out way back in 1934, when it introduced a 12-ounce bottle of soda for the same price as Coke's 6-ounce bottle (5 cents). In 1955 Coke introduced what it called "king size" drinks, which were 10- and 12-ounce single-serving bottles, to compete with Pepsi's 12 ounces. At McDonald's, Coke started out in 7-ounce servings; a large serving became 16 ounces around 1960, 21 ounces by 1974, and in the 1980s, the whopping 30 to 32 ounces we drink today.

> The standard serving size of soda used to be 6 ounces. That is half of what is considered a "child's size" at McDonald's today.

Pick any large drink you want on the McDonald's menu, or anywhere else for that matter. A large Dr Pepper has 17.5 teaspoons of sugar; a large Hi-C has 21 teaspoons of sugar. As the studies have indicated, just one soda a day is enormously problematic for our health. Even the "child size" Hi-C Orange Lavaburst (12 ounces) has 7.75 teaspoons of sugar, and since it has no fruit juice, that is straight sugar in the form of HFCS. Yet 50 percent of all Americans drink a sweetened beverage every single day. So do half the children in Australia. Mexicans drink two Cokes a day, not counting other brands of soda or sugary drinks. One-quarter of American teens drink a soda a day, and for the 12- to 19-year-old boys who do drink soda, the average is two 12-ounce servings daily. When we drink our calories, not only do we not feel full, but we're actually prone to eat more. Once we understand that, it's easy to see why fast food restaurants are so willing to supersize our drinks for next to nothing.

DRINK-ABETES
We simply weren't designed to handle the amount and the type of sugar now available to us in the food environment.

High sugar consumption has been implicated in weight gain, obesity, cardiovascular disease, metabolic syndrome,[2] diabetes, high triglycerides, dementia, macular degeneration, stroke, cancer—and, of course, tooth decay. There are studies blaming sugar for behavior problems, poor school performance, and violence. There are studies that demonstrate when we drink our calories, we get a jolt of insulin, or "sugar rush," and we tend to eat more.

---

2   A group of health issues—high blood pressure, obesity, high cholesterol, and insulin resistance —that can lead to diabetes and coronary artery disease.

Diabetes might as well be renamed drink-abetes.

As we were drinking all this sugar, type 2 diabetes rates around the world started to soar. According to the International Diabetes Federation, 382 million people in the world today have diabetes, and type 2 or "adult onset" diabetes accounts for 90 percent of the cases. By 2030 it is estimated that number will rise to 592 million people with more and more of them in the developing world. (The epidemic spread is even scarier when the WHO estimates there were around 30 million people with the disease in 1985.) In the US alone, health-care costs related to diabetes have reached $245 billion, or 1 in 5 of all health-care dollars.

In February 2013, the first large-scale study directly correlating sugar consumption with diabetes was published by the National Institutes of Health (NIH). The researchers used large population studies to demonstrate that the higher the sugar availability is in a region, the higher the level of diabetes. For every increase of 150 calories of sugar, the prevalence of diabetes rose 1.1 percent, even though they were controlling for other food consumed, obesity level, physical activity, age, economic status, and income. For every additional 150 *non-sugar* calories available to eaters, the prevalence of diabetes increased by only 0.1 percent, or 10 times less. This clearly illustrates that when calculating the risk factor for diabetes, a calorie is not just a calorie; eating more *unsweetened* food does not cause diabetes, but eating more sugar does. (The researchers were quick to point out that a 12-ounce can of soda contains about 150 calories of sugar.)

And if adults can't handle all the added sugar
from drinks, neither can kids.

Children drank three times more milk in the 1970s than they did soda; between 2003 and 2006, soda and milk consumption among kids was dead even, a fifty-fifty split. Today beverages are responsible for 47 percent of the added sugar consumed by children. Ironically, we pulled soda out of schools (which is good), but in its place we serve sugar-added, low-fat flavored milk instead. Even parents who would never dream of giving a child a soda will routinely allow chocolate milk and sports drinks like Gatorade, which are designed for adults who are elite athletes, not 50-pound second graders kicking a soccer ball after school. That 20-ounce Orange or Cool Blue Gatorade has 34 grams of sugar. That's 8½ teaspoons.

★ ★

Here is where it gets even scarier. All infant formulas contain some sugar to mirror the natural sugars in human milk, but some contain corn sugar and HFCS. New data show that compared with breast-fed babies, formula-fed babies have two and a half times the risk of being obese by age 2. Researchers believe this could be owed in part to the differences in the milk itself, but also may be due to the fact that it is easier for formula-fed babies to overeat. Even worse, we may be unwittingly programming infants to overeat even *before* they are born. A study done by Beverly Mühlhäusler, a senior research fellow at the University of Adelaide's FOODplus Research Center, in Australia, fed a large amount of sugar and fat to pregnant rats and found that their offspring required higher levels of sugar and fat to get the same "feel-good" opiate and dopamine brain response triggered by eating junk food than offspring of rats eating a healthy (low-sugar, low-fat) diet. Mühlhäusler speculated that expectant mothers who drink sugar-sweetened beverages (or other high-added-sugar foods) will have babies that tend to crave higher amounts of sugar to satisfy a sweet tooth developed in utero, because opioids produced by the mother after eating sweets pass through the placenta and create a high set point for the unborn child. She concluded:

> *"The take-home message for women is that eating large amounts*
> *of junk food during pregnancy and while breastfeeding will have*
> *long-term consequences for their child's preference for these foods,*
> *which will ultimately have negative effects on their health."*

Although many pregnant women hear messages about avoiding sushi or even coffee, snack junk foods and soda should arguably be added to the list. And pregnant women may be unaware that many foods and drinks that are considered healthy, such as juice, flavored waters, whole wheat bread, yogurt, peanut butter, even "healthy" breakfast cereals and canned soup, now have added sugars that may be predisposing their babies to crave sweets and potentially become overweight, even as infants. Despite a significant risk in childhood obesity in the past 30 years, a 2014 study in the *Journal of the American Medical Association* indicated a decline in obesity among 2- to 5-year olds in the past decade. Researchers noted this was likely due both to increased breastfeeding and decreased sugar-sweetened drink consumption. Parents can hear public health messages and change behavior—good news for future generations of eaters.

WHY WE KEEP TAPPING THE SODA FOUNTAIN

As humans, we are hard-wired to prefer the few sweet foods existing in nature, like fruits and honey, because they are rich in calories and full of nutrients, fiber, and vitamins. These natural sweets used to be only regionally available and seasonal, and therefore very scarce.

The brain science behind sugar addiction has received a lot of attention lately, particularly the research of Robert Lustig, a neuroendocrinologist and professor of pediatrics in the Division of Endocrinology at the University of California at San Francisco. Lustig is also the director of the Weight Assessment for Teen and Child Health Program at UCSF, for which he conducted groundbreaking work with children whose hypothalamus had been damaged either by brain tumors or by the surgery, radiation, or chemotherapy needed to treat them. A large number of the patients who survived the treatment became massively obese, and Lustig developed a theory as to why that was happening. He believes the damaged hypothalamus interfered with the hormone leptin, which regulates appetite. This created what amounted to a "starvation response" manifested by increased activity of the vagus nerve, which in turn increased insulin production. When he suppressed that insulin production, the patients lost weight.

Lustig then began evaluating the role of fructose as a mediator of both the hormone leptin and the production of insulin. He now argues that glucose that comes from the metabolization of carbohydrates is good, and that fructose and sucrose (sucrose is half fructose) are "poison." Lustig concluded that metabolic syndrome and its related diseases are solely a result of fructose consumption and largely due to increases in the consumption of HFCS in sweetened drinks. Between 1970 and 1990, American consumption of HFCS grew by more than 1000 percent, which is the biggest change of any of our intake of any food or food group. A 2008 study of daily intake revealed that a full 10 percent of all American calories came from fructose. Unlike the researchers in that 2010 Princeton study, he makes no distinction between sucrose and HFCS, but he does make a *giant* distinction between the fructose in fruit and the fructose we use as an added sugar. The fructose in fruit comes packaged with fiber, and the fructose in soda does not. That fiber is the "antidote" to what Lustig says we are suffering from: "fructose poisoning." As evidence, Lustig used a multivariate regression analysis (a mathematical tool to isolate cause from random correlations) and concluded what many might find shocking:

Removal of all sugary drinks would end the obesity epidemic.

According to well-accepted evidence, when we eat sugar, we consume too many calories because sugar (both sucrose and HFCS) blocks the signal in our brains that tells us we have eaten enough. If you want some anecdotal proof of this, just ask yourself if you have ever overeaten broccoli, or had so many string beans that you felt sick. The answer probably is no. When we eat healthy food, we tend to eat enough and stop. Cookies, ice cream, soda, and other sugary processed foods (including infant formula) create a totally different story, one that has become part of the modern dietary lexicon: *Sugar and sweets are addictive.*

ALL SUGAR MAY NOT BE CREATED EQUAL

Sugar is one of three simple carbohydrates: glucose, fructose, or sucrose. Sucrose—what we think of as table sugar and what comes from sugar cane or sugar beets—is a disaccharide made up of both fructose and glucose. Sucrose and fructose are both found in fruits and veggies, whereas glucose is made by the body. Known as "blood sugar," it is the energy source that our body makes when we metabolize carbohydrates. When we drink a sugary drink (made with either sugar or HFCS), enzymes in our bodies separate the fructose and glucose, but the difference in how our bodies handle these two monosaccharides is where it gets biologically interesting.

In a controlled study conducted by the University of California at Davis in 2012, researchers examined overweight or obese adults after the subjects consumed 25 percent of their total calorie intake from either a fructose-sweetened drink or a glucose-sweetened drink for 10 weeks. The group drinking the fructose-sweetened beverage, but not the group drinking the same quantity of glucose-sweetened beverages, had significantly increased indicators for metabolic syndrome—the collection of health issues that includes weight gain, hypertension, elevated triglycerides, and increased BMI, fasting plasma glucose, and LDL cholesterol, which together are known to lead to type 2 diabetes, cardiovascular disease, and even death.

Numerous studies comparing glucose and fructose indicate key differences between how our brains perceive these two sugars and how these sugars are metabolized by our liver. Glucose increases satiety (that feeling of being full), but fructose does not and, in fact, fructose has been found to raise the level of ghrelin, a hormone that increases appetite. Glucose, on the other hand, raises insulin, suppresses ghrelin, and stimulates leptin, a trio of hormones that work together to let us know that we have eaten enough. Fructose raises neither insulin or leptin. Further, there is compelling evidence that fructose can't be handled by the liver in the same efficient way that glucose can, so fat builds up at a greater rate.

There is also evidence that a diet high in fructose from any source during childhood leads to a higher level of abdominal fat, and that fructose inherently changes the maturing fat cells in children, making them less receptive to insulin. Fructose comes from all of the major sources of added sugar we consume: cane, beet, and corn. It also comes from fruit and fruit juice. The difference is that the fructose from whole fruit is hard to consume in large quantities because it also provides much-needed fiber and vitamins; the fructose in added forms, particularly soda, does not.

We know from studies like those above that too much sugar in the now ubiquitous fructose form is not doing our health any favors. A debate remains as to whether there is a difference between the sucrose we used to eat so much of and the HFCS we now eat even more of. Remember that chemically they are almost the same: Sucrose is roughly 50 percent glucose and 50 percent fructose, and HFCS-55 is 45 percent glucose and 55 percent fructose. But one of the key differences between HFCS and sucrose is HFCS's versatility and ubiquity.

In the past 30 years, HFCS helped create a constant stream of added sugar in our daily diets, turning up in so many of our processed foods and drinks because it has a lot of qualities that make it superior for processed food manufacturers even beyond price and taste. HFCS has a lower freezing point than sugar from cane or beets. It has better browning capability in baked goods. It offers an improved "chewy" texture for products like cookies, improved shelf life, diminished microbial growth, and better transportability (products made with HFCS are less sensitive to the temperature fluctuations of shipping). The fact that HFCS comes in a liquid form also makes it very easy to use in processing.

And, of course, since HFCS is made from corn—our favorite overproduced, highly subsidized grass—manufacturers can keep pumping foods with sweeter flavors and more shelf stability with help from our tax dollars.

FREE-MARKET LOVERS FOR SODA TAXES

In recent years, former New York City Mayor Michael Bloomberg and leaders in 24 other states proposed taxes on soda to help fund health care and healthier school lunches for kids and tried to implement size restrictions on sugary drinks in an effort to stem the obesity epidemic. However, the public, fueled by heavily financed marketing campaigns from the soda makers, expressed outrage at a "nanny state" levying yet another tax on consumers. Others decried such legislation as stripping them of free choice. Neither group, however, recognized these large drinks for what they really represent: corporate manipulation to convince consumers that we are getting value and "choice," when we're really just generating profit for them as we get addicted to sugar and get sick.

As this debate was raging, the beverage industry campaigns mocked Bloomberg's proposed drink-size limits, even though his plan might actually have helped we the eaters make real choices about what we can "afford" to drink. Government interventions like corn subsidies that have made soda artificially cheap and allowed manufacturers to lure consumers with low prices have led to the false perception that we can "afford" those larger drinks, from both a financial and health perspective. But if sugar-sweetened beverage taxes and size limits were passed, we would actually move closer to a drink size and cost that makes economic sense, and it might push us to rethink the real "value" of a supersized Slurpee.

There is another ongoing debate over whether the 47 million food-insecure Americans who receive federal Supplemental Nutrition Assistance Program (SNAP) benefits, or food stamps, should be able to buy soda and other junk food with these funds. Some other unhealthy products, like cigarettes and alcohol, are prohibited under SNAP benefits, but since soda is GRAS[3] and not categorically considered unhealthy, it doesn't fall under the same restrictions. And changing this will likely be an uphill battle. The USDA's position is that "soft drinks, candy, cookies, snack crackers, and ice cream are food items and are therefore eligible items." And people do buy them. According to a 2012 study conducted by Yale's Rudd Center for Food Policy and Obesity and published in the *American Journal of Preventive Medicine*, the federal government is spending a whopping $1.7 billion to $2.1 billion on just the soda purchases made by those using food stamps. That may be because low-income people, just like the rest of us, have a sweet tooth; or perhaps it is because buying soda when you have limited funds makes rational economic sense, since soda is insanely cheap for the amount of calories you are getting. Either way, this issue shines a critical light on pricing, nutrition, and falsely perceived "value" in the food space.

The Center for Science in the Public Interest (CSPI), a consumer advocacy group, is encouraging the FDA to reassess its classification of soda's current formulations as GRAS. With so many chronic diseases connected to sugar and soda intake, and with promises by the FDA to reconsider soda's status when new

---

3   "Generally regarded as safe" by the FDA.

health information is revealed, this could be an interesting opportunity for public health advocates to push for real change regarding the government's judgment of what are basically non-nutritious forms of liquid sugar that have become a significant part of our diets and a major contributor to our health problems. In response to CSPI's push, the American Beverage Association defended the industry by stating that, on average, people get "only" 7 percent of their total daily calories from soda.

A BRIGHT HOPE IN BEVERAGES?

The good news is that, according to the USDA, soda intake has been declining in recent years. Regular soft drinks available for consumption[4] rose consistently in the US to reach 39 gallons per capita in 1999, and then began to decline. Since 2003, likely thanks to a general focus on health, a growing awareness of the role of soda in weight gain, better public health campaigns, and rising concern over HFCS, soda consumption has fallen by around 40 percent.[5] (The steepest decline in soft drink revenue occurred between 2005 and 2009.) In the first few months of 2014, Coke shares fell by 7 percent. And research has shown that the average Coke drinker is 56—that's a problem for the future.

However, we're not out of the woods yet. In the past decade, as soda sales declined, sales of sports and energy drinks rose by 100 percent, and coffee drinks were up 50 percent, all of which typically are highly sweetened. As store sales of soda declined, the *Wall Street Journal* in early 2013 asked if this was "the end of the soft-drink era." But we should brace ourselves, because the soda companies and manufacturers of HFCS are not going to take these declines lying down.

> The new dark cloud is that we are switching to
> hyper-sweet teas and sugar water as we turn good drinks bad.

The tale of sugary drinks gets even bleaker when we consider that as we became increasingly aware of our soda consumption problem and started

---

4   "Available for consumption" is a measure of food production that does not account for industrial or consumer waste. It is a number lager than what we actually eat, but is an easy number to track.

5   Talk about mixed signals: As soda companies ran ad campaigns to put a damper on sugar intake, Pepsi signed a $50 million deal with Beyoncé and Diet Coke hired Marc Jacobs as its "creative director" and Taylor Swift as spokeswoman—both aggressive moves to attract teens and young adults.

drinking less of it, manufacturers introduced new product lines that are nothing more than sugar water fortified with vitamins and micronutrients to enable them to make lofty health claims to woo us back into the fold. By implying healthful benefits, these claims confuse consumers, who think they're getting healthier by moving away from soda and toward beverages like sports and energy drinks, teas, and "enhanced" vitamin waters, but often are not.

★ ★

The soda companies like Coca-Cola, Dr Pepper Snapple Group, PepsiCo, and others are introducing vitamin water and other enhanced water drinks branded with healthy catchphrases like "antioxidant" and "green tea," even as they load them with sugar. Glacéau Vitamin Water from Coca-Cola has 8 teaspoons of sugar in a 20-ounce bottle. SoBe Green tea (PepsiCo), also 20 ounces, has 12¾ teaspoons of sugar. Lipton Green Tea with Citrus, by Unilever, has 4½ teaspoons of sugar per 8 ounces. SoBe Lifewater Orange Tangerine has 6¼ teaspoons of sugar in a 20-ounce bottle. And even an 8-ounce serving of "old school" Schweppes Tonic Water contains 5½ teaspoons of sugar.

Most processed sweetened teas, like SoBe Green Tea, also have no meaningful amounts of antioxidants (polyphenols), or any of the health benefits associated with green tea. In fact, a study presented at the annual meeting of the American Chemical Society in 2010 looked at the levels of antioxidants present in popular brands of bottled teas and concluded that many "contain fewer polyphenols than a single cup of home-brewed green or black tea. Some contain such small amounts that consumers would have to drink 20 bottles to get the polyphenols present in one cup of tea." The processed food manufacturers are taking sugar water and implying that it has health benefits, either by fortifying it with added (read: lab-made, often in China) vitamins and minerals, or by capitalizing on our perceptions of what actually *are* healthful foods (after all, real green tea *is* very healthy). They are making healthy-sounding drinks into *health-destroying* drinks as they use both sugar *and* larger serving sizes to increase profit at the expense of our health.

The only other good news besides the soda decline is that plain water consumption is up by 50 percent (unfortunately this is for bottled water sales, which carries with it a host of its own environmental issues), indicating that at least some of the soda decline may be a shift to unsweetened beverages.

THE GROWTH OF GLOBAL COLA

While soft drink companies introduce new products to try to maintain domestic market share, they also continue to aggressively build foreign markets—which, for example, account for 60 percent of Coca-Cola's revenue and 50 percent of PepsiCo's. When asked about the decline in domestic soda consumption, a spokesperson for Archer Daniels Midland, which along with Cargill runs the plants that produce more than half of the HFCS made in the US, commented that the company will do just fine, because increases in exports of HFCS have *exceeded* the US decline.

> Today Mexicans consume more sugary drinks in general, and more Coca-Cola specifically, than any other country in the world.

And they have the type 2 diabetes numbers to show for it, along with the label of "the fattest country in the developed world." In Mexico, 15 percent of the population over the age of 20 has type 2 diabetes, and 70 percent of adults are overweight. The average Mexican drinks a staggering 728 eight-ounce servings of Coca-Cola a year (compared to 403 in the US). As I mentioned earlier in the chapter, that's two Cokes every day for every Mexican.

Ironically, taste tests and a bit of consumer folklore indicate that the primarily cane-sugar-sweetened Coca-Cola (with some HFCS) sold in Mexico tastes better than the all-HFCS-sweetened Coca-Cola sold in the US, and many people here go out of their way to buy "Mexican Coke." Regardless, as trade tension between the US and Mexico eased and tariffs were removed through the North American Free Trade Agreement (NAFTA), in Mexico the consumption of Coke, as well as other food products from the US, rose dramatically. Those 728 Cokes consumed per capita in 2011 is *two and a half times greater* than the amount consumed pre-NAFTA in 1991 (290 eight-ounce servings). NAFTA, which was meant to help facilitate trade between America, Mexico, and Canada, has led to a flood of US goods in the Mexican market, chiefly subsidized, and now import-duty-free, junk foods like soda, and obesity has skyrocketed. From a sociopolitical standpoint, much as we saw in Guatemala, access to cheap food crushed small local farmers and sent those farmworkers into cities—both Mexican and American. Many crossed the border illegally looking for jobs as cheap factory workers and farmhands, perpetuating the system of cheap food production. Cheap, illegal labor has become one more "subsidized" input that US taxpayers ultimately bear the brunt of.

As much as I am pointing the finger at trade policies, I am not diminishing the force of the beverage industry as it capitalizes on these markets to push sales. In September 2013, after a public awareness campaign funded by Michael Bloomberg's philanthropic organization, Mexico's president, Enrique Peña Nieto, proposed adding a sugar tax of 8 cents per liter to all sweetened drinks to try to curb the proliferation of obesity and type 2 diabetes. As expected, just as we saw here at home, the soda companies are fighting it.

AFRICA'S NEW BROWN WATER PROBLEM

As sales of soft drinks continue to stagnate and even decline in many developed countries like the US, soda companies look to the developing world for the next big growth opportunity. They want another Mexico; and they have found it in Africa.

In 2010, Coca-Cola, which already controls the dominant share of the soda market on the continent, doubled its marketing investment, committing to spend more than $1 billion per year over the coming decade to promote its products in Africa. But it gets complicated: Coke is not only the soft drink market leader, but also the largest private sector employer, providing jobs for more than 65,000 Africans. The company has 160 bottling plants on the continent, where the famous sodas as well as bottled water and, increasingly, juice brands, are produced. Thanks to its joint program with the Gates Foundation, Ugandan and Kenyan fruit farmers are expected to double their incomes by 2014 as they grow the mangoes and passion fruits for Coca-Cola's juice drinks. And those manual distribution centers (MDCs) that use bicycles, pushcarts, and boats to access rural areas are networks that *could* be used to deliver things like medicine or locally grown nutritious foods. The nonprofit ColaLife is working to piggyback on these MDCs to distribute necessities. The sad irony here is that as much as Coke is embedding itself in the local economy and food culture, employing local people and engaging in agricultural development, we know what will happen health-wise to the population if Coca-Cola doesn't shift what they are selling from soda and sweetened fruit drinks to water and healthier, natural juice or unsweetened tea beverages. *We know that based on what happened to us over the past 30 years.*

Among urban South African children between 12 and 24 months old, sweetened carbonated beverages are the third-most consumed food product after corn and tea.

In Ibadan, Nigeria, 16 percent of children ages 6 to 18 months
drink soda once a day because it's sometimes used to
wean babies from breastfeeding.

In Kampala, Uganda, 24 to 37 percent of children
10 to 14 years old drink soda daily.

In Coke's eyes, sub-Saharan Africa is a Mexico in the making. In Nigeria, annual per capita consumption of Coke in 2011 was only 27 eight-ounce servings, which means there is a lot of room to grow. Coke used the same MDC model to build market share and brand loyalty in Mexico that it has now established throughout Africa. And with the Mexican market saturated, Africa, with its growing middle class and established delivery routes, represents a massive growth market for sugary drinks.

And the beverage industry will likely build those markets in a dangerous way. The same marketing ploys we see in the US—namely, fortifying sugar waters and teas (and other junk foods) and labeling them as "healthful"—pose a greater risk if they are implemented in Africa, where beverage companies are sending the same confusing health messages we get in this country to a more vulnerable population. (Remember Nestlé's fortified chocolate drink, Milo, in Tanzania?)

FORTIFIED JUNK FOOD IS STILL JUNK FOOD

The widespread practice of fortification and enrichment of grains, oils, and dairy products with vital micronutrients through breeding plants or replacement or augmentation has spared millions of people around the world from diseases that result from deficiencies in, among other things, iodine, vitamin A, and folic acid. These programs, some of which are government mandated and others voluntarily initiated by food manufacturers, have been enormously successful in addressing a number of public health issues.

Yet at the same time that these programs are preventing disease and saving lives, food manufacturers are also misusing this system of fortification and enrichment in a way that is undermining our health. *Teddy Grahams are a good source of calcium, iron and zinc! Kellogg's Honey Smacks are a good source of vitamin D! SoBe Green Tea is full of antioxidants!* In order to understand what is both a massive public health system success and a massive public health system failure, we have to understand sugar and the role it plays in the process of food fortification and enrichment, and in the broader food system as well.

The World Economic Forum recommends fortification by private companies as a viable means to address malnutrition, and the prestigious journal *Pediatrics* published a paper in 2010 discussing the opportunity to use the soda industries' infiltration of these markets in Africa to address health issues with fortified soft drinks. The authors correctly, but perhaps naively, recommended that the soda companies engage in a "paradigm shift" to focus on low-sugar, fortified drinks. Africa's sugar consumption is expected to grow at an annualized rate of 3.4 percent, ahead of Asia (2.9 percent) and South America (2.1 percent), which means that not only is the Green Revolution headed to Africa, but the sugar revolution is, too. And fortified or not, sugar water destroys our health—no matter where we live. The fortification of sugar water is nothing more than a smoke screen for corporate profit.

ARTIFICIAL SWEETENERS: NOT A SWEET DEAL

A single can of soda containing the equivalent of 10 teaspoons of table sugar, if consumed every day for one year—assuming no other calorie adjustments—manifests as a 15-pound weight gain. Two cans a day? Thirty pounds a year. So the answer for many of the world's weight conscious was clear: *Switch to diet soda.*

And we did. Against the backdrop of all this sugar consumption, there emerged a sister crop of artificial sweeteners like aspartame,[6] acesulfame potassium,[7] saccharin,[8] sucralose,[9] and stevia.[10] The volume of diet beverages available for consumption in 1984 was 9.14 gallons per capita; by 2007 it was 14.94 gallons, an increase of more than 60 percent. The only problem was that in that same time frame, we got fatter. *A lot fatter.*

And there are other health concerns as well. The first diet beverages were sugar-free drinks for diabetics, such as No-Cal soda introduced in the late 1950s. No-Cal was artificially sweetened with cyclamate, which was taken off the market by the FDA in 1970 because it was found to cause cancer in rats. The drink makers switched to saccharin, but then there were concerns that saccharin might

---

6   NutraSweet and Equal.
7   Sunett and Sweet One.
8   Sweet'N Low.
9   Splenda.
10   A group of plants in the sunflower family.

be a carcinogen, so many soda manufacturers and drinkers switched to aspartame, and a few to Splenda (sucralose) and acesulfame potassium. All the while, we tried to ignore the fact that diet soda might just be bad for us, just because it promised to make us thin.

Nonnutritious sweeteners, what we know as "sugar substitutes," are considered by the FDA, just like sugar in soda, to be inert substances, or "generally regarded as safe." Yet a growing body of evidence suggests that drinks and foods with artificial sweeteners, which came to be in order to help people *lose* weight and *prevent* weight gain, have some of the same adverse effects that sugar-sweetened products do, and may even have a worse effect on our health. In numerous studies, *diet* soda has been linked to weight gain, metabolic syndrome, and type 2 diabetes, as well as increased risk for stroke, myocardial infarction, and vascular death—potentially because of how sugar substitutes interact with the brain by signalling "sweet" but delivering no calories. The Framingham Heart Study,[11] for example, found that individuals who drink *any* amount of sugar soda *or* diet soda have an elevated risk of developing metabolic syndrome, obesity, type 2 diabetes, and high blood pressure. Shockingly, diet soda drinkers fared the worst: Drinkers of two cans per day presented with a whopping 57 percent higher incidence of metabolic syndrome than non-soda drinkers. In a recent study, it was found that Splenda (sucralose) "affects the glycemic and insulin responses to an oral glucose load in obese people who do not normally consume nonnutritious sugars."[12]

These two issues—the potential health risks of sugar *and* artificial sweeteners—didn't bother the soda companies until consumers became aware of them and responded by buying less diet soda, therefore hurting their bottom line. In order to combat lost revenue (for example, sales of diet sodas at Coca-Cola fell 6 percent, and at PepsiCo 8 percent in the fist two quarters of 2013[13]), these companies are expanding their reach with line extensions, new products, and company acquisitions, as well as aggressively entering foreign markets.

As consumers cut back on soda, we've seen the new lineup of sugar waters and teas. But now consider that the beverage industry is also responding to

---

11   An ongoing, large-scale, longitudinal study of cardiovascular disease conducted by the National Heart, Lung, and Blood Institute that began in 1948.

12   An interesting fact about Splenda is that the fillers, which are 99 percent of the contents of both the packet and granular version of the product, are composed of maltodextrin and dextrose—both made from HFCS.

13   PepsiCo's North America unit reported a 5 to 6 percent decline in soda sales in the first half of 2013, but ended up with a 5 percent profit in the beverage division due to cost-cutting and price hikes.

concerns over sugar (sucrose), HFCS, *and* artificial sweeteners by *combining them in the same drink*. Pepsi introduced Pepsi Next, which has 60 percent less sugar than a regular Pepsi (15 grams for a 12-ounce serving). But here's the catch: It's sweetened with a mixture of HFCS *and* cane sugar *and* artificial sweeteners (to be specific, sucralose and acesulfame potassium). In other words, instead of offering a better (healthier) drink option, they are splitting the difference down the middle and offering a drink with a smorgasbord of bad health options. Dr Pepper did the same thing with Dr Pepper Ten, which is sweetened with HFCS, aspartame, and acesulfame potassium. It has only 4 grams of sugar per 20 ounces, but that is only because they opted for more artificial sugar and less HFCS than PepsiCo did with Pepsi Next. And believe it or not, these consumer-unfriendly new product introductions get even worse.

★ ★

The milk industry, which sells a lot of low-fat chocolate milk (especially to schools), filed a petition with the FDA to put aspartame in flavored milk to help combat obesity. Yet the lactose in plain milk is a natural disaccharide (galactose and glucose) present in a relatively small amount, and comes packaged with protein and calcium. The reason to use aspartame in milk would be to replace the *added* sugar used to flavor the milk (apparently necessary to get kids to drink it once the fat was removed) in order to make the high-sugar flavored milk appear to be *less* of a bad choice. Talk about falling down the rabbit hole of bad nutrition ideas! We arrived at diet chocolate- and strawberry-flavored milk by adulterating good food (whole milk) into a lesser food (low-fat sugary milk), then potentially into a lesser-lesser food (low-fat, artifically sweetened and flavored milk) for the sake of profit, with the intent of marketing it under a health banner (*Less sugar!*), when we *could* just serve plain, nutritious whole milk in the first place.

One cup of whole, unsweetened (white) milk has about 3.5 teaspoons (14 grams) of natural sugar (lactose) and about 150 calories. Depending on which brand you buy, the same size serving of chocolate- or strawberry-flavored milk has roughly twice the sugar (31 grams) and an additional 60 calories. And if your kids make that flavored milk themselves with strawberry or chocolate syrup, that flavored milk may contain even more added sugar, depending on how much syrup they add. If they have three servings per day, that's about 10 teaspoons of added sugar in their diets just from flavored milk—roughly the amount in a Coke.

NATURE'S SWEET NECTARS?

For many of us, it may come as a surprise to know that even 100 percent juice may contain too much sugar and lead to a rise in weight and cause sugar-related health issues. In fact, juice illustrates just how pervasive and perplexing the sugar problem is. An 8-ounce glass of Tropicana Pure Premium orange juice (a PepsiCo brand that was sued over its "100 percent pure and natural" claim because of the processing and pasteurization that the juice goes through before hitting the shelves) has the same amount of sugar as 2½ oranges. This may not seem that bad until we consider just how much juice some very small children are drinking. A toddler is an unlikely candidate to actually *eat* 7½ oranges, but may very well consume three 8-ounce servings of juice in a day, which represents 16½ teaspoons of sugar.

★ ★

We know that obesity is reaching epidemic proportions across all age groups and in many geographic regions of the world. Here in the US, a particularly tragic statistic is that the obesity rate in children ages 6 to 11 has increased nearly *fivefold* in only a few decades, rising from 4 percent in the 1970s to 18 percent in 2012. Today, a full third of children are overweight or obese.[14] The first thing a pediatrician will often ask a mother of even a child of healthy weight who reports that her 1- or 2-year-old isn't eating well is "How much juice is the baby drinking?" Similarly, the first thing Robert Lustig, whose research on fructose I discussed earlier, and who is a vocal advocate for sugar reduction, asks the parents of obese children is not "What are they eating?" but rather "What are they drinking?"

Some scientists and nutrition experts will argue that unrefined or minimally refined sugars such as honey and maple syrup are healthier options, as they contain antioxidants, trace minerals, and, in the case of maple syrup, calcium, potassium, and manganese. Raw honey, for its part, also offers vitamins, amino acids, and enzymes.[15] But there are other nutritionists and scientists in the food space who will tell us these differences are minuscule, and that there really is no

---

14   On a positive note, in the past few years the incidence of childhood obesity has dropped slightly. The Centers for Disease Control and Prevention reports that in low-income children ages 2 to 4, in 19 out of 43 states and territories examined, there was at least a 1 percent decline in obesity.

15   Raw or "real" honey, of course, is distinct from the widely available processed or filtered honey that we see in little ketchup packets or some plastic bear bottles that is sometimes made by feeding HFCS to bees.

difference at all between the sugar calories from honey or maple syrup and the highly refined sugars made from cane, sugar beets, and corn.

Even if you are willing to opt out of that debate, natural, local honey and 100 percent maple syrup have at least one healthy *economic* benefit over highly refined sugars that is undisputed: They are fairly priced. That is, *they are more expensive.*[16] A 12-ounce bottle of Mrs. Butterworth maple-flavored syrup made from HFCS and corn syrup (and no actual maple syrup) costs about $2.99. Twelve ounces of real maple syrup costs at least four times that; it typically runs about a dollar per ounce. The high prices of honey and maple syrup control how much of these products we eat. Cost limits the industrial use of unrefined, unsubsidized sugars as well.

> If it's not rendered artificially cheap through subsidies and price supports, we won't find it in most processed foods like soda.

We can sell a 2-liter bottle of soda sweetened with HFCS for under $2. Try replicating that with a honey- or maple-sugar-sweetened drink.

As we move away from processed, sugar-sweetened beverages, our first step should be to drink more water. The second is to sweeten any beverages we drink ourselves, and to do so only slightly and with sweeteners that have a built-in mechanism to control their use—price.

RELEARNING HOW TO DRINK

Many of the changes that have occurred in our drinking patterns over the past 30 years either went unnoticed, were perceived as good, or were implemented for what we *thought* were healthy reasons. We thought it was great that serving sizes got so big and soda got so cheap. It was convenient when we shifted to eating so many meals outside the home—meals that came bundled with large cheap sodas. We thought we were improving our health by switching from whole milk to low-fat flavored milk with added sugar. We didn't particularly notice that flavored milk and sugary drinks went from the occasional treat to the everyday fix. Or that we now serve soda, chocolate milk, and sugary fruit and sports drinks all day, every day, even to young children. Those cup holders that appeared in cars and shopping carts, and in strollers for both mom and baby, were perceived as a

---

16   There are government price supports for honey, but nothing like what we have for corn.

modern convenience, not a health hazard; we didn't see that they were just making it easier to always have a large cup of something sweet at our side. We hardly noticed that those drinks *kept* getting incrementally bigger and sweeter—or more artificial—so much so that 7-Eleven had to downsize a soda size it called the Double Gulp, which had 54 ounces of soda, 9 ounces of ice, 744 calories, and *46½ teaspoons of sugar,* which is just shy of one whole cup—not because people didn't want that much soda, but because there wasn't a motor vehicle with a cup holder that could handle a nearly half-gallon-sized single-serving drink.

When you look at it objectively, it doesn't seem possible that we didn't see something wrong with a half-gallon serving of soda, or chocolate milk for breakfast, or that there are now 12¾ teaspoons of sugar added to an antioxidant green tea. And we never dreamed that a zero-calorie diet drink could make us gain weight. It all goes down so sweet and easy, and seems like such good caloric and dollar "value" that we don't want to make the connection from these drinks to type 2 diabetes and obesity. We would much rather ignore the science that explains just how bad our drinking habits have become.

★ ★

Amazingly, despite our shifting drink choices, our fluid intake over time has been relatively stable. We each drink about 180 gallons of liquid a year. Since we simply adjust the specific type of liquid we consume, soft drink companies continue to compete for those gallons—and our dollars. They do so with established brands, and by creating new products that seem like they quench our thirst, but only bloat our bellies, and their bank accounts if we continue to buy them.

We have to start making different choices.

For starters, we can drink more tap water.

If we drink tap water, we not only get healthier, we also save some of the $65 billion we spend each year on soft drinks, which frees up money to buy better-quality foods and beverages. With bottled water consumption up 50 percent from 1988 to 2012, it indicates that some of the soda decline may be a result of a shift to water. But as much as drinking bottled water is a step up for our health if it means we are forgoing sweetened drinks, consumers should be leery of corporate messaging that bottled water is somehow healthier for us than tap water. Tap water, which is free—or close to it—or filtered water, which we can simply filter at home, is far better for our world than bottled water. It does not continue to empower the marketers of sugary drinks, who often also sell these waters. Drinking tap water means that all those plastic bottles won't end up in landfills, and the true environmental costs of transporting bottled water in trucks, from the fossil fuels to the resultant air pollution, will be saved. Plus, drinking tap water would free up another $11 billion—because that is what we collectively spend on bottled water every year.

> Next, we all have to cut back *dramatically* on
> the added sugars we drink.

We should drink simple teas and unsweetened coffee, or sweeten them ourselves with a *small* amount of organic cane sugar, raw unprocessed honey, or 100 percent pure maple syrup, and accept how much these sweeteners actually cost by using less.

Sugar *should* be expensive.

The signal we send up the demand chain every time we buy soda or other non-nutritional sugary drinks (or grab them when they are offered for free at events, conferences, and work meetings) is that these are the types of products we want. So the answer is to drink no commercially produced soda, sweet or diet. Ever.

Previously, "health conscious" young people, and women in particular, rushed to the diet drinks section of the soda aisle. But a recent report from Wells Fargo reported that in 2013, diet soda consumption was down 8.6 percent. As the industry scrambles to get more people to drink diet soda through new product introductions, at least some of us who used to be fooled by the word "diet" have moved on to safer waters.

Today's health-aware drinkers are not just bringing their own water bottles (which has pushed airports and other public spaces to add bottle fill stations to their fountains) and grabbing small servings of 100 percent juice instead of large servings of soda, they are also using beverages to push for global social change.

CHEERS: LET'S DRINK FOR CHANGE

Fair trade coffee and tea are staples on college campuses and, increasingly, the norm—from Starbucks to supermarkets. Since we don't grow coffee or much tea in the US, our caffeinated drink habit—and its partner in crime, sugar—has had a disproportionate impact on the developing world. This is slowly changing as growing interest in better-tasting coffee has led to an explosion of new coffee brands and houses that serve shade-grown,[17] sustainably sourced coffee that is purchased by paying fairer prices to ensure farmworkers a living wage, and a way out of poverty.

To wash down the typical American barbecue meal, a perfect accompaniment is a big glass pitcher of home-brewed sun tea. Buying fair trade, organic tea will help hungry regions of the world "grow themselves" out of poverty, without any chemical residue issues for the farmworkers or drinkers. It will also add some healthy antioxidants to our diets. Simply placing the tea bags with some mint leaves (which you can grow yourself) in a pitcher of water left to steep in the sun for a couple of hours will allow the tea to brew while you do other things. A little local honey, added as the sun heats up the pitcher, can sweeten it, and if you like, a few slices of lemon are a great way to add additional flavor.

Another way to improve the way we drink is to make our "adult beverages" bring positive economic growth and good agricultural practices to communities around the world. Unlike soda, beer and wine have no measurable sugar, and the US craft beer movement has been a harbinger of the local and artisanal food movement, supporting communities as it keeps our drink dollars close to home, uses less fuel, and keeps delivery trucks off the roads. If you're having a nice cold beer with your burger, find a local one from one of the 2,483 craft breweries in the US, or even one from the growing selection of organic beers (which have sales of more than $41 million a year, up from $9 million in 2003).

All across the US, small vintners are finding riverbanks and hillsides to grow grapes on and are restarting an industry of local wineries that go hand-in-hand with the agro-tourism movement. Getting people back to farms and vineyards has helped reacquaint eaters and drinkers with where their food comes from.

★ ★

As we shift what we drink, we should be very careful to monitor the liquid intake by children. We should end their addiction to flavored milk, sports drinks they don't need, and sodas bundled with fast food meals. We also need to pay close attention to the juices we drink, making sure we consume only 100 percent organic juice in *small* portions. Juice glasses used to hold just 3 to 5 ounces, not 8 to 12. Somewhere along the way, we forgot that.

---

17   Shade-grown coffee preserves the forest canopy and protects the birds that live there.

One incredible shift in beverage consumption that makes even the skeptical take note is the fast-growing trend of "green juice." Whatever the combination of pressed vegetables and fruits that makes it green also makes it nutrient dense and, often, a little less sweet. The so-called "juicing" habit of making your own fresh fruit and vegetable juice, and the new stores and chains of juice bars that make these drinks fresh to order, has also spawned a new line of pressed-juice supermarket brands. (As with any food or drink trend, beware the Big Drink companies creating shelf-stable green-colored juices that are high in sugar and low in fresh-pressed nutrients and enzymes.)

Although the price of an $8 bottle of juice is way too high for most people to afford—a signal that we don't need to drink it in large volumes—as more of we the eaters buy fresh juice, it will create new marketplaces and more supply, and push even organic veggie juice prices down. Now if we can only get celebrity spokespeople for kale and beet juice, like we have for Pepsi and Diet Coke!

Or we can look to the tech industry's new approach to corporate dining for inspiration. At a recent lunch meeting at Google's San Francisco office, I noticed that there were stacks of stylish metal cups placed on counters next to huge water dispensers flavored with sliced fresh fruit and mint. Meanwhile, all the soda was kept in refrigerators below the counter obscured by frosted glass. As a company composed mainly of hearty young people, Google might not need to be so vigilant about the soda intake of its employees. But as one that is very into analytics, the long-term health-care costs of liquid sugar show that shifting people's drinking habits from soda to water is a very smart money-saving technique. Using the same marketing tactics that the beverage companies have used to push us toward soda, like counter-height fountains and eye-height refrigerator placement, corporate dining facilities, restaurants, and stores can fight fire with . . . water.

By redirecting our beverage dollars, we will be telling the drink companies that we don't want sugar, and we don't want artificial sweeteners either. As we get the message out, first with our families' shopping dollars and then in our schools, college campuses, workplaces, and community events any way we can, we should share our concern about soda and sugar-added drinks with the rest of the world, knowing that if we the eaters *don't*, they the soda makers *won't*. If we don't make this our mission, we may eventually be calling on Coca-Cola to deliver insulin and diabetic supplies via those same bicycles, pushcarts, and boats they set up to deliver soda to rural villages in Africa. The people of African countries, just like the people of North America and everywhere else in the world, deserve to drink clean water, not Coke.

★ **7** ★

The Sweet We Eat

Dessert All Day and Really Real Fruit Flavors

AS WE'VE SEEN, about 50 percent of the added sugar in our diets comes from sweetened beverages. What that means is that the previous chapter told only half the sugar story. The remaining 50 percent of the added sugar in our diets is not only a little tougher to pin down, but also is a bit more difficult for us to correct. The reason the second half of the sugar story is so important for we the eaters to understand is that because we eat *so much* sugar, almost all of us are exceeding the healthy limit even before we take a sip of soda, or drink a sugar-added beverage of any type.

Admittedly, the amount of added sugar in our diets can be hard to estimate. Different sources put our current consumption levels anywhere from 18 to as high as 30 teaspoons per day, or roughly 70 to 100 pounds of added sugar per person, per year.[1] Further complicating the issue is the fact that foods containing

---

1   Michael Moss, the *New York Times* investigative reporter and author of *Sugar, Fat, Salt*, estimates that we eat, on average, 22 teaspoons a day; others put it higher. Most estimates on the upper end are based on sugar production, not consumption. The often-cited 156 pounds of added sugar per capita reported by the USDA, for example, is based on sugar "available for consumption"—not what we *actually* eat. The amount of sugar lost, from the growing fields to the refineries to the retail stores, restaurants, kitchens, and, ultimately, our plates, is almost impossible to calculate.

both natural sugar *and* added sugar are tough to evaluate for sugar content, since food manufacturers are not required to label "added sugar" separately from "naturally occurring sugar." If we want to know how much sugar is added to soda, since there's no natural sugar it's easy—it's indicated on the label. But for a flavored yogurt, which has natural sugar from the milk as well as any real fruit it might contain—and likely has added sugar from cane juice and high-fructose corn syrup (HFCS) as well—it's trickier. The only option is to estimate the added sugar by comparing the total sugar in the flavored yogurt to a container of the same size of that brand's plain yogurt, and then calculate the difference—it can start to feel like a calculus assignment just to eat well.

Yet even the most conservative estimates, and the most basic math, show that we are eating too much sugar. The problem is that once we start eating sugar, we might not be able to stop: Researchers from Connecticut College reported in October 2013 that Oreo cookies are as addictive for rats as both cocaine and morphine. Couple those findings with the work from researchers from the University of Utah who found that female rats eating the equivalent of 30 added teaspoons of sugar per day in an otherwise normal diet died at twice the normal rate, and we begin to see the scope of the problem.

DESSERT: IT'S NOT JUST FOR DESSERT ANYMORE

As you'd expect, processed sweets and desserts like cakes, cookies, ice cream, and candy are the second-largest source of added sugar in our diets. Grain-based desserts represent 12.9 percent of added-sugar calories, dairy desserts 6.5 percent, and candy 6.1 percent, for a combined total of 25.5 percent of our added dietary sugar intake. Just as we the eaters went from drinking the occasional small soda to drinking the frequent large soda, we also went from having the occasional sweet dessert to eating processed cakes, cookies, and sweet snacks *all the time*. In fact, it's hardly a coincidence that all those sweet drinks pair so well with all those sugary desserts.

This dietary trend toward sugary drinks and desserts exists for the simple reason that processing, affordability, shelf stability, and widespread availability colluded with the addictive qualities of sugar to make them popular with eaters and profitable for manufacturers. Food marketers have made sure that sugary treats and drinks are easy to grab anywhere: out of the cupboard, fridge, or freezer at home; in a vending machine; at a mini-mart; or off the conference table at work. They have crept into our diets to the point that for many, "dessert" has become an every day, even several-times-a-day, food choice—after lunch, school, sports practice, dinner, and even for breakfast.

Using the sugar-limit recommendation of the American Heart Association— 6 added teaspoons (24 grams) for women, 9 teaspoons (36 grams) for men—or even Lustig's higher limit (12½ teaspoons or 50 grams per day for someone eating 2,000 calories), most of us go well over all of these limits.

> A venti (large) nonfat Tazo green tea Frappuccino without whipped cream from Starbucks has 87 grams—almost 22 teaspoons—of sugar. That's almost *four days' worth of sugar for a woman* in a single drink.

If she bypasses the green tea frappuccino and orders an unsweetened black coffee or tea instead, but happens to pick out a "treat" like a Morning Bun to go with it, the bun alone has a full day's worth of added sugar—6½ teaspoons. That single pastry catapulted this eater past the healthy daily allotment with the first meal of the day. All of a sudden, that unhealthy 30 teaspoons of added sugar per day is no longer that hard to imagine, even if we don't drink sweetened beverages.

SOURCES OF ADDED SUGAR IN OUR DIETS

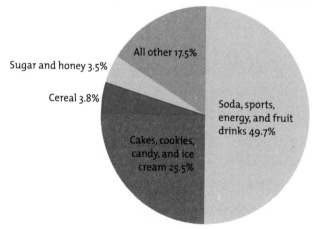

All other 17.5%

Sugar and honey 3.5%

Cereal 3.8%

Cakes, cookies, candy, and ice cream 25.5%

Soda, sports, energy, and fruit drinks 49.7%

Source: National Cancer Institute, 2005 to 2006

When you look at the chart above, the sweet drink and dessert problem is obvious, and together accounts for about 75 percent of our added sugar consumption. The amount of sugar and honey we add to food ourselves is reassuringly low, and the cereal number (which I will discuss later) is, perhaps, a bit surprising based on the dominant role processed cereal takes in the breakfast market.[2] The less obvious, and more insidious, source of added sugar in our diets falls into the "all other" category. That category represents the hidden sugar added to processed foods that really shouldn't be sweet at all.

★ ★

Added sugar shows up in a lot of unlikely places. Food manufacturers have pumped sugar into even "healthy" foods and meals, such as processed bread, fruit, and entrees, so we the eaters now face an almost constant stream of *hidden* sugar over the course of each and every day. There is hidden, added sugar in fast food hamburgers and salads, in processed foods like applesauce, tomato sauce, cold cuts, peanut butter, salad dressing, yogurt, crackers, and canned soup, to name just a few. Try to find a breakfast cereal or processed bread without sugar. You can, but you will have to hunt long and hard to do so.

Take a trip to a local fast food restaurant like McDonald's. Even ignoring the blatant sugar traps like drinks and desserts—the large Eggnog Shake, which has 29 teaspoons of sugar, and the large McFlurry with M&M candies, which has 32 teaspoons of sugar (all of these have a small amount of sugar from milk as well)—there's the Premium Southwest Salad with Crispy Chicken with Newman's Own Low Fat Balsamic Vinaigrette. Sounds healthy, right? It has 4 teaspoons of sugar.

Salad dressing and chicken should not contain added sugar.

And yet they do. Sugar grams and teaspoons add up quickly, and it's not just in fast food. Nor am I picking on McDonald's or any individual food purveyor. You can run the same numbers at Burger King, the school cafeteria, the vending machines at work, or anywhere else; you can get into the same trouble at an airport, in a Ugandan mini-mart, or just by eating at home. Substitute any restaurant or fast food company. *Pick any country.* Troll the aisles of the supermarket, or your fridge and cupboard at home. Sugar is lurking everywhere, and not just in soda and sweet desserts.

Lean Cuisine Bistro Chicken Salad contains 4½ teaspoons of sugar; the Grilled Chicken and Penne Pasta has 6 teaspoons. Most fruit yogurts have 4½ to 6½ teaspoons, some of it from the milk and fruit, but a lot of it from added sugar.

---

2   Data compiled from the National Cancer Institute, 2005 to 2006.

Yoplait 99% Fat Free Yogurt, Harvest Peach has 3½ teaspoons of sugar after the milk sugar (lactose) is subtracted. Even organic Stonyfield Farm Fat Free Chocolate Underground Yogurt has almost 9 teaspoons of sugar. Motts Original applesauce has 2¾ *added* teaspoons of sugar, not counting the sugar from the fruit. Two slices of Freihofer Double Fiber 100% Whole Wheat bread, which is made with HFCS, adds 1½ teaspoons of sugar to a sandwich. Ken's Steakhouse Fat-Free Sun-Dried Tomato Vinaigrette has 3 teaspoons of sugar *per 2-tablespoon serving.* Unbelievably, using 4 tablespoons of a healthy-sounding salad dressing has as much sugar as six Chips Ahoy! chocolate chip cookies. And Nutella, the chocolate–hazelnut sandwich spread, has 5¼ teaspoons of sugar per serving—more than two Tootsie Pops.

Even people who don't drink sweetened drinks or sugar-loaded coffees, teas, and waters, people who are trying to eat healthy food in the industrialized world of fast and processed food, will find it exceedingly hard to do so in an environment where a single meal of salad and chicken, along with a low-fat yogurt, has enough added sugar to exceed what should be our daily limit. If we now take a look at the food on the typical American barbecue table, we know there is added sugar in the form of HFCS in the soda and in any processed desserts, but it is also likely in the bun, the ketchup (of course), and the salad dressing.

As I reported earlier, we each consume about 56 pounds of HFCS each year. *That is a little over half our yearly consumption of added sugar, even though we never actually choose to eat any of it.* In fact, we couldn't add it to our food ourselves if we wanted to, because we can't buy HFCS—it's strictly an industrial ingredient. When it became widely available to manufacturers in the 1980s, the new, cheap HFCS, with all those added benefits I mentioned earlier, like improved browning and better shelf stability, made it advantageous to add it not only to soda, but also to previously healthy foods that never should have contained sugar in the first place. Foods like bread and "diet" chicken dinners.

Our first task as eaters is to cut out sweet drinks. Our second task is to cut way back on desserts. And our third is to cut out all of that hidden sugar in traditionally unsweetened foods by finding or, better yet, making the same foods we love, without the added sugar.

By buying different bread, different applesauce, and different peanut butter, a child's lunch can go from having about 5 teaspoons of added sugar to having none. If we can accomplish that meal after meal, day after day, we can make room on our plates for the occasional sweet dessert, as we make room in our closets for smaller clothes, room in our wallets for money not spent on medical care, and room on our calendars for longer, healthier lives.

When we read labels and cut out all that added sugar by buying different food, we can "afford" to indulge in the occasional dessert.

Ideally, a homemade dessert made with high-quality ingredients, like a seasonal apple cobbler, or homemade cherry pie, at the backyard barbecue.

DESSERT FOR BREAKFAST

Breakfast is a good place to begin to make the dietary shift away from those sugary products. In 2011 the cereal industry sold over $9 billion worth of products, the bulk of which were ready-to-eat cold cereals. That market is expected to grow to $9.8 billion by 2016. Even though cereal with added sugar accounts for only about 3.8 percent of the added sugar in our diets, we don't want to start the day halfway to our total added sugar consumption limit. Nor should we start the day with a sugar fix that very well may stimulate our appetite for more sugar as the day progresses.

This is especially true for kids. Take a serving of Honey Nut Cheerios. It has *three* different sugars: sucrose, honey, and brown sugar syrup. In total, that represents more than 2 teaspoons of sugar for only a ¾ cup serving. But does anyone actually eat a ¾ cup serving? The yellow, no-spill Cheerios snack container and Munchie snack mugs designed for toddlers *hold a full cup.*

By comparison, steel-cut oats have no added sugar and less than ¼ teaspoon of natural sugar. Yet the processed version of steel-cut oats, for example, instant Quaker Oatmeal Apples and Cinnamon, has *12 times that amount,* a full 3 teaspoons. And the more processed it gets, the higher the sugar total climbs. The Fruit and Maple Oatmeal at McDonald's has *8 teaspoons of sugar.* As I have been reporting, the maximum added-sugar consumption for women should be 6 teaspoons a day, yet a small child of half or a third of that size who consumes 1½ cups of Honey Nut Cheerios has eaten 4 teaspoons of sugar at breakfast. And the McDonald's customer who may think he or she made a good nutritional choice by picking oatmeal has been grossly misled by the system.

★ ★

Perhaps as a result of the recognition of the value of eating whole fruit for breakfast, there are myriad ads for children's cereal touting that they have "real fruit flavors." Inside these shelf-stable boxes and sealed plastic bags you'll find extruded wheat forced into fruit-shaped molds, then colored with dyes and coated in sugar. Alongside images of real fruit on the box will almost always be a list of the nutritious vitamins, minerals, and "whole grains" that the cereal provides—but often no real fruit.

One of the inherent problems with fresh fruits and vegetables, for growers, sellers, and eaters, is that, unlike so many of the processed foods we have become accustomed to eating, they don't have a long shelf life. This means almost guaranteed waste and less certain profit. Fresh strawberries and blueberries last for less than a week; Froot Loops, perhaps the most blatant example of a misleading, adulterated, processed version of fruit in the breakfast cereal category, has a shelf life of about a year because there is no actual fruit in the package, but there is the preservative butylated hydroxytoluene, a substance also found in petroleum products and embalming fluid that happens to be implicated in a variety of health issues like cancer and liver toxicity.

Additionally, the "Froot" colors in Froot Loops don't come from actual fruits such as blueberries or strawberries either, but from dyes like red 40, blues 1 and 2, and yellow 6 (which may be linked to behavior problems and hyperactivity in children). And of course, sugar is the most prevalent ingredient in Froot Loops, with 3 teaspoons per cup of cereal. Which means that a child who starts the day with 1½ cups of Froot Loops begins with 4½ teaspoons of sugar before he or she has had a single sugary drink or dessert and, of course, no fruit. That's about the same amount as in Honey Nut Cheerios, which, incidentally, doesn't contain any nuts—just "natural almond flavor." Now consider how many parents wouldn't dream of buying Froot Loops but *do* buy Honey Nut Cheerios because of a difference in the perceived health attributes of these two products.

In many of our diets, fortified, added-sugar cereals have replaced plain whole grains like oatmeal served with fresh fruit. The method of selling these high-sugar cereals involves marketing them as fun to kids and as healthy to parents, via a combination of high-budget, child-focused ad campaigns and parent-pleasing (and confusing) fortification.

In cereals, and now increasingly in drinks, fortification is used to sell desserts for breakfast and sugar in drinks throughout the day, giving consumers false reassurances that they are getting necessary vitamins and minerals or whole grains from what is actually a box or bottle of sugar.

Take Kellogg's Honey Smacks breakfast cereal. A banner across the box states that it is "a good source of vitamin D." Not because the content of the box is naturally rich in vitamin D, but because, as with many of its breakfast cereals, Kellogg's fortifies it with vitamins and micronutrients including iron; riboflavin; niacin; folic acid; and vitamins C, D, B_6, and B_{12}, which then allows them to make broad health claims. The problem is that Honey Smacks, which has 15 grams of sugar, happens to be more than *half* sugar (55.6 percent). The nonprofit organization that ranked Honey Smacks the "least healthy cereal for kids" based on sugar content, the Environmental Working Group, reports that a single ¾ cup serving of this breakfast cereal actually has more sugar than a Hostess Twinkie.[3]

If you are a parent standing in the cereal aisle of a supermarket contemplating buying a box of Kellogg's Honey Smacks, Froot Loops, or Honey Nut Cheerios—or any of the other fortified, ad-driven sugar products marketed by cartoons as nutritious food for kids—you might want to consider whether it would serve your child just as well to feed him or her 4 teaspoons of sugar straight from the sugar bowl, top it off with a multivitamin, and just forgo the cereal purchase altogether. Or better yet, the simple solution in the breakfast category is to add some real fruit to unsweetened whole grains ourselves, and avoid all of the added sugar completely.

SUGAR'S BITTER AFTERTASTE

Along with the damage it does to our bodies, sugar is a threat multiplier, affecting far more than our health. Earlier in the book we discussed the numerous environmental issues that arise from mono-cropping GM corn—from pesticide runoff and soil and water degradation to a loss of crop diversity that could potentially lead to widespread famine. The growing, refining, and processing of sugarcane and sugar beet crops around the world are responsible for widespread environmental damage as well: There is water pollution resulting from fertilizer use, and air pollution from the practice of burning the sugarcane during the harvest. A spot check around the world implicates sugarcane in phosphorus waste in Florida's Everglades, soil carbon decline in Papua New Guinea, and suffocation of fish and plant life from effluent runoff in the fresh waters of Cuba and Denmark.

Sugar cultivation has an infamous history of degrading the labor force as

---

3   A Hostess Twinkie is 41.8 percent sugar.

well. With demand high, and the need for cheap labor on sugar plantations and in the refineries, sugar was the driving force behind the African slave trade in the West Indies for centuries. Today sugarcane is grown in the "Global South" (in parts of Africa, Central and South America, and Southern Asia), regions of the world continually beset with poverty and hunger. Just as a single example, in 1997 the Rwandan government leased riverbed marshlands to a Ugandan sugar company to grow and refine sugarcane. In doing so, they displaced the local subsistence farmers who had lived off that land for generations. Working as laborers growing sugarcane for the Ugandan company, they no longer grow their own food, and they have seen the variety of the foods in their diets decline, right along with their overall standard of living. The company's Web site heralds its ownership of the sugar complex as a way into the markets of the Democratic Republic of Congo. Just what the Democratic Republic of Congo needs—some sugar and candy making on their current state of violence and humanitarian crisis.

> No matter where you look in the world—and in history—sugar
> production exploits the land it is grown on, the labor force
> that produces it, and the health of those who eat it.

And as a crop it is worth a bundle: Sugar is a $77.5 billion global enterprise, and growing.

Yet unlike any other agricultural crop grown and processed for human consumption, refined sugar has no real nutritional value other than the calories provided by its simple carbohydrates. It has no protein, fiber, vitamins, minerals, micronutrients, or antioxidants. Today 80 percent of the sugar sold in the global market is subsidized by the governments of the countries producing it, often as a direct response to US policy. In the US, aggressive sugar legislation began in 1789 with an import tax, and the government has been legislating sugar prices ever since. In 1937 Congress passed a comprehensive Sugar Act, a series of import quotas and tariffs to protect the states where sugar is grown. Import tariffs, loans, processor taxes, and price support programs for sugar continue in one form or another today. Comprehensive sugar legislation is included in the 2014 farm bill, and lobbyists from bakers and candy-making companies along with the American Beverage Institute and the Snack Food Association fought for cheaper sugar and lower tariffs, facing off against the American Sugar Alliance of growers, who want to continue to keep prices high and protect themselves from cheaper imports. Current sugar policies, yet again hailing from the early 1980s, allow companies that process sugar cane and beets into white refined crystals to borrow unlimited money from the USDA with sugar as collateral. In March 2013 prices plummeted to a 10-year low and it was reported that sugar processors defaulted on over $170 million in loans, despite the USDA buying over $106 million worth of sugar to try to increase prices. That's a high price for taxpayers to pay for cheap soda, diabetes, obese kids, shortened lives, and "muffin tops."

When we look at the global impact of sugar on the environment, the labor force, and our health, it appears that sugar functions in the marketplace more like blood diamonds or conflict minerals than a foodstuff. But despite all its faults, we can't seem to get enough of the stuff.

> The most important source of sugar in our diets should be the natural sugar in fresh fruits and vegetables, not the added sugar in processed foods.

THE FRUCTOSE WE *SHOULD* BE EATING: WHOLE FRUIT

Sweet fruit has been revered by the members of religions and cultures throughout time. Eve may very well have started it all with her lust for a sweet apple. The Greeks ascribed all kinds of aphrodisiac properties to the delicious, if difficult, pomegranate. The Chinese celebrate the New Year with sweet oranges, said to bring wealth and luck. In Spain people ring in the New Year by eating 12 grapes for good luck. The word *kwanzaa* literally means "first fruits" in Swahili. And in India, which produces 40 percent of the global supply of mangoes, mango season is a national affair.

The reason for all of this historical fruit reverence can be attributed, to a large degree, to the fact that these fruits were sweet and seasonal in a food environment where sweet was relatively rare. Since sugar is anything but rare in today's food environment, fruit is no longer perceived as a sweet, nor is it revered. And because of confusion over fruit's sugar content, it is sometimes shunned by dieters. Fruit has sugar, and yes, it is exactly the same as the fructose found naturally in corn kernels. The difference is that when we eat whole fruits, we are not stripping away the fiber and other nutrients. The sugar in whole fruit is not processed or refined, and whole fresh fruit has no *added sugar*. Almost all doctors agree that we should eat fruit more frequently. Here's why:

Since nature packaged fructose in a way that makes it difficult to eat in large quantities, it's very hard to overeat sugar if you are eating whole, unprocessed foods like fruit. The USDA, in a comprehensive analysis of fruit and vegetable consumption patterns, found that higher fruit consumption was correlated with healthier (i.e., lower) weight as measured by body mass index (BMI). If the more frequent fruit eaters are eating it in place of high-calorie snacks, it's easy to see how eating fruit is beneficial strictly on a calorie basis. In fact, the USDA also reported that higher fruit consumption was an even *better* predictor of low BMI than higher vegetable consumption; researchers speculated that this doesn't mean fruit is better for us than vegetables, but rather that fruit can "stand in" for unhealthy snacks more readily than vegetables can. In other words, you might bring an apple in your purse or bag and eat it instead of cookies, but you likely would not be carting broccoli around for an afternoon snack.

Even forgetting calories, fruit is packed with fiber and micronutrients, many of which have known health benefits. In 2011 a study found that people with precancerous lesions of the esophagus who ate large quantities of freeze-dried strawberries for 6 months either saw their lesions shrink or had a slowed rate of tumor growth. Yet every time a new study like this comes out suggesting that a certain fruit or vegetable is connected to a positive health outcome, instead of reinforcing fruit consumption as part of an overall healthy diet, it results in a rush to extract the single nutrient allegedly responsible for that health benefit. There are many reasons for this, but one of them is that companies can't make money from "branding" strawberries or grapefruits as a way to prevent cancer, and the only way to monetize these findings is to break down the nutrients and package them as "miracle cure" vitamin pills. The lead researcher in the strawberry study, Tong Chen, an assistant professor in the oncology division at Ohio State University, acknowledged that it isn't clear what the specific anticancer agent in strawberries is, since all fruits contain myriad vitamins, minerals, and phytochemicals, not to mention the thousands of ways those substances interact with each other.

★ ★

Thankfully, the American Cancer Society recognized the dangers of this type of reductionist science by stating on its website that "many studies have shown a link between eating foods rich in vitamin C, such as fruits and vegetables, and a reduced risk of cancer. On the other hand, the few studies in which vitamin C has been given as a supplement have not shown a reduced cancer risk." In fact, there are numerous studies pointing to the fact that supplements of vitamins C and E, for example, which were thought to be magic bullets for health, might do more harm than good in pill form. This reinforces the idea that it is far better for these vitamins to be ingested as part of an overall healthful diet in the form of whole foods.

Macro approaches to health like those inherent in the Mediterranean diet (low in sugar and high in vegetables, olive oil, wholesome grains, and whole fruits), or the diet and lifestyle recommendations outlined in Dan Buettner's book *The Blue Zones,* make this clear. Buettner isolated and analyzed cultures and regions of the world where the populations live far longer than most: Okinawa, Japan; Sardinia, Italy; Loma Linda, California; Nicoya, Costa Rica; and Ikaria, Greece. He demonstrates that the complexities of food interactions, lifestyle, and food culture matter much more than single vitamins and minerals supplied by dietary supplements used in an attempt to make up for low-quality-food intake and high-stress lives.

FRUITY-CONOMICS

Every year about 17,000 new food products are created and marketed, yet none of them is a "new" fresh fruit or vegetable. Today just 10 percent of US supermarket purchases are fruits and vegetables; if we want to raise that to 50 percent by 2020, consistent with USDA "My Plate" recommendations, we're going to have to shop and eat differently. Here's the best part: Whole fresh fruit has no added sugar at all, so it doesn't count toward our daily added-sugar intake, and there's no subsidized corn, soy, or wheat byproduct. It seems obvious to us now, but in order for us to eat more fresh fruit, farmers need to grow more. And in order for farmers to grow more, it has to make economic sense.

At the most simplistic level, domestic farmers should be able to produce apples and other fruits cheaper than factories can produce soda, bags of cookies, or little chocolate cakes full of synthetic fake cream and corn syrup. Yet, at the grocery store, prices don't seem to work that way. In the current system of agriculture policy, fruits and vegetables are considered "specialty crops" by the USDA and are not given the same subsidies that corn, soy, wheat, and cotton are. There are also more hidden benefits that fruits and vegetables are not afforded—research and development money is easier to invest in a few huge crops; mechanized harvesting systems have been developed to pick corn from the stalk, remove the husk, and thrash off the kernels, while most fruits and vegetables are harvested by hands; and the diversity of climates and soils in which varieties can

grow has made it impossible (and probably undesirable) to get the same economies of scale with fruit that are afforded to the ingredients of junk food.

Apples, native to the forests of Kazakhstan, originally found a great second
home in America: A USDA scientist cataloguing the fruit in 1904 estimated there
were more than 7,000 varietals growing in the US, and some heirloom apple spe-
cialties put the number as high as 15,000. Sadly, a recent report by Slow Food USA
estimates that 86 percent of those varietals have been lost, and most estimate that
there are 2,500 varietels grown in the US with many threatened with extinction.
Today only 11 varietals account for 90 percent of the apples sold in supermarkets,
41 percent of which are Red Delicious. And it's not just apples; the whole produce
section, from kale to kiwifruits to kumquats, takes a backseat to higher-profit
processed foods, as their genetic diversity has been discarded in favor of processors'
needs. These are needs defined by higher sugar content, longer shelf life, better
transportability, and uniformity, not sound agricultural practices and nutrition.

We need to re-center fresh whole fruits as the main source of sweetness in
our diets, and make sure the fruits we buy are helping to make the food system
better and supporting farmers and farm workers. Here's how we do that:

> Buy local when possible. Buy organic.
> Buy different varietals. And buy ugly.

Why ugly? As we're about to see, our consumption of fruits and vegetables
is hindered by more than just the food manufacturers' pushing high-sugar processed foods. It is also hindered by a staggering amount of food waste.

> Food waste is part of what makes apples cost more than cookies.
> And food waste is a big part of why higher yields are not the
> whole solution to global hunger.

In almost all regions of the world, government agencies and supermarket
chains set standards for fruit and vegetable size, shape, and general appearance
that contribute to the lack of crop diversity, as well as to misguided consumer
expectations. These policies promote mono-cropping and result in massive,
unnecessary food waste. They contribute to global hunger by removing good,
wholesome food from our global food supply and in effect, function to keep the
cost of produce high. This is something we the eaters can change by altering
what we buy, what we eat, and our perceptions of what good food looks like.

FOOD WASTE:
THE ULTIMATE BAD APPLE THAT SPOILS THE BUNCH

A full 50 percent of the fresh fruit and vegetables grown and supplied to the European market and 40 percent here in America ends up as waste, and not necessarily because that produce is overripe or rotten. Food waste starts with crops left to rot hanging on the vines, to food damaged during growing and picking, to food thrown away by contract buyers and supermarkets for not meeting preset standards. Fruits and vegetables are rejected for their size, color, shape, and small imperfections by growers, processors, and retailers alike. Our system of pushing yields to "feed the world" and then accepting waste by throwing away perfectly good food is a travesty in a world where almost a billion people are hungry and more than a billion more are overweight, as our landfills overflow with the healthiest food we produce—food that has been deemed "subpar" by a population consuming Twinkies and Froot Loops.

Waste is embedded in the food system at every step up and down the supply chain. In the US, there are about 3,900 calories available for every citizen, but in 2009, for example, the average American ate, on average, 2,594 calories per day (and most of us need only 2,000). Essentially, we built into the modern food supply an acceptable level of waste of at least 35 percent.

According to Tristram Stuart, a global advocate for ending food waste and the author of *Waste: Uncovering the Global Food Scandal,* the 40 million tons of food wasted in the US every year would be enough to feed the nearly 1 billion around the world who are hungry, and the water used to grow all the discarded crops around the world would be enough water to serve the domestic needs of the global population expected in 2050: 9 billion people. This waste begins with the harvest and ends on our plates. He's talking about the two end pieces of every loaf of bread that sandwich shops and restaurants discard every single day, and about acres of crops that "aren't the right size" for the contract grower, largely because of standards that often relate to appearance, not safety or nutrition.

One-third of all produce harvests don't meet supermarket standards.

And he's also talking about the 40 to 60 percent of European fish that are thrown back into the ocean dead, rejected by fisherman who have exceeded quotas, and/or who caught "the wrong fish" in their nets.

The EU recently loosened what were referred to as the "straight banana rules," which are largely standards of "quality" based on appearance, not nutrition.

These rules reject overly curved cucumbers, knobby carrots, imperfect bananas, and anything unconventional in size or appearance. In his September 2012 TED talk, Stuart showed slides of bins of discarded cooked food from supermarkets; massive mounds of oranges in California citrus fields headed for Dumpsters; acres of spinach rejected and left unharvested; tons of potatoes in Kent, England, that didn't meet the standards of buyers because they were too "oddly shaped" and were left to rot, or be plowed under, even as almost 1 billion people go hungry. He displayed towering mounds of "unacceptable" yet delicious-looking bananas piled up in Ecuador, a country whose people face staggering hunger.

We have developed a global standard of uniformity that is reinforced by mono-cropping and mono-expectations, as we falsely shape consumers' impressions of what fruits and vegetables should look like. These standards appear to be closer to the plastic produce in a child's play kitchen than anything that actually exists in nature. The funny shape, the different color, the crops and varietals that often deliver better nutrition and flavor and hardier, disease-resistant genetic stock have been discarded for bizarre standards of uniformity. Within the limited, mono-cropped varietals we grow and sell, there can be no individuality. Look at the produce in your supermarket; the mounds of apples and bunches of bananas are shockingly uniform in appearance. In the EU, those produce-shape regulations were absurdly exacting, stating that *cucumbers must not have a curvature of more than 10 percent.* If they exceeded this, they weren't even sold as second-class produce; farmers just threw them away.

An underground movement of self-proclaimed "freegans"(who are generally more outraged than broke), Dumpster dive in protest of food waste by retrieving the discarded food from supermarkets, green grocers, and even restaurants to bring home to eat. And we're not talking rotting garbage here: We're talking bins of organic lettuces from high-end supermarkets, day-old bread from bakeries, boxes of just-expired cereal, and fruit that is mildly bruised. Trader Joe's former president Doug Rauch is opening a new model of a discounted grocery store and restaurant based on selling meals and whole foods that are still perfectly healthy, but fall outside the expiration dates or expected appearance for conventional use. While some people are appalled by freegans and this approach to food waste, others applaud these radical efforts.

Due to increased pressure from activists, the media, and finally the now-aware public, the EU regulation was repealed in 2008. Going further, along with South Korea and Taiwan, the EU has created a system of fines for sending good food to landfills. Today, nudged by consumers in the UK and Germany, as well as smart business thinking, grocery stores are getting behind ugly or "wonky fruit and veg" campaigns and selling those foods at a discount instead of leaving healthy food in farmers' fields or trash dumpsters.

★ ★

The facts surrounding food waste poke a gaping hole in the food and agriculture science community's obsession with higher yields and producing more food. The inconvenient truth that as much as 40 to 50 percent of the food grown in the world today ends up *not feeding anyone* is one of the critical data points that has been overlooked and underfunded in food and agriculture research, which is instead focused on altering plant genetics and using more chemicals in order to grow more and more of the same few foods, even as the Dumpsters overflow with tons of uneaten calories and nutrients. And that waste extends beyond the food. There is the land, the labor, the water, the soil depletion, the chemical pollution—we lose on all counts when we dump good food.

> We the eaters need to demand a more efficient system
> of production, and a more efficient marketplace.

Food waste in the developing world takes on an even sadder hue. Postharvest losses due to poor storage, lack of refrigeration, poor roads and transportation, or a lack of hands to harvest the fields during that precious ripeness window means that in the developing hungry world, close to 40 percent of food goes uneaten as well. Those bananas piled sky-high in Ecuador are an incomprehensible level of food waste in a country, and a world, with such pervasive hunger and food insecurity.

Yet with all of the jaw-dropping statistics surrounding food waste, we may be missing the worst offense. The biggest travesty may not be the mounds of oranges, potatoes, and spinach that don't meet the standards of appearance or size and are tragically lost to food waste. We can add to those waste numbers a lot of the foods *we are eating.*

> As we overproduce cheap meat and dairy and grow monocultures
> of wheat and corn and soy to manufacture low-nutrition,
> added-sugar junk food that is making the world sick and degrading
> the planet, we are creating the largest food waste stream of all—
> what is not directly wasted is going straight to our waists.

BANANA REPUBLICS AND CROP DIVERSITY

Today a single varietal of banana, the Cavendish, is grown in massive mono-crop farms in Latin America and makes up 99 percent of the banana export market. It is most likely the only banana many of us have ever eaten, even though there are more than 1,000 varietals of banana grown as staple foods across Africa. This once-rare tropical fruit, which is only grown thousands of miles from America and Europe, is both cheaper than most apples grown here at home and eaten as often in America as all apples and oranges combined. Just as with other cheap, mono-cropped foods, two American companies, Dole and Chiquita, control more than half the global banana trade. Goldfinger, Red Dacca, Blue Java, and Karat (the Karat has 100 times the beta-carotene as the Cavendish), are just a few of the bananas we could be eating if our systems of food production supported variety.

Our Western obsession with cheap and easy, even in healthy foods like bananas, causes unseen misery for the people who grow the cheap and make the easy. Top banana-exporting countries include Ecuador (which provides 30 percent of all bananas globally), Costa Rica, and Colombia, followed by Guatemala, Honduras, and Panama. Sadly, like in most banana republics, the inequitable distribution of land and oppressive social and economic characteristics of these countries mean that most Ecuadorians are not seeing the financial boon of their country's global market dominance of this key food staple around the world.

According to the UN World Food Program, the malnutrition rate in Ecuador is roughly 26 percent, and is estimated to be as high as 92 percent in children under 5 in rural indigenous areas, where more than 62 percent of these children also suffer from anemia. As is now common in the hungry countries of the developing world, there is also crippling weight gain—more than 52 percent of women in Ecuador are overweight. In fact, besides the ignorant rigidity of our mono-crop agriculture systems that provide growers with the scale they need to keep bananas priced under a dollar a pound and our policies of legislated food waste, the only thing that could make things worse for the many banana-dependent populations of Latin America is if there were no bananas to sell at all.

And that is exactly the future they may be facing.

★ ★

What we didn't learn from the Irish potato famine, we may end up learning from the Cavendish banana. Since both the potato and the banana propagate by cloning, both produce fruits that are genetically identical to the parent, which leaves them highly susceptible to being wiped out by a single disease. The Cavendish banana, a fruit varietal bred to meet the standards of uniformity dictated by government agencies, grocers, and eaters, is mostly straight, plentiful, long lasting, and, of course, cheap. And it may now be headed for extinction.

In the 1950s, a single fungal disease called Panama disease (Tropical Race 1) virtually wiped out the global banana crop. The dominant species at the time was called Gros Michel. Today a sister fungus called Tropical Race 4 is affecting the roots of the Cavendish, which became the cultivar exported to most of the world when we lost the Gros Michel. The Cavendish banana was resistant to the original fungus, but is susceptible to the new strain. Sadly, many of the people in Africa, Southeast Asia, and Latin America whose diets and national economies are dependent on the crop are about to learn what a mistake they made by planting a single varietal of a crop. We the Western eaters need to have the nutritional foresight to see that we have been disserved by the mono-cropping, high-waste model our food systems have engineered for fruits and vegetables. And we need to seek out diversity beyond the supermarket standards for produce by supporting small farmers who are trying to produce variety as a means to building a better genetic foundation for our food systems, better nutrition for eaters, and more financial stability and control for themselves as growers.

SLAVES FOR CHOCOLATE

With all this talk of sugar and sweets, we can't forget about chocolate. Close to three-quarters of the world's cocoa beans are grown on small farms in West Africa, and the bulk of them are from Ivory Coast. UNICEF reports that hundreds of thousands of very young children work under deplorable conditions, many as slaves, to provide the multinational chocolate companies with cheap chocolate for processing. Advocates for industry reform recommend buying no cocoa beans from Ivory Coast, and recommend instead buying cocoa beans from the South and Central American organic cocoa bean growers who do not employ child labor. Nestlé, Hershey, and the Italian maker of Nutella, Ferrero Rocher, pledged to eradicate child labor from their supply chains by 2020. *We the eaters should let them know that is not soon enough.* The Food Empowerment Project provides a list on its website of companies that use only ethically sourced chocolate, a list that includes Whole Foods 365 Dark Chocolate, Justin's Nut Butter, and Newman's Own, to name a few. Theo Chocolate is producing fair trade organic chocolate in Seattle that it buys direct from farmers, and Kopali Organics is pushing eaters to enjoy chocolate-covered fruit while supporting the triple bottom line of people, planet, and profit. These are the types of small changes that we the eaters can employ to effect change in our health and the health of the world around us.

Once again, it isn't the foods per se that are inherently problematic. A serving of whole fruit, a small piece of dark chocolate, or even whole grain desserts are not dietary pitfalls in and of themselves. As with so many other foods discussed in this book, it is the systems that now surround these foods that degrade their quality, the land they are grown on, the environment in which we live, the farmers who produce them, and, ultimately, the health of those who eat them. Not surprisingly, the big cocoa exporters also happen to be some of the big corn exporters—namely, Archer Daniels Midland and Cargill.

By supporting those new companies and farmers that produce treats that treat the world better and demanding sweetness in a more natural and nutritious way, we the eaters can help create *real* choice in the marketplace and support the entrepreneurs pushing the system forward.

Chocolate can help sum up the problem with the global food system in two sentences:

> Chocolate can be a fair trade, environmentally friendly, antioxidant-rich treat in the form of a piece of high-quality, ethically sourced, 100 percent dark chocolate.
> Or chocolate can be an HFCS- and palm oil–infused, environmentally degrading piece of processed candy made from cocoa beans harvested by child slaves.

We the eaters, although we often don't realize it, actually get to choose which of those two chocolate options we buy and eat. This is the metric we should use for as much of the food we eat as possible, as we seek out the better version of all foods that have been diminished by our global food production systems.

THE NEXT "APPLE": OLD-SCHOOL SOLUTIONS MEET NEW TECHNOLOGY

Right in step with—and often in the same communities as—tech start-ups, a new generation of eaters is creating the farms, brands, markets, and recipes for the future of agriculture entrepreneurship. One high-tech group of statisticians at Ghent University and Wageningen University are hoping to help reduce food waste as part of a European research project called Veg-i-Trade. They are working out statistical models to help growers, processors, transporters, and sellers more efficiently handle the seed-to-mouth supply chain in order to prevent high levels of food waste.

Meanwhile, a great young start-up called FenuGreen makes a product called Fresh Paper, which is infused with the herb fenugreek—once used by the founder's grandmother to preserve fresh foods—to keep produce fresh two to four times longer, curtailing food waste at home. One Silicon Valley area farm— Pie Ranch, so named for the property's shape and because the farm grows all the ingredients needed for a pie: wheat, butter, eggs, and apples, pumpkins, strawberries—runs a great educational and productive farm, but is working to bring fresh produce to companies like Google through an innovative farm-to-company CSA. And many, many other young farmers are getting into specialty fruit and vegetable crops, farmers' markets, and direct sales.

In 2011 the US secretary of agriculture, Tom Vilsak, said we would need 100,000 new farmers to provide for the food needs of a growing nation. If that's not an economic opportunity, I really don't know what is! The organic food sector has been growing at about 10 percent per year for the past few years, and creating jobs, according to the Rodale Institute, at "four times the national average." And in a counterintuitive, retro-hipster sort of way, young people in and near cities and in rural communities are heading "back to the land."

In December 2008, I attended the first Young Farmers Conference at the Stone Barns Center for Food and Agriculture in Pocantico Hills, New York. At a time when I was starting to wonder about the best way to effect change in the global food system, even as FEED was providing funding for school meals for thousands (and soon, millions) of children around the world, the conference connected me to a whole new constellation of people with their hands literally in the dirt. I learned there that even though the average US farmer today is 57 years old, the average organic farmer is 34. And consistent with movements toward more socially conscious business in other sectors (which FEED helped pioneer in fashion), the National Young Farmers Coalition includes in its list of values its aim to maintain independent family farms, practice sustainability and fair labor, and encourage diversity. The nexus for the coalition is a group of young people who wanted to go into agriculture for a living, but found the existing system has been structured to make accessing land and capital virtually impossible for new farmers.

To help young people who are not actually from farm families get on the ground to learn, places like Stone Barns and Quail Hill Farm in New York, the

Michael Fields Agricultural Institute in Wisconsin, and Pie Ranch in California offer training and apprenticeship programs, and the World Wide Opportunities on Organic Farms (WWOOF) network has offered people short to long farm-work stays since its founding in the UK in 1971. WWOOF's US website lists 1,800 organic farms in all 50 states in America that will host a person for short-time work. At the Young Farmers Conference, I learned that young people in and around New York City, as well as in rural Pennsylvania and coastal Maine, were digging around to find loans and land to use, growing for community-supported agriculture (CSA) programs and high-end restaurants, and building a system of social networks and data right along with old-fashioned seed sharing, all of which are helping to infuse the profession with new energy and, more importantly, hope.

★ ★

Young farmers today see themselves as entrepreneurs, and the linkages are deep and wide between start-up farmers and tech mavens. Organizations such as the National Grange, through its website NationalGrange.org, are gathering farmers online and giving them tools and resources. For the past 30 years, all too often the local USDA Cooperative Extension offices have focused on helping only big commodity farmers, so entrepreneurial farmers need these online sources to access information. The National Young Farmers Coalition has utilized innovations from both new media and the tech start-up world; they have produced a documentary film, *The Greenhorns,* about the need to support young farmers; and they have a regular Farm Hack meeting series to help spur open-source agricultural technologies (often a huge barrier to entry is getting decent and working farm implements) and sharing ideas for making farmers more sustainable and productive. Farm Hack is like the new-school barn raising, except you bring your laptop and possibly a 3-D printer instead of your logging saw to participate in a community that is developing and sharing all sorts of agricultural design ideas.

This new generation of farmers is cropping up not just in the US, but also in countries around the world, and new ways to bring healthy fruits and vegetables to increasingly overweight populations are helping to restore both rural and urban livelihoods and health. In 2011, at the World Food Prize event in Des Moines, Iowa, I met a peasant woman farmer from Colombia amid the Big Ag and Big Aid bureaucrats. Her name was Nelly Velandia, and she had come to share her story of being a part of the Bogotá Farmers Markets, a joint venture by Oxfam International and the Colombian government. This program, just like farmers' markets in the US, allows urban dwellers to access fresh and healthy produce, but also helps keep small farmers farming. Eighty percent of Colombian farms are less than 3 acres, and in order to keep them going and growing fruits and vegetables (and not coca or other lucrative drug crops), they need smart urban–rural links. Colombia has a chance to keep small farmers on the land, growing good food for local and global markets, and keeping much of its agricultural land organic.

The tech and entrepreneurial space is also playing a role in the growth and success of farmers around the world. Information communication technologies (ICTs) are revolutionizing how farmers are trained and connect to markets. Digital Green in India uses transportable projectors to train 1,650,000 farmers in best practices and how to grow new crops, and Esoko in Ghana is a mobile platform that connects rural farmers to real time price information so they can sell their crops for the highest return at market. Tractors for Peace gets used tractor donations from the Midwest to Ghana; Open Source Ecology has what it calls a Global Village Construction Set, which is "an open technological platform that allows for the easy fabrication of the 50 different industrial machines that it takes to build a small civilization with modern comforts."

In other words, you can use its designs and instructions to locally build and maintain machines like a hay baler, a dairy milker, a microtractor, and a rototiller. As founder Marcin Jakubowski said in his 2011 TED talk, "it's kind of a civilization starter kit."

As for the rest of us, we just have to support these young farmers by eating well.

GETTING OUT OF THE STICKY BUN SITUATION

The good news is that the solution is just as sweet and delicious as the problem. If we eat nutritious and diverse fruits, sourced sustainably from farmers close to home, we can reposition the sweets in our diet as sources of essential nutrition and help promote the production of healthy foods around the world. Our cover photo of a delicious apple-cherry pie—the type you might enjoy at your backyard barbecue—showcases tart cherries as it illustrates an awesome story of how fruit can mean health to a whole community. Almost three-quarters of all US tart cherries, the ones that become pies and jam with the addition of a little honey, are grown in the Traverse City, Michigan, area. Cherry farmers and their new neighbors, local wineries and microbreweries, have helped maintain the beauty of the region as they reinvigorate the local economy. The area has attracted a slew of environmental start-ups and now has a strong agro-tourism sector. These young entrepreneurs are creating a high demand for CSAs, along with great local restaurants and coffee shops, and have ensured that the local population has increased in the past 10 years even as the rest of Michigan's has declined.

A world away, in the beautiful countryside of Ethiopia, another type of natural sweetness is leading to economic growth as well. Ethiopia is Africa's largest producer of honey, and beekeeping supports nearly 2 million people. New programs like women's cooperative farming groups and training from international organizations like Oxfam and Concern Worldwide are helping to ensure long-term economic growth and greater gender equality in agriculture—especially since women in Ethiopia usually don't own land, and you don't have to be a landowner to keep bees. Promoting the local honey economy is also helping Ethiopia maintain an essential part of its dietary culture, giving people an economic incentive to preserve the forests and fields that host bees, and helping supplement the honey markets of the US, Europe, and South America, where bees are suffering from colony collapse disorder. Closer to home, when we buy local honey at the farmers' market or plant some mint or sunflowers, we are helping to protect bees in a way that in turn will help our local farmers grow more food.

By combining the natural sweet treats of pesticide-free organic fruit and local honey, we can make a delicious dessert for our barbecue. Unlike the packaged, processed toothache-sweet pastry that would be easy to grab in your supermarket center aisles, we the eaters can use our sweet tooths to reposition a healthier food system for the whole planet. Better fruits and natural fair-trade sweeteners mean better agriculture and put built-in economic limitations on our sugar intake. By making this sweet fix "just dessert," we are also promoting a healthier, longer life for the family and friends we invite to our tables.

★ 8 ★

Reset the Table and *Really* Change Dinner

Beyond the Corn, the Meat, the Dairy, the Wheat, and the Sugar Is That Single Healthful Meal That Changes Everything

EATERS HAVE ALWAYS evolved with their food supplies. As soon as humans began to experiment with the technology and systems called agriculture about 10,000 years ago, our eating habits started to change. We learned to make bread and feed and care for animals so they stayed nearby, and we chose the seeds of tastier varieties of plants to save and plant again. We developed recipes and cuisines and saw our species become healthier and live longer—and we learned from our parents and tribes what to eat. From agriculture and recipes came food cultures and even whole societies and empires built on salt (the root of the word "salary") and spices and cod and cotton.

We learned to exploit the ability of plants to use sunlight and rain from the sky and soil from below to nourish themselves so they grow and become our food. The incredible and simple blade of grass makes its own food and then becomes food for herbivores that carnivores and omnivores like us eat. Along the way, there is energy lost from the sun, to the plant, to the animal, to the human, so we've always needed to have more plants than animals and more plants and animals than people. To make sure we've got enough plants and animals to eat, we've employed technologies to improve yields and created complex markets and incentives. We the eaters can't do the incredible and simple thing a blade of grass does and produce food from sunlight ourselves, but we can build food systems that produce food for us.

★ ★

All along the way, we've worried that Thomas Malthus just might be right. Maybe population growth *will* exceed our ability to feed the world. He saw what was coming, and he knew, even in the 1700s, that in order for us to survive, we, the apex predators, would have to outsmart, outpace, and outthink population growth. And so as our population continued to grow, we demanded that the systems of food production be made more productive; we demanded that they overproduce because we overproduced. We had to, because there were too many hungry people and, so it seemed, not enough food.

Why accept small yields when we can push them beyond what had ever been imagined? Two times, three times, ten times the yields for corn and wheat and milk. With a focus on production and higher yields, we didn't consider that, just maybe, we already produced enough food—food that is lost to waste and inefficiency.

> Between 1 and 2 billion metric tons of food produced
> in the world goes to waste every year. That's one-third to
> one-half of what we produce.

Think of the man-hours and the unnecessary petrochemicals, water, and money it takes to produce that wasted food, and the unnecessary environmental damage that results from it. And then think of the hungry and the food insecure who might be better served if we focused more on nutrition-per-acre *efficiency* than on calorie-per-acre *yield*. Why don't we shift the focus from growing *so much food* and think about growing *more diverse and better food,* and growing it in places and ways that are accessible to all eaters. And while we're at it, why not ask if we are growing too much of the *wrong* foods, or if there are better ways, beyond the ways we have already taken, to harness the sun to make food that feeds and nourishes more people?

We built food systems with epic expectations. We structured them around smart science, and then not-so-smart science. After all, a calorie is a calorie. Or so we thought. We erroneously believed it didn't matter what that calorie was made of. And of course, we structured all of these advances around profit. Profit gives incentives for great inventions, hard work, and innovation. It motivates efficiencies and scale. But it can also corrupt, and embed us in systems that may not be working.

In the process of cultivating and industrializing, we forgot what mattered about food. This could have been a reasonable approach if what we sacrificed was a *little* nutrition, and a *little* health, and a *little* of the environment as we sought to gain *a lot* and feed the hungry of the world. But despite all this effort, all this goodwill, all this science, and all this profit, there are *still* almost 850 million hungry people in the world, and 30 percent of the global population are micronutrient deficient. And now, these nearly 2 billion people who are not fed well *enough* have been joined by a billion and a half who are overweight, many of whom are rapidly stampeding toward obesity and other diseases.

Because we lost sight of what the real goal should be:
feeding the world well.

We created hybrid plants, higher yields, bigger fruit, larger grain, and pest-resistant crops. We produced chemical fertilizers to try to replenish the soil those high yields depleted. We manipulated DNA and fractured the norms of nature by crossbreeding species of plants and animals that could never crossbreed themselves as we engineered seeds that could kill the weeds and pests that interfered with their growth. In the process, we created bigger pests and bigger weeds, and now we need more powerful pesticides. And on we march, fooled by the flavorful fruits of the flawed system.

We created legislation to push farmers to grow more calories. We expanded cropland as we diverted rivers toward the arid and deforested the lush. Along the way, we built, automated, and replicated agribusiness models, factory farms, and algorithmic weather predictors; we computerized and built sophisticated financial structures around farming, food production, and distribution and spent billions on food aid for the hungry, who stayed hungry as we ourselves became increasingly overweight.

We didn't mean to, but we created a food-aid system for the developing world that often crushes their local agriculture and small farmers, even contributing to and lengthening conflicts. Our food systems got so big that we lost sight of all things small, like subsistence farmers, vibrant soil, hungry children, and wholesome, nutritious food.

Yet if we stopped eating bad food long enough to look around, we might have seen what was wrong, and what was coming. We might have noticed that there are nearly the same number of hungry people as there were before, and now, standing side by side with those hungry are the rising billion and a half of overweight and increasingly obese—a lot of them children. *Our children.*

We find ourselves captive in a food system that clearly isn't working, where even those who know enough to want out can't find a way. An alarming number of small farmers in India who listened to our promises and adopted our technology (which helped some succeed but failed many) to grow pesticide-coated cotton for our fast, cheap fashion habit are still going hungry. And 3,000 Indian children are still dying from hunger every day as we wait in lines in big-box supermarkets and at fast food drive-thru restaurants clutching coupons for a dollar off a "value" meal, slowly ending our lives and cutting our kids' lives short, too.

We're told we have options. We're told that our rising weight and declining health are *our fault* because of the way we *choose* to eat.

So we make a different choice. As we are sitting in that line at a drive-thru window deciding whether we should supersize a meal that just might kill us if we were to eat it every day, we acknowledge that we have the option to change our minds, pull away, and change another input in this system of energy exchange. We can decide to improve our diets, cook for ourselves, and eat better. So we drive to the supermarket, where we buy a perfectly round tomato that was picked by an underpaid laborer who can't afford to eat, a tomato that required so many chemicals to produce that we polluted the groundwater hundreds of miles away just to grow it.

It doesn't even taste like a tomato, but we don't know that because we never ate a tomato with a name like Brandywine or Big Rainbow, grown without chemicals and picked fresh from the vine, its flesh still warm from the sun. Tomatoes like that aren't suited for large production farms or tractor-trailer transport, and would bruise too easily for the big, stackable boxes needed to stock the mounds of perfectly uniform fruit preferred by super-stores. Even still, we bring our tomato home, along with some low-nutrition ground beef sourced from hundreds of animals in concentrated animal feeding operations (CAFOs) that were cornfed and pumped full of antibiotics, all the while standing knee deep in their own manure, manure that pollutes the aquifers we all need to survive. These animals likely were slaughtered and processed by another group of exploited, underpaid workers whose often illegal immigration status and tenuous economic situations greatly affect the communities where they live and work—communities we don't really see because they're nowhere near where we live. We fry the meat, slice the tomato, and put it all between a roll baked from hybrid wheat that just might be messing with our metabolism and is likely loaded with HFCS. HFCS that was made from genetically engineered corn classified by the FDA as a pesticide, subsidized by that same government, and sold so cheaply it wreaks havoc on the agricultural landscape and economies of countries thousands of miles away that we've never visited, but where we've been told children can find a Coke more readily than a glass of clean water. Countries where children die every day from complications that arise from stunted growth and malnutrition, even though they live in communities where they used to grow their own food before a bunch of politicians wielding acronyms like NAFTA and CAFTA got involved.

We slap some fake mayonnaise on the roll, not noticing it is likely made with GM soybeans and HFCS, and top it off with ketchup, made with more of those tomatoes and sweetened with more HFCS, then we pour ourselves bottled green tea to go with our hamburger and tomato sandwich, believing it to be so much healthier than the fast food meal and the soda we decided to drive away from. But that "green tea" is made by one of those soda companies, and if we read the label, we would see it is loaded with sugar and has no real antioxidants. No omnivore was supposed to consume the amount of sugar in these large drinks, let alone consume it in such large quantities day after day after day.

While eating what we have served ourselves, we didn't realize that it's all way more than a serving size—information that is buried on the side of a supersized package. We hardly noticed that our plates and cups, and the bottles and jars and bags that we buy our food in, got so big. And we never suspected that there was something about all that sugar, and the always-accompanying salt and fat, that would lead us to eat and drink more than we should. As we eat our lunch, we innocently think we've made a step in the right direction—and also earnestly believe we sent our kids off to school in the morning well fed, too.

After serving them bowls of cereal with names sounding more like cartoons or cookies than breakfast food, we tried to ignore the fact that some of these cereals are more than 50 percent sugar by concentrating on the banners across the front that say things like "good source of vitamin D" or "whole grain" as we poured fat-free milk into their bowls. It caught our eye that on the milk carton there was an idyllic picture of a cow grazing in a pasture, and nowhere did it say this milk was produced by animals with infected udders made sick by overmilking, fed the same corn and antibiotic–hormone mix that will be present in our meat later that day. We were just looking at the cow and the green pasture, and thinking how great it is to have such an abundance of food in this country.

We feel pretty good about the fact that we're sending the kids off with homemade lunches instead of subjecting them to the low-nutrition slop they serve in the school cafeteria or those premade Lunchables they beg us for every time we bring them to the supermarket.[1]

We know better than *that*.

The lunch we made for our kids, lovingly and with good intentions, is composed of nutritionally stripped white bread, processed with HFCS and preservatives so it stays "soft and fresh," just like the label promises it will, for weeks. One of those preservatives happens to be something called azodicarbonamide, a blowing agent (whatever that is) used in the rubber and plastics industry. You get thrown in jail if you're caught using it in Singapore, and it is illegal as a food additive in Europe and Australia, but we assume we have the USDA and the FDA making sure our food is safe. I mean, this *is* the United States of America, and we don't put blowing agents used by the rubber industry in our bread. *Do we?*

Onto that bread we spread some of that shelf-stable peanut butter loaded with added sugar and hydrogenated oils that all the "choosy mothers" choose, along with some jelly that has no fruit in it at all. We don't know that, because it certainly looks like real fruit, even though it's just a whole lot more HFCS along with some plain old regular corn syrup and some fruit juice concentrate. Silly us for thinking someone might have actually thrown a whole grape or two into that bottle full of sugar.

We tossed boxes of chocolate milk into the lunch bags, not realizing just how much added sugar the milk has, because, once again, we're feeling pretty good since the milk is fat-free, and no good parent would serve a child whole milk these days. We don't bother anymore with the carrot sticks or slices of apple; the kids told us point-blank they throw them in the trash. Turns out fruits and veggies don't fare very well against the artificially cheap Cheetos and chocolate cream Twinkies in the sugar-amped, black-market barter-exchange system of school cafeterias. But we don't realize just how much sugar they're eating and we toss in a few cookies. And we don't consider that there's a pretty good chance it's

---

1   The Lunchables Uploaded Ultimate Deep Dish Pizza with pepperoni also includes Kool-aid Tropical Punch, Cheez-its, and a Fruit Roll-up, and it doesn't sound too healthy. So I checked the www.lunchablesparents.com Web site, but it didn't list the nutrition facts or ingredients; it only noted that it's a "good source" of calcium, vitamin C, iron, and protein.

someone's birthday today, and at least one of our kids will be eating a sugary sweet (or two) that afternoon, because in a classroom of 30 students, there's bound to be a Dunkin' Donuts or cupcake birthday party roughly every 6 days.

We do all of this, all the while feeling pretty good about ourselves for feeding our families so well. We don't recognize how helpless and confused and duped we are, even as we try to do the right thing. We're not even sure what good food is anymore for the simple reason that what used to be *good, whole food* has been reengineered into *bad, processed food* right under our noses, and we didn't even notice. How could we? This bad food comes packaged with a whole lot of very sophisticated marketing and food science that works against the consumer and against our health, because it is cloaked in deception and geared toward profit at any cost. Just like the corn-fed cattle dying of organ failure while standing knee deep in manure, we are victims of this food system, too. We the eaters are not a whole lot different from the CAFO cattle being fattened up for the slaughter; we're eating a lot of the same corn they are. It's in our meat, bread, jelly, ketchup, cereal, and milk. In fact, corn is in every single food item in the menu above except the tomato. We've all been treated by the system with the same disregard as a 6-month-old calf without long to live was, and now we are facing the possibility of a truncated life pumped up with medication that won't delay our dispatch date as much as we'd like either.

★ ★

It is hard for we the eaters to remember about systems, food chains, and photosynthesis. It's hard to remember that food begins with the sun beating down on a blade of grass, or fescue, or clover, and transpires in a complex web of energy exchanges that end in a feedlot, a supermarket, a fast food restaurant, and, ultimately, a doctor's office. We don't see the oppressed immigrant workers in the slaughterhouses, or the growing fields across the ocean (or even around the corner). We don't know the plight of the farmers in Mexico and the rest of the developing world facing the complexities of NAFTA and competing with our corn–soy blend and the brawn of big agribusiness companies like Monsanto, or understand how the high costs of seeds and fertilizers can be too high to handle even if, in theory, they will produce higher yields. We don't see the farmers who lose their farms, or the families who lose their fathers who have to migrate *here* to work illegally in a bacon factory, as a citrus picker, or in a slaughterhouse to send money back *there* so their children can eat, because the small farmers in countries that used to grow food for themselves can't farm anymore for reasons that are too complicated for even an economist to decipher. We don't see the overweight teen-agers in Central America or Africa who started their lives suffering from wasting and stunted growth and will end with diabetes and obesity, and who at no single moment in their lives will actually be *fed well.* And we might chalk up the obesity epidemic in America to too much self-indulgence, too much fast food for a slow life in the Western world of affluence, coupled with long stints seated in cars and in front of TVs and computers. But lately it's been getting harder to blame it all on that, when we are now seeing *obese infants and toddlers.* And it's getting harder to keep blaming ourselves as individuals when we are witnessing the same dra-matic rise in obesity all around the world as well, even in places where people might have TVs but no electricity to turn them on, and certainly no cars. That alone should make us start thinking that the problem is bigger than our high-tech sedentary lives and poor individual choices.

★ ★

But it just might be those individual choices that will change the system that makes it so hard for so many of us to be healthy. I remember all of this when I am at a food conference in Switzerland, looking at the pastries and soft drinks on the conference table and the intimidating group of CEOs and food industry lead-ers around it. Those CEOs are driven to protect and promote the status quo of the big companies they are minding and the agricultural policies and systems that their industries helped craft. These are generally good people, motivated by their companies' profits, with boards of directors, shareholders, market shares, policy positions, and revenue gains to protect, and often also motivated by the long-standing belief that what they are doing to solve hunger and obesity would work if we just kept doing it longer.

I, on the other hand, am there as an advocate for we the eaters (while trying to ignore the pastries even though they are the only option for breakfast): the child in Guatemala with stunted growth; the obese teenager in Nova Scotia heading to Dairy Queen to hang out with friends; the *matoke* farmer in Ruhiira deciding which bananas to eat and which to sell, and the American working mom thinking how easy and cheap, albeit unhealthy, it would be to hit the fast food drive-through window with the kids for the third time this week. I am sitting in the conference room thinking about the axiom that got me into food policy work in the first place—that *a hungry man is an angry man;* and a hungry child, a *really* hungry child, doesn't want to hear about investments and yields, or input costs and trade agreements. It made me think that instead of just *talking* about new ideas to feed the world, we need to *eat* new ideas to feed the world.

★ ★

Just like the first law of thermodynamics, which states that energy can neither be created nor destroyed, that it just transforms in a constant shape-shifting dance of joules and carbon and kilocalories, our collective consumer dollars could be channeled away from bad food and toward good food, away from bad food policy and toward good food policy, away from bad health and toward good health and good food systems that will feed all of us *well*. That can change *everything*.

Redistributing our consumer food dollars and reframing the way we think about food gives us the power to reset our tables, change our dinner and our health, as it impacts jobs, economic development, education, food policy, crop diversity, pollution, water quality, human rights, animal welfare, human dignity, the strength of our communities, and our families as it increases global stability and harmony.

In the past few decades, a food system based on cheapness and convenience has pushed us to get out of the kitchen and have time for "more important" pursuits. But our health, our kids' health, and that of our communities and the world *are* the most important pursuits, and it's time we re-created a food system that supports that view. Getting back to our kitchens means reframing how we view cooking as power, learning new tasks, and sharing the burden with our family and friends. Instead of feeling tied to the banality of kitchen drudgery (like our grandmothers and many women have felt for generations),

> the fridge and pantry can become our new arsenal, the kitchen table our base of operations, as we regain control of the food we consume and the systems we invest in.

But changing dinner will mean more than just shifting our dollars from the bad fast food of restaurants to the bad fast food of supermarkets. It requires a new way of buying food, new technologies to connect eaters to farmers, and new thinking on how we convene with our favorite people around the table. We need to invest our dollars into a whole new system. If we can take back the dinner table, then we have the power to not only change dinner, but also change the world. Here's how.

CONCLUSION

Action Steps:
30 Food Shifts to Better Health and a Better World

WHEN YOU LOOK back to try to decipher where we went wrong with food, a number of key events emerge, many of which occurred around the year 1980. Obesity rates began to rise; US policy shifted away from international agricultural aid toward food aid; the US Supreme Court allowed seeds to be patented; fast food spending increased exponentially at home and many countries around the world; multinational agriculture and food companies consolidated, funneling control of our food into fewer hands. The global Cola Wars—kicked off in the late 1970s with the "Pepsi Challenge," boosted by the shift in the US to cheaper HFCS in 1984, and the continuing advertising and marketing skirmishes in almost every corner of the globe—have made both soda giants winners, with we the eaters (and drinkers) everywhere as the casualties.

To be fair, in the past 30 years, we have also made some progress in alleviating hunger around the world. But it's not nearly enough. And now, added to the global problem of persistent hunger, we have an epidemic of global obesity—and its related cadre of chronic ills, like heart disease, diabetes, cancer, and stroke. We have sloughed it off and blamed our affluence and sedentary lives (which are certainly partial causes), but the fact that obesity has become prevalent in poor and hungry communities should be the single hair-raising data point that underscores the magnitude of the problem. We have the choice of continuing on the path we are on and scoffing at the data—or we can change direction. The reward for we the eaters who do shift our diets is that when we eat differently, from day one, we are improving our own health as we simultaneously become part of the collective force needed to re-create a healthy food system that feeds the world well too.

Many of us are already moving in the right direction. In just the few years since 2008, the number of farmers' markets in the United States has grown by roughly 60 percent, and the system of buying directly from farmers through community supported agriculture (CSA) has spread throughout the country. Although many of our current farmers are aging toward retirement, a new movement of young farmers is going back to the land and even rooftops—from Brooklyn to Beijing to Hawaii to Hyderabad—to grow fresh, local (often organic) produce. Joining this wave of new farmers in America are many military veterans, who have the work ethic and love of country to return to their home states (or head to new ones) and grow good food, benefitting both themselves and their broader communities as they engage in healthy and meaningful work. New organizations to support emerging farmers such as the Greenhorns and the Farmer Veteran Coalition, and training programs such as the Veterans Sustainable Agriculture Training program in Southern California, help returning vets learn skills and start businesses. In Kentucky, Mike Lewis, a veteran himself, pushed the state to establish a "Homegrown by Heroes" label for local produce and helps train veterans in farming as part of a program called the Growing Warriors Project.

Along with growers, food start-ups are helping us find new ways to buy food that will challenge the dominance and the power of the superstores. These include everything from gardens in schools to refrigerators in city apartment building lobbies for CSA deliveries of fresh food from regional farms. Many of the entrepreneurs and start-ups in the food and agriculture space today will be the power players tomorrow—if we the eaters support these efforts by diverting our food dollars toward change. If we want a better food system and a reverse of the trends of hunger and obesity of the past 30 years—we can start with 30 food shifts today.

1. *Eat more family dinners.*

Whatever family means to you (nuclear family, friends, roommates, or a faraway loved one on a webcam), make a point to gather people to the table to share meals—at a backyard barbecue or in your kitchen. Nearly all cultures around the world value the tradition of communal food preparation and gathering people together to eat. We can honor that with everything from heirloom recipes to rituals of prayer or giving thanks before meals. Whatever that looks like at your table, try to reestablish those habits.

There are tangible benefits if you do: A study published in the *Archives of Family Medicine* found that regular family meals were associated with adolescents eating more fruits, vegetables, and grains, and drinking less soda. The practice of eating dinner together as a family has other benefits for children: It correlates with lower drug and alcohol abuse, less depression and suicide risk, delayed sex, and even larger vocabularies. Kids who eat more often with their parents tend to get better grades in school and are more willing to try new foods. For families, it's one of the easiest things we can do to impact the lives of our children.

And the trend toward family dinner goes beyond the traditional definition of "family." Today on college campuses, more and more young people are cooking, frequenting on-campus farmers' markets, and reading publications like *College & Cook,* which features food stories from 40 campuses and reaches more than 10,000 students.

The college cooking movement is yielding a slew of new start-ups that are building on the low-tech/high-tech opportunity of next-generation homemaking. The table and, more broadly, the home have taken on a cool new centrality in the lives of so many young people, both men and women, and there is no shortage of new faces that are being defined, or are defining themselves, as "the next Martha Stewart." So be the next Martha Stewart yourself and have some people over for a dinner that will help create change.

2. Rethink the idea that healthy food costs too much.

In 2011 Americans spent $65 billion on soft drinks, $11 billion on bottled water, $7.7 billion on cereal, and $117 billion on fast food. Not to mention more than $40 billion on obesity-related health care. And if that's not enough money to channel in a more positive way, we can tap into the $17 billion we spent on video games, the $5 billion we spent on ringtones, the $2.3 billion we spent on tattoos (I'm talking to you, navy friends!), and the $310 million we dedicated to Halloween costumes for our pets. Pick any category you want and allocate your funds just a little bit differently. Most of us can afford to spend more on good food by recapturing all the money we spend on "bad food" and regularly eating out and redirecting it toward good food, and more eating in. Think of food and mealtimes as investments in physical and mental health for both you and your relationships. In both the short and long term, you can reap the benefits of spending money on good food instead of on doctor's bills, prescription meds, and bigger clothes. We the eaters have a budget for food; let's spend it better.

3. Rethink the idea that healthy food takes too much time.

Speaking of things we can spend differently, our time is one of the best and worst examples. Americans, and those around the world who are quickly adopting not only the Modern American Diet, but also our Modern American Lifestyle (MAD and MAL couldn't be more appropriate acronyms), have treated dinner preparation and eating well as chores to be outsourced. A global survey of TV viewing in 80 countries found that people spend an average of 3 hours and 10 minutes watching TV every single day. Eating in front of the TV also leads people to eat more, and eat more junk—and kids are especially susceptible. So let's really separate our time in the kitchen from our time on the couch. If we took 1 hour away from watching a cooking show, we could actually make, eat, and clean up after a really great meal.

Television isn't the only screen competing for our time. A company called eMarketer found that Americans are spending an average of 5 hours and 16 minutes consuming digital media—on computers, tablets, and smartphones—and we are watching an average of 4 hours and 30 minutes of TV. Although often we are multitasking our media forms and tweeting about our favorite shows, it makes for an insane 9 hours and 45 minutes of screen time on average every day. If only a fraction of that multitasking could include following an online recipe or listening to the news in the background while we are chopping vegetables, we could be consuming a whole lot more healthy food with our limited schedules.

4. Change your plate, and shake the system.

You might feel like one lone person, but the acts of individuals, spreading the word to families and friends, is the only thing that pushes the healthier food movement, or any movement, forward. Although this book examines a system of issues that make it difficult for eaters to access the most nutritious foods and more easily eat a healthy diet, we can and must break down the existing system and rebuild it better—first for ourselves and eventually for those who have the least power to effect change. Remember: Our consumer habits have spread fast, cheap, fat, and sweet around the world. We can spread CSAs, more rational meat eating, and heirloom grains, too. Our shopping bags are like our own personal slingshots that can be used to knock down the Goliaths of the grocery store.

Speaking of shopping bags, the lessons from the start of FEED Projects offer some of the most compelling motivation for individuals shaking the system. The power of FEED was that it shifted just a small fraction of consumer dollars from the developed world in a pointed and potent direction. Companies like FEED looked like a trend in 2007, a blip in the massive machine that is retail, but years later we see that companies big and small have adopted corporate social responsibility (CSR) programs and created their own give-back products and one-for-one programs in order to stay relevant and competitive. The system changed because the early adopters, people who could afford to buy the FEED bags that feed hungry kids, helped make it possible for many other consumers to access this type of product as it changed the retail marketplace. And our food dollars and our dinner tables represent a far greater financial force than our tote bag dollars—even though that tote bag budget funded 60 million meals in 4 years!

5. *Change your plate, and help end global hunger.*

Don't forget that our food dollars don't stop at our shores: The impact of the system built in America and the wealthy world is global. Shop for the hungry by supporting local and regional food (to ensure the economic health of our neighbors and nearby rural communities); buy fair trade (which means farmers and laborers and the environment are treated better), heritage grains (so you don't send money to seed companies pushing our food system on the rest of the world), and heirloom vegetables (which help promote crop diversity and foster a greater variety of choice). Those shifts will not only make us healthier, they will also disempower the large manufacturers making most of the processed foods that hurt us, hurt the hungry around the world, and hurt the environment.

Then do something small but dramatic: Buy two cows. Or parts of two cows, anyway. You can buy directly from a farmer for your own family a "cow share," which will bring you a more economical source of pastured meat, and another one for a poor family in the developing world, through Heifer International. Those two cows will connect your family with a local farmer who is working hard to improve our meat production system against many barriers, and with hundreds of families in another part of the world—and will make everyone healthier. Or for $25, you can join others who are loaning a subsistence-level farmer somewhere in the developing world the money to buy a cow on the microloan site Kiva.org. When your $25 is paid back (remember, it's a loan), send that same $25 to another farmer.

6. *Buy local and regional.*

Buy some locally grown, locally produced foods. It reduces your carbon footprint and reduces your health-care footprint. It also keeps your food dollars in your community, which supports your local and regional economy. Local food economies have kick-started the refurbishment of downtown areas and propelled the building of walkable, more connected communities, while increasing local land and home values and promoting area employment. Supporting local businesses is a patriotic act, and it's a smart health move to know your farmers and food producers.

Realistically, we can source much of our food from regional food sheds that include our own state or groups of neighboring states. Meat, milk, vegetables, fruits, and many grains can be produced across our diverse country, and rebuilding regional distribution is a very tangible goal for the food system of the future. Saving fuel, promoting freshness, and keeping money and jobs close by are all bolstered by the additional big-picture benefit of true food security that comes with producing our basic necessities closer to home.

7. *When you do buy global, think fair trade and low impact.*

"Fair trade" is a certification that is given to food producers who pay farmers and workers an equitable wage. Tea, coffee, chocolate, and sugar are products that can be leveraged to alleviate hunger and spur real agricultural and economic development, if we divert our dollars to small and fairly paid growers around the world and away from the multinational food companies who don't commit to fair prices or wages. Consumer spending in these categories can directly benefit (or harm) farmers and farmworkers and affect global migration patterns, hunger, and obesity. Fair pricing for imports is essential for smart global agricultural development and decent farming jobs. Since fair trade versions of sugar, chocolate, and coffee might cost a little more—as they should—it means we will eat less of them, too.

When we can't see the farms or meet the farmers who grow our food, especially foods from countries we've never been to, we still need to try to make sure the growing practices are not degrading the planet or the people. Various global certification programs—such as Fair Trade, Rainforest Alliance, Marine Stewardship Council, Quality Assurance International, and Ecocert—ensure that foods are grown sustainably and reduce the impact of chemically intensive, factory-like growing practices. When food producers pollute the air in China, chop down the Amazon for cheaper meat and soybeans, and destroy ocean ecosystems for cheap seafood in Southeast Asia, it affects the people of those regions—and it also affects us. Pollution, low wages, and unhealthy farming practices that are outsourced through our global food systems will still affect our air, water, food, and society.

8. *Embrace the idea that food equals health.*

"Let food be thy medicine and medicine be thy food."

—*Hippocrates*

Obesity in America has escalated since 1980. Today close to 70 percent of adults in America are overweight, and a staggering 31.8 percent of the population is classified as obese. When we look beyond our shores, we can also see how quickly obesity is reaching epidemic levels in developing countries: A 2014 report from the Overseas Development Institute estimated that more than 900 million adults in the developing world are overweight or obese, which means that there are twice as many obese people in poor countries as in rich ones. With extra weight comes a whole host of diseases such as diabetes, cancer, heart disease, and stroke, and a huge strain on health care systems everywhere.

As fast as pharmaceutical companies are developing drugs to help with the symptoms of overconsumption, food and beverage companies are coming out with "new" foods containing novel combinations of the same old sugar, fat, and salt that send us to the doctor.

We don't need gimmicky diets or pills to cure this underlying disease, we need better food policies that will support the growing and marketing of fruits and vegetables, healthy whole grains, and better-quality meat and dairy. If we eat our medicine today, we won't pay the doctor—or Big Pharma—as much tomorrow. Don't forget the drug companies are the ones visiting your doctor with samples and information—the broccoli and strawberry growers are busy in the fields growing our health.

9. *Remove hidden corn from your diet and help end our addiction to it.*

Ground zero for improving your family's health and US food policy: Read every label in your kitchen and shift to products with no HFCS, corn syrup, dextrose, corn syrup solids or any other processed corn ingredients. This will be tricky—all industrialized meat is made from corn-fed cattle, and so is most milk and dairy—so look for grass-fed and pastured. Beyond that, processed foods, breads, cookies, cereals, yogurt, crackers, frozen dinners, and jelly can all be found without HFCS and other corn-based sweeteners. Hunt for them. This will send a message to manufacturers that we won't buy products made with artificially cheap processed corn. It's also a great way to remove the junk foods from your cabinets and make room in your wallet and home for healthy, whole foods.

But let's make sure to not punish the corn growers themselves. Iowa is the largest producer of corn in the US, but the vast majority of it is shipped out of state by processors to go into soda as HFCS and into burgers in the form of cheap animal feed. Those farmers are working hard to provide the yields we have been demanding for the past few decades, and we need to work with them to move slowly away from mono-cropping corn and soy and to grow a greater diversity of crops. After all, the Delicious species of apple was first discovered in Iowa, a harbinger of what could be if our agriculture systems reflect our changing food preferences.

Changing our agricultural landscape will take time, but farmers are entrepreneurs, and they will see the shift and grow what we demand. So as we move away from processed corn, let's remember the farmers and invest in solutions that will help them stay in business and steward their land well!

10. *Cut added sugar.*

The biggest culprit and source of added sugar in our diets is soda and other sweetened drinks, from teas to coffees to chocolate milk. But added sugar is hidden everywhere. Watch out for bread, applesauce, tomato sauce, and salad dressing. Buy steel-cut oats, not instant flavored oatmeal with added sugar. Buy real maple syrup, not the fake stuff. When you reduce added sugar hidden in processed foods, the natural sugars in food actually taste deliciously sweet, and the sugars in the fruit come bundled with all sorts of nutrients and fiber. Globally, the sugar trade can be a bitter business, and both the sugar production and consumption of cheap sugar have enslaved people for hundreds of years. Just avoid all added sugars as much as possible.

11. *Avoid processed foods.*

Although many breads, crackers, salsas, cheeses, and yogurts are perfectly reasonable food options, the vast majority of things in a shelf-stable box, can, or jar are not really worth the savings when we see what they actually cost (remember the added cost to families' health care, the environment, and our tax dollars). We have become accustomed to the idea that cheese can be a neon orange powder packet, and that meat comes in a can of pasta, and that sugary tomato sauce can sit in your cabinet for years. The further the food is from its natural state, the less nutritious it is likely to be.

That said, some "processed" foods such as ground nut butters, whole fruit jams, simple crackers, and some soups can be great options for fast and healthy meals. The goal is to find foods with very few ingredients, and ingredients that you can actually pronounce. Bread should contain flour, yeast, salt, and water, not HFCS, mono- and diglycerides, calcium propionate, grain vinegar, calcium sulfate, datem, citric acid, sodium stearoyl lactylate, azodicarbonamide, and ethoxylated mono- and diglycerides.

12. *Don't buy or drink commercially produced soda. Ever.*

About half of the added sugars in our diets come from sweetened soda and energy, sports, and fruit drinks. And consumption of sugary drinks is correlated with poor food choices overall. Be leery of veiled health promises on bottles of sugar water. Stop buying packaging; instead, buy ingredients. Read labels. And drink tap water—lots of it. Add a splash of 100 percent juice to seltzer water in place of soda. Brew real fair trade teas at home. Beware of soda or sweetened, artificial junk masquerading as a health tonic. For example, SoBe Green Tea doesn't deliver on good health, despite its touting of antioxidants; the 12¾ teaspoons of sugar in the 20-ounce bottle is about the same as 11 Oreos. Our soda purchases empower global soda's spread—let's stop a cola colonialism.

13. *Make sweets a treat.*

Speaking of Oreos, bake cookies at home—with real butter and quality chocolate. Eat sweets with real sugar just once in a while so it's really a treat. Remember, if we remove the added sugar from our diets, occasional desserts become okay. And if you make your desserts at home or only get them from your local bakery, it takes time and effort, which helps define them as "treats" in the first place.

And have that small piece of chocolate, but buy fair trade, organic chocolate, with one ingredient: chocolate. (Or, at most, a scant few, such as chocolate and vanilla, or dried fruit and almonds.) Ignore candy with HFCS or hydrogenated palm kernel oil, and steer clear of the highly processed, packaged sweet stuff that lines the checkout areas of stores. We need to get treats out of our everyday life. Instead, let's indulge in the rare, well-made, small treat that treats the world well.

14. *Avoid "diet" foods.*

When you do eat something sweet, don't get caught in the Snackwell trap—we now know that fake sugars and unsaturated fat in the form of partially hydrogenated oils are unhealthy and result in weight gain when we overeat. That includes diet drinks. Diet soda and fake sugar waters don't help us eat less, are linked with the same bad health effects of regular sugar water, and contain a long list of chemical ingredients that don't break down in our bodies and are often found in local water supplies.

The weight-loss industry is part of the Big Food industry and sells us processed diet junk food, which keeps them in business, but they also profit from diet books, supplements, even group meetings. These products and methods might work for some, but they are not as foolproof and inexpensive—or nearly as healthy—as just eating healthy, whole foods. If someone is trying to sell you low-carb carbs, low-fat fats, and high-protein candy bars, they are still trying to sell you something that's not an apple or a glass of local milk. All those "diet" processed foods are supporting the current food system. Break away.

15. *Quit fast food.*

For an example of food gone wrong here in America, consider the fast food chain Long John Silver's Big Catch[1] fish meal, called "the worst restaurant meal in America" and "a heart attack on a hook" in 2013 by the Center for Science in the Public Interest (CSPI). Weighing in at 1,320 calories and containing what CSPI estimates to be 2 full weeks' worth of trans fats when ordered with onion rings, the meal will set you back only $4.99. It is a piece of batter-fried haddock that comes with hush puppies (a deep-fried cornmeal cake) and an additional side. With onion rings, it has almost 3,700 milligrams of sodium, 19 grams of saturated fat, and 33 grams of trans fats. Haddock, corn, and onions are three healthy, low-calorie, nutrient-rich foods that have been adulterated into a diabetes-inducing cardiovascular time bomb. Imagine the fast and healthy meal you could make with those simple ingredients, bought in a more sustainable way. That is the real value meal. We spend $117 billion a year in this country on fast food, money that could otherwise go a long way toward buying healthful food.

Eating in fast food restaurants just twice a week was found to increase the risk of coronary heart disease by a staggering 56 percent. Accept that once you walk through the door of most fast food restaurants, you have made a nutritional commitment to an unhealthy meal. Even if you order a salad, they will get you with high-sugar salad dressing. And don't be seduced by the other "healthy options" offered by fast food, either. A Burger King veggie burger with cheese has 430 calories; that's even more than a double bacon cheeseburger, which has 390.

Even Burger King's "Satisfries," the reduced-fat french fries lauded as a "good step" by the fast food restaurant, are part of the problem, not the

---

1   Long John Silver's Web site notes that the Big Catch is a limited-time menu item and, in January 2014, the chain removed all trans fat from its menu.

solution. They have less fat and calories than regular fries, but are far from healthy. And, of course, they are considered a "side" to a burger. The president of Burger King North America, Alex Macedo, predicts that the calorie-reduced fries "will grow, just like diet soda grew over time." Too bad that in 2013, sales of diet soda had fallen by 7 percent.

McDonald's recently announced it will offer milk, juice, or water and stop advertising that soda is an option in Happy Meals. It also announced a rollout of Happy Meals with fruit or veggies in place of the fries, to reach 85 percent of its franchises by 2020. This is an attempt to win back moms who have chosen not to get their kids hooked on junk food, but I doubt most of these moms will be going back in 2020. And remember that the quality of the milk, juice, and veggies served at these fast food restaurants matters too, as these foods will likely not be grown or processed in ways that make the new "healthier" options all that much healthier.

These companies are making small changes to keep us coming in through the door and feeling okay about it. We should head for the exit and take our dollars with us. That will also send a message through the global marketplace that we don't want American food to be synonymous with a tsunami of sweet, salty, greasy junk and a soon-to-follow wave of obesity.

16. DIY "fast food" by making slow food.

The best way to fight the urge for fast food is to have slow food standing by and ready to eat. Create a new food tradition in your house by making lots of "slow food" one day a week. Cook your way to a fridge full of healthful choices to make easier meals during the busy week. A platter of oven-roasted vegetables; a slowcooker of chili; a bunch of servings of quinoa; a vat of steel-cut oatmeal with dried fruit to substitute for Pop-Tarts, frozen waffles, or sugary instant oatmeal in the mornings. Make chicken fingers yourself with organic, free-range chicken, lightly dusted in flour and paprika and baked on an olive oil-coated tray, then freeze them for your kids. Prepare cut veggies and fruits all at once. Make the good food the easy food.

Not coincidentally, all this advice is the same advice you'd get if you wanted to "diet" or lose weight. That's the power of eating our values by eating food that's better for the world: It's better for our waistlines as well.

17. *Redefine the "value" meal.*

Food used to be grown by people who were going to eat it themselves, or sell it to their neighbors and local community. Seeing the energy and patience and work that goes into growing and making food is a great reminder of what a truly valuable thing a colorful, fresh salad is. Compare that with the factory assembly lines that create the other kind of "value" meal, and you get a stark contrast.

Early in the book, I stated that we the eaters forgot what food is and why we eat it. When food production leaves the dirt-stained hands of farmers and enters the manufacturing plants of the processors, it loses part of its true value, while creating monetary value for a corporate CEO. Ninety percent of the food consumed in the farm state of Iowa is imported from outside the state; Iowans could be growing more fruits and vegetables and keeping more of their 8 billion food dollars in the state, but instead they are eating more imported and more processed foods. Sadly, more than 30 percent of them are obese. Let's recognize what's wrong with this.

We need to remind ourselves that what actually gives food value is not yield and cost; it's nutrition, flavor, healthfulness, culture, community building, and its role in a healthy environment. Let's also remember that everything we buy, especially food, is a display of values. Values like loyalty to one's family and community, commitment to leaving the world better than we found it, and concern for our fellow man are things we don't want to sacrifice three times a day with every meal.

18. *Buy and cook for quality over quantity.*

A half-gallon of soda is not for one person, even if it is a "good deal." If we start out with a larger package, research says we eat more. It's as simple as that. We don't need a portion of meat in a meal larger than the size of our palm, and we don't need more pasta or quinoa or potatoes than the size of our fist. If we really rethink what a healthy "full" plate looks like, we can afford to get that grass-fed steak and the whole wheat with spinach linguini instead of the cheaper meat and carbs. We all know that most of us should be eating less; let's actually let the economics of real, well-produced food help us limit our intake while we improve our health. Remember that artificially cheap is an artificial choice, so if all those subsidized, processed foods are off the grocery list, it's easier to focus on all the options for good stuff.

In our current food system, we have unprecedented obesity but also unprecedented food waste. Estimates suggest that almost 40 percent of food that is grown is discarded or left to rot before it gets eaten. We are literally buying supersized, two-for-one deals that are either going to our waists or to waste. We can save dollars and shave pounds by actually buying less of great quality, well-produced food.

19. *Reduce waste.*

About that 40-ish percent of food that is wasted around the world: Our constant desire for newer, cheaper, more convenient goods has had a measurable impact on the eating habits of people everywhere. We have also been told we need to grow higher and higher yields in order to "feed the world." Unfortunately, those two goals have left us with a crisis of food waste and "dumping" through food aid. Food is so cheap that in the wealthy world we don't think twice about throwing about half of it away. At every stage in the food production chain, our goal of cheap and easy has created enormous waste; food is heading to the landfill instead of to hungry stomachs. In the developing world, a focus on fertilizers and expensive seeds instead of food storage, infrastructure, and basic home processing has meant that almost half of all food grown by poor farmers goes to waste, too, often rotting in the fields during harvest and rendering it unavailable a few months later during the hunger season. Food waste is a direct result of our current system, and it's something we can change by altering our buying and eating habits. Buy better food, buy less food, plan your meals, eat your leftovers, and conserve. Like your mom said—eat your veggies because there are hungry kids still and it's a shame to waste.

The massive waste in our modern food system also includes the packaging—paper, plastic, and foil—that much of our food comes in or on. Not only do most of these materials enter the waste stream rather than a recycling bin, but the natural resources used to make them, and the industrial chemical byproducts their manufacture and disposal yield, are not healthy for people or planet. Buy in bulk and avoid wasteful packaging when you can. And carry your food home in a less waste-generating way, too.

Thanks to the movement that FEED helped to jump-start, many of us now bring reusable bags to the store to carry our groceries, which is one of those small but big things that can create a ripple effect of change. Reusable bags remove a source of waste from landfills and oceans (where fish end up eating little pieces of the bags, and then we eat the fish). Plastic bags have only been around for about 50 years, so we're not sure how long they take to decompose; estimates range between 500 and 100,000 years, and the bags become more toxic in the process. By not using plastic bags, we remove a source of profit for polluting natural gas and oil companies, and a source of litter in our communities. Like some places in America (for example, San Francisco, Seattle, and the Outer Banks of North Carolina) and around the world (including Italy, India's Punjab state, Pakistan, and Dhaka, Bangladesh), the country of Rwanda banned plastic bags in 2006, since they were causing such an environmental eyesore and hurting the market for traditional Rwandan baskets. The waste of petrochemicals to make the fertilizers, plastics, and fuel that grow, package, and ship food we throw away goes hand in hand with the general misuse of resources that food waste creates, and we can change that.

20. *Grow something edible. And help your kids grow food, too.*

Plant garlic or mint with your kids, your neighbors, and your friends. Buy tomato and lettuce seedlings and grow your own salad. Stephen Ritz did it in the South Bronx; Ron Finley planted vegetables all over South Central LA; and families in the overcrowded slums grow produce out of recycled food aid bags. We can certainly find some dirt where we live. If you live in the suburbs, plant asparagus crowns with your toddlers and plan on eating them with your big kids; asparagus is a perennial vegetable that keeps producing for many years. Plant herbs in a pot and put it on a windowsill. Visit farms and farmers' markets, and look for "grown locally" stickers in the supermarkets. Learn how your food is grown by visiting a local farm or ask a farmer at your farmers market.

We can also help spread the power of fresh-picked food to fight hunger in our communities by supporting farmers' markets and farmers themselves to provide gleaning help or discounted sales of end-of-the-day produce to local food banks. And consider helping kids around the world grow their own veggies, too. From supporting small nonprofits that help plant school gardens globally to supporting big aid organizations and legislation that is finally seeing the benefits of locally grown school feeding and food aid, we can promote this truly universal solution to growing the next generation of healthy kids.

Guerilla gardener Ron Finley said, "If kids grow kale, kids eat kale." We've seen the school garden movement explode because it works to nudge kids toward healthier foods. If kids grow food, visit farms, and cook, kids will learn to respect food, respect their health, and respect the environment on a deeper level.

21. *Eat entrepreneurially by supporting healthy-food entrepreneurs.*

Supporting local, start-up food entrepreneurs improves our local economies, supports our communities and neighbors, and pulls money away from the large manufacturers who engage in the food practices that hurt us in the first place. Local coffee shops, farm-to-table restaurants, and local brands create jobs and keep food dollars in the community instead of sending them to a remote corporate headquarters. Try out a new app to find your favorite produce, or buy a new brand of kale chips or fair trade tea to invest in new companies entering new markets that are not yet dominated by the few big food conglomerates. Just as with almost every other industry, early adopters, the first to buy new and demand better food, will help make it more and more accessible to everyone.

As an example, only a few years ago cell phones used to be owned only by the wealthy, but today we know that Africa has more cell phones than the US or European Union. People say that organic food and, in particular, Whole Foods Market are just for the affluent, but like all spreading technologies, as more and more of we the eaters demand better food, companies will create ways to get better food to all of us, and at different price points. New food systems will be built with new technologies and applications that connect producers who are making new and better (read: healthier) food with consumers who demand it.

22. *Eat high tech, but low impact.*

Along with new apps and food delivery start-ups, new agricultural technologies are being developed to grow greens on rooftops, use water more efficiently with drip irrigation, and increase transparency for eaters. Look for brands that let you scan the QR codes on their products to see what the farm and farmers look like, or check out new technologies like home aquaponic growing systems and wall-hanging vertical herb gardens.

Just because something is high tech doesn't mean it's chemically intensive or genetically engineered. Farm hacks inventing new smart uses for agricultural tools, small farmers around the world using cell phones to monitor weather, and more ecofriendly packaging and fresh food storage both in our own kitchens and in the developing world are all technological innovations we can rally around.

Theoretically, everyone should support the idea that growing more healthy food with fewer off-farm, chemical inputs is a good idea. Let's get behind farmers, brands, and stores that use high-tech solutions to disrupt the status quo, reduce dependence on petrochemical and mined agricultural inputs and ingredients, and that bring us good, old healthy food in creative new ways.

23. Buy food differently. Try a new kind of food vendor.

It might be true that highly consolidated and centralized big-box stores and supermarkets will never, ever sell diverse local foods because of the economies of scale. But we can choose other retail options for many food purchases. The supermarket was invented in 1916 by an entrepreneur in Tennessee; it's not like it's the only way people have ever bought food. In reality it's just the current system and, like other technologies, it can be phased out when something better comes along that consumers prefer. We can be those consumers by supporting farm-direct purchasing, co-operative grocers, mobile grocery trucks, online and app-based stores, farmers markets, local cheese and fish mongers, whole animal butchers, and health-conscious brands.

Right now, artificially cheap is an artificial choice, and those who pay the slotting fees hold the sway. Find places to buy food that stock the shelves according to your values, so it's easier to make choices among foods that are all better to eat. And find brands—both big and brand new—that make you feel good about eating.

24. Take a walk.

Although weight loss per se is not the focus of this book, exercise is an essential part of the solution to the global obesity epidemic, so walking is in general just a good idea. But I'm talking about walking to your next meal. The shift away from walkable downtown shopping areas, sidewalks and green grocers and farm stands and coffee shops embedded in our living communities to superstores with cornfield-sized parking lots and strip malls with the same repeating restaurant chains mirrors the same 30-year changes that have dramatically increased our weight. Starting in the post-WWII era, the suburban sprawl and car-focused communities begot Walmarts and infinitely replicable shopping center restaurants and drive-throughs. None of this driving has done our health or our local food economies any favors.

But change is afoot. A 2011 survey of Realtors found that Baby Boomers and Millennials are looking for housing in walkable, urban, or small-town environments, and that only 12 percent of people buying homes are looking for one in the overdeveloped, car-centric "fringe" suburbs. This shift away from sprawl will help revitalize our local restaurants, which help local farmers and suppliers, and smaller food markets, which often means fewer two-for-one 2-liter bottles of soda, since they are hard to carry home in your reusable shopping bag.

And, by continuing to support more walking-centric urban design in America, we will also be helping to disempower the system that is creeping into the developing world as well. More and more strip malls and parking lots have started appearing in places like Mexico, China, India, and Kenya, as the same mall developers and superstores (Walmart is growing in Central America, and the UK's Tesco is in India) are vying for widening pockets and waistlines. We can do much to help the world—demand walkable and bikeable communities and reimagine what the middle-class lifestyle means if we start by doing it at home. Walking to your next meal or to your neighborhood farmers' market is a great place to start.

25. *Use your table as your activist platform.*

Americans are the most generous nation, comparing our private donations with those of other developed countries. We are especially concerned and generous when disasters that lead to hunger happen around the world. But, at the same time, we spend less on food than any other country in the world. Charitable giving in the US represents around 2 percent of GDP. Food purchases are 10 percent, and consumer goods, many of which are tied to the table, are another formidable source of spending. We can do so much more to improve the world by changing how we spend our food budget than by just giving a portion of our disposable income to charity.

With our food dollars we can impact the environment, worker's rights, women's income equality, children's opportunity to go to school instead of the fields and factories, hunger alleviation, global health—and also local health and food availability, local water, air and soil quality, greater economic growth, more jobs, and more open space in the form of well-managed farms (which can serve to increase home values).

Instead of our philanthropy being one budget line and our food and consumer goods being another (meaning that we buy cheap food for ourselves and donate even cheaper food or money to the hungry), we can have a much greater impact by altering our buying and eating habits to support smart global and local economic development and environmental practices. A major cause of continued hunger in the developing world is the increase in droughts, floods, and major natural disasters along with new pests as changes in the climate have a dramatic impact on already poor infrastructure and people. These climate shifts are partially caused by our petrochemical and carbon-heavy food systems, but are felt more intensely by farmers and eaters on the other side of the world. Reducing our food's environmental impact will have positive impact for our own farmers as well as those who are one drought away from hunger.

With our tables as platforms for change, we can teach our family and friends about food in a very fundamental and valuable way as we pivot the food systems in a healthier direction.

26. Occupy your kitchen! Learn how to cook.

It might sound too easy, but cooking might be the greatest act of protest and social rebellion that we have, and it's right at our fingertips. By buying our own ingredients and deciding how much and exactly what types of salt, sugar, and fat we want to use to make our fruits, veggies, meat, dairy, and grains taste delicious, we are reclaiming control over our health and our waists. If we make our potatoes and burgers at home, we can take them back from the dangerous realm of junk food. If we don't want giant conglomerates to control our laws and governments, then we should not let them into our kitchens.

Our parents and grandparents (or mostly mothers and grandmothers) were told to release the bonds of their apron strings and let companies cook for them, but after years of processed, additive-jacked and fast food, this looks like a deal with the devil. The answer is not drudgery but creativity; it's not to stay home tied to the stove, but to come home armed with real healthy food options—well-prepared meals and raw ingredients. Let's all put our aprons back on sometimes—moms, dads, kids, college students, professionals, and grandparents. We can be change agents, humanitarians, and global citizens, just by getting back into the kitchen.

27. Teach your family and friends, as well.

Just like in-school antismoking campaigns helped send kids home to get their parents to quit, today school gardens and the Jamie Olivers of the world who are promoting healthier eating are also getting kids to ask for veggies at home. But it's not just elementary school kids—Millennials are teaching their parents about the joys of kale and the tastiness of a veggie burger. Young people can introduce their parents to cooking and CSAs just like they are showing them Twitter and Instagram. And the knowledge transfer goes both ways: As parents become more aware of the health risks of fast and processed food, they can engage their kids in a new way of cooking and eating to prevent those issues for the next generation.

Sharing a love of food and the stories behind your meal is not just for families, though. Invite friends to a Change Dinner Barbecue and show them that eating in a way that changes the food system for the better can be delicious and fun. Giving others a taste of a delicious, but not super-sized, grass-fed burger on a whole grain bun surrounded by a plate full of vegetables is the best way to educate eaters.

28. Be conservative.

Smaller portions should mean less expenditure, which should mean more resources available to buy that local food that keeps your money in your community and region. Traditionally "conservative" values of strong families, investing in local solutions, reducing government costs (by reducing Big Ag subsidy programs and government financial support for private-sector agribusiness pollution), nudging people to support themselves (by ensuring a fair wage for farm and food-service workers, so they don't need food stamp benefits), and allowing real consumer and farmer freedom (by letting the true costs of food be accounted for) are things that all eaters can agree on.

We should be more conservative with our spending, too. If we start to judge food purchases based on nutrient density instead of how many calories we get for the dollar, we will buy more fruits, veggies, and whole foods. If we make sure that farmers near and far are paid a fair margin of our food dollars for their work—and not subsidized on the back end by our tax dollars or foreign aid—local and fair trade might seem like a real deal. If we consider how expensive food transportation is for our environment and energy demands, eating in-season fruits and vegetables starts to look a lot cheaper.

We need to incorporate more *values* into our food system instead of just a narrow definition of value that is plastered on a sign by the buy-one-get-one "free" jumbo bags of Doritos. By reclaiming control of what our family eats from Big Government and Big Food, we can redistribute health back to our communities and our bodies.

29. *Be radical*

Just like no one can exercise for us, no one controls our food intake except ourselves. Outsourcing something as important as our daily sustenance to a marketing company or multinational junk-food provider seems like the ultimate way to surrender our freedom and take whatever "the man" is feeding us. For years people were mistrustful of fake pink margarine and blue sugar milk drinks, and rightfully so. It's time we get back a little of that revolutionary spirit and not let a big, powerful machine decide what we put in our mouths.

We shouldn't be outsourcing the culture of our dinner tables either. Setting the table, lighting candles, using special utensils, passing around the bread or wine, and engaging in conversation with the people you eat with is an important part of our social structure. We don't want to be defined by golden arches, or cardboard boxes and buckets, or the mass, generic, commercial "American food culture" created by large food companies.

Ironically, the counterculture generation of the 1960s and 1970s who didn't want to "take it" from "the establishment" ended up feeding themselves and their kids all the processed junk that "the man" offered them. And the image of a young eater lined up at a fast food drive-through window blaming today's brand of "screw the man" music and reaching for that multinational corporation-branded paper bag with an anti-establishment tattoo-branded arm is also a bit ironic. Let's actually rebel and redefine our own food culture.

30. *If we rebuild the system, it will change.*

As much as these watchwords sound like they are telling the individual consumer that it's all up to them to make better choices, there is something deeper and more complete in the way we can effect change. Fundamentally, there is a problem with the system—our food system was built on metrics such as fast, cheap, sweet, salty, and fatty, and that is a not the fault of individual eaters, individual farmers, or individual corporations. But the system needs to change, and the only way to change it is to use our power as consumers to make different choices and nudge the current alternatives to become more of the norm so more of us can eat into a better system.

If we think differently and act in all the above ways toward our food purchasing and eating, this shift will continue to happen. Like the first cellphone users re-created global communication for everyone, and the first car owners pushed the planet toward an interconnected network, we the eaters will slowly shift the food system to be healthier and better for all. The power of capitalism is that our dollars matter, and the power of innovation and "creative destruction" is that entire systems actually can be changed.

The winners of this seismic shift toward better, healthier, truer foods, and different ways of buying that good food, will be all of us. If we push capitalism in the direction of real and fair costs for truly valuable food, we will be surrounded by those kinds of choices at every turn, just as the opposite has inundated us—in both Mbarara, Uganda, and JFK Airport—with rows of junk food and few options for something truly nutritious. If we the eaters demand change and put our money where are mouths are, great companies and smart farmers will step up and give us a changed dinner—and a better world.

EAT GREAT FOOD WITH GREAT PEOPLE.
FEED YOURSELF AND YOUR FAMILY WELL.

Change dinner ... and change the world.

A cheeseburger on a bun with lettuce, pickles, and a tomato with a side of fried potatoes, an ear of corn, a salad, a cold sweet drink, and dessert can either be the worst meal on the planet and the embodiment of how the Modern American Diet has hurt the world—or the meal that will change everything.

In order for a burger to change the world, we have to eat them less often, which will be easy if we make burgers from really high quality meat, raised on pasture, and ensure the farmer a fair price for her role in stewarding the land. Buying healthier, whole grain or even sprouted wheat bread will be better for the eaters around your table, as will every purchase that nudges the marketplace to have more of these options and fewer highly processed, bleached carbs masquerading as a food group. Eating fresh corn on the cob is a summer treat that so many of us remember as our main dietary encounter with corn. We should try to eat corn only in forms in which we can identify the kernel—or the ground cornmeal of whole grain cornbread or tortillas.

In too many restaurant burger or barbecue meals, "fresh" vegetables only show up in a little plastic cup of coleslaw. At home, though, a fresh salad (maybe including some greens you grew in a little patio planter) is so easy to make and brings flavor and nutrition to any meal.

Although sweet drinks and dessert can be the downfall of even the most well-meaning eaters among us, making those sweets healthier is easier than it seems. Sun tea is a cool and rare opportunity to use solar energy in modern food preparation, and using real fruit instead of the canned, sugar-soaked kind in a homemade dessert leaves a little room for some local ice cream or homemade whipped cream.

To show your family and friends (and yourself!) how delicious it is to use your dinner table to change the world, invite them over for a Change Dinner Barbecue. The menu below can be adjusted from six people to as many as you need, and you can easily substitute a few portobello mushroom caps marinated in balsamic vinegar and olive oil for the guests who don't eat meat.

MENU FOR A CHANGED DINNER

Serves 6

A Homemade Burger

1.2 pounds grass-fed, organic ground beef

1 onion, finely chopped

1 free-range organic egg, beaten

Sprinkle of turmeric, paprika, and oregano

Salt and pepper to taste

6 thin, firm local cheese slices

6 whole grain rolls or sprouted whole wheat English muffins, toasted

6 slices heirloom tomato

1 head organic lettuce

Pickle slices, either from a farmers' market or naturally fermented

Combine ground meat, onion, egg, turmeric, paprika, oregano, salt, and pepper. Form into six burgers. Cook on the grill or on a grill pan on the stove at high heat for 3 to 4 minutes each side. Add cheese after cooking the second side.

Serve on a roll or muffin with a slice of locally grown heirloom tomato, a few leaves of lettuce, and some pickles.

Sweet Corn on the Cob

6 ears corn, shucked

⅓ stick pastured butter, softened, or 2 Tbsp extra virgin olive oil

⅓ cup freshly grated Parmesan cheese

Black pepper to taste

Fresh chopped parsley (optional)

Prepare the grill for medium-high heat. Coat corn with butter or olive oil, then sprinkle with Parmesan cheese and black pepper, and wrap each ear in recycled aluminum foil. Place the corn on the grill for about 10 minutes, turning 2 to 3 times. Serve with a sprinkle of chopped parsley and a dusting of Parmesan.

Sweet Potato or Local Fingerling Potato "Fries"

For Sweet Potato Fries:

3 large sweet potatoes, washed and cut into ¼- to ½-inch medallions

1-2 Tbsp coconut oil (melted) or extra virgin olive oil to coat

Sprinkle of salt and rosemary

Preheat the oven to 425°F degrees. Mix medallions in a bowl with oil to coat, and season with salt and rosemary. Roast the potatoes on a baking sheet for 15 minutes, then flip the potatoes and roast 10 to 15 minute on the other side, until the potatoes are fork tender.

For Fingerling Potatoes:

1 pound fingerling potatoes, scrubbed, dried, and cut length wise

1-2 Tbsp extra virgin olive oil or grapeseed oil

2-3 sprigs of fresh thyme, sage, or rosemary, chopped

Salt and pepper to taste

Preheat the oven to 425°F. Mix potatoes in a bowl with oil to coat and then add salt, pepper, and fresh herbs. Roast the potatoes on a baking sheet for 10 minutes, then flip the potatoes and roast 10 to 15 minutes more, until the largest potato is fork tender.

Serve both with locally made ketchup or hot sauce for a kick.

Fresh and Colorful Summer Salad

6 cups any combination of kale, spinach, red lettuce, arugula

1 large carrot, shaved into "chips" with a vegetable peeler

6 radishes, thinly sliced

10-12 marinated artichoke hearts, chopped

For dressing:

⅔ cup extra virgin olive oil

1 Tbsp Dijon mustard (make it 2 Tbsp for spicier dressing)

2 Tbsp lemon juice

2 Tbsp white wine vinegar

2 minced garlic cloves

Fresh ground pepper

Salt

Combine all dressing ingredients in a mason jar or old sauce jar and shake right before spooning over the salad.

Mint Green Sun Tea

4 organic fair trade green tea bags   4 sprigs of fresh mint
  (for 1 gallon of water)

In a large glass pitcher, add tea bags and mint and set in a sunny spot for 3 to 5 hours. Take out the tea bags when brewed to your liking (check the color for how strong it is brewed). Chill the tea in the fridge before serving.

To lightly sweeten the tea, stir in a few tablespoons of honey when the tea is still warm from brewing, before putting it in the fridge to chill. Serve with lemon wedges and ice cubes.

Homemade Apple-Cherry Crumble

For filling:
3-4 apples, thinly sliced (can use   season)
  peaches if they are in season) $\frac{1}{3}$ cup dried cherries
1$\frac{1}{2}$ cups pitted cherries, fresh or   1 Tbsp lemon juice or orange juice
  frozen (or a local berry varietal in   Pinch sugar

For topping:
1 cup rolled oats   2 Tbsp ground flaxseed
$\frac{1}{3}$ cup whole wheat, spelt or other   3 Tbsp brown sugar
  wholegrain flour   3 tsp ground cinnamon
$\frac{1}{3}$ cup mixed seeds and chopped nuts, $\frac{1}{3}$–$\frac{2}{3}$ cup butter, melted
  such as sunflower seeds, flaked
  almonds, chopped pecans, or
  walnuts

Lightly butter a baking dish. Preheat the oven to 350°F. Mix apples, cherries, dried cherries, and juice in the baking dish and sprinkle with a pinch of sugar. In a separate bowl, combine oats, flour, mixed seeds and nuts, flaxseed, brown sugar, and cinnamon, then add the butter and stir. Generously sprinkle the crumble topping on the fruit and set aside.

You can turn the oven down a bit after you finish the potatoes and put the dessert in the oven when you sit down for your barbecue. Bake for 35 minutes—the topping should be starting to brown. Serve warm alone or with some freshly whipped cream or local ice cream.

SOURCE NOTES

INTRODUCTION

Rebecca Greenwald. "Getting to the Root of Africa's Agriculture Challenges: TropAg and AfSIS Partner to Improve Soil Fertility." *State of the Planet*, August 18, 2011. http://blogs. ei.columbia.edu/2011/08/18/getting-to-the-root-of-africa's-soil-problems

Millennium Village Project. "Ruhiira, Uganda." n.d. www.millenniumvillages.org/ the-villages/ruhiira-uganda

Ellen Gustafson. "Partners' Meeting Notes from Project FEED." September 29, 2009. www. millenniumvillages.org/field-notes/partners-meeting-notes-from-project-feed

Patrick Jaramogi. "Millions of Ugandans Suffer from Food Poisoning Annually." *New Vision,* March 9, 2012.

Food and Agriculture Organization of the United Nations. "Crop Biodiversity: Use It or Lose It." October 26, 2010.

Henk-Jan Brinkman and Cullen S. Hendrix. "Food Insecurity and Violent Conflict: Causes, Consequences, and Addressing the Challenges." World Food Program Occasional Paper No. 24, July 2011.

Wenonah Hauter. *Foodopoly: The Battle Over the Future of Food and Farming in America.* New York: New Press, 2012.

Tom Philpott. "How Your College Is Selling Out to Big Ag." MotherJones.com, May 8, 2012.

National Center for Chronic Disease Prevention and Health Promotion. *Obesity: Halting the Epidemic by Making Health Easier.* At a Glance 2011. Atlanta: Centers for Disease Control and Prevention, 2011.

"Chocolate Milk Exonerated! Schools That Banned Sweet Beverage Forced to Bring It Back After Complaints from Experts." *Daily Mail,* April 12, 2011.

World Health Organization. "Uganda." *Noncommunicable Diseases Country Profiles 2011.* September 2011. www.who.int/nmh/countries/uga1/4en.pdf

Brooke Jarvis. "Can a Farm State Feed Itself?" *Yes!* September 4, 2009. http://www. yesmagazine.org/new-economy/eating-in

Economic Research Service. "Table 7: Food Expenditures by Families and Individuals as a Share of Disposable Inome." US Department of Agriculture, November 13, 2013. www. ers.usda.gov/data-products/food-expenditures.aspx#.Um7gdxZEZvk

CHAPTER ONE: THE HUSK, THE COB, AND A KERNEL OF TRUTH

United Nations Conference on Trade and Development. "Infocomm—Commodity Profile: Maize." *Infocomm: Market Information in the Commodities Area,* April 25, 2012.

Janet Larsen. "Grain Harvest: Global Grain Stocks Drop Dangerously Low as 2012 Consumption Exceeded Production." Earth Policy Institute, January 17, 2013. www.earth-policy. org/indicators/C54/grain1/42013

Jennifer Bremer. "Crop Scientist: 300-Bushel Corn Yields Are Possible." *High Plains Journal,* December 9, 2009.

Dairy Herd Management. "A Comparison of World Corn Yields." October 11, 2013. http://www.dairyherd.com/dairy-news/latest/A-comparison-of-world-corn-yields-227415201.html

"Obesity Rates in US: Half of Illinoisans to Be Obese by 2030." ABC7 News, September 18, 2012.

Jo Robinson. *Eating on the Wild Side: The Missing Link to Optimum Health.* New York: Little, Brown, 2013.

Worldwatch Institute. "Genetically Modified Crops Only a Fraction of Primary Global Crop Production." *Vital Signs Online,* December 3, 2008.

Economic Research Service. "Recent Trends in GE Adoption." *Adoption of Genetically Engineered Crops in the U.S.* Washington, DC: US Department of Agriculture, July 9, 2013. www.ers.usda.gov/data-products/adoption-of-genetically-engineered-crops-in-the-us/recent-trends-in-ge-adoption.aspx#.UnUp3RZEZvl

Economic and Social Development Department. "Food Security: Food Security Indicators." Food and Agriculture Organization of the United Nations, December 20, 2013. www.fao.org/economic/ess/ess-fs/ess-fadata/en

Brendan Koerner. "How Much of Our Food Is Bioengineered?" Slate.com, May 22, 2003.

Jason Koebler. "Herbicide-Resistant 'Super Weeds' Increasingly Plaguing Farmers." *US News and World Report*, October 19, 2012.

Food and Agriculture Organization of the United Nations. "World Hunger Report 2011: High, Volatile Prices Set to Continue." October 10, 2011.

Dan Flynn. "Corn Growers Turn to Pesticides After Genetically Modified Seeds Fail." *Food Safety News,* May 28, 2013.

International Assessment of Agricultural Knowledge, Science, and Technology for Development. "Agriculture at a Crossroads—Global Report." 2009. http://www.unep.org/dewa/assessments/ecosystems/iaastd/tabid/105853/default.aspx

Economic Research Service. *An Initial Assessment of the Payment-in-Kind Program.* Washington, DC: US Department of Agriculture, April 1983.

Tadeusz Patzek, Davd Pimentel, Michael Wang, Christopher Saricks, May Wu, et al. "The Many Problems with Ethanol from Corn: Just How Unsustainable Is It?" Phoenix Project Foundation, May 2004.

David Biello. "Can Ethanol from Corn Be Made Sustainable?" ScientificAmerican.com, February 20, 2013.

Meghan Sapp. "Chevron Predicts Increased Gasoline Prices Due to Ethanol Mandate." *Biofuels Digest,* June 12, 2013.

George Sale, George Psalmanazar, Archibald Bower, George Shelvocke, John Campbell, and John Swinton *The Modern Part of an Universal History: From the Earliest Account of Time.* Vol. 39. London: T. Osborne, et al., 1763.

Bryan Walsh. "Beepocalypse Redux: Honeybees Are Still Dying—and We Still Don't Know Why." Time.com, May 7, 2013.

Tara Parker-Pope. "A New Name for High-Fructose Corn Syrup." *New York Times,* September 14, 2010.

US Census Bureau. "Table 212: Per Capita Consumption of Major Food Commodities: 1980 to 2007." *Statistical Abstract of the United States: 2010.* Washington, DC: US Census Bureau, 2009. www.census.gov/compendia/statab/2010/tables/10s0212.pdf

US Department of Agriculture. "Chapter 2: Profiling Food Consumption in America." *Agriculture Fact Book 2001–2002.* Washington, DC: US Department of Agriculture, March 2003. www.usda.gov/factbook/chapter2.pdf

Bob Yirka. "Researchers Find High-Fructose Corn Syrup May Be Tied to Worldwide Collapse of Bee Colonies." Phys.org, April 30, 2013.

Miriam E. Bocarsly, Elyse S. Powell, Nicole M. Avena, and Bartley G. Hoebel. "High-Fructose Corn Syrup Causes Characteristics of Obesity in Rats: Increased Body Weight, Body Fat and Triglyceride Levels." *Pharmacology, Biochemistry and Behavior* 97(1):101–106, 2010.

American Medical Association. "AMA Finds High Fructose Syrup Unlikely to Be More Harmful to Health Than Other Caloric Sweeteners." PRNewswire.com, June 17, 2008. [news release]

Mary Clare Jalonick. "Senate Passes Half-Trillion Dollar Farm Bill." *Huffington Post,* June 10, 2013.

CHAPTER TWO: HERE'S THE BEEF

Ann Crittenden. "Consumption of Meat Rising in the Developing Countries." *New York Times,* August 25, 1981.

US Environmental Protection Agency. "Major Crops Grown in the United States." April 11, 2013. www.epa.gov/agriculture/ag101/cropmajor.html

Economic Research Service. "Corn: Background." US Department of Agriculture, December 16, 2013. http://www.ers.usda.gov/topics/crops/corn/background.aspx#.UchNXJVx4ZY

Michael Pollan. *The Omnivore's Dilemma.* New York: Penguin, 2006.

Eric Sorensen. "Billions Served." *Washington State Magazine,* Fall 2011.

Elanor Starmer and Timothy A. Wise. *Feeding at the Trough: Industrial Livestock Firms Saved $35 Billion from Low Feed Prices.* Policy Brief No. 07-03. Medford, MA: Global Development and Environment Institute, Tufts University, December 2007.

Eric Schlosser. *Fast Food Nation: The Dark Side of the All-American Meal.* Boston: Houghton Mifflin, 2001.

Ravi Krishnani. "McDonald's in Russia—Defeated Communism with a 'Happy' Meal." *Business Today,* n.d.

Jennifer Stewart. "Reduced Cattle Herd Could Mean Bigger Profits Starting Late 2013." Purdue Agriculture News, August 22, 2012. [news release]

Cynthia A. Daley, Amber Abbott, Patrick S. Doyle, Glenn A. Nader, and Stephanie Larson. "A Review of Fatty Acid Profiles and Antioxidant Content in Grass-Fed and Grain-Fed Beef." *Nutrition Journal* 9:10, 2010.

American Meat Institute. "The United States Meat Industry at a Glance." n.d. www.meatami.com/ht/d/sp/i/47465/pid/47465

Central Intelligence Agency. "A Spotlight on World Obesity Rates." April 30, 2013.

Frontline. "*Modern Meat:* Interview: Michael Pollan." PBS.org, April 2002. http://www.pbs.org/wgbh/pages/frontline/shows/meat/interviews/pollan.html

Anthony Gucciardi. "Cattle Now Being Fed Cookies and Candies Instead of Real Food." *Natural Society,* September 24, 2012.

Carolyn Dimitri, Anne Effland, and Neilson Conklin. *The 20th Century Transformation of US Agriculture and Farm Policy.* Economic Information Bulletin No. 3. Washington, DC: US Department of Agriculture, June 2005.

Alan Barkema, Mark Drabenstott, and Nancy Novack. "The New U.S. Meat Industry." *Economic Review,* 2nd Quarter, 2001. www.kc.frb.org/Publicat/econrev/pdf/2q01bark.pdf

Worldwatch Institute. "Global Meat Production and Consumption Continue to Rise." *Vital Signs Online,* October 11, 2011.

National Family Farm Coalition. "The Facts Behind King Corn." NFFC Fact Sheet, July 30, 2008. www.nffc.net/Learn/Fact%20Sheets/King%20Corn%20Fact%20Sheet.pdf

David A. Kessler. "Antibiotics and the Meat We Eat." *New York Times,* March 27, 2013. [opinion]

Bill Tomson and Helena Bottemiller Evich. "'Pink Slime' Returns to School Lunches in 4 More States." *Politico*, September 9, 2013.

Maureen Morrison. "McDonald's Has a Millennial Problem." *Advertising Age,* March 25, 2013.

Food Revolution Team. "The 'Pink Slime' Story Continues." Jamie Oliver's Food Revolution, March 28, 2012.

Dan Barber. "Food Without Fear." *New York Times*, November 23, 2004. [opinion]

National Center for Chronic Disease Prevention and Health Promotion. *Obesity: Halting the Epidemic by Making Health Easier.* At a Glance 2011. Atlanta: Centers for Disease Control and Prevention, 2011.

Centers for Disease Control and Prevention. "Overweight and Obesity: Adult Obesity Facts." August 6, 2013. http://www.cdc.gov/obesity/data/adult.html

Stemple Creek Ranch. "Buy Our Meats." StempleCreek.com, n.d. http://stemplecreek.com/buy-our-meats/buy-online/whole-beef

Critical Care Pediatrics. "Basal Energy Expenditure: Harris-Benedict Equation." Joan and Sanford I. Weill Medical College, Cornell University, October 3, 2000. www-users.med.cornell.edu/~spon/picu/calc/beecalc.htm

Dan Witters and Diana Liu. "In U.S., Poor Health Tied to Big Losses for All Job Types." Gallup Well-Being, May 7, 2013.

Savory Institute. "Allan Savory: Founder and President." n.d. www.savoryinstitute.com/about-us/allan-savory

Jo Robinson. "The Label Says Grass-Fed, But Is It?" *Mother Earth News,* April/May 2008. www.motherearthnews.com/homesteading-and-livestock/usda-grass-fed-label.aspx

Jo Robinson. "Getting Wild Nutrition from Modern Food." EatWild.com, January 15, 2014.

CHAPTER THREE: DAIRY

Hayden Stewart, Noel Blisard, and Dean Jolliffe. *Let's Eat Out: Americans Weigh Taste, Convenience, and Nutrition.* Economic Information Bulletin No. 19. Washington, DC: US Department of Agriculture, October 2006.

American Cancer Society. "Recombinant Bovine Growth Hormone." February 18, 2011. www.cancer.org/cancer/cancercauses/othercarcinogens/athome/recombinant-bovine-growth-hormone

Masai of Kenya. "Maasai Food and Diet." n.d. www.masaikenya.org/MAASAI1/4FOOD1/41/41/4DIET.pdf

Elliot M. Fratkin, Eric Abella Roth, and Martha A. Nathan. "When Nomads Settle: The Effects of Commoditization, Nutritional Change, and Formal Education on Ariaal and Rendille Pastoralists." *Current Anthropology* 40:5; 729-735, 1999.

Shadrack Oiye, Joseph Ole Simel, Ruth Oniang'o, and Timothy Johns. "Chapter 11: The Maasai Food System and Food and Nutrition Security." In Harriet V. Kuhnlein, Bill Erasmus, and Dina Spigelski, eds. *Indigenous Peoples' Food Systems: The Many Dimensions of Culture, Diversity and Environment for Nutrition and Health.* Rome: Food and Agriculture Organization of the United Nations, 2009.

David S. Ludwig and Walter C. Willett. "Three Daily Servings of Reduced-Fat Milk: An Evidence-Based Recommendation?" *JAMA Pediatrics* 167(9):788–789, 2013. [opinion]

Rebecca J. Scharf, Ryan T. Demmer, and Mark D. DeBoer. "Longitudinal Evaluation of Milk Type Consumed and Weight Status in Preschoolers." *Archives of Disease in Childhood* 98(5):335–340, 2013.

Tara Parker-Pope. "A New Name for High-Fructose Corn Syrup." *New York Times*, September 14, 2010.

E. Melanie DuPuis. *Nature's Perfect Food: How Milk Became America's Drink.* New York: New York University Press, 2002.

James McWilliams. "How Journalists Got the Cheese Lobbying Story Wrong." TheAtlantic. com, November 17, 2010.

International Dairy Foods Association. "Cheese Sales and Trends." IDFA.org, December 2012.

Liesbeth A. Smit, Ana Baylin, and Hannia Campos. "Conjugated Linoleic Acid in Adipose Tissue and Risk of Myocardial Infarction." *American Journal of Clinical Nutrition* 92(1):34–40, 2010.

F. Sofi, A. Buccioni, F. Cesari, A. M. Gori, S. Minieri, et al. "Effects of a Dairy Product (Pecorino Cheese) Naturally Rich in *cis*-9, *trans*-11 Conjugated Linoleic Acid on Lipid, Inflammatory and Haemorheological Variables: A Dietary Intervention Study." *Nutrition, Metabolism and Cardiovascular Diseases* 20(2):117–124, 2009.

Clement Ip, Sebastiano Banni, Elisabetta Angioni, Gianfranca Carta, John McGinley, et al. "Conjugated Linoleic Acid–Enriched Butter Fat Alters Mammary Gland Morphogenesis and Reduces Cancer Risk in Rats." *Journal of Nutrition* 129(12):2135–2142, 1999.

S. K. Jensen, A. K. Johannsen, and J. E. Hermansen. "Quantitative Secretion and Maximal Secretion Capacity of Retinol, Beta-Carotene and Alpha-Tocopherol into Cows' Milk." *Journal of Dairy Research* 66(4):511–522, 1999.

Matthew Herper. "Fish Oil or Snake Oil? Study Questions Omega-3 Benefits." Forbes.com, June 11, 2012.

Barry Estabrook. "A Tale of Two Dairies." *Gastronomica* 10(4):48–52, Fall 2010.

Barry M. Popkin. "Global Changes in Diet and Activity Patterns as Drivers of the Nutrition Transition." *Nestlé Nutrition Workshop Series: Pediatric Program* 63:1–10, 2009.

Grain. *The Great Milk Robbery: How Corporations Are Stealing Livelihoods and a Vital Source of Nutrition from the Poor.* Barcelona: Grain, December 2011.

Cancer Prevention Coalition. "International Scientific Committee Warns of Serious Risks of Breast and Prostate Cancer from Monsanto's Hormonal Milk." March 21, 2003. [news release]

Paul D. Fey, Thomas J. Safranek, Mark E. Rupp, Eileen F. Dunne, Efrain Ribot, et al. "Ceftriaxone-Resistant Salmonella Infection Acquired by a Child from Cattle." *New England Journal of Medicine* 342(17):1242–1249, 2000.

Jeffrey M. Smith. "In-Depth Look at rbGH." *Spilling the Beans,* April 6, 2009.

Jesse Rhodes. "Food Dye Origins: When Margarine Was Pink." Smithsonian.com, April 7, 2011.

E. Melanie DuPuis. "Not in My Body: rBGH and the Rise of Organic Milk." *Agriculture and Human Values* 17:285–295, 2000.

The NPD Group. "The Tale of Yogurt: Tracing the Source of Growth." https://www.npd.com/lps/FFT/index3.html

Carolyn Dimitri and Catherine Greene. *Recent Growth Patterns in the U.S. Organic Foods Market.* Agriculture Information Bulletin No. 777. Washington, DC: US Department of Agriculture, September 2002.

Organic Trade Association. "Six Myths Busted by Organic in 2011." n.d. www.ota.com/organic/standards/Organic-Mythbusters.html

John Stevens-Garmon, Chung L. Huang, and Biing-Hwan Lin. "Organic Demand: A Profile of Consumers in the Fresh Produce Market." *Choices* 22(2):109–115, 2007.

CHAPTER FOUR: GLOBAL WAVES OF GRAIN

Leonor Hurtardo. "Corn Price Crisis in Mexico and Guatemala." Food First/Institute for Food and Development Policy, February 22, 2007. [opinion]

U.S. International Trade Commission. *U.S.–Central America–Dominican Republic Free Trade Agreement: Potential Economywide and Selected Sectoral Effects.* Investigation No. TA-2104-13, USITC Publication 3717. Washington, DC: US International Trade Commission, August 2004.

Deborah James. "Food Security, Farming, and the WTO and CAFTA." Global Exchange, n.d.

Catie Duckworth. "The Failures of NAFTA." Council on Hemispheric Affairs, June 19, 2012. www.coha.org/the-failures-of-nafta

Donovan Webster. "Haiti: Two Years after the Earthquake, Where Did the Money Go?" January 10, 2012. www.globalpost.com/dispatch/news/regions/americas/haiti/120110/haiti-earthquake-aid-rice

Michael Economides. "Ethanol Isn't Worth Costlier Corn Flakes and Tortillas." Forbes.com, May 17, 2011.

Kevin Drum. "Ethanol Subsidies: Not Gone, Just Hidden a Little Better." MotherJones.com, January 5, 2012.

Stephen Parker. *Agricultural Progress in the Third World and Its Effect on US Farm Exports.* CBO Publication No. 490. Washington, DC: Congressional Budget Office, May 1989.

World Bank. *World Development Report 1987.* New York: Oxford University Press, 1987.

Timothy A. Wise and Marie Brill. *Fueling the Food Crisis: The Cost to Developing Countries of US Corn Ethanol Expansion.* Washington, DC: ActionAid International USA, October 2012.

Won W. Koo, Richard D. Taylor, and Jeremy W. Mattson. *Impacts of the U.S.–Central America Free Trade Agreement on the U.S. Sugar Industry.* Special Report 03-3, Center for Agricultural Policy and Trade Studies, North Dakota State University, December 2003.

Index Mundi. "Guatemala Wheat Domestic Consumption by Year." IndexMundi.com, n.d.

Minnesota Association of Wheat Growers. "Background on Central America's Wheat Imports." *Small Grains Update,* Issue 179, December 31, 2003.

World Bank. *Guatemala—Nutrition at a Glance.* Report No. 77167. Washington, DC: World Bank, April 1, 2011.

Daniel J. Hoffman, Ana L. Sawaya, Ieda Verreschi, Katherine L. Tucker, and Susan B. Roberts. "Why Are Nutritionally Stunted Children at Increased Risk of Obesity? Studies of Metabolic Rate and Fat Oxidation in Shantytown Children from São Paulo, Brazil." *American Journal of Clinical Nutrition* 72:702–707, 2000.

Talea Miller. "Malnutrition Plagues Guatemala's Children." *PBS Newshour,* February 16, 2011.

Abay Asfaw. "Does Consumption of Processed Foods Explain Disparities in the Body Weight of Individuals? The Case of Guatemala." *Health Economics* 20(2):184–195, 2011.

María Elena Hurtado. "Processed Foods Contribute to Obesity in Guatemala." Javier Torres, trans. Environmental News Network, January 13, 2010.

Ricardo Uauy, Cecilia Albala, and Juliana Kain. "Obesity Trends in Latin America: Transiting from Under- to Overweight." *Journal of Nutrition* 131(3):893S–899S, 2001.

B. C. Curtis. "Wheat in the World." In B. C. Curtis, S. Rajaram, and H. Gómez Macpherson, eds. *Bread Wheat.* FAO Plant Production and Protection Series, No. 30. Rome: Food and Agriculture Organization of the United Nations, 2002.

Grain. "A New Green Revolution for Africa?" Grain.org, December 17, 2007.

William Davis. *Wheat Belly Cookbook.* New York: Rodale Books, 2012.

Simon Romero. "Quinoa's Global Success Creates Quandary at Home." *The New York Times,* March 19, 2011.

Marc Bellemare. "Quinoa Nonsense or Why the World Still Needs Agricultural Economists." January 22, 2013. http://marcfbellemare.com/wordpress/2013/01/quinoa-nonsense-or-why-the-world-still-needs-agricultural-economists/

Heather Day and Travis English. "In Kenya, Farmers Grow Their Own Way." *Yes!* October 4, 2010.

"Food: We Want Wheat—Africa's Growing Cereal Demand." IRINNews.org, October 10, 2012.

US Environmental Protection Agency. "Pesticide Fact Sheet: *Bacillus thuringiensis.*" Office of Prevention, Pesticides and Toxic Substances, November 29, 2011. www.epa.gov/pesticides/biopesticides/pips/smartstax-factsheet.pdf

Peter Thomison. "Managing 'Pollen Drift' to Minimize Contamination of Non-GMO Corn." Ohio State University Extension Fact Sheet, Agronomy Series, AGF-153-04, n.d.

Jack Kaskey. "Monsanto to Charge as Much as 42% More for New Seeds (Update3)." Bloomberg.com, August 13, 2009.

Zia Haq. "Ministry Blames Bt Cotton for Farmer Suicides." *Hindustan Times,* March 26, 2012.

Adam Pugen. "Are GM Seeds to Blame for Indian Farmer Suicides?" *International,* February 21, 2013.

Eli Rogosa. "Seeds for Peace." Rodale Institute, December 14, 2006. http://newfarm.rodaleinstitute.org/international/features/2006/1206/ancientseed/rogosa.shtml

Jessica Fanzo, Danny Hunter, Teresa Borelli, and Federico Mattei. *Diversifying Food and Diets: Using Agricultural Biodiversity to Improve Nutrition and Health.* 2013.

Colin K. Khoury, Anne D. Bjorkman, Hannes Dempewolf, Julian Ramirez-Villegas, Luigi Guarino, Andy Jarris, Loren H. Rieseberg, and Paul C. Strvik. "Increasing Homogeneity in Global Food Supplies and the Implications for Food Security." *PNAS,* March 3, 2014. D01:10.1073/pnas.1313490111. [e-pub ahead of print]

CHAPTER FIVE: THE FRENCH FRIES, THE KETCHUP, AND THE ORPHANED WORLD OF REAL VEGETABLES

Charles Siebert. "Food Ark." *National Geographic,* July 2011.

Esra Capanoglu, Jules Beekwilder, Dilek Boyacioglu, Ric C. H. De Vos, and Robert D. Hall. "The Effect of Industrial Food Processing on Potentially Health-Beneficial Tomato Antioxidants." *Critical Reviews in Food Science and Nutrition* 50(10): 919–930, 2010.

Nanci Hellmich. "'Eat Your Vegetables': For Kids, It Means Fries." *USA Today,* March 3, 2009.

Sarah Nassauer. "Old Ketchup Packet Heads for Trash." *Wall Street Journal,* September 19, 2011.

Javier E. David. "The Ketchup War That Never Was: Burger Giants' Link to Heinz." CNBC, February 15, 2013.

Anne Marie Thow and Corinna Hawkes. "The Implications of Trade Liberalization for Diet and Health: A Case Study from Central America." *Globalization and Health* 5:5, 2009.

Kenneth F. Kiple and Kriemhild Coneè Ornelas (eds.). *The Cambridge World History of Food.* 2 vols. Cambridge, England: Cambridge University Press, October 2000.

National Potato Council. "US per Capita Utilization of Potatoes, by Category: 1970–2001." n.d.

University of Oregon. "Begin Early: Water with Meals May Encourage Wiser Choices." *Science Daily,* May 14, 2012.

Andrew O. Odegaard, Woon Puay Koh, Jian-Min Yuan, Myron D. Gross, and Mark A. Pereira. "Western-Style Fast Food Intake and Cardio-Metabolic Risk in an Eastern Country." *Circulation* 126(2):182–188, 2012.

McDonald's. "McDonald's Food Facts: Ingredients." January 20, 2014. www1.mcdonalds.ca/NutritionCalculator/IngredientFactsEN.pdf

Matthew Guariglia. "Burger Rivalry: McDonald's Drops Heinz Ketchup after Ex-Burger 'King' Named CEO." Heavy.com, October 26, 2013.

Joseph Stromberg. "Scientists Finally Pinpoint the Pathogen That Caused the Irish Potato Famine." Smithsonian.com, May 21, 2013.

R. L. Mikkelsen. "Tomato Flavor and Plant Nutrition: A Brief Review." *Better Crops* 89(2): 14–15, 2005.

Rachel Champeau. "UCLA Researchers Create Tomatoes That Mimic Actions of Good Cholesterol." University of California–Los Angeles, March 19, 2013.

Marion Nestle. "Ketchup Is a Vegetable? Again?" Atlantic.com, November 16, 2011.

Sarah Henry. "Berkeley's New School Food Study: A Victory for Alice Waters." Atlantic.com, September 23, 2010.

United States Department of Agriculture Economic Research Service. "Tomatoes." October 9, 2012. www.ers.usda.gov/topics/crops/vegetables-pulses/tomatoes.aspx#.UubtvP2tt0s

Deborah K. Rich. "California—Tomato capital of the nation." San Francisco Chronicle, August 23, 2008. www.sfgate.com/homeandgarden/article/California-tomato-capital-of-the-nation-3199159.php#page-1

"Our Dwindling Food Variety." National Geographic, July 2011. http://ngm.nationalgeographic.com/2011/07/food-ark/food-variety-graphic

Linda Calvin and Roberta Cook. "North American Greenhouse Tomatoes Emerge as a Major Market Force." Amber Waves, April 2005. http://webarchives.cdlib.org/wayback.public/UERS1/4ag1/41/20120419161004/http:/www.ers.usda.gov/AmberWaves/April05/Features/GreenhouseTomatoes.htm

McDonald's USA Ingredients Listing for Popular Menu Items. http://nutrition.mcdonalds.com/getnutrition/ingredientslist.pdf

CHAPTER SIX: THE SUGAR WE DRINK

Sarah Boseley. "Adults Should Cut Sugar Intake to Less Than a Can of Coke a Day, says WHO." *The Guardian,* March 5, 2014.

"Global Sugar, Sweeteners Market to Hit 97 Billion by 2017." *Food Product Design,* April 18, 2013.

Harvard University School of Public Health. "Sugary Drinks and Obesity Fact Sheet." Nutrition Source, June 2012. www.hsph.harvard.edu/nutritionsource/sugary-drinks-fact-sheet.

Travis A. Smith, Biing-Hwan Lin, and Jonq-Ying Lee. *Taxing Caloric Sweetened Beverages: Potential Effects on Beverage Consumption, Calorie Intake, and Obesity.* Economic Research Report No. 100. Washington, DC: US Department of Agriculture, July 2010.

Sanjay Basu, Paula Yoffe, Nancy Hills, and Robert H. Lustig. "The Relationship of Sugar to Population-Level Diabetes Prevalence: An Econometric Analysis of Repeated Cross-Sectional Data." *PLoS One* 8(2):e57873, 2013.

B. G. Gibbs and R. Forste. "Socioeconomic Status, Infant Feeding Practices and Early Childhood Obesity." *Pediatric Obesity,* April 2, 2013. DOI: 10.1111/j.2047-6310. 2013.00155.x [e-pub ahead of print]

University of Adelaide. "Maternal Diet Sets Up Junk Food Addiction in Babies." April 30, 2013. [news release]

Katrina Trinko. "No Food Stamps for Soda." *National Review Online.* September 14, 2013. www.nationalreview.com/article/358490/no-food-stamps-soda-katrina-trinko

Tatiana Andreyeva, Joerg Luedicke, Kathryn E. Henderson, Amanda S. Tripp. Grocery Store Beverage choices by Participants in Federal Food Assistance and Nutrition Programs." *American Journal of Preventive Medicine* 43(4): 411–418, 2012.

Susanna M. Hofmann and Matthias H. Tschöp. "Dietary Sugars: A Fat Difference." *Journal of Clinical Investigation* 119(5):1089–1092, 2009.

American Chemical Society. "Bottled Tea Beverages May Contain Fewer Polyphenols Than Brewed Tea." August 22, 2010. [news release]

Alan Bjerga. "U.S. Losing Taste for Corn Sweetener as Dieters Shun Soda." Bloomberg.com, January 22, 2013.

Barry M. Popkin. "Patterns of Beverage Use Across the Lifecycle." *Physiology and Behavior* 100(1):4–9, 2010.

Mike Esterl. "Is This the End of the Soft-Drink Era?" *Wall Street Journal,* January 18, 2013.

Lenny R. Vartanian, Marlene B. Schwartz, and Kelly D. Brownell. "Effects of Soft Drink Consumption on Nutrition and Health: A Systematic Review and Meta-Analysis." *American Journal of Public Health* 97(4):667–675, 2007.

"Coca-Cola Taste Test: High Fructose Corn Syrup vs. Sugar." *Huffington Post,* March 6, 2012.

Rob Walker. "Cult Classic." *New York Times,* October 8, 2009.

Judy Bankman. "Mexico: Public Health, Rising Obesity and the NAFTA Effect." *Civil Eats,* July 17, 2013.

Juan A. Rivera, Simón Barquera, Fabricio Campirano, Ismael Campos, Margarita Safdie, and Victor Tovar. "Epidemiological and Nutritional Transition in Mexico: Rapid Increase of Non-Communicable Chronic Diseases and Obesity." *Public Health Nutrition* 5(1A): 113–122, 2002.

Janet M. Wojcicki and Melvin B. Heyman. "Malnutrition and the Role of the Soft Drink Industry in Improving Child Health in Sub-Saharan Africa." *Pediatrics* 126(6):e1617–e1621, 2010.

Jon Entine. "Slimming Down: Food and Beverage Companies Cut 1.5 Trillion Calories, Accelerating Obesity Rate Decline." *Forbes,* May 30, 2013. [opinion]

Gary Taubes and Cristin Kearns Couzens. "Big Sugar's Sweet Little Lies." *Mother Jones,* November/December 2012.

David Leonhardt. "What's Wrong with This Chart?" *New York Times,* May 20, 2009.

Susan E. Swithers. "Artificial Sweeteners Produce the Counterintuitive Effect of Inducing Metabolic Derangements." *Trends in Endocrinology and Metabolism* 24(9):431–441, 2013. [opinion]

Hannah Gardener, Tatjana Rundek, Matthew Markert, Clinton B. Wright, Mitchell S. V. Elkind, and Ralph L. Sacco. "Diet Soft Drink Consumption Is Associated with an Increased Risk of Vascular Events in the Northern Manhattan Study." *Journal of General Internal Medicine* 27(9):1120–1126, 2012.

Harvard University School of Public Health. "Sugary Drinks or Diet Drinks: What's the Best Choice?"

Endocrine Society. "Fructose Sugar Makes Maturing Human Fat Cells Fatter, Less Insulin-Sensitive." *Science Daily,* June 21, 2010.

M. Yanina Pepino, Courtney D. Tiemann, Bruce W. Patterson, Burton M. Wice, and Samuel Klein. "Sucralose Affects Glycemic and Hormonal Responses to an Oral Glucose Load." *Diabetes Care* 36(9):2530–2535, 2013.

Foreign Agricultural Service. *Sugar: World Markets and Trade: Gap Narrowing Again Between Global Sugar Production and Consumption.* Washington, DC: US Department of Agriculture, May 2013.

CHAPTER SEVEN: THE SWEET WE EAT

Center for Nutrition Policy and Promotion. "Figure 3-6: Sources of Added Sugars in the Diets of the U.S. Population Ages 2 Years and Older, NHANES 2005–2006." In *Dietary Guidelines for Americans: 2010.* 7th ed. Washington, DC: US Department of Agriculture and US Department of Health and Human Services, December 2010. www.cnpp.usda.gov/Publications/DietaryGuidelines/2010/PolicyDoc/PolicyDoc.pdf

Connecticut College. "Student–Faculty Research Suggests Oreos Can Be Compared to Drugs of Abuse in Lab Rats." Connecticut College News, October 15, 2013. [news release]

James S. Ruff, Amanda K. Suchy, Sara A. Hugentobler, Mirtha M. Sosa, Bradley L. Schwartz, et al. "Human-Relevant Levels of Added Sugar Consumption Increase Female Mortality and Lower Male Fitness in Mice." *Nature Communications* 4:2245, 2013.

Food Advisory Committee. "Background Document for the Food Advisory Committee: Certified Color Additives in Food and Possible Association with Attention Deficit Hyperactivity Disorder in Children." Food Advisory Committee Meeting, US Food and Drug Administration, March 30–31, 2011.

"Study Ranks '10 Worst' Kids' Cereals for Sugar." CBSNews.com, December 11, 2011.

American Heart Association. "Sugars and Carbohydrates." January 7, 2014. www.heart.org/HEARTORG/GettingHealthy/NutritionCenter/HealthyDietGoals/Sugars-and-Carbohydrates1/4UCM1/43032961/4Article.jsp.

Alexandra Wexler. "Despite Defaults, USDA Sweetens the Pot." *The Wall Street Journal,* November 18, 2013.

Biing-Hwan Lin and Rosanna Mentzer Morrison. "Higher Fruit Consumption Linked with Lower Body Mass Index." *Food Review* 25(3):28–32, 2002.

Tristram Stuart. "The Global Food Waste Scandal." TED Talk, May 2012. www.ted.com/talks/tristram1/4stuart1/4the1/4global1/4food1/4waste1/4scandal.html

Guy Fagherazzi, Alice Vilier, Daniela Saes Sartorelli, Martin Lajous, Beverley Balkau, and Françoise Clavel-Chapelon. "Consumption of Artificially and Sugar-Sweetened Beverages and Incident Type 2 Diabetes in the Etude Epidémiologique Auprès des Femmes de la Mutuelle Générale de l'Education Nationale–European Prospective Investigation into Cancer and Nutrition Cohort." *American Journal of Clinical Nutrition* DOI: 10.3945/ajcn.112.050997, January 30, 2013. [epub ahead of print]

Muriel Veldman and Marco Lankhorst. *Socio-Economic Impact of Commercial Exploitation of Rwandan Marshes: A Case Study of Sugar Cane Production in Rural Kigali.* Rome: International Land Coalition, January 2011.

The World Bank. "The Transformational Use of Information and Communication Technologies in Africa." 2012. http://go.worldbank.org/CXS4GFJDE0

Shekhar Anand and Gizachew Sisay. "Engaging Smallholders in Value Chains: Creating New Opportunities for Beekeepers in Ethiopia." Programme Insights, Oxfam GB, April 2011.

RESET THE TABLE AND *Really* CHANGE DINNER

Kathleen Page, Owen Chan, Jagriti Arora, Renata Belfort-DeAguiar, James Dzuira, Brian Roehmholdt, Gary W. Cline, Sarita Naik, Rajita Sinha, Todd Constable, Rupert S. Sherwin. "Effects of Fructose vs. Glucose on Regional Cerebral Blood Flow in Brain Regions Involved with Appetite and Reward Pathways." *The Journal of American Medical Association,* 309(1):63-70, 2013.

United Nations Environment Program. "Food Waste Facts." n.d. www.unep.org/wed/quickfacts

"Digital Set to Surpass TV in Time Spent with US Media." eMarketer, August 1, 2013. www.emarketer.com/Article/Digital-Set-Surpass-TV-Time-Spent-with-US-Media/1010096

ACKNOWLEDGMENTS

A BOOK ALWAYS takes a village and a book about food also takes farmers, chefs, waiters, home cooks, grocery store clerks, food policy wonks on Twitter, and all the eaters who have fed me or dined with me—I am thankful for you all.

I have been honored to work with the whole company of Rodale Inc. My editor, Alex Postman, is brilliant and has the best "bedside manner" of anyone as accomplished and driven as she is. And to other great Rodale people—Mollie Grewe, Erin Williams, Emily Weber Eagan, my high school pal Ursula Cary, Elissa Altman, and the friendly 8th floor receptionist, Maria Barreto—I hope to continue to work with you all. Special thanks to Maria Rodale, a hero to the food movement, and I'm glad to have met so many of the Rodale family members who each gracefully carry on their powerful family name.

Big thanks and love to my friend and agent James Marshall Reilly and the whole team at The Guild Agency, especially Tori Marra and Jared Shahid. You have believed in me and in my message and have allowed me to reach the world with it. Thanks also to the Summit Series community and leadership for introducing me to James and to some of the greatest folks in the world.

I'm so grateful to the awesome Danielle Nierenberg for her leadership of Food Tank and deep passion for improving the global food system. I'm also grateful to my cadre of former colleagues who have helped me learn and grow, including: Lauren Bush Lauren and the FEED team; Lisa Shields and Admiral Jeffrey Fowler, USN (Ret.) from the Council on Foreign Relations; Professor Jeff Sachs and Dr. Prabhjot Singh from Columbia University; Howard G. Buffett and Howard W. Buffett for your tireless work to end hunger and make the world better for all people; and the great Josette Sheeran, formerly of the UN World Food Program, for being a leader to the world's neediest. Thanks to all of my teachers, and food service providers, from kindergarten to Columbia University, for feeding my brain and teaching me how to learn. And to all members of the navy and military family—thank you for your service, and stay safe.

So many talented people have helped to turn my ideas into written words, but no one as much as the incredible Kathy White—thanks for sharing your knowledge of writing a book with me. Thanks to my friend and colleague Dr. Jessica Fanzo and to the great Raj Patel for reading early manuscripts and giving your thoughts.

My love of family dinner starts with my incredible husband and wonderful parents, and extends to my huge extended Gustafson, Nevin, and now Campbell families: Thanks for feeding me with love and always lots of food. Special thanks to Gran for the rule of salad at every dinner, AK for my love of hummus, and all my aunts for recipes like Swedish rye bread and layered dip. And, finally, to my awesome circle of friends, I am lucky to have such wonderful people to share life, laughter, and meals with.

INDEX

Boldface references indicate illustrations.

A

Africa. *See also specific African locations*
  agricultural problems in, v
  Green Revolution in, 93
  hunger in, v–vi, vii, x, xvii, 33, 37
  soda and sugar consumption in, 129,
    131, 144–45, 146, 154
  US aid to, xiv–xv
Agent Orange, 12
Agricultural Adjustment Act of 1933. *See*
  Farm bill
Agricultural aid, xiv–xv, 23, 24, 26, 47,
  124, 188
Agricultural development, 22, 66, 83–84,
  124, 144, 193, 194
Alliance for a Green Revolution in Africa,
  93
Amber Waves Farm, 101–2
Antibiotic-resistant bacteria, 42, 43, 69
Antibiotics
  in foods, 55–56, 65, 183
    reduced use of, 43
  livestock given, 34, 38, 42, 55–56, 69,
    182
Apple varietals, loss of, 167
Artificially cheap foods, 14–16, 17, 20,
  23, 27, 55, 140, 184, 195, 200,
  204
Artificial sweeteners, 146–48

B

Bad food
  corn-based, 26, 27, 28
  ill effects of, xii, xiii
money spent on, 187, 191
in typical meal, 182–85
Banana crops, threats to, 171–72
Beans, grown with corn, 3
Beef. *See also* Meat
  corn-fed, 30, 34–36, 182
  grass-fed, 35, 50, 51, 52, 53, 63
  pink slime in, 41, 44, 47
Beers, craft, 153
Belly fat, from HFCS, 21
Beverages, sweetened. *See* Sweetened
  beverages
Biofuel, corn for, 3, 17. *See also* Ethanol
Bloomberg, Michael, xvi, 139, 140, 144
Borlaug, Norman, 88, 89, 90–91, 92, 93,
  94, 95, 98, 103, 106
Bottled water, 151–52
Bread
  food waste from, 168
  sprouted grain, 101, 210
  unhealthy ingredients in, 158, 159, 183,
    184, 196
  wheat for, 89, 92, 98, 99, 100, 102,
    183, 210
Breakfast, sugary foods for, 160–62. *See
  also* Cereals, added sugar in
Burgers
  annual consumption of, 1, 2
  better buns for, 100–101
  corn-fed beef for, 30
  in fast food industry, 44–46
  homemade, 210, 211
  soda consumed with, 110
  unhealthy, 183
Butter, 73, 74, 75

C

CAFOs. *See* Concentrated animal feeding operations
CAFTA, 81, 183
Cattle producers, consolidation of, 40–42
Central American–US Free Trade Agreement (CAFTA), 81, 183
Cereals, added sugar in, 127–28, 157–158, **157**, 160–162, 183
Change Dinner Barbecue, 207, 210–13
Cheap food. *See also* Artificially cheap foods
    negative effects of, 27, 37, 40, 41, 49, 143, 206
    obesity from, 37, 49
Cheese
    artisanal, demand for, 76, 77
    increased consumption of, 60, **60**, 63
    natural coloring of, 74–75
    organic, ingredients in, 65
    processed, 74, 75
Cherry farming, 176
Chocolate, 172–73
Chronic diseases
    causes of, xiii, 128, 134
    health-care spending on, xv, xvi
    obesity-related, 49, 72, 188, 194
CLAs, in milk, 63, 70–71
Coca-Cola, x, xi, 37, 58, 129, 130, 131, 134, 141, 142, 143, 144, 145, 147, 154
Coffee, 84, 141, 152–53, 193, 194, 196
Colony collapse disorder, 21, 177
Community supported agriculture (CSA), 29, 102, 174, 175, 177, 189, 192, 207
Concentrated animal feeding operations (CAFOs), 38, 40, 44, 50, 52, 55, 64, 66, 68, 70, 182, 185
Conjugated linoleic acids (CLAs), in milk, benefits of, 63, 70–71
Conservation Reserve Program, 15, 16
Conservatism, 207–8
Consolidation
    in dairy industry, 65–67, 69–70, 71, 72

    of food growers and producers, 39, 40, 41, 42–44, 123
    of tomato plant breeding, 104–5
Consumer spending, power of, xviii, 101, 152, 154, 191–92
Contract farming, 103–4
Cooking, at home, 187, 191, 206
Corn
    artificially cheap, 14–16, 17, 23, 195
    benefits of, 2–3
    bred for sweetness, 8
    Bt, 11, 48, 94
    developing nations growing, 25
    early European description of, 2
    farm bill and, 22–23
    farming of, 3–7
    fresh, on the cob, 26–27, 210, 211
    genetically modified, 2, 8, 9, 10, 12, 14, 25, 27, 30, 33, 95, 96, 162
    as global currency, 23–25
    government subsidies for, xvi, 5, 16, 17, 27, 30, 33, 35, 36, 73, 81, 82, 128, 130, 139, 140, 183
    hidden sources of, 195
    for international food aid, 22–23, 79, 80
    multicolored, 3, 8
    nixtamalization of, 7, 87
    overabundance of, 15, 16
    reduced diversity of, 105
    role of, in food production, 1–2
    uses for, 3, 5–6, 17–18, 27, 28 (*see also* Ethanol; High-fructose corn syrup; Livestock feed, corn as)
    US exports of, 80, 81–82
Cows
    antibiotics given to, 34, 38, 42
    corn-fed, 34–35, 38–39, 42, 185, 195
    grass-fed, 35, 37–38, 42, 49, 52, 55, 63, 74
    treatment of, 38–39, 55–56, 182
Cow shares, 52, 193
Crop diversity
    encouraging, 172, 195
    loss of, xiii, 105, 114, 123
    story about, 29–30
CSA. *See* Community supported agriculture

D

Dairy farms, 65–66, 71–73
Dairy-free eating, 77
Dairy industry, consolidation in, 65–67, 69–70, 71, 72
Dairy Management Inc., 61–62
Dairy products. *See also* Cheese; Milk
  best sources of, 77–78
  from corn-fed animals, 30, 55
  fortified, 63–64
  lobbying groups promoting, 61–63
  nutritionally degraded and cheap, 55–56
  organic, 56, 77
  rBGH-free, 69
  rBGH-treated, 56, 68–69
Dairy Queen, 72, 73
Darfur, vii
Deforestation, 33, 74
Desertification, 50–51
Desserts
  added sugar in, 127, 156–57, **157**, 184–85
  better choices of, 176–77
  cutting back on, 159, 197
  homemade, 160
    Homemade Apple Cherry Crumble, 213
Diabetes, xiii, xv, 49, 72, 87, 100, 122, 128, 135, 138, 143, 144, 147, 151, 164, 186, 188, 194, 198
Diet foods, avoiding, 197–98
Diets, variety of, xvi
Digital media, time spent on, 191
Diversification, agricultural, 102. *See also* Crop diversity
Domino's pizzas, 61, 62, 64–65
Drinking patterns, 150–54

E

Eating habits, evolution of, 179
Ecuador, hunger and malnutrition in, 169, 170, 171
Egypt, wheat consumption in, 92
Enriched foods, xv, 58, 64, 146

Entrepreneurs
  healthy-food, 176–77, 203
  young farmers as, 102, 175–76, 189
Ethanol, 6, 8, 17–18, 23, 30, 35, 82, 85, 87, 100
Ethiopia, honey production in, 177
Ethylene, for ripening produce, 114–15

F

Factory farms, 5, 6, 17, 33, 38, 39, 42–43, 44, 64, 70, 71, 181
Fair trade, 152, 153, 172, 173, 177, 192, 193–94
Family dinners, 53, 189–90
Farm bill, 5, 15, 16, 17, 19, 22, 23, 24, 36, 83, 163
Farmers
  cattle-raising profits of, 39
  connecting with community, 102
  declining number of, 41, 185–86
  encouraging crop diversity from, 195
  entrepreneurial, 102, 175–76, 189
  overweight and obesity among, 6–7
  seed collecting by, 93–94
  suicides among, 97
Farmers' markets, 76, 102, 104, 120, 124, 174, 175, 177, 189, 190, 202, 204, 205
Farms
  declining number of, 4, 40, 41, 65, 72, 90
  factory (*see* Factory farms)
Fast food. *See also* McDonald's
  added sugar in, 158
  changing demand for, 47–48
  death rates from, 110
  effect on food systems, 44–46
  in foreign countries, vi, 45–46, 67, 85, 86
  fries and ketchup (*see* French fries; Ketchup)
  increased consumption of, 61
  obesity from, 72
  quitting, 198–99
  soda consumed with, 110
  spending on, 190

Fat, dietary, sources of, 59–60, 61
FEED Bags, ix, 129, 192
FEED Health Backpacks, ix–x
FEED Projects, ix, xviii, 79, 174, 192,
        201
Fertilizers, vi, 5, 16, 17, 25, 34, 39, 90,
        93, 94, 96, 97, 104, 105, 107,
        162, 181, 185, 201
Finley, Ron, 118, 119–20, 123, 202
Fish, corn-fed farmed, 30
Fish oil supplements, 64
Food aid, international
    corn for, 23, 24, 79, 80, 81
    problems of, 23–25, 26, 81, 83–84,
        96, 181
    US policies on, xiv, xv, xvi
Food costs
    decline in, xv, 36
    for healthy vs. unhealthy foods, 132,
        190–91
    HFCS for lowering, xv, 128, 130, 131,
        188
    income spent on, 49
Food culture, redefining, 208
Food deserts, xii, 7, 27, 73, 111, 119,
        121
Food for Life bread, 101
Food for Peace, 84
Food insecurity, vii, viii, xix, 37, 57, 80,
        82, 89, 92, 140, 170, 180
Food production
    changes in, xv–xvi, 4, 37, 45, 46, 95
    consolidation in, 39, 40, 41, 42–44,
        123
    corporate-controlled, xiv, 10, 47
    failures in, 82
    increased, 89
    measure of, 141
    positive, 102
    role of corn in, 1–2
Food purchases
    as activist platform, 205–6
    alternative methods of, 204
    conservative, 207–8
    decline in, xv
Food shifts, for better health,
        189–209

Food start-ups, 173–75, 189, 203
Food systems, current
    changing, xvii, xviii–xix, 29–30,
        98–99, 101, 102, 118–21, 123,
        124–25, 167, 174, 177, 180, 187,
        189, 192, 193, 203, 206, 207,
        208–9
    origin of, xiii–xiv, 130
    problems of, xii, xiii, 14, 23, 34,
        36, 37, 47, 75, 81, 91, 106,
        114, 117, 145, 168, 172,
        173, 180–81, 182, 185, 187,
        194, 198, 200–201, 204,
        206, 209
Food Tank: The Food Think Tank,
        xviii
Food waste, 167–70, 173–74, 180,
        200–202
Fortified foods, xv, 58, 59, 63–64, 67,
        98, 142, 145–46, 161–62
Frankenfoods, 9–11. See also Genetically
        modified (GM) foods; Genetically
        modified organisms (GMOs)
French fries, 106–7, 108, 109, 110,
        111–12, 116, 117, 124, 198–99
Fruit juices, 149, 153–54
Fruits
    disincentives for growing, 117–18,
        166–67
    fresh, short shelf life of, 161
    health benefits of, 164–66
    historical reverence toward, 164
    increasing consumption of, 166, 167,
        210

G
Gardens
    home, 124, 202, 203
    school, 121, 202, 207
    urban vegetable, 118, 119–21
Gasoline prices, 18
Genetically modified (GM) foods
    corn, 2, 8, 9, 10, 12, 14, 25, 27, 30, 33,
        95, 96, 162
    tomatoes, 115, 117
    wheat, 10, 95–96

Genetically modified organisms (GMOs)
  bans on, 10
  controversies about, 9–11, 14, 16,
    95–97
  creation of, 94–95
  health concerns about, 13–14, 25
  increased herbicide use with, 11–12
  as ineffective solution to world hunger,
    12, 16, 25
Genetic engineering, 2, 8, 11, 14. *See also*
    Genetically modified (GM) foods;
    Genetically modified organisms
    (GMOs)
Glyphosate, 11, 12
GMOs. *See* Genetically modified
    organisms
Government subsidies, agricultural, xiii,
    xvi, 16, 23, 24, 25, 28, 53, 143,
    207
  corn, xvi, 5, 16, 17, 27, 30, 33, 35, 36,
    73, 81, 82, 128, 130, 139, 140,
    183
  ethanol, 82
  fruits and vegetables excluded from,
    117–18, 166
  grain, xvi, 22, 25
  meat, 39, 44, 50
  rice, xvi, 24, 36
  sugar, 130, 150, 163
Grains. *See also specific grains*
  alternative, 101
  subsidies for, xvi, 22, 25
Grasslands, restoring, 51
"Green juices," 154
Green Revolution, 88, 90, 91, 93, 97–98,
    146
Growth hormones, 56, 65, 68–69, 76
Guatemala
  food economy of, 80–82, 84–85
  increased wheat consumption in,
    85–86, 87
  malnutrition and hunger in, 80, 81, 82,
    84, 85, 86, 87, 100, 108
  obesity in, 85, 86, 87, 108
  stunted growth in, 79, 80, 82, 84, 85,
    86, 87, 100
Gulf of Mexico, dead zone in, 5

H

Hamburgers. *See* Burgers
Health-care expenditures
  for chronic diseases, xv, xvi
  increase in, xv–xvi, 49
  obesity-related, 28, 49, 190
Heinz, 28, 94, 103–4, 105–8, 112, 118,
    120
Herbicide-resistant weeds, 11
Herbicides, xiii, 5, 11, 12, 27, 34, 96
High-fructose corn syrup (HFCS), 30,
    100, 130
  advertising of, 62
  attributes of, 139, 159
  consumption of
    increased, 20, 137, 159
    refusing, 28, 195
  creation of, 19
  food sources of, 20, 108, 112, 118, 128,
    130–31, 139, 148, 183, 184
  government corn subsidies and, xvi,
    128, 183
  health effects of, 20, 21, 128, 132, 137
  increased exports of, 143
  increased production of, xiv
  for lowering food prices, xv, 128, 130,
    131, 188
Holistic planned grazing, 51
Honey, 149–50, 157, **157**, 177
Honeybees, colony collapse disorder and,
    21, 177
Hunger
  in Africa, v–vi, vii, x, xvii, 33, 37
  climate shifts causing, 206
  disasters causing, 205
  in Ecuador, 169, 170, 171
  in Guatemala, 81, 82, 85, 86
  increasing awareness of, viii, 186–87
  in India, 182
  obesity related to, xii, xiii, xvii, 66, 87,
    188–89
  population growth and, 97
  solutions to
    effective, viii, ix, xviii–xix, 51–52,
      93, 118–21, 124–25, 189, 192–93,
      193–94, 202
    high-yield wheat as, 89–90, 92, 106

Hunger *(cont.)*
    solutions to *(cont.)*
        ineffective, xii, 9, 12, 13, 15–16, 22–23,
            24, 25, 66, 82–83, 86, 122, 167
        progress with, 188
    statistics on, 13, 37
    violence connected to, vii–viii, xviii, 24, 92
Hybridization, 94, 95

I
India
    farmer suicides in, 97
    hunger in, 182
    loss of crop diversity in, xiii
Infant formula, 66–67, 136
Irish potato famine, 113, 114, 171

J
Juices, 149, 153–54

K
Kentucky, farming improvements in,
    122–23
Ketchup, 106, 107, 108, 109, 110, 112,
    116, 118, 183

L
Labor abuses, 43–44, 162–63, 172, 182, 185
Livestock feed, corn as, 30, 33–36,
    38–39, 42, 55
Locally grown food, 18, 27, 102, 118,
    123, 124, 167, 193, 202
Low impact foods, 193–94, 203–4
Lustig, Robert, 137, 149, 157

M
Maize cultivation, Mayan, 80
Malnutrition
    contributors to, 2, 22
    countries with, vi, 57, 80, 82, 84, 85,
        86, 87, 100, 108, 171, 183
    GMO goal to end, 12

Maple syrup, 149, 150
Margarine, 73–74, 75
Masai people, diet of, 26, 33, 57–59,
    66
Matoke, x, xi, 2
Mayans, agricultural practices of, 80
Mbarara, Uganda, x–xii, xix, 209
McDonald's, 44, 45–46, 47, 86, 107,
    111–12, 131, 134, 158, 160,
    199
Meat. *See also* Beef
    antibiotics in, 42
    consumption of, 33, 36, 49, 53
    grass-fed, 31–33, 50, 51, 52, 53, 63
    higher-cost, benefits of, 49
    production of, 33–34, 35, 51–52
    subsidies for, 39, 44, 50
Meatless Mondays, 53
Meat-locker shares, 52
Menu for a Changed Dinner, 211–13
Mexico, soda consumption in, 143, 144
Milk
    best source of, 73
    childhood obesity and, 60–61
    flavored, added sugar in, 148, 184
    fortified, 64
    as gateway food, 66
    from grass-fed vs. grain-fed cows, 63
    low-fat and fat-free, 59, 60, 61, 64
    organic, 56, 65, 76
    pasteurized, 70, 71
    processed alternatives to, 58–59
    production of, 56, 69–70
    raw, 70–71, 72, 73
    rBGH-free, 69
    rBGH-treated, 56, 68–69
    sweetened drinks replacing, 60, 61, 135
    swill, 70
    whole, 59–60, **60**, 61, 63, 64
Millennium Villages Project (MVP), ix,
    25
Milo cocoa drink, 58, 59, 64–65, 66, 67
Modern American Diet, xiii, 33, 108, 191,
    210
Mono-cropping, xiv, 5, 24, 80, 90, 92, 93,
    106, 108, 114, 123, 124, 162, 167,
    169, 171, 172, 195

Monsanto, xiv, 8, 9, 10, 11, 12, 41, 56, 68, 69, 76, 93, 94, 95, 96, 97, 104, 115, 185

N

NAFTA. *See* North American Free Trade Agreement
Nairobi, Kenya, urban gardens in, 121
Nestlé, 57, 58, 64, 66–67, 73, 172
Nixtamalization, of corn, 7, 87
North American Free Trade Agreement (NAFTA), 80–81, 143, 183, 185

O

Oatmeal, processed, sugar in, 160
Obesity and overweight
    causes of, 13–14, 20, 21, 48, 72, 92, 98, 128, 136, 151, 186
    childhood, xvi, 60–61, 136, 149, 182
    deaths related to, 72
    diseases related to, 49, 72, 188, 194
    epidemic of, xiii, xvii, 149, 186, 188, 194
    among farmers, 6–7
    food shifts for reversing, 189–209
    in foreign countries, xvii, 85, 86, 87, 108, 143, 144, 171
    health-care expenditures for, 28, 49, 190
    hunger related to, xii, xiii, xvii, 66, 87, 188–89
    incidence of, xvii, 37, 49, 181, 182, 194, 200
    solutions to, 124–25, 137, 139, 204–5
Omega-3 and omega-6 fatty acids, 63, 64
Organic foods, 56, 65, 76–77, 174
Osteoporosis, 77
Overgrazing, desertification from, 50–51
Overweight. *See* Obesity and overweight

P

Palm oil, 74
Pasteurized milk, 70, 71

Patent-protected seeds, 5, 9, 10, 25, 26, 93, 95, 96, 188
Pepsi, 28, 127, 130–31, 134, 141, 142, 143, 148, 149, 154, 188
Pesticides, xiv, 5, 11–12, 13, 17, 26, 27, 34, 65, 90, 94, 96, 97, 104, 107, 162, 181, 182, 183
Photosynthesis, 37, 38, 179, 185
Pink slime, 41, 44, 47
Pizza
    cheese consumption and, 61, 62, 63
    Domino's, 61, 62, 64–65
    homemade, 78
    organic, demand for, 76
    soda consumed with, 110
    as "vegetable" source, 116, 118
Pizza cheese, ingredients in, 65
Plastic bags, waste from, 201–2
Population growth, 89, 97, 112, 180
Portion sizes, 200–201
Posilac, cows given, 56
Potatoes
    french fried (*see* French fries)
    Heinz's sales of, 108
    history of, 112–13
    preserving genetic diversity of, 113
    raw, calories in, 112
    shifts in consumption of, 109–10, **109**, 124
    Sweet Potato or Local Fingerling Potato "Fries," 212
Pregnancy, foods to avoid during, 136
Processed foods
    added sugar in, 156, **157**, 158–59
    avoiding, 196
    backlash against, 75–76
    in developing nations, x–xii, xix, 24
    diet foods, 197–98
    HFCS-free, 195
    money spent on, xiii
    pizza ingredients as, 65
    prevalence of, xviii
    tomato-based, 105, 117, 118
    in US, xii
    wheat-based, 98, 99, 100
Public Law 480, 84

Q

Quality protein maize (QPM), 2, 9
Quinoa, 101

R

rBGH, 56, 68–69, 76
Recipes
  Fresh and Colorful Summer Salad, 212
  Homemade Apple Cherry Crumble, 213
  A Homemade Burger, 211
  Mint Green Sun Tea, 213
  Sweet Corn on the Cob, 211
  Sweet Potato or Local Fingerling Potato "Fries," 212
Recombinant bovine growth hormone (rBGH), 56, 68–69, 76
Restaurant meals
  home cooking vs., 53
  increased consumption of, 61
  less meat in, 53
  organic pizza, 76
Reusable bags, 201
Rice
  as food aid, 24
  genetic engineering of, 2
  subsidies for, xvi, 24, 36
Ritz, Stephen, 118, 120–21, 123, 202
Roundup, 11, 12
Ruhiira, Uganda, v–vi, viii, ix, 25
Russia, 45, 46, 92
Rwanda, 4, 129, 163, 202

S

Salads, 210, 212
School feeding, international, viii, ix, 79
School gardens, 121, 202, 207
School lunches, 41, 75, 116, 118, 139, 184
Seed prices, 95, 96–97
Seeds, patent-protected, 5, 9, 10, 25, 26, 93, 95, 96, 188
Seed saving, 94, 95
Serving sizes, 183
Silage, 3

Slaughterhouses
  animals sent to, 34, 38
  consolidation of, 39, 40
  immigrant labor in, 43–44, 185
Slow food, 121, 199
Soda. See also Sweetened beverages
  abstaining from, 152, 196–97
  added sugar in, 128, 130, 133, 134, 156
  alternatives to, 196–97
  attempts to limit, xvi, 139–41, 144
  consumption of
    with calorie-dense foods, 110
    declining, 141, 143, 151, 152
    increased, 127, 128, 129, 134, 188
  diet, 146–48, 152, 197, 199
  in foreign markets, 143–45
  health risks from, 147
  HFCS in, 130–31
  oversized servings of, xvi, 133–34
  pricing of, 131–32, 150
  replacing milk consumption, 60, 61
Squash, grown with corn, 3
Stunted growth, 2, 183, 186
  in Guatemala, 79, 80, 82, 84, 85, 86, 87, 100
Subsidies. See Government subsidies, agricultural
Sugar
  added
    cutting back on, 159–60, 196
    estimated consumption of, 155–56
    increased consumption of, 127, 133
    recommended limits on, 128, 133, 157
    sources of, 127–28, 130, 134, 136, 147–49, 155–59, **157**, 160, 183, 184–85
  addiction to, 137–38, 156
  body's handling of, 138–39
  consumption of
    diseases associated with, 134–35, 147
    statistics on, 20–21
    weight gain from, 20, 21, 146

cultivation of, 162–63
HFCS replacing, 130–31
in ketchup, 108, 110
natural sources of, 129–30, 133, 137,
    156, 164
pricing of, 19–20, 163–64
subsidies for, 130, 150, 163
Sugar substitutes, 146–48
Sun tea, 153, 210, 213
Supermarkets, alternatives to, 204
Supplements, money spent on, 64
Sweetened beverages. *See also* Soda
    abstaining from, 159
    added sugar in, 128, 134, 155, 157, **157**,
        183
    alternatives to, 150, 151–52
    decreased consumption of, 136
    fortified, 142, 145, 146
    HFCS in, 21
    increased consumption of, 141
    oversized, 150–51
    replacing milk consumption, 60, 61,
        135
    spending on, 190
Swill milk, 70

T

Tanzania
    agricultural challenges in, 57–59, 66,
        67, 71
    school gardens in, 121
Tap water, 151–52
Tea, 141, 142, 145, 147, 152, 155, 183,
    210, 213
Technologies, agricultural, 203
Terrorism, hunger related to, vii, viii,
    xviii, 24
30 Project, xvii–xviii, 29
Thousand Gardens Project, 121
"Three sisters," 3
Tomatoes, 182, 183
    crossbreeding of, 103, 104
    genetically modified, 115, 117
    heirloom, 78, 102, 105, 118, 121, 124
    for ketchup (*see* Ketchup)

in processed foods, 105, 117, 118
    reduction in varieties of, 105
    vine- vs. ethylene-ripened, 114–15
Trans fats, 73, 74
TV viewing, time spent on, 191
2,4-D, 12

U

Uganda. *See also* Mbarara, Uganda;
        Ruhiira, Uganda
    grass-fed meat in, 31–33
    hunger and obesity in, xvii
    soda consumption in, 145
Urban vegetable gardens, 118, 119–21

V

Value of food, redefining, 199–200
Vegetables
    consumption of
        inadequate, 116, 117
        increasing, 124, 210
        recommended vs. actual, 115–16
    disincentives for growing, 117–18,
        166–67
    food products classified as, 116–17,
        118
    fresh, short shelf life of, 161
    homegrown, 124
    Kentucky-grown, 122–23
    from urban gardens, 118, 119–21
Violence, hunger connected to, vii–viii,
        xviii, 24, 89, 92
Vitamins and minerals, from supplements
        vs. food, 165–66

W

Walkable communities, 204–5
Water consumption, 141, 150, 151–52,
    154
Weeds, Roundup-resistant, 11
Weight gain. *See also* Obesity and
        overweight
    from sugar consumption, 20, 21, 146

Wheat
  African demand for, 93
  consumption of
    in Guatemala, 85–86, 87
    shifts in, 99
  domestication of, 88
  genetically modified, 10, 95–96
  healthier, demand for, 100–102
  high-yield, development of, 88–90, 98,
    103
  obesity linked to, 98
  overdependence on, effects of, 92

  processed, 98, 99–100
  semidwarf, health problems from,
    100
Wineries, local, 153

Y

Yogurt, sugar in, 156, 158–59

Z

Zea mays. See Corn

Higher Unlearning:
39 Post-Requisite Lessons for Achieving a Successful Future

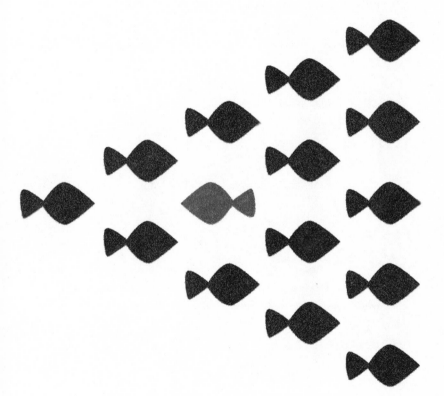

Jack Uldrich
Author of *Unlearning 101:*
101 Lessons in Thinking Inside-Out the Box

ISBN 13: 978-1592984188

Library of Congress Catalog Number: 2011928807
Printed in the United States of America
Second Printing: 2012
15   14   13   12   5   4   3   2

Cover and interior designs by Emsster Design Company.

Beaver's Pond Press, Inc.
7108 Ohms Lane,
Edina, MN 55439
(952) 829-8818
www.BeaversPondPress.com

To order, visit www.BeaversPondBooks.com or call 800-901-3480.
Reseller discounts available.

VOLUMES NOT FOR INDIVIDUAL SALE.

Higher Unlearning:
39 Post-Requisite Lessons for Achieving a Successful Future

Jack Uldrich
Author of *Unlearning 101:*
101 Lessons in Thinking Inside-Out the Box

To my children,
Meghan and Sean,
never stop learning —
and unlearning.

Table of Contents

Introduction 1

Pre-Quiz 5

Lesson 1: Knowledge Can Kill – Unlearn or Die 13

Lesson 2: Don't Climb the Highest Mountain 18

Lesson 3: Become Uncomfortable in Your Own Skin 23

Lesson 4: Argue with Yourself (It's Not Debatable) 27

Lesson 5: Do Not Feed Creatures of Habit 30

Lesson 6: Study at an Anti-Library 33

Lesson 7: Question the Wisdom of Experts 36

Lesson 8: Bite the Hand That Feeds You 40

Lesson 9: Unlock the Keys to Failure 43

Lesson 10: See What Isn't There 46

Lesson 11: If It Goes Without Saying, Question It 49

Lesson 12: Think Small 53

Lesson 13: Practice Intentional Imperfection........................56

Lesson 14: The Grass Isn't Greener on the Other Side 59

Lesson 15: Cast a Narrow Net 63

Lesson 16: Bet Against Yourself 66

Lesson 17: Do the Math Until It Doesn't Add Up 69

Lesson 18: Don't Follow the Money 72

Lesson 19: Grow From Your Inexperience 76

Lesson 20: Mix Up Your Mind 79

Lesson 21: Know Doubt 82

Lesson 22: Lose Sight of the Shore 85

Lesson 23: Ignore the Eclipse and Admire the Sunset 88

Lesson 24: Playing it Safe is Risky 91

Lesson 25: Put One Foot in Back of the Other 94

Lesson 26: Stop Looking for Patterns 97

Lesson 27: Show Your True Colors: Fear Commitment 101

Lesson 28: Do Stop Believing 104

Lesson 29: Don't Reach for the Stars 107

Lesson 30: Zone Out to Zone In 111

Lesson 31: Engage in Situational Unawareness Training 114

Lesson 32: Don't Just Do Something, Sit There 117

Lesson 33: Shoot "Granny" Style 120

Lesson 34: Don't Mind Your P's & Q's 123

Lesson 35: Put on Some Rose-Colored Glasses 128

Lesson 36: See the Whole Picture 132

Lesson 37: Tread Cautiously on Thick Ice 36

Lesson 38: Develop a Healthy Dose of Unconfidence 139

Lesson 39: Ignorance isn't Bliss, but It May Hold the

Key to Wisdom 142

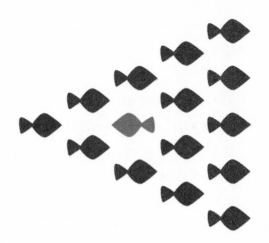

Introduction

What if learning more, acquiring ever-increasing amounts of information and completing all the mandatory prerequisites at school, work and in life were no longer sufficient for guaranteeing future success? What if, instead, there were post-requisite lessons that require you to unlearn much of what you have previously learned?

This future has arrived, and as Alvin Toffler so presciently wrote forty years ago, "The illiterate of the twenty-first century will not be those who cannot read and write, but those who cannot learn, unlearn and relearn." Great emphasis has always been paid to learning and, recently, more attention has been placed on relearning but the middle concept—unlearning—has been widely ignored. Alas, some new learning can't take place until some unlearning occurs first. The following thirty-nine lessons are easy to digest and designed to get you started down the productive and profitable path of unlearning.

The format for each chapter is straightforward. Each begins with a quotation and is followed by a simple question. At the end, a short "homework assignment" is given. The purpose of this structure is threefold. First, as Benjamin Disraeli once said, "The wisdom of the wise and the experience of the ages are perpetuated by quotations." I agree and I have selected a unique quotation to begin each lesson to emphasize the idea that while my words on unlearning may be new, the concept is not. In fact, the importance of unlearning has been recognized for eons—from Aristotle and Zeno to more contemporary individuals as varied as architects and authors, business gurus and Buddhist scholars, Catholic and Confucian philosophers, feminists and futurists, poets and professors, statesmen and science fiction sages alike. All have agreed unlearning is a necessary and vital skill.

Second, I have chosen to follow each quotation with a question because, as Francis Bacon wrote more than 300 years ago, "A prudent question is one-half of wisdom." Each question was selected for one reason: Most people believe they know the answer to the questions being asked, but their answers are almost always wrong. In other words, each question selected demonstrates that 1) most people think they know more than they do and 2) the recognition of their faulty knowledge will serve as a tangible reminder that continued advancement is often as much a matter of stepping back and unlearning as it is advancing forward in the form of new learning. Because I immediately provide the answer to each question after it is posed in each chapter, I strongly encourage all readers to first attempt to answer all thirty-nine questions in the Pre-Quiz beginning on Page 5. If you are confident in your knowledge, I invite you to write down your answers in ink—especially the answer to Question 38.

Lastly, each chapter will conclude with a "homework assignment" to both demonstrate that unlearning has broad applicability as a life skill, and to reinforce the idea that in order to reap the full benefits of unlearning, one must understand that it is a skill that must be constantly honed and applied.

Before going any further, let me say that I don't consider myself an expert on unlearning. Rather, this book has its humble origins in a file I began compiling back in 2005 of various facts, assumptions, habits and beliefs I found I needed to unlearn. In fact, most of the questions posed in this book were chosen because I originally provided the wrong answer and subsequently had to unlearn what I thought I knew. I therefore approach the topic of unlearning with a great deal of humility; I do, however, believe it is a critical skill and I hope that by the end of the book you'll agree.

I now conclude this brief introduction with a quotation from Aristotle who said, "It is the mark of an educated mind to be able to entertain a thought without accepting it." I invite and encourage you to approach this book in this same open-minded spirit. Feel free to entertain each lesson without being compelled to accept it. I say this not because I lack confidence in the concept or importance of unlearning, but because it is the nature of unlearning that we must all—and I include myself in this category—embrace the idea that someday in the future we may even have to unlearn how we think about unlearning.

In this spirit of intellectual humility, let the unlearning commence!

Pre-Quiz

Question 1: Estimate the number of people you expect to die in the United States from the following causes over the course of the following year:

    A. Homicides _____   or   Suicides _____

    B. Floods _____   or   Tuberculosis _____

    C. Tornadoes _____   or   Asthma _____

Question 2: What is the world's tallest mountain?

Question 3: Take a look at the picture below. What do you see?

Question 4: If you had to select one of these two tables to fit into a long, narrow space, which would you select?

Question 5: On a game show, you are given the option of choosing a gift behind one of three doors. Behind one door is a new car; behind the other two are goats. After you have made your selection, the game host (who knows what's behind each door) opens one of the doors to reveal a goat, and then gives you the option of switching your selection. Is it in your best interest to do so?

Question 6: Which of these animals is more likely to kill you: a shark or a deer?

Question 7: Write or trace the letter "E" on your forehead. (That's it. No other instructions will be provided.)

Question 8: In hospitals, what action is estimated to reduce the risk of infection from catheters by as much as 90 percent?

Question 9: Who coined the phrase, "The survival of the fittest"?

Question 10: Does a rusted nail weigh more or less than the original, non-rusted nail?

Question 11: Why does it get hotter in the summer? (In general terms.)

Question 12: If the average temperature of the earth increases due to global climate change, what will be the primary cause of rising sea levels?

Question 13: If a poor man can make one cigarette from six butts, how many can he make from 36 butts?

Question 14: Are there more words that begin with the letter "K" or that have "K" as their third letter?

Question 15: This is a two-part question and you will need a pencil, a single piece of paper and a timer:
Part 1) For 20 seconds, list all of the white things you can think of.

Part 2) The second part of the question will need to be answered once you get to Lesson 15.

Question 16: Which of the following characteristics has a higher correlation to the success of a Hollywood movie: the involvement of a famous movie star or the location(s) where the movie is shot?

Question 17: Which is greater: 1 or 2? What about 100 or 10,000?

Question 18: This is another question with two parts:
1) Does $50 always equal $50?

2) Which amount of money would you prefer to earn over a three-year period $110,000 or $150,000?

Question 19: Which is the more likely scenario?

  A. Roger seemed happily married. He killed his wife.

  B. Roger seemed happily married. He killed his wife because he wanted her inheritance.

Question 20: According to the latest research, IQ accounts for what portion of career success?

  a. 50 to 60 percent

  b. 25 to 49 percent

  c. 23 to 34 percent

  d. 11 to 22 percent

Question 21: How much of the earth is water?

Question 22: There is a small town that has only one street. The street runs in an east-west direction and is exactly one mile in length. The town council recently granted liquor licenses to two taverns with the proviso that the establishments be situated so that each town's inhabitants and the tavern owners experience maximum convenience. Where along the one-mile street should the establishments be located?

Question 23: In 2003, what money-losing product far exceeded its sales projections for the year in spite of the fact that the manufacturer made no material upgrades to the product and spent less money on advertising?

Question 24: Do more people die jaywalking or in the designated crosswalk?

Question 25: Imagine that the Roman numeral equation below is made out of ten toothpick sticks such that "I" equals one stick and the "X", "+" and "=" all represent two sticks:

XI + I = X

Fashion the correct answer by moving around as few sticks as possible. (Translated, the equation currently reads 11 + 1 = 10.)

Question 26: If you flip a coin 14 times, which scenario (A or B) is more likely to occur?
    A. The coin will land on heads (H) 14 straight times:
       H–H–H–H–H–H–H–H–H–H–H–H–H–H
    Or
    B. The coin will land with the random outcome of tails (T) and
       heads (H): T–T–H–T–H–H–H–T–T–H–T–H–T–T

Question 27: What do chameleons do?

Question 28: True or false: Hypnosis is useful in helping witnesses accurately recall the details of crimes.

Question 29: How many planets are there in our solar system?

Question 30: Consider these three words: eye, gown and basket. Can you think of another word that relates to all three?

Question 31: A yield sign has two colors. What are they?

Question 32: If five frogs are sitting on a log and four decide to jump off, how many are still sitting on the log?

Question 33: In both 1995 and 1996, David Justice of the Atlanta Braves had a higher batting average (1995: .253; 1996: .321) than the New York Yankees, Derek Jeter (1995: .250; 1996: .314). Who had the higher two-year average?

Question 34: On a pond, there is a single lily pad. Every day the number of lily pads doubles. If it takes 30 days for the lily pads to cover the entire pond, how long would it take for the patch to cover half of the pond?

Question 35: Estimate the odds of the following two events:
    A. A large flood somewhere in America in which more than one thousand people die.
    B. An earthquake in California causing large flooding, in which more than one thousand people die.

Question 36: Study the logo below. Do you notice anything unusual?

Question 37: You are in Las Vegas and are offered a $1 bet in which you have a 99.9 percent chance of winning $10 and a mere 0.1 percent chance of losing $11,000. Would you take the bet?

Question 38: (See Lesson 38) For fun, estimate the percentage of questions for which you provided the correct answer for the 39 questions in this pre-quiz.

Question 39: Where is the universe expanding to?

Extra Credit: To demonstrate your understanding of exponential growth, estimate how tall a piece of paper would grow if it could be folded 50 times. (See the answer in Lesson 3.)

Lesson 1: Knowledge Can Kill— Unlearn or Die

"The most necessary part of learning is unlearning our errors." — Zeno

Question 1: Estimate the number of people, you expect to die in the United States from the following causes over the course of the following year:

A. Homicides _____ or Suicides _____

B. Floods _____ or Tuberculosis _____

C. Tornadoes _____ or Asthma _____

If you're like most people, you will rate the number of deaths from homicides, floods and tornadoes as being higher than suicides, tuberculosis and asthma, but this is wrong. In fact, the numbers for the latter have been consistently higher than each of the former since records have been kept.

The reason so many people get the answer wrong is because homicides, floods and tornadoes are more vivid and easier to recall. Unfortunately, what people recall often bears little or no correlation to the facts. The result is that people commonly expose themselves to greater risks for longer periods of time; or alternatively, they worry about the wrong things—such as being whisked away by a flood or a tornado.

If you wish to bolster your odds of surviving in the future, unlearning could be critical, as the following story highlights.

In 1601, James Lancaster, an English sea captain, set sail from England to India. Overseeing a crew of 278 sailors on four separate ships, Lancaster conducted an experiment to evaluate the effectiveness of a treatment to prevent scurvy. He administered three tablespoons of lemon juice to the members of his ship and left the crews of the other three ships untreated—effectively creating a control group. Halfway through his journey, Lancaster's experiment yielded startling evidence: none of the sailors on his ship had died of the disease, but 110 of the sailors on the other ships—or 40 percent— had succumbed to the dreaded malady. With such clear and compelling evidence, one might have expected the British Navy to begin immediately administering lemon juice to sailors. It did not.

Nearly a century and a half later in 1747, James Lind, a British Navy physician who was familiar with Lancaster's work, carried out the first example of a scientifically controlled clinical nutrition study of the disease. He prescribed oranges and lemons to patients suffering from scurvy and found they were cured in a matter of days. Six years later in 1753, Lind published his seminal work, "A Treatise of the Scurvy."

Armed with this well-documented information, one might again have expected the British Navy to make haste in prescribing regular doses of citrus fruits to all of its sailors. It did not. In fact, it took an additional forty-eight years for the disease to be eradicated.

Why did it take the British Navy almost two centuries to adopt a new, albeit simple, method for treating a disease that could have spared the lives of untold numbers of its sailors? A variety of factors were at work, but prominent officials and the sailors alike had different ideas for the best way to prevent scurvy, and these erroneous ideas prevented them from being receptive to new knowledge. In short, before they could fully assimilate the new information, they had to unlearn their old beliefs.

It is easy to dismiss the scurvy case as an isolated example from history and chalk it up to poor scientific knowledge, the slow diffusion of new information, bureaucratic inertia or just plain stupidity. Unfortunately, the British Navy isn't alone in its slowness to unlearn.

Consider the case of Australian physician Barry Marshall. In 1984, Marshall traveled to Brussels, Belgium, to a prestigious conference of ulcer specialists to present his research suggesting that ulcers were caused by bacteria. His presentation was greeted with laughter because the audience of ulcer experts judged the idea to be preposterous.

A year later, after drinking a vial of bacteria and giving himself an ulcer, Marshall returned with even more compelling evidence, but was shouted down with a chorus of boos by the group. It took the American Medical Association a full decade before it accepted Marshall's research and announced that the vast majority of ulcers are caused by bacteria and not by stomach acids, stress or spicy foods as leading ulcer experts had erroneously believed. In 2005, Marshall and his researcher partner, Dr. Robin Warren, were awarded the Nobel Prize in medicine.

This begs the obvious question: Why were hundreds of thousands of ulcer patients treated with unnecessary, costly and often ineffective treatment for more than twenty years? The answer is because many people, including highly educated medical specialists, have a difficult time unlearning old knowledge.

It would be reassuring to think that society has progressed much since 1984 and that it won't repeat similar errors in the future, but it would be wise to remain humble. To demonstrate, I'd like to share a mildly shocking insight with you: Six times as many people died in their cars as a result of the terrorist attacks on September 11, 2001, as did those in the planes that crashed into the World Trade Towers, the Pentagon and in the rural farm field in Pennsylvania—combined.

Impossible, you say? Not if you change your frame of reference and consider that since September 11, 2001, millions of Americans have decided to forego flying and instead have chosen to drive to their destinations. In this light, the numbers become more plausible because, statistically speaking, driving is far more risky than flying. In fact, it has been estimated that since 9-11 more than 1,700 Americans have died in automobile accidents than otherwise would have if only those travelers had chosen the safer method of travel—flying.

Alas, before people can accept that airplanes are more likely to get them safely to their destination, they first need to unlearn that driving is safer than flying. This isn't an easy or even natural thing to do, but just as sucking on a lemon has saved and prolonged the lives of numerous sailors roaming the high seas, so too can unlearning prolong and maybe even save your life.

Homework Assignment 1: Research the following question: Which is the greater threat to a child's safety: your neighbor's swimming pool or the unlocked gun in his closet? (The answer will also be provided later in the book.)

Lesson 2:
Don't Climb the Highest Mountain

"In some sense our ability to open the future will depend not on how well we learn anymore but how well we are able to unlearn."
— Alan Kay

Question 2: What is the world's tallest mountain?

Did you say Mount Everest? You're wrong. The answer is Mauna Kea and, as measured from its base to its summit, it is 33,465 feet high—or 4,436 feet taller than Mount Everest.

Mauna Kea's distinguishing characteristic is that three-fourths of the mountain lies under water. Mount Everest remains the *highest* mountain as measured from sea level to summit, but Mauna Kea is the *tallest* as measured from the bottom of its base to its top.

Both the question and the answer serve as a useful metaphor for the concept of unlearning, which I define as follows:

18

unlearn: v. [the act of unlearning; verbal n, to unlearn]

1. the act of releasing old knowledge

2. to see the world not as one would like to see it, but as it really is

3. to be un-uninformed

4. to acquire wisdom either by replacing old information that has been supplanted by new knowledge, or alternatively, by relinquishing known falsehoods

Unlearning is a critical skill, especially in today's world of rapid and accelerating change. To understand why, consider this: scientific and technical knowledge is now doubling every seven years.

This may sound a tad astounding until one considers that there are now 6 billion-plus people populating the globe and 90 percent of the scientists ever to roam the planet are alive at this very moment. Moreover, these scientists and their growing legions of students are adding new knowledge in fields as varied as biotechnology, chemistry, genomics, material science, nanotechnology, neuroscience, robotics, quantum physics and numerous other fields at a prodigious rate.

Aided in their quest, the world's researchers and entrepreneurs are now armed with a bevy of sophisticated new tools capable of doing everything from probing and plumbing subatomic particles deep inside the human body to visualizing the outer expanses of the universe. Further accelerating matters, these discoveries are now being enhanced with the aid of wickedly powerful supercomputers, and then shared with fellow researchers on the other side of the globe, via social networks and wireless and fiber optic connections, in the proverbial blink of an eye.

One often overlooked implication of this growing tsunami of scientific knowledge is that as impressive as our knowledge base is today, it will represent only half of what society will know in just seven short years and a mere 25 percent in fourteen years.

To get a glimpse of the near future, it helps to go back in time, let's say fourteen years, and consider how the advances in just two fields (semiconductors and fiber optic bandwidth) have enabled the creation of the cell phone and Internet and how those devices, in turn, have transformed society.

If you think of future knowledge as an iceberg, the portion of the iceberg that lies above the water can be thought of as representing existing knowledge. The portion that resides below the water is the equivalent of future knowledge. And, just as the hidden part of Mauna Kea causes many people to overlook the fact that it is the tallest mountain in the world, future knowledge will also cause people to overlook obvious trends that will have an impact on their businesses.

Unless, that is, they are open to unlearning.

Unlearning, unfortunately, is neither a natural skill nor is it an easy one to acquire, and it is here that the metaphor of an iceberg is particularly apt. Imagine you are the captain of a ship entering waters conducive to the creation of icebergs. To survive it is important to beware not only of the presence of the growing number of icebergs, you must also understand that the greater threat is that portion of the icebergs that are submerged and can't be seen.

And just as a modest-size iceberg sank the "unsinkable" *Titanic*, the growing number of future "icebergs" (e.g, biotechnology, nanotechnology, robotics, the semantic web, RFID, quantum physics, etc.) will similarly take down the most "unsinkable" of industries. To avoid this fate, it'll be necessary to change course quickly and often, and unlearning is an essential skill every leader and organization must possess in order to safely navigate the future. Or, as Mark Twain once said about his time as a riverboat captain on the Mississippi River, "Two things seemed pretty apparent to me. One was in order to be a pilot a man had to learn more than any man ought to learn; and the other was that he must learn it all over again every twenty-four hours."

In between the old learning and the new learning, however, resides the often overlooked requirement of unlearning; but, just as the bulk of Mauna Kea or the majority of an iceberg can't be seen, it is necessary to be aware of its dimensions. Thus, one of the first tricks to unlearning is to simply acknowledge its existence as a vital component of the broader "mountain" of learning.

Homework Assignment 2: In 2001, Wikipedia was created by one man beginning with 100 entries. In its tenth full year (2011), more than 684 million people access 10 million different encyclopedia articles that were drafted by 75,000 individuals in 264 different languages. Describe how knowledge providers such as encyclopedia companies and teachers have had to unlearn as a result of Wikipedia.

Extra Credit: Describe how voice and speech recognition technologies, e-Books or social networking tools will require further unlearning in the future.

Lesson 3: Become Uncomfortable in Your Own Skin

"If they give you ruled paper,
write the other way."
— Juan Ramon Jimenez,
winner of the 1956 Nobel Prize for Literature

Question 3: Take a look at the picture below. What do you see?

Do you see an older woman or a younger woman? Most people see one or the other, but with some effort you can train your brain to see both images. In many ways, the journey of unlearning is comparable. This is to say that unlearning provides a different perspective on learning, but you must train your mind to view it as an equally legitimate educational outcome.

As with many journeys, it helps to begin with small steps. To get started, it may first be beneficial for you to become uncomfortable in your own skin. One effective strategy to remind you of the importance of unlearning is to develop a modest, easy-to-implement unlearning habit. In my case, whenever I think I may be in need of unlearning, I fold my hands the opposite way.

To demonstrate, clasp your hands as if you were in prayer. There are only two ways to do this. You can either place your left thumb and fore-finger over your right thumb and forefinger or vice versa. Regardless of which way you do it, most people consistently do it the same way every time.

Now take a moment and fold your hands in the opposite manner. (Go ahead. I'll wait.) It feels different, doesn't it—almost unnatural? Of course, it isn't.

Unlearning can also feel unnatural in the beginning, but it is really just a different way of thinking about learning.

Therefore, whenever you feel you may be in need of unlearning I encourage you to fold your hands opposite your normal way—think of it as an exercise in becoming uncomfortable in your own skin. You may also choose to fold your arms the opposite way. Personally, I'm fond of this method because often when people are not open to an idea or another person's thinking or line of reasoning, they may defiantly fold their arms against their chests. By actively unfolding your arms and refolding them in an opposite manner this, too, can serve as a powerful physiological reminder of the importance of being open to unlearning.

In keeping with this spirit of folding, I'd like to highlight another un-learning folding exercise. How many times can you fold a piece of paper in half? Conventional wisdom holds that a strong person can do it only seven times, at which point the paper gets too thick to fold.

In January 2002, Britney Gallivan, in an attempt to solve an extra-cred-it problem for her high school math class, became the first person in the world to fold a piece of paper nine times. For good measure she then went on to fold it a tenth, eleventh and twelfth time.

Gallivan did so by questioning everything. First, she began by using ultra-thin toilet paper. Next, she used a very long strip of paper (about the length of six city blocks) and lastly, she didn't limit herself to folding the paper precisely in half after every fold. Instead, she sometimes folded the paper in different lengths and directions. A more detailed explanation can be found in her book, *How to Fold Paper in Half Twelve Times: An "Impossible" Challenge Solved and Explained.*

In this same way, unlearning also requires us to fold old problems in new, different and innovative ways. One good way to remind you of this is to create opportunities to become uncomfortable in your own skin and fold your hands and arms differently on occasion.

Homework Assignment 3: Think of a problem that has been vexing you for some time. Challenge three basic or underlying as-sumptions about that problem and then develop new tools or approaches to tackle the problem.

Extra Credit: To demonstrate your understanding of exponential growth, estimate how tall a piece of paper would grow if it could be folded 50 times.

Answer: Approximately 100 million kilometers — or 62 million miles

Lesson 4:
Argue with Yourself
(It's Not Debatable)

"I have what I call an iron prescription that helps me keep sane when I naturally drift toward preferring one ideology over another and that is: I say that I'm not entitled to have an opinion on this subject unless I can state the argument against my position better than the people who support it. I think only when I've reached that state am I qualified to speak."
— Charlie Munger

Question 4: If you had to select one of these two tables to fit into a long, narrow space, which would you select?

Did you say the table on the left? If so, you are correct. If, however, you opted for the other table, you are also correct. Why? Because both tables have the exact same dimensions. Don't believe me? Measure the width and the length of the two tables.

The optical illusion and the above quotation from Charlie Munger (Warren Buffett's right-hand man for more than 40 years) offer both visual evidence and worldly advice for anyone wishing to stay open to the importance of unlearning. They also serve as useful reminders that it is important to consider all sides of something—be it a table or an issue.

Munger's practice of arguing opposite sides of a question is a practice dating back thousands of years. As Nassim Taleb recounts in his book, *Fooled by Randomness*, in 155 BC the Greek philosopher Carnaedes traveled to Rome to argue against a penalty that had been levied upon the Athenians. With unmatched eloquence, Carnaedes sang the praises of Roman justice and convinced his audience of the merits of his position. Alas, that wasn't the point he was trying to make. The very next day Carnaedes dissected his previous arguments and proceeded to convince the same audience the opposite was true.

So where did Carnaedes really stand on the issue of the penalty? We don't know. But that doesn't matter because what he wanted to advocate was a doctrine of "uncertainty of knowledge." Carnaedes was a "radical skeptic" and believed that all knowledge is impossible to know—except for the knowledge that all knowledge is impossible to know. Or, as Taleb writes, "Carnaedes stood all his life against arrogant dogma and belief in one sole truth."

This philosophy calls to mind a quotation from F. Scott Fitzgerald "The test of a first-rate intelligence is the ability to hold two opposed ideas in the mind at the same time, and still retain the ability to function." This ability to deal with ambiguity is not a luxury reserved only for ancient philosophers and poets. In 1988, a study by the American Management Association found the leadership characteristic most essential for steering organizations through troubled and complex times was "the ability to deal with ambiguity."

One strategy for preparing to deal with such ambiguity is (like Munger and Carnaedes) to familiarize oneself with all sides of an issue. In this way, whenever new—and perhaps contradictory—information becomes available, the holder of the opinion can assimilate this new information into their decision-making process. This, in turn, may make it easier to unlearn a position, in spite of having voiced support for it in the past, because you have at least acknowledged the merits of the opposite side of the issue.

Why might this be so? Because the previous work in understanding the opposing viewpoints will have created the space for a different but equally plausible idea—or even a table—to fit.

Homework Assignment 4: List all of the reasons why your competitors' products or services are superior to your own, and why its revenue growth, profits and stock performance may outperform your own over the next three years. For individuals, identify your favorite stock and list all the reasons it may underperform in the broader S&P index in the coming years.

Lesson 5:
Do Not Feed Creatures of Habit

"Not choice, but habit,
rules the unreflecting herd."
— William Wordsworth

Question 5: On a game show, you are given the option of choosing a gift behind one of three doors. Behind one door is a new car; behind the other two are goats. After you have made your selection, the game host (who knows what's behind each door) opens one of the doors to reveal a goat, and then gives you the option of switching your selection. Is it in your best interest to do so?

If you're like most people, you won't change because you believe you still have a one-out-of-three (33.33%) chance of having made the right decision. The statistically smart thing to do is to accept the host's offer and switch your vote. In fact, this act doubles your probability of winning from 33.33% to 66.67%.

This result is so counterintuitive that when this question and its answer were presented in a *Parade* magazine article in 1990, some 10,000 readers, including nearly 1,000 PhDs, responded afterward that the proposed solution (switching) was wrong. Alas, it was they who were wrong. (For a more detailed explanation of the statistics behind the solution, visit Wikipedia.org/wiki/Monty_Hall_Problem).

The choice of whether you choose to unlearn or not is, of course, your own. But if you feel the act won't confer a distinct advantage on you or your organization, you may want to consider just a small sampling of findings that, like the above problem, may challenge your intuition:

- In the long run, not listening to your best customers could be a wiser strategy than catering to their every whim.
- Taking more risks, embracing failure and practicing imperfection can produce better results than the relentless pursuit of perfection.
- The collective opinion of a random group of independent individuals will, more often than not, be superior to the opinion of an expert.
- For the health of your organization, older workers should be encouraged to seek out younger and more inexperienced colleagues as mentors rather than vice versa.
- Under-scheduling your day, turning off your cell phone, taking more naps and going on more vacations can bolster productivity.
- The interview question most likely to be indicative of long-term employee success has nothing to do with a person's educational background or past experience.
- Using money as a financial incentive to bolster employee productivity can be counterproductive and lead to disastrous results.

- Telling an employee (or a child) that he or she is smart can hinder creativity and problem-solving skills.
- Acknowledging what you and your company *don't know* is far more important than what you do know.

It's perfectly understandable if you find yourself resisting many of these findings. As I said, the choice to unlearn or not is yours alone. You are entitled to your opinions. If, though, you do get in the habit of feeding your curiosity and not your habits of thought, I can guarantee you—statistically speaking—your odds of future success will be much improved.

Homework Assignment 5: Regardless of which leg you normally put in first when putting on your pants, try placing the opposite leg in first. The exercise will feel odd in the beginning, and it may even be difficult for some people, but stick with it for an entire week. If you do, your balance will improve. Afterward, on occasion, use the exercise as a tangible reminder that in order to lead a well-balanced life, it's in your best interest to starve some of your creatures of habit on occasion.

Lesson 6: Study at an Anti-Library

"There is a huge difference between
what people actually know and how much
they think they know."
— Nassim Taleb

Question 6: Which of these animals is more likely to kill you: a shark or a deer?

The right answer is the deer. In fact, the contest isn't even close. You are 300 times more likely to be killed at the hands—or the "hoof," if you will—of a deer than a shark. The reason a vast majority of people answer this question incorrectly is because shark attacks, although quite rare, are easy to imagine and vividly recalled. For example, it is not uncommon for television news stories to report shark attacks even when those attacks occur thousands of miles away. And, if you are over the age of forty, you may viscerally recall the movie *Jaws*. On the other hand, instances of drivers striking deer on remote country roads and dying in the resulting collision are much more common. They occur with such startling regularity that they rarely warrant more than a passing mention on the local news.

The discrepancy between the relative danger of sharks and deer is a poignant reminder of that old adage: What we don't know is more important than what we do know. One of the better ways to remind ourselves of our ignorance—and to remain open to the concept of unlearning—is to keep our ignorance top of mind. One of the more effective strategies for doing this is to create an anti-library. As Nassim Taleb recounts in his provocative and insightful book *The Black Swan,* an anti-library is a collection of books that one *hasn't* read.

Unlike a shelf or bookcase filled with previously read books, an anti-library serves as a tangible reminder of all unread books—books that may contain valuable information or insights—that a person hasn't yet had the opportunity to access. With an estimated 3,000 new books being published daily and the rate of scientific knowledge purported to be doubling every seven years, it is safe to assume that there is a growing body of knowledge that is relevant to you and your business but of which you remain blissfully unaware.

It is also impossible to know everything. Therefore, the best one can do in such a deplorable situation is to use the awareness of this ignorance as a method for staying intellectually humble. By extension, a person is more likely to remain open to the necessity of unlearning if they occasionally remind themselves of what they don't know.

Of course, you are free to ignore this advice, but remember this: What you don't know can kill you—almost as easily as a deer.

Homework Assignment 6: If your financial situation permits, start creating an anti-library. Alternatively, using an online tool such as Shelfari, begin compiling a list of books that may contain useful knowledge that you don't or won't have the time to read. Add a minimum of one book a week for a year to your anti-library.

Lesson 7:
Question the Wisdom
of Experts

"I can't understand why people are
frightened of new ideas. I'm frightened
of the old ones."
— John Cage

Question 7: Write the letter "E" on your forehead. (Go ahead, I'll wait. You may also just trace the letter on your forehead if that's more comfortable for you). Did you write the letter in a self-oriented fashion such that it would appear backward to those viewing it, or did you write it backward so that it would appear legible to others?

In a fascinating study conducted by Adam Galinsky of Northwestern University's Kellogg School of Management, Galinsky and his colleagues found that the more power an individual possessed, the more likely the person was to draw the letter from their perspective, making it appear backward to others. In fact, individuals assigned to a high-power group were three times more likely to draw a self-oriented "E."

The study concluded that power causes individuals to assign too much weight to *their* own viewpoint and makes them less capable of adjusting to, or even considering, another person's perspective.

This finding is worth keeping in mind when listening to any expert who discusses a new idea. For instance, in 1899, Lord Kelvin, then recognized as one of the brightest individuals in the world, dismissed the work of aviation enthusiasts by saying, "Heavier-than-air machines are impossible." A mere four years later, Kelvin was forced to eat his words when two bicycle repairmen from Dayton, Ohio—Orville and Wilbur Wright—struck out from the sandy dunes of Kitty Hawk, North Carolina, and achieved flight.

In the mid-1980s, a conference full of ulcer experts ridiculed the work of Barry Marshall when he proposed that ulcers were not caused by acid or spicy food (as ulcer experts assumed at the time) but rather were caused by bacteria. It took ten years but eventually the American Medical Association (AMA) agreed and, in 2005, a full two decades after he first proposed his theory, Marshall and his colleague, Robin Warren, were awarded the Nobel Prize in Medicine.

That experts should be threatened by new ideas is to be expected. After all, it is difficult to accept the notion that years of well-intentioned study, research and effort were misplaced. It is equally problematic to accept that the foundation of one's power (one's status and standing in the eyes of society) was based on a flawed premise.

What is even more troublesome is that rather than keeping an open mind and entertaining new ideas, which may challenge one's expertise, many experts do just the opposite and perform the equivalent of writing a backward "E" on their forehead and refuse to consider new alternatives. Often, they'll even go a step further and use their status as experts to ridicule and belittle the new idea in question.

The problem is further compounded because experts are often extremely intelligent and are able to lay out in articulate and plausible sounding—but, ultimately wrong—arguments as to why the new ideas should be dismissed.

New ideas, by their very nature, challenge old ideas. It is dangerous, therefore, to cede sole control of the assessment of new ideas to the very group that would be most threatened by the adoption of these ideas.

It is, of course, entirely reasonable that experts be allowed a role in assessing new ideas. But before anyone accepts their word as "gospel," they should insist that the experts take a moment and write the first letter of "expert" backward (instead of in a self-oriented way) as a reminder that expertise doesn't necessarily equal correctness and that they must stay open to new perspectives.

Homework Assignment 7: In 1933, what brilliant scientist uttered this famous quotation: "There is not the slightest indication that nuclear energy will ever be obtainable"? Hint: His name began with "E" and he later publicly reversed his position in a letter to President Franklin D. Roosevelt.

Extra Credit: After the near meltdown of the global financial market in 2008–2009, what other group of experts might have benefited from entertaining a new perspective?

Lesson 8:
Bite the Hand
That Feeds You

"The mastery of transformation is the process of unlearning what you have already learned."
— Unknown

Question 8: In hospitals, what action is estimated to reduce the risk of infection from catheters by as much as 90 percent?

The answer may surprise you: systematic hand washing. That's right—if more health care professionals (the very people charged with healing you) would simply scrub their hands more diligently, countless numbers of preventable infections would be averted, an estimated 25,000 lives would be saved and billions of dollars in unnecessary health care costs could be avoided.

The fact that hand washing saves lives is nothing new in the health care system. More than a century and a half ago, Ignaz Semmelweis discovered that if doctors would wash their hands and sterilize their equipment prior to performing childbirth, the mortality rate among women would also plummet. So how long did it take doctors to adopt Semmelweis's simple, life-saving technique? Almost twenty years.

It would be comforting to think of this painfully slow transition as a historical anomaly, but it has been estimated that it still takes seventeen years, on average, before a health care-related "best practice" will be adopted by a majority of medical professionals.

Getting otherwise intelligent and well-intentioned people to change habits can be hard. This is especially so when these folks are considered experts in their field. One way to challenge this arrogant behavior (and avoid it yourself) is to "bite the hand that feeds you" and constantly challenge your best practices and ideas.

One rule to help get you started on this path is this: It is OK to be in love with *what* you do but not with *how* you do it.

For example, in the 2000s, IBM was quick to adopt open-source software because it wasn't "in love" with how software was provided. The same couldn't be said for Microsoft, which stubbornly resisted the transition for a longer period of time. Netflix has similarly avoided falling in love with how movies are delivered to consumers. Today, less than a decade after disrupting the movie rental market by mailing DVDs, it is now streaming videos via the Internet. Amazon is doing much the same by embracing cloud computing and electronic books. This company understands it is not in the business of distributing physical books but rather distributing digital content.

Even Tiger Woods, one of the greatest golfers to play the game, makes it a habit to regularly revisit everything from his swing to his grip. Famously, after winning an unprecedented six consecutive tournaments, Woods announced to the world that his swing "sucked." He then proceeded to retool virtually every aspect of his game in order to ascend to an even higher level.

Woods and other companies that systematically attack their successes do so because they have embraced the wisdom of the late management guru Peter Ducker, who once said, "Every organization has to prepare for the abandonment of everything it does."

Rarely will you be handed the next great opportunity in life. More likely, you are going to have to grab it, but this won't always be possible if your hands are still filled with yesterday's bounty. So go ahead and bite the hand that feeds you—it may just free you to grab the next rung on the ladder of success.

Homework Assignment 8: Create an anti-resume: Make a list of skills or knowledge you and/or your company *don't* possess. If you had any of these skills or knowledge might it change how you do your business? If so, is it worth it to stop honing your current strengths and instead start developing some new skills?

Extra Credit: Research how Bethlehem Steel went from being named *BusinessWeek*'s "best managed company" in 1989 to bankruptcy by 2001. Next, explain how the company might have avoided its fate of having the Smithsonian Institute purchase its once impressive steel manufacturing plant for the purpose of converting it into the National Museum of Industrial History if it had had the courage to "bite the hand that fed it".

Lesson 9: Unlock the Keys to Failure

"To kill an error is as good a service, and sometimes even better than, the establishing of a new truth or fact."
— Charles Darwin

Question 9: Who coined the phrase, "The survival of the fittest"?

Did you say Charles Darwin? If so, you are mistaken. The honor belongs to Herbert Spencer, who first used the phrase in his book *The Principles of Biology* in 1864. To be fair, Spencer's book was inspired by Darwin's theory of evolution and Darwin himself later acknowledged that the phrase might be both more convenient and accurate than his own term, "natural selection." Nevertheless, Spencer, and not Darwin, deserves credit for coining the popular phrase.

It is worth noting at this juncture that Darwin's paradigm-shattering book was only written because he had the temerity to ignore the advice of a well-intentioned but, ultimately, misguided editor who, after reading the first chapter of Darwin's treatise, urged him to write a book on, of all things, pigeons.

Darwin's *On the Origin of Species* went on to become an immediate best seller and, arguably, the most influential book of the nineteenth and twentieth centuries. It is further worth reflecting on the courage Darwin displayed in publishing the book. As another British intellectual, John Maynard Keynes, once observed, "Worldly wisdom teaches that it is better for the reputation to fail conventionally than to succeed unconventionally." Darwin could have easily chosen to "fail conventionally" by writing a book on pigeons; and yet, in spite of the scorn and ridicule he knew would be heaped upon him, he chose to publish his intellectually challenging theory anyway.

The reason was because Darwin was a scientist and he understood that science could only progress if ideas were put to the rigorous test of other scientists. In this sense, Darwin understood that risking failure was integral to long-term success. Outside the field of science, this important lesson is rarely taught and even less frequently encouraged. This is unfortunate and the notion that failure only has negative attributes is a belief worth unlearning if people and organizations wish to achieve future success.

By embracing the positive attributes of failure, individuals can free themselves from the fear of failure. Once so relieved, individuals are more willing to confront and overcome the inhibitions of presenting society with unconventional ideas and products. Or, as one sage once said, "If you are not prepared to be wrong, you will never end up with anything original."

One of the benefits of embracing failure is that often in the marketplace of ideas and products, the market doesn't even know what it wants until after someone has showed them something completely original—a sentiment neatly captured in Henry Ford's famous quip, "If I had asked people what they wanted, they would have said faster horses." Luckily, Ford, like Darwin and countless other iconoclasts and innovators, chose to succeed unconventionally, and you can, too—but only if you first have the courage to unlock the keys to failure and venture forth with your bold, controversial and far-out ideas.

Homework Assignment 9: Look up the definition of the word "theory" and see if the definition—as used in a scientific sense—corresponds with your understanding of the term. (Hint: A theory is distinct from a hypothesis and it doesn't mean "an idea that isn't certain.") Next, explain how many of the best scientific theories are often the product of multiple failures.

Extra Credit: Explain how the concept of unlearning may be vital to your own evolution and, thus, long-term success.

Lesson 10:
See What Isn't There

"You don't understand something until you
understand it more than one way."
— Marvin Minsky

Question 10: Does a rusted nail weight more or less than the original, non-rusted nail?

It weights more. This finding, discovered by Antoine and Marie Lavoisier in the late eighteenth century, was rather startling because it drew attention to the unobservable notion that a rusting object was somehow drawing the attraction of an element that people could not see. In this case an iron nail is attracting oxygen molecules and converting the metal into iron oxide.

This idea of "not seeing" what is there is an important element of unlearning. Consider the case of Abraham Wald. During World War II, Wald and a team of researchers were charged with protecting Allied bombers from German anti-aircraft guns. As part of their work the researchers diligently recorded where on the body of the plane each returning bomber was struck by gunfire. The most common areas were the wings and the tails.

In response, the researchers advised the military command to reinforce those bullet-struck areas. Everyone, that is, except Wald, who suggested that those areas of the plane *not* struck by gunfire—largely the fuselage—be reinforced. His recommendation was met with incredulity by his peers and superiors.

Eventually, Wald convinced them of the wisdom of his logic. The mistake his peers made was that they were observing only those planes that returned *safely*. What they were not seeing were those planes that didn't return. Wald reasoned correctly that if a plane could safely return with bullet-ridden wings and tailfins, then those areas didn't need reinforcement and, counterintuitively, the parts of the plane without bullet holes were the areas requiring additional armor.

Similar situations occur every day. Millions of people play the lottery because they see photos of smiling winners holding humongous checks in the newspaper or on TV. What they don't see are the millions of losers who consistently drop one dollar, or five dollars or more, to play the game every day.

Academic and corporate research often falls prey to a similar prejudice. For example, in the wake of the horrific 1999 Columbine High School massacre in which twelve students were gunned down, scores of academic researchers received grants to study student aggression. Their conclusion was that aggression leads to bad behavior and that bad behavior is uniformly associated with negative consequences.

One problem with these findings was that the vast majority of these researchers were only looking for negative consequences. Subsequent researchers have now discovered that aggression can also have positive consequences. Many people—but especially teenagers—perceive aggression as a "cool" trait and reward those individuals who exhibit it with popularity. (Interestingly, according to recent research, popular kids are more likely to abuse alcohol and drugs and, therefore, have a different but no less serious set of problems than the "quiet, loner type.")

What is the moral of the story? Just as a tetanus shot can help prevent an infection from a rusty nail, unlearning can help inoculate you against other rare and difficult-to-see threats.

Homework Assignment 10: Some parents don't allow their children to walk home from school or down to a friend's house and, instead, drive them because they are concerned that their child could be kidnapped or otherwise harmed by a stranger. What aren't the parents seeing? (Hint: Think obesity and diabetes.)

Lesson 11:
If It Goes Without Saying, Question It

"We only hear those questions for which
we are in a position to find answers."
— Friedrich Nietzsche

Question 11: Why does it get hotter in the summer?

In the late 1980s, for the production of a movie entitled *A Private Universe*, the filmmakers posited this question to twenty-three graduating seniors of Harvard University. Twenty-one of the twenty-three students provided incorrect answers. The overwhelming majority responded with something to the effect that it's because the earth draws closer to the sun.

Intuitively, this answer makes sense—after all, if you step closer to a fire you get warmer—but it's wrong. The reason it gets hotter is because the tilt of the earth's axis changes and exposes those areas of the world experiencing summer to more direct and sustained sunlight.

It may be comforting to believe this shockingly high degree of ignorance is limited to Harvard Yard, but many people respond with a similar answer. What is ironic is that most students are taught this basic lesson of

49

astronomy in grade school and yet, such is the power of embracing intuition that this fact is overridden as we grow older. (Perhaps you could say this fact is "unlearned" in a negative way.)

The problem of relying on our intuition has, unfortunately, been compounded in recent years due to the popularity of Malcolm Gladwell's book *Blink: The Power of Thinking Without Thinking*, which encourages people to rely more—and not less—on their intuition.

Of course, intuition is a powerful idea and it has its place. But should people really "think without thinking"? Let me ask another simple question and trust your answer to intuition: When you look at a wooden table, where does the material from the tree that makes the wood come from? More succinctly, from what does a tree derive the majority of material from which it is made?

Did you say the ground and dirt? Perhaps you said water. Some material comes from these sources, but the vast majority—approximately 85 percent—comes from the air. Trees process carbon dioxide (in the air) and convert it into stored carbon—or wood.

Was your intuition correct?

Now allow me to ask a few more questions: What does your intuition tell you about the relative danger of driving while talking on a cellphone versus speaking on a hands-free device? If you are a parent, what is more dangerous to your child: a neighbor with a gun in his house or one with a swimming pool? And speaking of swimming, do you think you could easily recognize when someone is drowning?

In each case, the truth might surprise you. According to research, using a hands-free phone is no safer than using a regular cellphone. A child is fifty times—fifty times!—more likely to die in a neighbor's swimming pool than at the hand of their gun, and many drownings occur directly in front of people for the simple reason that unlike in the movies, victims don't flail, make splashing noises or even cry out for help. In fact, for physiological reasons, none of the acts commonly associated with drowning are likely to occur. For example, a drowning person doesn't wave or flail her arms. Instead, the arms are typically pressed flat against the water in a desperate attempt to keep the head above water. And if the person is fortunate enough to achieve this goal, her first act will be to breathe—and not cry out for help—because that is what the respiratory system was designed to do.

These surprising findings beg the obvious question: Where else might your intuition be leading you astray? For example, what does your intuition tell you your best skills are? What is your core business or what are your key competitors? How do you rely on it to select key employees?

What if your intuition is wrong about these things?

To avoid getting burned, the best strategy is just to ask this simple question: What if I'm wrong? And if you don't think you need to answer this question because the answer goes without saying, then definitely question it.

Homework Assignment 11: Around whom does your world revolve? Your spouse or partner? Your parents? Your children or grandchildren? Perhaps it's your friends, employees or even your customers? Do they know this? Do they really? When was the last time you actually told the most important people in your life how much they mean to you? You may assume this knowledge goes without saying, but what if they don't know how you feel? For your homework, tell them.

Lesson 12: Think Small

"If we are to achieve results never before accomplished, we must employ methods never before attempted."
— Sir Francis Bacon

Question 12: If the average temperature of the earth increases due to global climate change, what will be the primary cause of rising sea levels?

Did you say melting ice caps and glaciers? Wrong. While it's true the water from these sources will contribute to the problem, the primary cause of rising sea levels will be the thermal expansion of ocean water.

This problem of misidentifying the root cause of a problem can manifest itself in an equally problematic behavior worthy of unlearning: the idea that big problems always require big fixes.

It would be easy to begin this lesson with the famous story of how NASA engineers spent a million dollars to design a pen that worked in the zero-gravity conditions of outer space (when a humble pencil would have sufficed). Or to retell the story of the young boy who, upon watching a group of firemen and engineers struggle to free a large truck that had lodged itself under a bridge, proposed that they begin by deflating the tires of the truck. Alas, both stories are urban legends.

Nevertheless, these anecdotes have gained a near mythical status in today's contemporary society because of their strong emotional appeal. Many people suspect a large number of solutions are "over thought" and "over engineered."

What is not an urban myth is the fact that Ignaz Semmelweis helped save the lives of hundreds of thousands of women by getting doctors to engage in the simple act of washing their hands prior to assisting in the delivery of a newborn child. (Unfortunately, it took the medical community nearly two decades to unlearn their unhealthy habits and, even today, health care professionals still aren't scrubbing their hands often enough.)

In the field of agriculture, it was the simple addition of ammonium nitrate (a cheap but effective crop fertilizer) that allowed the world's farmers to feed a billion more people using the same amount of land, and it was the installation of the seat belt that saved the lives of thousands of motorists. This occurred in spite of the fact that the device was initially ridiculed as "inconvenient, costly and just a bunch of damn nonsense" by auto executives.

As implausible as it may sound, the problem of hurricanes may also require only a simple fix. As Steven Levitt and Stephen Dubner outline in their book *Super Freakonomics*, it may soon be possible to prevent hurricanes (which, since 2005, have inflicted more than $150 billion in damage on the U.S. economy) by deploying a few thousand "hydraulic heads" to help keep the ocean water cool in those areas where hurricanes begin. The estimated cost: $1 billion.

On the bigger problem of climate change, Levitt and Dubner also explain how "Budyko's Blanket" (a massive chimney-like structure) may pump sulfur dioxide into the atmosphere and could theoretically cool the planet for a mere $250 million.

Now, to be fair, both "hydraulic heads" and "Budyko's Blanket" may not work. But, the broader point is that when faced with big problems there is absolutely no reason why we must first look to "big answers"— such as moving the entire city of New Orleans or requiring every citizen in the world to modify his or her behavior and consume only products that use no fossil fuels or emit little carbon dioxide—as the solution. Often, big problems can be solved with small, easy-to-implement solutions—and that's no myth.

Homework Assignment 12: Identify your company or organization's largest problem. Break into two groups and have one group brainstorm solutions that cost no money while the second group considers only inexpensive solutions. Have the two groups come back together and share their ideas. Repeat the brainstorming session with everyone in the room.

Extra Credit: Post your call for solutions to a broader community on the Internet. If necessary, offer a modest prize for the best practical solutions.

Lesson 13:
Practice Intentional Imperfection

"Perfecting oneself is as much unlearning
as it is learning."
— Dijikstra

Question 13: If a poor man can make one cigarette from six butts, how many can he make from 36 butts?

Seven. He makes six cigarettes, smokes them, and uses the six new butts to make a seventh cigarette.

In the rush to calculate the answer, it is easy to overlook the creation of seventh cigarette. In this same way, it is easy to overlook how quantity can have a quality all its own. In an often told story, a ceramics teacher once asked half her class to concentrate on producing as many cups as possible. To the other half, she instructed them to focus on quality. At the end of the class, which half of the class do you think produced the higher quality cup? It was the half that focused on quantity.

The reason is because the "quantity" group learned from their mistakes and continually improved while the quality group theorized about perfection, fretted over the smallest of details and chose not to take any imaginative risks for fear of failure.

As society continues to become more saturated with information and the means by which to share this information (e.g., smartphones, social networks, instant messaging, email, etc.), it is easy to fall into the trap of "analysis paralysis." All too often, people and organizations put off making decisions because they are under the illusion that additional information will lead to a better decision and thus, a better and higher quality product. This is not true and it's a habit or belief that needs to be unlearned.

In a study, a group of experts was once asked to rate five jellies (jams) according to taste. Their rankings corresponded closely to the most popular consumer brands. When they were asked to rate the jellies on a variety of characteristics including aroma, texture and spreadability, how-ever, they ranked less popular brands higher because they assigned more value to characteristics, such as spreadability, which were not really that important to the end customer. In this case, the input of additional infor-mation led to a poor decision.

In an era where it's easy to communicate with colleagues halfway around the world and gain their input, it is possible certain people will provide keen and useful insights. But it is also just as plausible they will raise questions, concerns, barriers and obstacles that serve no useful pur-pose. (For example, if your job is to focus on making a jelly that can be easily spread, it is only natural to want to delay the release of a new jelly until it is perfectly spreadable—even if that trait isn't critical to the product's ultimate success.)

To circumvent this conflict, it is worth unlearning perfection and to embrace instead the habit of practicing imperfection. To better understand this concept, consider the practice of Persian rug weavers who intentionally include imperfections in their rugs. Their purpose is twofold. First, this habit keeps the weavers humble and reminds them that while true perfection can be pursued it can rarely be attained. Second, this habit makes it easier for them to ship a product to market because they don't needlessly worry about creating the perfect product. As a result, they end up producing more rugs and getting progressively better with each one they create.

Amish quilt makers and Navajo artisans employ similar policies with regard to their wares, but an old Persian proverb best captures the essence of practicing imperfection: "A Persian rug is perfectly imperfect, and precisely imprecise."

The best way to get better is to stop worrying about perfection and, counterintuitively, begin practicing imperfection, because it will actually get you closer to the goal of perfection.

Homework Assignment 13: Find an area in your life where you would like to be more productive. For instance, perhaps you'd like to write more, produce more art or music, or start a new habit or hobby. Next, begin practicing imperfection.

Lesson 14:
The Grass Isn't Greener on the Other Side

"He who hesitates because he feels inferior is being surpassed by those who are busy making mistakes and becoming superior."
— Henry Link

Question 14: Are there more words that begin with the letter "K" or that have "K" as their third letter?

With words such as kangaroo, kitchen and kite readily springing to mind it is easy to assume there are more words beginning with the letter. This is incorrect. Surprisingly, there are three times as many words with "K" as their third letter. The reason many people get the answer wrong is because it's relatively easy to think of words beginning with K. It is far harder to conjure up words such as acknowledge, irksome, unknown and wake.

In this same way, it is easy to understand our own situation because it is always top of mind and far more difficult to understand the plight of others because the context of their life is not so clear. This bias is one reason why the grass often appears greener on the other side of the fence.

In fact, there is a scientific explanation for the "greener grass" phenomenon. From a person's viewpoint atop a patch of grass it is easy to notice the bare spots—just look down. When the grass is farther off, a person's viewpoint will impose a slant on the grass and their angle will only enable them to observe the tops of the blades of grass. (See image.) The result is that bare spots remain obscured from their line of sight and they only see the tops of green blades of grass. Only as they draw nearer do the ugly blotches and bare spots become noticeable.

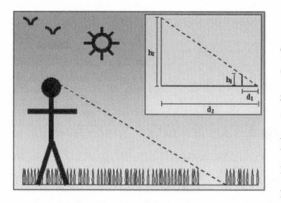

The same is true with other aspects of our lives. Obviously, a person has an up-close view of the "bare spots" in his or her life—be it a lower balance in the checking account, mounting credit card debt, an aching back, family issues or any number of things. The view of a neighbor's life—one who has a larger house, newer car or perhaps a happier family—is more difficult to discern. Like spotting words with "K" as their third letter, it is trickier to assess other people's "bare spots"—be they in the form of internal house repairs, larger car payments or well-concealed dysfunctional family issues.

The problem runs deeper than misplaced envy. Many times people will feel as though their patch of grass is cursed. For example, have you ever noticed how the line you are standing in at the grocery store is always the slowest moving? If you feel this way there is good news. You aren't cursed. You simply notice such instances more often.

If you think about this for a moment, this makes sense. Because you are waiting and since you have little else to do, it's easy to concentrate on those who don't share your plight (i.e., the people in the quicker-moving lanes). On the other hand, when you are briskly moving along you are less likely to consider your good fortune. Instead you just move ahead—oblivious to the envious glances of those poor souls in the slower-moving lines.

All of this is not to deny that there are bald spots on your grass and that sometimes you have chosen the slow lane. The challenge, in such situations, is to view your situation from a new perspective.

Over the past few years a number of companies have done exactly this. For instance, when Yellowtail, an Australian wine company, recognized that many people were foregoing wine purchases because they were intimidated by their lack of knowledge in selecting a nice wine, they created and marketed a low-cost quality wine. This took the apprehension out of buying wine for many people who had previously never purchased wine because of the expense, and sales skyrocketed. In essence, they converted a "bare spot" into a lush green pasture of opportunity.

By unlearning the idea that the grass is always greener on the other side you will stop chasing an illusion. The extra time you save can then be used toward making the grass upon which you are standing greener.

Homework Assignment 14: Next time you find yourself standing in a slow-moving line at the grocery, take the opportunity to gain a new perspective on your life by making a list of the things that are going well in your life or, alternatively, try studying a "bare spot" in your business or life from a different angle and figure out how to make it greener.

Lesson 15:
Cast a Narrow Net

"It's what you learn after you know
it all that counts."
— John Wooden

Question 15: This is a two-part question and you will need a pencil, a single piece of paper and a timer:

Part 1) For 20 seconds, list all of the white things you can think of. (Read no further and make the list.)

Part 2) Next, on the opposite side of the paper, in 20 seconds make a list of all the white items inside of a refrigerator.

Surprisingly, most people can record just as many items on the second list—even though the universe from which they can select is decidedly smaller. Some people, in fact, find the second part of the question easier to answer.

How can this be? How can people get just as many—or more—ideas from a smaller sample? Aren't we always encouraged to cast a wide net?

63

Casting a wide net is, of course, often an effective strategy. This is especially true if time isn't an issue (as it was in this exercise) because a wider net will usually yield a higher number and quality of ideas—but not always.

The key to understanding this paradox resides in understanding the issue of concreteness, which is defined here as focusing a person's attention on a specific task.

This paradox is appropriate when considering the idea of a mentor. Over time many people have come to think of mentors as individuals possessing more knowledge and experience than they have themselves. It is natural, therefore, to seek out mentors with these attributes.

In order to unlearn, though, I encourage you to seek out a reverse mentor—a person younger or more inexperienced than you. For starters, such individuals are likely to possess some knowledge you don't. More important, in today's era of accelerating change, it is not always the quantity or quality of knowledge that is most important, but rather the ability to bring a fresh perspective to an existing base of knowledge.

By providing uncommon insights on what may be coming next or exposing individuals and organizations to a new way of seeing an old problem, a reverse mentor can be just as valuable as an "experienced" mentor.

Like thinking of white things in the refrigerator, the life experiences of reverse mentors may be more limited, but by identifying overlooked opportunities or spotting future threats to your business, they just may make sure you don't end up with egg (white) on your face or crying over spilled milk.

Homework Assignment 15: Identify at least two potential reverse mentors—one within your field of expertise or industry and one outside—who are either younger or more inexperienced than you. Meet quarterly with these individuals and spend the majority of the time listening—not talking.

Lesson 16:
Bet Against Yourself

"Don't wanna learn from nobody
what I gotta unlearn."
— Bob Dylan

Question 16: Which of the following characteristics has a higher correlation to the success of a Hollywood movie: the involvement of a famous movie star or the location(s) where the movie is shot?

The answer, to the surprise and chagrin of many Hollywood producers, is the latter. The fact that Johnny Depp, Angelina Jolie, Jack Nicholson or any other Hollywood "A" list actor performs in the movie has only a small correlation to its ultimate success. As Ian Ayres recounts in his book *Super Crunchers*, a company named Epagogix uses a proprietary neural network equation that relies on little more than the information found in a movie's screenplay to predict—with a higher level of accuracy than Hollywood's most experienced directors and producers—how financially successful the movie will be. Not surprisingly, this finding has not been warmly received by most Hollywood elites because it highlights how little they actually know about which characteristics matter most to a movie's bottom line.

This trait highlights another behavior individuals may need to unlearn as they move into the future, and this is the idea of assigning too much weight to one's own opinions or intuition. Extraordinary new capabilities in data mining and computer processing power, when paired with equally powerful advances in algorithms, neural networks and predictive analysis software, are proving that machines are frequently far better judges than humans for many important tasks.

For example, researchers have found that for patients with uncommon medical conditions, Google is now more reliable at assessing those conditions than doctors. Considering that the average doctor has access to only two million pieces of medical information and Google a thousand times more, this isn't that surprising. What is worth considering is the idea that as computer hardware and software improves exponentially, so too will Google's ability to diagnose a growing number of diseases with an even higher rate of accuracy.

In the rarified field of oenology (the study of wine), Orley Ashenfelter has produced a sophisticated regression equation that can predict more accurately than the wine industry's top judges which vintages of red wine will be the most valuable in the future. Ashenfelter cares nothing for swishing wine around in his mouth in search of subtle hints of oak, cherry, tobacco or blueberry but instead relies on weather-related data.

For wine collectors who invest in wine futures, Ashenfelter's information is giving them a distinct competitive advantage over those who can't or won't unlearn their reliance on so-called wine "experts." And only recently have many Las Vegas hotels and casinos unlearned the idea that its most valuable customers are limited to the ranks of wealthy high rollers. Thanks to complex algorithms there are hundreds of middle-aged, middle-income individuals who are now being aggressively courted. If you've ever wondered why your ne'er-do-well Uncle Ned is being "comped" to stay at a nice hotel in Las Vegas twice a year, it's because a computer program has figured that it is likely to make the most money off him.

Therefore, if you ever happen to receive a free weekend in Las Vegas courtesy of a hotel-casino, my advice is to bet against yourself and stay home. It'll save you money.

Homework Assignment 16: Recalling that it took Galileo years to convince people that light objects fell as quickly as heavy objects even though they could see the results with their own eyes, how long—if ever—do you think it will take before all doctors will be required to confirm their diagnoses of patients with a machine? Defend your answer.

Lesson 17: Do the Math Until It Doesn't Add Up

"Let me see: four times five is twelve, and four times six is thirteen, and four times seven is—oh dear! I shall never get to twenty at that rate."
— Lewis Carroll in *Alice in Wonderland*

Question 17: Which is greater: 1 or 2? What about 100 or 10,000?

The correct answer is that it depends upon context. As Shel Silverstein recounts in his famous poem "Smart," context is everything. The poem tells the story of a young boy who trades one dollar for two quarters because "two is more than one." Next, he swaps the two quarters for three dimes because "three is more than two," and then three dimes for four nickels because "four is more than three." The poem concludes with the boy trading four nickels for five pennies because, as you may have guessed, "five is more than four."

It would be nice to believe Silverstein's poem is just a cute little piece about a misguided youth. Unfortunately, many otherwise intelligent adults continue to make comparable mistakes every day, and it is a habit worth unlearning.

Consider the recent push among businesses and marketers to get followers on the social media site Twitter. On its face, it would appear to be better to have 10,000 followers than 100 followers. What matters, though, is not the total number of followers a business or person has but rather the willingness of those "followers" to spread their ideas, thoughts and opinions.

As Seth Godin reminds us, if a person begins with 10,000 followers and has a tweet with a net pass-along rate of 0.8 (implying her 10,000 followers will forward it to 8,000 new people, who will then pass it along to 6,400, etc.), the tweet has a relatively short shelf life and the idea will soon die out. If, however, she has 100 loyal followers and creates a noteworthy tweet that is passed along to a net of 1.5 new people, her idea will first reach 150 new people after the first tweet and eventually it will overtake the tweet of the person with 10,000 followers after the thirteenth generation. (See graph.) If her idea was only slightly better—say it had a 1.7 net pass-along rate—the effect would be even more dramatic. (See the purple line.)

The point is that it is the *idea* that matters most and not the raw number of followers. Still, many people and organizers obsess over the raw numbers and miss the more important point of providing meaningful, insightful and creative content. Why? Because, like the boy in the Silverstein poem, everyone knows "10,000 is more than 100."

Alas, this isn't always so. Less can be more when you concentrate on the right things.

Homework Assignment 17: For one week, record the number of phone calls and emails you respond to at work. Also count the number of meetings you attend. Next, make a conscious effort to reduce the number in each category by 25 percent. What is the impact on your productivity? Did fewer meetings increase productivity?

Lesson 18:
Don't Follow the Money

"Education is one of the few things a person is willing to pay for and not get."
— William Lowe Bryant

Question 18: This is another question with two parts:

1) Does $50 always equal $50?

2) Which amount of money would you prefer to earn over a three-year period: $110,000 or $150,000?

While it is true that $50 will always equal $50 and $150,000 is, of course, more than $110,000, it is also true that many people ignore these obvious facts and work contrary to their financial interests. If you see a little of yourself in either of the examples below, you may need to unlearn some of your financial behaviors.

Let's first consider the case of the $50. If you were about to purchase a $100 mobile phone and then suddenly learned the same model was being sold for $50 on the opposite side of town, would you drive across town to save the extra $50? When surveyed, an overwhelming number of people stated that they would.

So far, so good.

When the scenario was changed, however, and the product in question was a $40,000 automobile and they were informed that the same model was available on the other side of town for the price of $39,950—or the exact same $50 savings—a majority of people indicated they wouldn't make the trip.

The reason is that a $50 savings on a $40,000 product is miniscule compared to its overall price. Whereas when one purchases a $100 product, a $50 savings is quite significant. The reality is that a $50 savings is a $50 savings, and a person's wallet or bank account doesn't know or care how they accumulated the extra savings. In a perfectly rational world people would work to save $50 regardless of the situation.

One real-world manifestation of this behavior can be found in retail shops. It is a well-known tactic that if a person were to go into a high-end retailer and tell the sales clerk they were interested in buying some socks, shoes and a suit, the clerk would first attempt to get them to buy the suit. Why? Because if they are successful at selling the customer a $1,500 suit, a $300 pair of shoes and $40 for a pair of socks suddenly seems less consequential. If, however, the customer were to begin shopping for socks first, not only would he be less likely to spend $40 on socks, he would also probably think longer and harder before dropping any money on expensive shoes and suits.

The second question stems from another fascinating study in which people were provided a choice between two different scenarios. In the first, they earned $30,000 in year one; $40,000 in year two; and $50,000 in year three. In the second scenario, they earned $60,000 in the first year; $50,000 in the second; and $40,000 in the third.

When asked to select which scenario they would prefer, a surprising number chose the first scenario. This is in spite of the fact that they would earn a total of $30,000 less. (In the first the total equals $110,000 and in the second it equals $150,000.) It is well documented that many people experience the pain of losing money more (as is experienced in the second scenario) and will go to great lengths—including missing out on an extra $30,000—to avoid that pain.

For a real-world implication of this behavior, consider the case of a bargain flight from San Francisco to New York. Imagine the price is $300 on Monday but suddenly jumps to $400 on Tuesday. Many people will skip the deal. If, however, the same flight was originally $800 and then dropped to $600, more people would rush to book the flight because it was a "deal"—even though it is $200 more expensive than the first scenario.

Often, people prefer the illusion of a good deal (a $600 flight that was $800) to the reality of a much better deal (a $400 flight that was $300). My advice: Don't always follow the money, because sometimes it can lead you astray.

Homework Assignment 18: Which are you more likely to sell: a $50 stock that has appreciated $25, or a $50 stock that has declined by $25? Explain and defend your answer.

Lesson 19: Grow from Your Inexperience

"Human beings, who are almost unique in having the ability to learn from the experiences of others, are also remarkable for their apparent disinclination to do so."
— Douglas Adams

Question 19: Which is the more likely scenario?

A. Roger seemed happily married. He killed his wife.
B. Roger seemed happily married. He killed his wife because he wanted her inheritance.

Many people select "B" because it sounds more plausible. But it's the wrong answer. The correct answer is "A" for the simple reason that logically, the more broadly worded description depicted in scenario A not only includes scenario B but also every other possible reason why Roger may have killed his wife, including reasons of anger, jealousy, mental illness or accident.

The relevance of this common mistake of focusing on the specific to the exclusion of the general can be found in how many people think about insurance. After September 11, 2001, many people were more inclined to purchase insurance to protect against acts of terrorism even though injury or death due to terrorism was already covered under the terms of most general insurance policies. Rental car companies also play off people's inexperience when they encourage customers to buy "extra" insurance. The rental companies know it is easier for people to imagine the specific experience of getting into an automobile accident in a new city with a rental car, and they use this knowledge to get the customer to purchase additional (and unnecessary) insurance.

It is not sufficient to merely get others to stop profiting from our inexperience; there are additional ways to profit from your own inexperience—provided you're willing to unlearn.

In many cases, we can learn from those who have experienced something we have not. Unfortunately, this is more difficult to do than it may sound because people don't like to believe they are "average" and that their experiences will mirror the experiences of those who have gone before them.

In his book *Stumbling Upon Happiness*, Dan Gilbert documents how people who win the lottery are not happier a year after winning the lottery. Nevertheless, the overwhelming majority of lottery players are convinced they are unique (or "not average") and, unlike those other poor saps who won the lottery and didn't achieve happiness, winning will definitely make them happy. This illusion keeps them playing (and, for the most part, losing) even though it might have been avoided by applying other people's real-world experiences to their hypothetical future experience.

The second way to unlearn from our inexperience is to become cognizant of the fact that often our most vivid memories come from the most unlikely experiences. This causes people to believe these rare experiences are more common than they actually are. For example, do you "always" get in the slowest lane at the grocery store or on the highway during rush hour? The reality is that you don't. You just don't recall all the times your lanes are moving at a normal or faster-than-normal clip.

The same effect is at work when people refuse to fly in an airplane after a bad plane crash. Airline accidents are exceedingly rare and, statistically speaking, it is far more dangerous to drive than fly. Because people can more easily and vividly recall these unlikely plane crashes, however, they are more likely to select a different—and far more dangerous—mode of transportation.

By reminding yourself of the totality of your experiences—as well as the experiences of others—not only can you gain a clearer picture of reality, you may even grow enough from your inexperience to extend your life.

Homework Assignment 19: Think of someone who has made an unfavorable first impression on you but receives high praise from others. Using those experiences from other people, make a list of the person's favorable characteristics. Next, construct a list of things that you have not experienced about the person. Now, explain how your first impression might have been wrong.

Lesson 20:
Mix Up Your Mind

"The mind is like an iceberg, it floats with one-seventh of its bulk above the water."
— Sigmund Freud

Question 20: According to the latest research, IQ accounts for what portion of career success?

a. 50 to 60 percent

b. 25 to 49 percent

c. 23 to 34 percent

d. 11 to 22 percent

The answer is between 4 and 10 percent. In other words, "none of the above." This question comes compliments of Dan Pink, who used it in his best-selling book *A Whole New Mind* to suggest the idea that confining oneself to the answers presented is "a symptom of excessive left-directed thinking."

In order to unlearn, however, it is not enough to train yourself to use right brain-directed thinking—although this is helpful. A person or an organization must also intentionally mix up their thinking in order to get a clearer picture of reality.

For example, did you know that if a person scores low on an IQ test they are likely to spend more time reading articles that refute the validity of the IQ test? The reason is because once an outcome has been determined and the experience can no longer be changed, people look for ways to change their view of the experience.

The same is true with the stocks we buy, the cars we purchase and the schools where we send our children. In each case, after the fact, people prefer finding information confirming—rather than refuting—their decision. This process may make them feel better, but it is unlikely to lead to better decisions in the future.

What, then, is a person to do? One strategy is to mix up your thinking. Specifically, look for information that contradicts your interpretation of the situation, consider the situation from multiple viewpoints or actively solicit input from people with a different perspective.

Google and Proctor & Gamble (P&G) provide a good example. In the past, the companies swapped two dozen key employees. For its part, Google was interested in winning over a larger portion of P&G's $9 billion annual advertising budget, while P&G was concerned that only a small fraction of its advertisement budget was being spent online and it wanted to better understand the Internet's potential.

The intentional mixing of the two cultures allowed each company the opportunity to see their current business dynamic—as well as future opportunities—in a different (and, perhaps, clearer) light by forcing employees to challenge key assumptions about how they viewed their business environments. P&G, for example, wasn't inviting influential bloggers to attend press conferences for the roll out of new products, and Google didn't fully appreciate how important colors were to building brand image.

Mixing up your mind need not always involve others. Sometimes it can be as simple as changing your mind-set. In an influential study, Ellen Langer studied 84 women who cleaned hotel rooms. One group of women heard a brief presentation explaining how their work qualified as good exercise. The other group did not. The two groups then continued on with their regular work routine. Surprisingly, the group that heard the presentation displayed more weight loss and experienced larger declines in blood pressure. In short, they became healthier by virtue of nothing more than a change of perspective.

Langer's studies and the Google-P&G employee swap are tangible reminders that if you are serious about seeking new insights and achieving better results, you don't need a high IQ. All you need to do is "mix up your mind."

Homework Assignment 20: Locate a regular optometrist's eye chart which begins with the largest letter on top. Test your vision. Make note of the last line you could read. Next, locate an eye chart that begins with the smallest print on top. Make note of the last line you can read. Did your results improve?

Lesson 21:
Know Doubt

"Doubt is not a pleasant condition,
but certainty is absurd."
— Voltaire

Question 21: How much of the earth is water?

Did you say somewhere between two-thirds and 75 percent? If so, you are incorrect. As John Lloyd and John Mitchinson explain in their delightful book *The Book of Ignorance*, "Seven-tenths of the earth's surface is *covered* by water but water accounts for less than a fiftieth of one percent of the planet's mass."

If it makes you feel any better, more recent research suggests there may be five times as much water dissolved deep under the earth's crust. If true, the answer may need to be revised upwards to the neighborhood of 0.1 percent.

In many ways our knowledge is analogous to the amount of water covering the earth's surface. It may look substantial—indeed—it may even be the reason for our survival, but there will always be so much more that we will never know.

The task then is to unlearn the false confidence that our knowledge provides and replace it with the less pleasing, but ultimately more realistic, strategy of harboring more doubt.

How can this be done?

The answer, in part, can be found in the work of Irving Janis, who in his seminal book *Groupthink* outlined six methods to help individuals and groups of like-minded people to challenge the confidence of their knowledge prior to relying on it to make a difficult decision. Specifically, Janis advised leaders to:

1. Assign the role of "critical evaluator" to everyone involved in the decision-making process so they can freely air concerns, objections and doubts.
2. Keep their opinions to themselves so as to prevent subordinates from tailoring their advice or withholding dissenting opinions.
3. Set up independent groups to work on the same problem.
4. Effectively examine all alternatives.
5. Actively solicit the opinions of outside experts.
6. Appoint a devil's advocate.

Janis used the Kennedy administration's ill-fated invasion of the Bay of Pigs as a classic example of how groupthink can lead to overconfidence in a group's knowledge, but the global financial meltdown brought on by the subprime mortgage fiasco is a more recent example. Of course, hindsight is 20/20, but if everyone in the banking and insurance industries from the CEOs down to the government regulators and the consumers themselves (who overextended themselves) had been less certain of themselves and embraced some doubt, the outcome may have been less severe. For example, the parties involved might have tempered their feelings of excessive optimism and pierced the illusion of the housing market's inevitable and continuous rise if they had conducted an objective survey of alternatives and more thoroughly examined the risks. Similarly, by actively seeking outside experts, diverse opinions and engaging the services of a devil's advocate, the parties involved may have been made aware of their biases, conducted better information searches, and spent more time developing contingency plans.

As a wise person once said, "The only thing I am certain of is that there is too much certainty in this world." In this spirit, then, it would be unwise to expect that all foolish and poor decisions can be avoided in the future. But they can perhaps be spotted earlier, be better contained and dealt with more swiftly and effectively if more people would occasionally substitute confident statements of "no doubt" with the more modest philosophy of "to know doubt."

Homework Assignment 21: What world-famous inventor said, "We don't know a millionth of one percent about anything"?

Lesson 22: Lose Sight of the Shore

"The real voyage of discovery consists not in seeking new landscapes but in having new eyes."
— Marcel Proust

Question 22: There is a small town that has only one street. The street runs in an east-west direction and is exactly one mile in length. The town council recently granted liquor licenses to two taverns with the proviso that the establishments be situated so that each town's inhabitants and the tavern owners experience maximum convenience. Where along the one-mile street should the establishments be located?

Did you say that the taverns should be positioned on opposite sides of the street at the half-mile point? This ensures both taverns will draw an equal number of patrons, but the locations are not maximized for the customers' benefit. To do this, the establishments must be located at the one-third—and two-thirds-mile marks. Under this scenario both taverns draw an equal number of people, but no one in the town walks more than one-third of a mile. The difference is that in the first scenario the tavern owners optimize the situation for their own benefit, but that didn't yield the best solution for the town's residents.

The situation has comparable real-world implications, and it is a behavior worth unlearning because it can lead to missed opportunities. In his book *Guns, Germs and Steel*, Jared Diamond writes that one of history's greater curiosities is the fact that the large island of Madagascar, which sits only 225 miles off the coast of Africa, wasn't discovered by Africans. It was discovered by peoples from Indonesia—a country thousands of miles to the east. Much the same dynamic is at play when large and established businesses miss big opportunities close to home.

W.Chan Kim and Renee Mauborgne argue persuasively in their book *Blue Ocean Strategy* that one of the best methods for achieving success is not to go head to head with the competition (as in the aforementioned example of placing one tavern directly across the street from another), but instead to delve into unknown market space or what they refer to as Blue Ocean opportunities.

This is precisely what Cirque do Soleil chose to do when it reimagined the circus. It didn't try to compete with Ringling Bros. and Barnum & Bailey with longer trapeze sets or larger and better-trained elephants. Instead, it created an entirely unique experience that didn't rely on any animals and rather emphasized theme and artistic music, along with a rich and diverse pool of dance and performance art.

In the beginning Cirque du Soleil was considered cutting edge and avant-garde (and it still is). But by venturing forth into unchartered waters, it has redefined the meaning of the circus and has brought its art to millions of people around the world.

As was mentioned in Lesson 7, unlearning requires a willingness to "see what isn't there," and it is impossible to see far beyond the shore when you are tethered to it. Or, as Andre Gide more eloquently wrote, "Man cannot discover new oceans unless he has the courage to lose sight of the shore."

Homework Assignment 22: In 2008, Nintendo was able to recapture a large share of the video gaming market by developing a new gaming console (the Wii), which could be used by its non-customers (seniors). Today, the 55—to 65—year-old demographic is the fastest-growing segment of the video gaming market. Consider and design a product for a group of people who are not your customers today.

Lesson 23:
Ignore the Eclipse and Admire the Sunset

"We must unlearn the constellation
to see the stars."
— Jack Gilbert from the poem "Tear It Down"

Question 23: In 2003, what money-losing product far exceeded its sales projections for the year in spite of the fact that the manufacturer made no material upgrades to the product and spent less money on advertising?

The answer is Oldsmobile, and its success was all the more surprising because its parent company, General Motors, had decided to discontinue the line after 2004 due to consistently weak sales. In retrospect, this paradoxical outcome was driven by the realization by potential customers that Oldsmobile was only going to be available for a limited time.

The idea that something is special just because it is limited in number—or even rare—is worth unlearning on a limited basis. Sometimes limited items and objects are special and deserving of our attention. Often, however, they are not.

Consider, for example, sales of other products that are advertised as being available for a "limited time." This time-honored marketing tactic has been employed for one simple reason: it works. People fear the potential loss of the product more than the actual benefit it will deliver. If you have ever ended up with buyer's remorse or wondered why you are donating a pair of shoes you never wore to charity, it is possible you fell prey to this trap.

The "scarcity principle"—the idea that since something may be going away it makes sense to buy it—is part of the same theme. The problem becomes more pernicious when even more people are clamoring for the scarce item. If you've ever witnessed the insanity of a preholiday rush as a store's patrons sprint to secure the last few remaining versions of a Cabbage Patch doll, Tickle-Me-Elmo, Beanie Baby or the latest "must-have" toy, you get the general idea. Many people are motivated by nothing more than the fear of being left empty-handed.

This habit of confusing scarcity with value leads to the unusual title of this unlearning lesson. During my sophomore year of high school, I recall being dragged outside during the middle of the school day to view a rare full eclipse. The only problem is that I wasn't actually allowed to look at the eclipse as it occurred, lest I do irreparable damage to my eyes. To avoid this cataclysmic fate, my fellow classmates and I were instructed on how to construct a "pinhole projector." As I recall, we punched a hole in the flimsy piece of poster board and held the board up so that it blocked our view of the event and, in its place, cast a shadow of the eclipse onto the ground. It was, to say the least, a decidedly unsatisfying experience.

I mention this because during high school I was never once advised or encouraged to get up early to enjoy the radiant beauty of a sunrise or to slow down at the end of a day to admire the magnificence of a setting sun—even though both are far more beautiful than a solar eclipse.

The relationship between quantity (or availability) and value is often tenuous at best and sometimes can be as weak as the shadow of an eclipse cast upon the ground through a makeshift pinhole projector.

Homework Assignment 23: While enjoying either an early morning sunrise or a late afternoon sunset, make a list of common items that have great value to you and compare it with a second list of those scarce items you possess but hold little value.

Lesson 24:
Playing It Safe Is Risky

"Beware of false knowledge, it is
more dangerous than ignorance."
— George Bernard Shaw

Question 24: Do more people die jaywalking or in a designated crosswalk?

The answer is the crosswalk. The reason is because people are lulled into a false sense of security due to the allure of existing rules such as painted crosswalks and flashing signs. As a result, they don't feel as compelled to pay close attention to the actions of others. When jaywalking, people are under no such illusion and remain vigilant and fleet of foot.

This lesson is appropriate in today's business environment in two important ways. First, too many business leaders and organizations are lulled into complacency by tradition, existing rules and the power of the status quo. Like the white painted lines on a crosswalk, the protection their market position or brand offers is often nonexistent. Worse yet, much as the flashing lights and warning signs provide a false level of security to a pedestrian, the signals customers send businesses also offer illusionary protection against an accelerating future. The problem is that by the time a person or organization realizes the danger they are in, it is too late and they are run over.

Clayton Christensen, in his excellent and now classic book *The Inno-vator's Dilemma*, provides numerous examples of industry leaders refus-ing to heed the oncoming sounds of new threats because they were so at-tuned to the needs of their best customers—customers who were primarily focused on incremental product improvements.

This purportedly safe approach (i.e., "the customer is never wrong") left them vulnerable to new competitors who were willing to ignore exist-ing rules and opted instead to jaywalk in the direction of those "risky" fringe customers. Over time, the niche markets serving these small com-munities mature and the product's features or capabilities that were ini-tially only demanded by those on the fringe come to be seen as valuable to mainstream audiences. Unfortunately, by the time this becomes evident to the existing players, it is too late and they ceded the marketplace to an upstart company. Think about how IBM was caught flat-footed by the personal computer in the 1980s, large book retailers by the Internet in the 1990s and the music industry by digitalization in the first decade of the twenty-first century.

What's next?

Industries destined to feel a similar effect in the future include the en-ergy, gaming and manufacturing industries. Advances in nanotechnol-ogy are fueling startling advances in solar and fuel cell technology. These technologies, many of which are now expensive and limited in capability, don't appear to represent much of a threat today, but as they improve they will create a vastly more decentralized energy distribution network and transform the energy paradigm. If existing leaders in the energy sector ignore these signs they will be run over. The same is true with how hand-gesture and 3-D technology will transform gaming culture, and advances in 3-D printing are poised to lead to radical new manufacturing and supply chain distribution models.

What, then, is a person or organization to do? Jaywalk. That's right. Break the rules. Doing so will not only make you more aware and and alert to the dangers around you, but you'll also be more likely to chart a quicker path to future customers.

Remember, unlearning isn't risky. What is risky is playing it safe.

Homework Assignment 24: Did you know that after childproof lids on medicine bottles were introduced, the change led to a significant increase in the number of child poisonings? The reason is because parents became *less* careful about keeping the bottles away from their children. With this analogy in mind, explain how a supposedly safe strategy your organization is implementing may actually be risky.

Extra Credit: Identify at least one area where the rules in your business are changing and explain how a supposedly risky strategy may actually be safer.

Lesson 25:
Put One Foot in Back of the Other

"Every mile you go in the wrong direction
is really a two—mile error. Unlearning is twice
as hard as learning."
— Unknown

Question 25: Imagine that the Roman numeral equation below is made out of ten toothpick sticks such that "I" equals one stick and the "X," "+" and "=" all represent two sticks:

$$XI + I = X$$

Your mission, should you choose to accept it, is to fashion the correct answer by moving around as few sticks as possible. (Translated, the equation currently reads 11 + 1 = 10.)

If you answered that you move one stick—by placing the "I" on the left side of "X"—to create this new equation: IX + I = X, you solved the problem, but you did not get the correct answer. The correct answer is that you move zero sticks. The solution merely requires you to flip the equation over backward providing the following result:

$$X = I + IX$$

What is interesting about this problem is that when students had their brains scanned while solving the problem, the brain waves associated with memory and conventional mental activity experienced abrupt decreases just prior to the solution becoming apparent. This result has led researchers to theorize that thinking spatially may be one way to expand problem-solving potential.

Earlier in the book I encouraged you to "become uncomfortable in your own skin" by unlearning the regular way you fold your hands or cross your arms. I'd now invite you to take this a step further and identify a few other daily rituals that you can do in a spatially different manner.

For example, if you are right-handed, try using your left hand to brush your teeth or move the mouse on your computer. You may also consider putting your pants on with the leg opposite the one you normally choose first. Other ideas include eating corn on the cob differently (e.g., if you normally nibble corn horizontally along the rows, try consuming it in vertical fashion by mowing up the columns) or eating your pie from the outer edge.

Such activities sound frivolous, but in each case the brain is required to reactivate seldom-used neural connections. Sometimes these new connections can lead to innovative insights that may facilitate unlearning older and more conventional problem-solving approaches.

For instance, eating pie from the edge was instrumental in causing pizza companies to experiment with making the crust more enjoyable by infusing it with cheese. And the analogy to the Roman numeral quiz is apropos of the engineer who was charged with making elevators run more quickly in order to appease growing customer dissatisfaction with long waits. When faced with safety concerns that limited the speed of the elevators, the engineer flipped the question on its head and asked the seemingly ridiculous question: "What would we do if we wanted to make the passenger wait longer for the elevator?" The result led him to install mirrors by each elevator. The tactic didn't change the speed of the elevator, but it did take passengers' minds off the delay and caused the underlying problem to go away.

Homework Assignment 25: In 1996, Guinness was plagued by plummeting sales due to consumers growing impatient with the time it took to properly pour a Guinness (the process takes about two minutes). To overcome the problem, company officials made no changes to their beer and instead turned the "problem" of slowness into a virtue by creating a new ad campaign slogan: "Good things come to those who wait." This, in turn, converted a supposed liability into an asset. Your assignment is to identify one problem or trouble area in your business and turn the issue on its head. List at least one outcome from this process.

Lesson 26:
Stop Looking for Patterns

"We are so good at seeing patterns that, often,
we see them where they don't exist."
— Michael Mauboussin

Question 26: If you flip a coin fourteen times, which scenario (A or B) is more likely to occur?

A. The coin will land on heads (H) 14 straight times:
  H-H-H-H-H-H-H-H-H-H-H-H-H-H

Or

B. The coin will land with the random outcome of tails (T) and heads (H): T-T-H-T-H-H-H-T-T-H-T-H-T-T

The answer is that the odds of each scenario occurring is exactly the same: 1 in 16,384. And yet to most people, the first outcome is viewed far differently and is seen not as a random outcome but instead as part of a clear and established pattern.

To demonstrate the point, consider one of the more statistically improbable outcomes from the world of sports: For the past fourteen Super Bowls (1998 to 2011), the team from the National Football Conference (NFC) has won the coin toss.

Now, the NFC team has not always called "heads." In fact, the NFC team has been just as likely to call "tails." Moreover, the NFC team only calls the coin toss every other year. Still, the NFC has defied the odds by being on the winning side of the coin toss fourteen consecutive times.

This outcome is no more likely than fourteen straight heads, fourteen straight tails or 16,383 other permutations. The NFC's streak is, to be sure, a matter of extraordinary good fortune, but it is not part of an established pattern from which you can discern anything about the future other than the fact that the odds of the NFC team winning the coin toss for a fifteenth straight time is only 50 percent.

This won't stop countless individuals from believing there is a clear pattern. To better understand why this behavior is worth unlearning, consider this map of London showing where German V-2 rockets hit the city during World War II.

1.3.
Map of London showing V-1 rocket strikes (Adapted from Gilovich [1991])

From the above map, it appears as though the area in and around the River Thames (in the lower right-hand corner) was being targeted. This pattern may cause a person to take the seemingly logical action of moving to the neighborhood in the upper right-hand corner on the assumption it is safer.

Watch what happens, however, when the boundaries of London are re-configured into a diagonal pattern (see the map below). The distribution of the bombs now appears much more evenly distributed even though where those bombs fell hasn't changed. The result is a visual reminder that our perception of reality can be framed by arbitrary randomness around which we place boundaries—or patterns—after the fact.

In the world of business, the situation is far worse because frequently

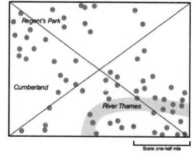

ap of London showing V-1 rocket strikes (Adapted from Gilovich [1991])

people "see" established "patterns" after only one or two examples. For instance, how often has a board of directors hired a CEO who was suc-cessful in his past job, or a university lured a football or basketball coach who had a winning season at his last school, only to watch him fail mis-erably in his new position? The CEO or coach may have looked like a safe choice (much like the one London neighborhood looked safe), but "bombs" have a way of catching up with people if they lull themselves into believing they have discerned a pattern that does not, in reality, exist.

Homework Assignment 26: If a stockbroker advertises she has beaten the market for three consecutive years, how much credence should you assign to the claim?

Extra Credit: If LeBron James, a career 53 percent shooter, has hit his last eight shots in Game 7 of the NBA finals, how likely is he to hit to next shot?

Lesson 27: Show Your True Colors: Fear Commitment

"A foolish consistency is the hobgoblin of little minds."
— Ralph Waldo Emerson

Question 27: What do chameleons do?

They do many things, but the one thing they don't do (as many of us believe) is change color to match their background. Chameleons do change color in response to changes in light and temperature. They also change appearance when frightened or when attempting to gain the attention of a member of the opposite sex.

This distinction between changing to meet *every* change in external conditions and changing only in response to those factors critical to one's long-term well-being or survival is an important one.

From a human perspective, the difference can best be seen in the actions of a "yes man" (someone who too readily modifies his message to match the viewpoints or beliefs of his audience) versus a person who changes his mind in response to new information.

There is, for example, a big difference between the lone juror who has reservations about the guilt of the defendant, but goes against her convictions and votes "guilty" with the other jurors for the sake of expediency, and the juror who had originally sided with the majority but, when presented with compelling, new information, changes her mind based on the principle of fairness.

The distinction is an important one especially in a social climate where changing one's mind has become something of a liability. To this end, how often have you heard a politician skewered by an opponent because he or she has changed position on an important topic? "Candidate so-and-so was *for* it before he was *against* it!"

Distinguishing when someone is changing positions for expediency's sake and when they are doing it as a matter of principle can be difficult to assess, but one strategy for avoiding such situations yourself is to "fear commitment" and steer clear of making unnecessary public declarations in the first place.

It has been scientifically demonstrated that once a person publicly commits to a course of action or proclaims a belief, he is far less likely to change his position. The remedy then is to keep an open mind and maintain a position of "non-commitment" as long as possible. Of course, as anybody in a long-standing romance where one partner refuses to commit to the relationship can attest, this strategy is not without risks, but these can be minimized. In fact, the solution can be found by emulating the actions of the chameleon.

Again, it is not true that these creatures change in response to every external change—and neither should you. Rather, the key to survival is to contemplate which external factors are critical to your survival and change only in response to those. In the case of the chameleon, they change to regulate their temperature, hide from predators or procreate. In other words, they commit to changing only when one of three criteria has been met: 1) their external environment has changed; 2) to avoid being killed; or 3) to survive and propagate as a species.

Their behavior is worth mimicking. It is probably true that at some point everybody will "show their true colors," but it is also equally likely that every person's true colors will change in response to external factors. The trick, then, is to avoid committing to a one-color policy in a multi-color world.

Homework Assignment 27: Think of a time when either you or your organization made a public commitment that you later regretted. How did that commitment either slow you down or prevent you or your organization from making a positive change?

Lesson 28:
Do Stop Believing

"Man prefers to believe what
he prefers to be true."
— Francis Bacon

Question 28: True or false: Hypnosis is useful in helping witnesses accurately recall the details of crimes.

False. Hypnosis helps people recall more information, but not more *accurate* information. Yet, according to a scientific study, 61 percent of people still falsely hold this belief about the power of hypnosis. In addition, 65 percent of people also believe that they can sense when someone is staring at them from behind; and an even higher percentage (76 percent) believe that subliminal messages in advertisements can cause people to buy things. As with the hypnosis theory, the latter two beliefs have also been scientifically proven to be untrue.

With apologies to the band Journey and their 1981 hit "Don't Stop Believin'," to effectively engage in unlearning it is, in fact, healthy to stop believing. Please note that I'm not saying, nor am I advocating, that people rashly drop all of their beliefs—only that they temporarily stop believing.

Specifically, there are three things people can do to become more open to unlearning. First, they must learn to suspend their beliefs. To do this one need only admit the possibility (however remote or unlikely) that one's belief may be misguided or wrong. Second, once someone has engaged in this thought exercise and allowed a thin crack of light to pierce the belief, he or she should actively seek out the opinions of those who believe differently. At this stage, a person should merely listen to the arguments of others regarding their beliefs and try to do so without judging those beliefs.

Next, if those who believe differently raise legitimate counterpoints, the person who is unlearning should use those points to further explore his or her own beliefs. Better yet, if there were surprising observations (for example, scientific studies highlighting how hypnosis doesn't improve accurate recall, how people can't tell if someone is staring at their head or proof that the person [James Vicary] who originally claimed that subliminal ads in movies increased sales of Coca-Cola admitted his study was a fraud), they should turn those surprises into question marks and use those questions to further investigate why they believe what they do.

In the Paris riots of 1968, students spray-painted signs on walls saying, "We demand the right to contradict ourselves." It is easy to laugh at this statement and dismiss it as the epitome of sophomoric indiscretion. It is much harder to view it as a wise statement. Alas, it has been said that the "wiser one becomes, the more one is able to contradict one's own ideas."

The problem is that modern society has made self-contradiction a shameful act. It isn't. What is shameful is an inability to change one's mind when presented with new and contradictory information. The ability to change one's mind—even on long-held beliefs—is not a weakness, it's a strength.

Ironically, by submitting your beliefs to continuous and rigorous examination, the beliefs you do choose to hold on to will likely come to rest on a more stable and solid foundation.

Homework Assignment 28: Do you believe that humans only utilize 10 percent of their brain capacity? Or do you believe that listening to classical music will improve a young child's intelligence? If so, suspend your belief and seek out people who believe differently from you. What were the results of your research?

Lesson 29: Don't Reach for the Stars

"When it becomes necessary to develop a new perception of things, a new internal model of reality, the problem is never to get new ideas in, the problem is to get old ideas out."
— Dee Hock

Question 29: How many planets are there in our solar system?

The answer is eight. If you said nine don't feel bad because that was the correct answer until August 24, 2006, when the International Astronomical Union (IAU), in its infinite wisdom, declared Pluto a planet no more.

In addition to delivering a crushing blow to Pluto's planethood by ignominiously demoting it to "dwarf planet" status, the IAU also single-handedly rendered obsolete the famous childhood mnemonic for recalling the names of the then nine planets of Mercury, Venus, Earth, Mars, Jupiter, Saturn, Uranus, Neptune and Pluto: My Very Excellent Memory Just Served Up Nine Planets.

In terms of unlearning, however, it is not Pluto that concerns us, but rather Uranus. This is because between 1690 and 1769, the planet was observed no fewer than eighteen times—six times by the English astronomer John Flamsteed, and an additional twelve times by the French astronomer Pierre Lemonnier. In each instance, the orb was not recognized as a planet and was instead believed to be a star because of its dimness and slow orbit.

It was not until William Herschel observed the planet on March 13, 1781, and, in a subsequent report to the Royal Society described it as a "comet," that experts began to consider that it might be something other than a star. Still, it took an additional two years before most astronomers agreed the celestial body was neither a comet nor star but, in fact, a new planet. The story reminds us that when we are predisposed to see something in a certain way, it can be challenging to see it from a different perspective.

In a landmark psychology study, Jerome Bruner and Leo Postman showed a group of twenty-eight college students a series of playing cards. Most of the cards were normal but some were incongruous. On the incongruous cards, the colors and suits were reversed so that, for example, the three of hearts was black and the six of clubs red.

Whereas most students quickly identified the normal cards, it took, on average, four times longer for them to correctly identify the incongruous cards. There were three typical reactions. The most common was what the authors called a "dominance reaction." In such cases, the hearts on the cards were seen as red regardless of whether they were colored black.

A second outcome was what Bruner and Postman called a "compromise reaction." A black heart may be described as "purple" or "brown." In essence, the "red" heart the subject expected to see would blend with the black heart on the paper and merge in the subjects' minds to create a compromise color. Lastly, in a few rare instances, the subject would recognize something was wrong but be unable to articulate the appropriate solution.

For unlearning, the real-world implications of this study and the Uranus story are evident in many aspects of our lives. In his book *Moneyball* Michael Lewis describes how many baseball scouts eschew a player's statistics and assess (and ultimately draft) baseball prospects on their physique because "they look like a baseball player."

Voters do much the same with political candidates. In a recent study, people were shown the pictures of two opposing candidates—with no other information—and were asked to identify the more competent candidate. Surprisingly, their selections corresponded with the winning candidate 70 percent of the time. The finding strongly suggests that voters, when engaged in one of the most important civic duties in a democracy, are taking into consideration things other than performance-based information when selecting political candidates. Put another way, "looking the part" plays a large role in helping voters determine whom to vote for.

Like Uranus, baseball scouts and voters may believe they know a "star" when they see one, but they may be better off using this new mnemonic for recalling the eight planets: Many Vain Experts Must Just Study Unlearning Now. If you do, you may just stop reaching for the "stars" and come to perceive the world a little more clearly.

Homework Assignment 29: Could a politician with the physical appearance of Abraham Lincoln or the physical disabilities of Franklin Delano Roosevelt be elected president today? If not, why not, and are there similar prejudices in how CEOs, doctors or "star" marketing executives and salespeople are selected and hired?

Lesson 30:
Zone Out to Zone In

"We must be willing to sit on the edge of mystery and unlearn what has helped guide us in the past but is no longer useful."
— Robert Wicks

Question 30: Consider these three words: eye, gown and basket. Can you think of another word that relates to all three?

If not, don't fret. Zone out. That's right, don't focus, concentrate, "zone in" or even try to get "in the zone." Just allow your mind to wander.

Of the many beliefs and habits society must unlearn, one is the idea that the traits of concentration and focus are undeniably positive attributes. This is not to imply these traits are bad. They aren't. In fact, for the most part, concentration and focus are instrumental to a person's or an organization's success.

As with so many other things in life, however, moderation is necessary. With this caveat in mind, I'd like to therefore give you permission to daydream and zone out on occasion. New scientific research suggests that "mind wandering" can yield positive results; and, if you have ever come up with a clever, creative or innovative solution to a pesky problem while walking, exercising or taking a hot bath or shower, you can testify to its benefits.

Scientists theorize that while zoning out people are more apt to engage different parts of their brain. This facilitates the creation of new connections which, in turn, lead to new insights and the development of creative solutions.

In his excellent book *Drive: The Surprising Truth About What Motivates Us*, Dan Pink recounts the work of psychologist Karl Duncker and his "candle problem." In its simplest form, people are given a candle, a box of tacks and a book of matches and told to attach the candle to a wooden wall in such a way that no wax drips on the table. (See figure 1.)

Figure 1

Most people begin by attempting to adhere the candle to the wall with a tack or by melting the bottom of the candle and sticking it to the wall. Neither strategy works. Before the problem can be solved people must overcome what is termed "functional fixedness." In this case, participants must see the box of tacks as a platform for the candle that can also be attached to the wall. (See Figure 2.)

What is more interesting is that when another psychologist offered students a financial incentive to solve the problem, he discovered it took the students an average of 3.5 minutes *longer* to solve. The reason is because the inducement of a financial reward caused most of the students to narrow their focus. In other words, they zoned in on a misguided solution and it hindered their ability to see the problem from a different (and ultimately more constructive) perspective.

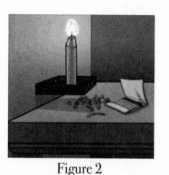

Figure 2

Now, return to the question at the beginning of this section. Have you arrived at the correct solution? If not that may be because you have kept your eye on the ball too closely. You'd have been better off taking a break and playing with a ball or perhaps shopping for a ball gown. (If you still haven't arrived at the solution the word that related to all three is *ball*.)

Homework Assignment 30: Identify at least one way you can give yourself or your employees permission to "zone out." Alternatively, figure out how to carve out more time in your day to stay *unfocused*. If you still can't come up with any ideas, get away from your office or desk and go for a walk, take a hot shower or just daydream and see if there is anything in particular that comes to mind.

Lesson 31:
Engage in Situational Unawareness Training

"Be very, very careful what you put into that head, because you will never, ever get it out."
— Thomas Cardinal Wolsey

Question 31: A yield sign has two colors. What are they?

Did you say yellow and black? That answer would have been correct if *Marcus Welby, M.D.* were the top-rated TV show, Richard Nixon still occupied the White House and NASDAQ had yet to become a leading stock market index. Since 1971, the yield sign has been red and white. Interestingly, a large number of people (including many born after 1971) still erroneously believe the yield sign is yellow and black.

This phenomenon demonstrates that once a thing has been learned—even something as common as the color of a sign—it can be very difficult to unlearn. This occurs, in spite of the fact that people have been observing (and hopefully, obeying) red and white yield signs for four decades.

Compare this situation to the actions of computer industry executives in the 1980s who, having learned about computers in the era of mammoth mainframes, were accustomed to producing their own proprietary hardware and software, as well as having internal sales teams market and sell the expensive products they created.

With the advent of the personal computer the rules suddenly changed, and companies began relying on microprocessors and packaged software, and using third parties to distribute and sell the product. A handful of computer companies adjusted but many others, such as Digital Equipment, Wang and Burroughs, did not because they either didn't unlearn the old rules or were late in responding to the new signs.

The same situation occurred more recently in the telecommunications industry. Prior to the creation of the iPhone, service providers dominated the telecom industry and dictated to phone manufacturers the terms of agreement. The creation of Apple's multi-touch, gesture interface and "apps"-laden device changed the industry virtually overnight. In a matter of months, millions of people switched providers and began using mobile devices to access the Internet (with a user-friendly browser), watch videos, read electronic books and, together with the growing universe of software applications, do everything from locating their parked car at an airport to keeping their child mildly amused with an easy-to-download "fart app."

In each case, the signs of change were not immediately obvious, but they could have been picked up on if industry leaders had engaged in some situational "unawareness" training by stepping outside their industry's existing paradigm and scanning the environment for subtle changes in technology, consumer behavior and the competitive landscape.

For example, in the automotive industry, new advances in nanomaterials and battery power may lead to radical new designs; the continued growth of social networking may demand that the cars of the future maintain constant connectivity and improve the driving experience; and advances in robotics and rapid prototyping could transform the manufacturing process and revolutionize the global supply chain. In each case, automotive industry professionals will have to unlearn what a car looks like, how it is made and powered, what it is expected to do and with whom they will have to partner in order to build the car of the future.

Virtually every other industry, including education, energy and health care, faces comparable changes, and one excellent way to prevent yourself and your organization from being run over by these emerging trends is to stop focusing on what you think you know and become more recognizant of how unaware you actually are.

Homework Assignment 31: Using Starbucks as a case study, identify three emerging trends in technology, consumer behavior or the beverage/food industry that may necessitate company officials unlearning some aspects of its current business model.

Lesson 32:
Don't Just Do Something, Sit There

"When men know not what to do, they ought not to do what they know not."
— Abigail Adams

Question 32: If five frogs are sitting on a log and four decide to jump off, how many are still sitting on the log?

The answer is five, because *deciding* to do something isn't the same as actually doing it.

From childhood, we are instilled with a bias for action. In many cases, it's a useful trait. It's even possible our bias for action is a genetic hand-me-down from our prehistoric ancestors, and it enabled us to avoid being devoured by predators by reacting with haste to the slightest rustling in the bushes. (Better safe than sorry, right?)

Is this bias toward action something then that we really need to unlearn? The answer is a qualified yes. To understand, consider that the scientists studying the odds of goalies trying to stop penalty kicks concluded that a goalie's best strategy was to stay put. If they had followed this course of action, goalies would have successfully stopped the shot 33 percent of the time. According to the data, however, goalies only employed this strategy of "staying put" 6 percent of the time.

There is a reason for this: people don't like "doing nothing." In fact, people who don't act often feel a deep emotional pang of guilt over their inaction. In the case of a goalie during a shootout, for instance, the goaltender would feel worse for standing there than if she had dived left on a kick to the right. This is true even though the outcome would have been the same—a goal. In common parlance, the feeling can best be summed up with the phrase, "At least she did *something.*"

The example of a goalie staying still may seem trivial, but the implications for staying put can have real-world implications. Consider the stock market. It is not uncommon for people to rush in and buy a certain stock when others are doing the same. The result, as a spate of investing "bubbles" have recently demonstrated, is the creation of artificially high and, ultimately, unsustainable stock prices. Counterintuitively, many people also follow the actions of others when selling a stock. They sell only because other people are selling—not because the underlying of the fundamentals of the stock has changed.

Warren Buffett is one of the world's richest men, but his sage partner, Charlie Munger, says, "Half of Warren's time is spent sitting on his ass reading; the other half is spent talking on the phone or in person to a highly gifted person that he trusts and trusts him." In other words, Buffett has a bias toward inaction. Most other stockholders would also be better off financially if they also employed a "buy-and-hold" approach as opposed to trying to time the market.

A bias toward inaction can also reap other unexpected benefits. Have you ever been traveling down the freeway and spotted other cars moving over into a more crowded lane? What is occurring is that drivers in the trailing cars believe that the action of the drivers in front of them are based on the knowledge of something that they can't yet see and so they decide to mimic the action. Sometimes there really is something ahead in the road, but often it is the result of nothing more than two cars simultaneously shifting lanes for arbitrary and unrelated reasons. The problem quickly grows, however, as this faulty logic gains momentum and an increasing number of drivers shift lanes, thus creating more "evidence" for others to do the same.

If you want to get ahead on both the freeway and in life, it behooves you to wait to "jump off the log" until you actually have access to compelling information that requires movement.

Homework Assignment 32: For the top five stock holdings in your portfolio, write down your rationale for holding the stock as well as the length you expect to hold it. Next, list the conditions under which you will sell the stock. Before you sell the stock, revisit your notes.

Lesson 33:
Shoot "Granny" Style

"It's not what you don't know that hurts you; it's what you know that just ain't so."
— Satchel Paige

Question 33: In both 1995 and 1996, David Justice of the Atlanta Braves had a higher batting average than the New York Yankees, Derek Jeter. Who had the higher two-year average?

The answer is Derek Jeter. The anomaly, known as Simpson's Paradox, occurred because in the first year Jeter had only 48 at bats and 12 hits for an average of .250, while Justice batted 411 times with an average of .253. The following year Jeter batted 582 times and hit for a .314 average, while Justice hit .321 but had only 140 at bats.

In other words, when you combine the players' totals for both years Jeter comes out on top' as the table below demonstrates. In this particular case, Jeter's two-year average was forty points higher.

	1995	1996	Combined
Derek Jeter	12/48 .250	183/582 .314	195/630 **.310**
David Justice	104/411 **.253**	45/140 **.321**	149/551 .270

The sporting world is ripe with unlearning examples. One of my favorites occurred on December 30, 1936, when 17,000 fans crowded into the old Madison Square Garden to watch Long Island University, then the country's top-ranked basketball team, take on Stanford University. It was slated to be a great game. Long Island was putting its forty-three-game winning streak up against the reigning Pacific Coast Conference champions.

More than that, though, people were eager to watch Hank Luisetti, Stanford's star sophomore. What made Luisetti unique is that he was the only player known for shooting the ball with one hand while jumping up in the air. At the time, every other basketball player in the country shot with two hands or took hook shots. Luisetti's jump shot was so radical, in fact, that it caused Nat Holman, the legendary coach of City College of New York (and a man known as "Mr. Basketball") to remark, "That's not basketball! If my boys ever shot one-handed, I'd quit coaching."

Luisetti and Stanford went on to crush Long Island University and, two years later, Luisetti became the first college player ever to score fifty points in a game. Today, it is impossible to find a single player at either the collegiate or professional level who shoots two-handed.

It took a long time for basketball players (and their coaches) to unlearn the two-handed shot, but this story and Jeter/Justice anomaly remind us that unlearning can be both counterintuitive and paradoxical.

To this end, while it is true that a return to two-handed shooting is unlikely, it may make sense in one area of the basketball court: the free-throw line. Consider the case of Rick Barry. Although Barry used an unorthodox underhand "granny-style" technique for his free throws, he is the National Basketball Association's (NBA) second most accurate free-throw shooter in history with an average of .900. Today, though, not a single player shoots free throws underhand. This is in spite of the fact that the average accuracy rate in the NBA is roughly 75 percent and many games are determined by just a few points.

For those players and coaches with the courage to unlearn their current free-throw shooting style, it could lead to an "above average" outcome because even a modestly higher free-throw average could result in a handful of more victories each season.

Homework Assignment 33: Explain why you think no one in the NBA shoots underhand free throws.

Extra Credit: Name at least two NBA players who may want to unlearn their current form and consider shooting "granny style." (Hint: At 52.4 percent, Shaquille O'Neal is only the second worst free-throw shooter.)

Lesson 34:
Don't Mind Your P's & Q's

"The curious thing is that with these exponential changes, so much of what we currently know is just getting to be wrong. So many of our assumptions are getting to be wrong. As so, as we move forward, not only is it going to be a question of learning, it is also going to be a question of unlearning."
— John Seely Brown

Question 34: On a pond, there is a single lily pad. Every day the number of lily pads doubles. If it takes 30 days for the lily pads to cover the entire pond, how long would it take for the patch to cover half of the pond?

The answer is 29 days.

In his best-selling book *Only the Paranoid Survive*, Andy Grove, then CEO of Intel, recounted the story of his discussion with Gordon Moore regarding the future of the company in the wake of its profits dwindling from $198 million to less than $2 million in the mid-1980s. "I looked out the window at the Ferris wheel of the Great American amusement park revolving in the distance when I turned back to Gordon, and asked 'If we got kicked out and the board brought in a new CEO, what do you think he would do?' Gordon answered without hesitation, 'He would get us out of memories.' I stared at him, numb, and then said 'Why shouldn't you and I walk out the door, come back, and do it ourselves?'

Grove did exactly that by abandoning the memory market and jumping into the microprocessor market. A few years later Grove made the then-controversial decision to begin branding Intel's technology with the "Intel Inside" slogan. During his tenure, the company grew at an impressive annual compound rate of 30 percent.

Undoubtedly, Grove was an intelligent, capable and visionary leader, but what really lay behind his extraordinary leadership? It was his ability and willingness to unlearn. Before Intel could become a microprocessor company it had to unlearn that it was a memory manufacturer, and before it could adopt an innovative marketing campaign, it had to unlearn the idea that a technology company could only appeal to consumers based on raw computer processing power. In a culture dominated by engineers this was no easy feat.

Unlearning is hard work. In fact, it often requires a brutal act of will. Intel only recovered from Grove's decision after it laid off 8,000 employees and suffered through a one-year loss of $180 million.

Throughout his reign, Grove kept Intel successful by keeping an open mind and displaying a willingness to set aside everything he knew—or thought he knew. It may be easy to think the semiconductor industry is somehow unique and more responsive to change because the industry's underlying technology (the transistor) is constantly changing (the number of transistors that can be placed on a chip doubles roughly every eighteen months). Perhaps this is true, but it is no reason for complacency.

We now live in an era of accelerating change, and every industry must embrace the concept of unlearning or risk perishing. For example, Wikipedia, the open-source movement, virtual and augmented reality, electronic books, social networking, gaming dynamics and free online courses are whipsawing educational institutions; and yet, amazingly, many teachers and administrators are reluctant to embrace new paradigms and new ways of doing business. Why? It's because they can't unlearn the old ways of doing things. This is true even when confronted with overwhelming proof that the system and its current models aren't working.

Similarly, the health care industry is about to be bombarded with a wealth of new genomics data that will fundamentally alter both patients' and doctors' understanding of diseases. Before the industry can take advantage of these new findings and treatments, medical professionals will need to unlearn much of what they think they know about how diseases are caused and how those ailments are best treated.

Mobile communication, radio frequency identification (RFID) technology, vast networks of "smart" sensors and flexible electronics are poised to revolutionize everything from advertising and marketing to how consumers shop for goods. Unless these related industries can unlearn some of their current behaviors' they will be at a severe competitive disadvantage to those who aren't wedded to old ways of doing business.

Advances in rapid prototype manufacturing (3-D printing), robotics and material science threaten to disrupt the manufacturing industry. Breakthroughs in solar power, fuel cell technology, demand management tools and other more far-fetched energy technologies such as wave power, synthetic biology and, perhaps, even nuclear fusion could also force energy providers to unlearn what they currently believe to be the most economical, cleanest and convenient energy sources.

Add to this amazing array of technological progress the as-yet-unknown technological advances; combine them with the accelerating power of the Internet, mobile and social communication tools, advanced algorithms and artificial intelligence; and then sprinkle on top of that voice and speech technology, which will help information flow more easily to hundreds of millions of aspiring entrepreneurs all across the globe, and it is easy to understand how many forecasters are predicting a wave of innovation unlike anything ever experienced in the history of humankind.

Like a surfing novice paddling to catch her first wave, the prospect is both thrilling and terrifying. If you approach the wave with an open mind—one that is ready to unlearn and jettison old skills that are no longer suitable for the new environment—your prospects for a successful adventure improve markedly. If you are rigid and cling to your old ways, the wave will either pass you by, leave you far from shore or, worse yet, slam your stiff and inflexible body (and thinking) onto the shoals of future progress.

Returning to Andy Grove now for a moment, if you looked out the window of your office and saw a large wave approaching and it was doubling in size every few moments, what would you do?

Homework Assignment 34: Rank the previously mentioned technologies (computer processing power, wireless technology, RFID, rapid prototype manufacturing, social networking, robotics, genomics, biotechnology and nanotechnology) in terms of their ability to necessitate unlearning within your organization.

Lesson 35:
Put on Some Rose-Colored Glasses

"Before people can begin something new, they have to end what used to be and unlearn the old way."
— William Bridges

Question 35: Estimate the odds of the following two events:

A. A large flood somewhere in America in which more than one thousand people die.

B. An earthquake in California, causing large flooding, in which more than one thousand people die.

Did you rate the second scenario (B) as being more probable? Many people do even though the first scenario (A) is more likely. If you reflect on the two options for a moment this should be obvious because, as a general condition, Scenario B would naturally also be included under Scenario A.

The reason many people misdiagnose the odds is because the second scenario (a California earthquake) is easy to perceive, whereas the first is more abstract. In much the same manner, people frequently misdiagnose situations based on their perception. This truism is often characterized as seeing the glass as either half full or half empty. The true impact of this distinction, though, goes far beyond this cliché.

The difference between optimists and pessimists has been succinctly delineated by Martin Seligman, the author of *Learned Optimism*, who explains it thusly: When bad things happen to optimistic people, they tend to see the event as: 1) temporary (limited in duration); 2) external (being caused by something outside their immediate sphere of influence); and 3) specific (affecting only a partial or isolated area of their life). Pessimistic people, by contrast, view negative events as: 1) permanent (or at least lasting a long time); 2) personal (they are somehow to blame); and 3)pervasive (affecting all aspects of their life).

A person's outlook on life—be it optimistic or pessimistic—may seem a matter of personal disposition, but Seligman's research suggests otherwise. Pessimism can be unlearned, and the benefits are not inconsequential because optimists have been found to lead longer, healthier, happier and, ultimately, more successful and fulfilling lives.

Consider just one of Seligman's studies on optimism. In 1985, while working with Metropolitan Life Insurance Company, 15,000 potential applicants took Met Life's regular career profile test along with an Attributional Style Questionnaire (ASQ) that measures optimism. One thousand applicants were hired as salespeople on the basis of the career profile alone. Met Life, however, still had a shortage of insurance agents and took the unusual step of hiring an additional 100 employees solely on the basis of those who scored in the top half of the ASQ. In other words, they hired only optimistic people for the additional openings.

What Met Life discovered was that the special hires (those who didn't pass muster on its regular career profile) outsold the pessimists in the regular force by 57 percent. This was the result of a few different factors. For starters, optimism helped these people push ahead in the face of failure. Rather than accepting setbacks as a mark of personal failure, they adopted an outlook closer to that of the great inventor Thomas Edison, who once remarked: "I have not failed. I have found 10,000 ways that didn't work." And failure, as we saw in Lesson 9, can have the counterintuitive effect of enhancing the quality of a product (or in this case, a sales pitch) by virtue of continuous improvement.

Optimism also encourages risk. This isn't always a positive trait, but in an era of continuous change, risk-taking can call forth two qualities likely to deliver success in a fast-changing environment: innovation and agility.

Unlearning pessimism merely requires you to adopt an optimistic explanatory style as your default setting when describing undesirable events. Instead of focusing on the negative, strive to put adverse matters in a positive light and, where possible, view them as temporary, external and limited in nature. In other words, put on rose-colored glasses.

Homework Assignment 35: If one were required to compile a list of "the best things that could ever happen," it would be hard to imagine that "being jilted by a lover" would make the list. To better understand how to adopt a positive explanatory style, explain how being left at the altar by an erstwhile lover could, in fact, come to be described as the best thing that ever happened to a person.

Lesson 36:
See the **Whole** Picture

"We don't see things as they are,
we see them as we are."
— Anais Nin

Question 36: Study the picture below. Do you notice anything unusual?

It is one of the world's most recognizable corporate logos and although most people see it every day, only a small percentage of people have ever noticed the clever arrow hidden between the letters "E" and "x."

It is a fitting analogy for how many people view the world. We like to believe—and, in fact, we're quite confident—that we're seeing the whole picture. Often, though, there is a glaring hole in our knowledge. To this end, did you notice the double entendre in the title of this lesson? Did you see that the word "hole" was bolded in the word "**Whole**"?

What else aren't we seeing? This, of course, is impossible to know because we can't see what we can't see. Nevertheless, it is safe to assume we're seeing less than the complete picture, and it would behoove us to unlearn the assumption that our vision is infallible.

The video "Gorillas in our midst" has become one of the best-known and widely used studies in all of psychology, and it is one I personally use in speeches and keynote presentations all around the world. The thirty-second video shows a group of students passing a basketball back and forth. The six students are divided into two groups with one set wearing white shirts and the other black shirts. Viewers are then invited to count the number of times the students in the white shirts pass the basketball.

Normally about half the audience responds with the correct answer of thirteen. When audience members are then asked if they noticed anything else unusual in the video, typically about 20 percent respond in the affirmative. And when asked what they saw, they will say "a gorilla." The answer usually draws a good laugh from the disbelieving audience. But when invited to watch the video again (this time without concentrating on the basketball passes), they are amazed to see a person dressed in a gorilla suit walk directly onto the screen and into the middle of the students. It then stops, beats its chest and slowly walks off screen. In total, the gorilla is on screen for a full ten seconds.

Many people are so astounded that they could have missed something so blatantly obvious that they believe it is a different video. It is not. The video and the study are a tangible reminder that while people love to believe they are seeing the whole picture, the reality is that often they are missing large things that are staring them directly in the face.

It is easy to dismiss the video as a clever college psychology experiment with no practical application, but this is far from the case. The emerging field of data mining, for example, is exposing an ever-increasing number of business metrics to new findings that contradict conventional wisdom and people's intuition. In a well-documented case, McDonald's had great difficulty accepting the finding that a large number of its shake buyers weren't interested in the taste, texture or temperature of the milkshake. This wasn't particularly surprising because the vast majority of consultants it hired to study the issue were concentrated on those factors.

By studying the whole picture, one consultant, Gerald Berstell, however, uncovered a surprising fact: Many McDonald's shake buyers were buying shakes in the morning. When he delved into the matter, Berstell discovered these consumers were "hiring" the shake to perform a very specific job. What these buyers really wanted was something they could hold with one hand and wouldn't easily spill (e.g., hot coffee) or stain their clothes (e.g., a sausage McMuffin), and yet provide them some sustenance during their long morning commutes.

Like the gorilla, the data was perfectly clear: Customers were purchasing a large number of shakes in the morning. The problem was that McDonald's and its consultants were focused on the wrong things, such as taste, texture and aroma. Once they were able to unlearn their myopic view of the world, McDonald's was able to create new marketing opportunities to increase sales of shakes.

The moral? Sometimes the 800-pound gorilla isn't being talked about for the simple reason that no one can see it.

Homework Assignment 36: Data mining is uncovering a wealth of nuggets across a spectrum of industries. Readers interested in learning more are encouraged to pick up a copy of Ian Ayer's outstanding and insightful book *Super Crunchers: Why Thinking the Numbers Is the New Way to Be Smart* in order to understand how data mining can help them see the whole picture—or, should I say, see the hole in their view of the world.

Lesson 37:
Tread Cautiously on Thick Ice

"Beware of false knowledge; it is more dangerous than ignorance."
— George Bernard Shaw

Question 37: You are in Las Vegas and are offered a $1 bet in which you have a 99.9 percent chance of winning $10 and a mere 0.1 percent chance of losing $11,000. Would you take the bet?

The odds suggest that if you were to take the bet one thousand times you would win $10 a staggering 999 times. The wise choice, however, would be to refuse. Why? Because the expected gain from your victory is less than your expected loss. In more practical terms, for every ten dollars you bet, you would gain $9.99 but lose $11.

This is an important point because the world is ripe with such asymmetrical situations, and it is important to unlearn the idea that it is not the *frequency* of correctness but rather the *magnitude* of correctness.

I personally experienced such a situation on January 1, 2008. My family and I were staying at a friend's lake cabin in Northern Wisconsin and after celebrating New Year's Eve with one too many libations, my wife and I decided we were in need of a little exercise. My friend suggested we go snowshoeing across the lake.

My wife, having noticed a thin layer of slush above the ice on the lake, was concerned that the ice wasn't safe. My friend, after drilling through the ice to create an ice-fishing hole, assured her there were eight solid inches of ice and pointed to numerous snowmobilers gliding across the lake on their heavy sleds as visual evidence of the lake's ability to withstand our weight.

Bearing these common-sense points in mind, my wife and I confidently proceeded toward a small island ensconced in the middle of the lake. Once there, we continued across a marshy area until we heard a crack. Before we could stop to assess the situation, my wife had broken through the ice.

Luckily, I was standing on solid ground and she only plunged up to her waist before grabbing hold of the ice edge. After a fearful minute, I assisted her out of the water and onto solid ground. We then hastily made a beeline back across the lake—careful to follow our precise tracks back to the warmth and safety of the cabin.

In retrospect, everyone involved in the situation made the mistake of confusing the probability of falling through the ice (which was admittedly small) with the magnitude of the consequences of falling through the ice. (Had my wife and I both been just a few feet farther to the left, the outcome could have been fatal.)

In his book *Think Twice* (which cleverly and appropriately has the double entendre of "thin ice" in the title), Michael Mauboussin encourages people to focus on process and not outcomes when making decisions that involve probability.

Returning to the opening question, a focus on outcome leads a person to take a $10 bet with a chance of winning 999 out of 1,000 times because they will win an overwhelming percentage of the time. A focus on process suggests the decision is still a poor one because the magnitude of the rare possibility of losing $11,000 outweighs the benefits.

In other words, even if the thickest layer of ice has a remote chance of being thin somewhere, it behooves you to think twice about crossing it because the result could be a cold and painful dose of reality.

(Please note that this habit of focusing on process versus outcome is not inherently conservative, nor does it eschew risk taking. Quite to the contrary, if the odds were reversed so that you lost ten dollars 99.9 percent of the time but won $11,000 just 0.1 percent of the remaining time, it would be a good bet.)

Homework Assignment 37: Nine of your ten board members believe your company's sales will grow a modest 3 percent this year, but one board member estimates sales will plummet 50 percent. How do you modify your strategic plans to account for this possibility?

138

Lesson 38: Develop a Healthy Dose of Unconfidence

"There is a huge difference between what people actually know and how much they think they know."
— Nassim Taleb

Question 38: In his book *Super Crunchers: Why Thinking-By-Numbers Is the New Way to Be Smart*, Ian Ayres writes, "People think they know more than they actually know." To prove this point, he asks his readers to answer 10 questions such that they are 90 percent confident that their answer is correct. For example, if asked, "What is the length of the Mississippi River in miles?" you would respond by setting the parameters to your answer between any two figures (of your own choosing) so long as you were 90 percent confident the correct answer would fall somewhere between those two figures. In this case, even if you don't know the precise length of America's longest river, you may be 90 percent confident the correct answers falls somewhere between a low of 500 miles and a high of 5,000 miles. (The correct answer is 2,320 miles.)

Now take a minute to answer the following 10 questions:

	Low	High
1. What is the length of the Nile River in miles?	___	___
2. What was Martin Luther King Jr.'s age at death?	___	___
3. How many countries belong to OPEC?	___	___
4. How many books are there in the Old Testament?	___	___
5. What is the diameter of the moon in miles?	___	___
6. What is the weight of an empty Boeing 747 in pounds?	___	___
7. In what year was Mozart born?	___	___
8. What is the gestation of an Asian elephant in days?	___	___
9. What is the air distance from London to Tokyo in miles?	___	___
10. What is the deepest known point in the ocean in feet?	___	___

The answers are listed below. Did you get at least nine answers correct? You should have; after all, you were allowed to set your own confidence parameters. If not, don't worry—you're not alone. Most people get a lot more than one answer wrong because they are overconfident in their knowledge. More often than not we know less than we think we know.

This finding should lead most people to have some intellectual humility. It also points out that one of the first things worthy of unlearning may be our artificially high level of confidence in our knowledge.

The trait of overconfidence takes on a more ominous note when we are asked to judge ourselves. For example, did you know that 94 percent of all university professors rank themselves in the top fiftieth percentile of teachers? Pure statistics dictates that 44 percent of these ivory-tower academics are deluding themselves about their skills. It is, of course, easy to poke fun at arrogant university professors, but overconfidence abounds almost everywhere. When asked if they are better drivers, athletes, spouses or lovers, most people grade themselves above average. (They can't all be correct unless they hail from Lake Wobegon where "all the children are above average.")

Developing a healthy dose of unconfidence may sound like an unhealthy thing to do but, counterintuitively, it isn't. Instead, it will lead to a more accurate assessment of one's knowledge and skills, and this self-knowledge can be used to identify those areas of knowledge and skills that most need improvement.

Homework Assignment 38: According to you and your management team, which aspects of your business are you 90 percent confident are immune to economic, social, financial, political and technological forces? Now review the list and consider the implications if one or more is not only wrong but way off base.

Extra Credit: Make a list of economic, social, political, financial and technological changes that could influence your business in the next three years.

(Answers: (1) 4,187 miles; (2) 39 years; (3) 13 countries; (4) 39 books; (5) 2,160 miles; (6) 390,000 pounds; (7) 1756; (8) 645 days; (9) 5,959 miles; (10) 36,198 feet.)

Lesson 39:
Ignorance Isn't Bliss, but It May Hold the Key to Wisdom

"The greater our knowledge increases
the more our ignorance unfolds."
— President John F. Kennedy

Question 39: Where is the universe expanding to?

The honest answer is that nobody is entirely sure. According to Einstein's theory of general relativity, the space-time continuum cannot remain stationary and must either expand or contract; and, since there is no indication the universe is currently collapsing upon itself, it is believed the universe is expanding. But this begs the obvious question posted above: What is our universe expanding into?

One leading theory encourages people to think of the universe as an expanding balloon with its billions of galaxies as dots on the outer surface of the balloon. From this perspective, it may appear as though the galaxies are moving away from one another, but actually they remain in the same relative position (i.e., the same longitude and latitude on the balloon), and it is only the fabric that is expanding.

It is, to say the least, an unsatisfying answer and it may even be proven to be wildly off base at some point in the future. In fact, some string theorists believe there may be eleven or more dimensions and our universe is but one "balloon" in a weird and sorted pack of balloons. Not withstanding this possibility, the notion of an expanding universe is a fitting metaphor upon which to end this book on unlearning.

As the quotation from President Kennedy that started this chapter (which he spoke in his famous speech declaring it America's goal to place a man on the moon and safely return him), the idea that our ignorance is unfolding faster than we can acquire knowledge is a cold, hard fact.

This sounds like a depressing statement and, perhaps, it is; but it is one that anyone serious about unlearning must embrace. To understand, consider the sheer growth of scientific and technical knowledge. As smart, intelligent or knowledgeable as any person or organization may be about continued advances in information technology, biotechnology, nanotechnology and the countless other fields and disciplines that populate our world, it is impossible to keep abreast, let alone make sense of all of this new knowledge.

In other words, even as our knowledge increases, it is a sure bet our ignorance—or that which we don't know—will grow even faster. And it is a certainty that contained within this growing category of unknown knowledge will be new knowledge that will require unlearning that old knowledge which has become obsolete.

The challenge was wonderfully captured in this quotation from Henry David Thoreau, who once said, "How can we remember our ignorance, which our growth requires, when we are using our knowledge all the time?"

The answer is that we needn't stop using our knowledge. That's not only impractical, it's foolish. Rather, the solution is to keep our ignorance—our growing ignorance—top of mind. We must always strive to be intellectually humble and remain cognizant of "what we don't know."

And what, precisely, is the benefit in acknowledging our ignorance? It may be real knowledge. Over two thousand years ago, Confucius said, "Real knowledge is to know the extent of one's ignorance."

It may even be wisdom. Olin Miller, a veritable quotation machine but about whom little else is known, once quipped, "If you realize you aren't so wise today as you thought you were yesterday, you are wiser today."

More simply put, by acknowledging all that you *don't know* today, you may just become wiser tomorrow—and well into the future.

Homework Assignment 39: What do you think Lao Tzu meant when he wrote: "To attain knowledge, add things every day. To attain wisdom, subtract things every day"? Now, find one thing to subtract today—and continue to do so every day into the future.